NEW MEXICO
Sunrise

D0174563

**FAITH AND LOVE HOLD
GENERATIONS TOGETHER
IN FOUR COMPLETE NOVELS**

Tracie Peterson

BARBOUR
PUBLISHING, INC.
Uhrichsville, Ohio

ISBN 1-58660-123-7

Cover design by Robyn Martins.

All scripture quotations, unless otherwise indicated, are taken from the King James Version of the Bible.

Published by Barbour Publishing, Inc., P.O. Box 719, Uhrichsville, Ohio 44683 http://www.barbourbooks.com

ecpa Member of the
Evangelical Christian
Publishers Association

Printed in the United States of America.

TRACIE PETERSON

Tracie Peterson, best-selling author of over forty fiction titles and one nonfiction title, lives and works in Topeka, Kansas. As a Christian, wife, mother, and writer (in that order), Tracie finds her slate quite full.

First published as a columnist for the *Kansas Christian* newspaper, Tracie resigned that position to turn her attention to novels. After signing her first contract with Barbour Publishing in 1992, her first novel appeared in 1993 under the pen name of Janelle Jamison, and the rest is history. She has over twenty-three titles with Heartsong Presents' book club and stories in six separate anthologies from Barbour, including the best-selling *Alaska*. From Bethany House Publishing, Tracie has several historical series, as well as a variety of women's fiction titles.

Voted favorite author for 1995, 1996, and 1997 by the Heartsong Presents readership, Tracie enjoys the pleasure of spinning stories for readers and thanks God for the imagination He's given. "I find myself blessed to be able to work at a job I love. I get to travel, study history, spin yarns, spend time with my family, and hopefully glorify God. I can't imagine a more perfect arrangement."

Tracie also does acquisitions work for Barbour Publishing and teaches workshops at a variety of conferences, giving workshops on inspirational romance, historical research, and anything else that offers assistance to fellow writers.

See Tracie on the Internet at http://members.aol.com/tjpbooks/

Dear Readers,

*I'm happy to tell you about the re-release of eight previously published **Heartsong Presents** romances. First issued under the name Janelle Jamison, this collection launched my fiction writing ministry.*

New Mexico Sunrise *is book one in a two-book collection that follows the lives of the Lucas, Monroe, and Dawson families.*

I hope you'll enjoy the collection in this book, as well as the one which follows in book two, New Mexico Sunset. *God bless you!*

Tracie Peterson

A Place to Belong

Chapter 1

The Kansas heat was enough to wilt the sturdiest flower. Humid air hung thick and heavy, but certainly no heavier than the atmosphere inside the Intissar parlor on that June day.

"I won't go!" Magdelena Intissar announced at the top of her lungs. She stamped her small foot, just in case her words weren't enough to make her decision clear.

"Maggie, lower your voice," Sophia Intissar said patiently. The stately old woman was used to her granddaughter's temper. The only other person in the parlor was the subject of Maggie's displeasure.

"I won't go with that man, Grandmother. And that's final!" Maggie's blue eyes blazed at Garrett Lucas. He shifted uncomfortably.

Sophia smiled sympathetically at the young man. He had appeared on her doorstep only hours earlier, and with him had come the news that Maggie's father was sending for his daughter.

With a swish of her English afternoon dress, Sophia moved gracefully to a chair and took her place. "I suggest you sit, Magdelena," she said, pointing to a brocade parlor chair. "This issue will not be easily dismissed. We must talk."

Maggie never took her eyes off Garrett Lucas as she followed her grandmother's instructions and sat down.

"Please continue, Mr. Lucas," Sophia requested.

"As I said, Ma'am," Garrett began. "Your son, Jason Intissar, instructed me to come to Topeka and return to New Mexico with his daughter. I have two train tickets." He pulled the tickets from his vest pocket and held them up for both women to see.

"So what! You have two train tickets," Maggie interrupted, enraged at the presumption that this should make any difference.

"Grandmother," she said, turning to Sophia Intissar. "You can't trust him. Anybody can buy train tickets. He's probably some kidnapper who thinks Father will pay a high price for my return."

Garrett chuckled, but Maggie ignored him.

"Grandmother, it wouldn't be appropriate for me to travel unchaperoned with this man. What would our friends say?" Maggie knew she was grasping at straws. Neither she nor her grandmother had ever given much thought to neighborhood gossip.

Sophia took the tickets, reviewed them, and returned them to Garrett Lucas's well-tanned hand.

"I also have this letter," Garrett said. Reaching into his pocket, he pulled out a sealed envelope.

Sophia took the letter and used it to fan herself for a moment. The high collar of her gown framed her thin, aged face. Signs of quality were evident from her gleaming white hair to the sweep of her elegantly tailored gown. Lifting her chin slightly, she drew a deep breath.

"I believe you are who you say you are, Mr. Lucas. I believe this letter will explain that my son has sent you to retrieve his daughter. We all know he's tried many times before. What I don't understand is why you must leave today on the four o'clock train."

"The letter will explain, Ma'am. Mr. Intissar was afraid his daughter might react as she had before and run off."

"How dare you!" Maggie could take no more. "How dare you talk about me as if I weren't even here! You don't know me. My father doesn't know me. He deserted me to my grandmother's care when my mother died. I was eight years old, and I've only seen him twice since then!" The bitterness in Maggie's voice was not lost on her listeners.

"Maggie, remember your manners," Sophia interjected firmly, but not without gentleness. She'd known the pain of that eight-year-old girl as she knew the pain of the young woman who sat angrily before her. "Mr. Lucas does have a point," she continued.

Maggie knew her grandmother was right. Her father had sent for her on a dozen other occasions, but Maggie had always managed to be away from Topeka or hiding out with friends when he had arrived to take her home. She'd never been able to get past the pain of being left behind, and in her heart, Maggie had held an anger toward her father that seemed to grow each year.

Now, Garrett Lucas had arrived. If she were forced to leave with him, Maggie knew it would not be easy to escape and return to her grandmother. But no matter how difficult flight might prove to be, Maggie was determined to defy her father's wishes. She had no desire to face him or the wounds that stood between them.

"It seems your father has outwitted you, my dear," Sophia was saying. Maggie jerked her head up.

"You'll have to drag my dead body to that train!" she shouted, jumping to her feet. Garrett's lips drew back in a wide grin. The girl had spunk, and he had to admire her ability to stand up to people.

Maggie noticed the smile and felt her heart skip a beat. Garrett Lucas was quite handsome, especially when he smiled. His skin was tanned from many years spent outdoors, and Maggie lost herself in his intense blue eyes. Just then she remembered he was grinning because of her.

Maggie raised herself to her full height. "I mean it. Go back and tell my father I refuse to come to New Mexico. I have friends and family here, and that's enough for me. Furthermore, in less than two months I will be eighteen years old. I think I am more than mature enough to make my own decisions, and my decision is to remain here."

As Maggie's tantrum played out, silence fell over the parlor. Sophia quietly read her son's letter. From time to time, a faint breeze fluttered the lace parlor curtains, bringing with it the sweet scent of honeysuckle.

Maggie refused to look at Garrett, but she was well aware that he studied her intently. How she wished she could run from the room.

Sophia let the letter fall to her lap. It confirmed that her son was determined to form a relationship with his child. Pity he'd allowed Maggie to have her way for so many years. There were so many miles and scars to overcome. But Maggie must face her father's decision. Scars or no scars, it was time for her to go home.

Sophia broke the silence. "Maggie, I have no choice. You will go with Mr. Lucas."

"What? You can't be serious, Grandmother. You would trust this man, this. . .this devil?"

"Magdelena!" Sophia admonished, and Garrett Lucas broke into a hearty laugh, causing both women to look at him.

"Excuse me, Ma'am," Garrett said to Sophia. "I meant no disrespect."

"I apologize for my granddaughter, Mr. Lucas. She doesn't yet understand that being grown up often means making unpopular and unwanted decisions."

Maggie came to stand in front of Sophia. "Grandmother, what are you saying? Will you really let him take me away?"

"Maggie, I must. Your father has made it very clear in this letter. He has his reasons, and now I have mine. Run upstairs and pack your things."

"She doesn't need to take too much," Garrett offered. "Jason's bought her quite a bit already. She'll have enough clothes to be the envy of any woman in the territory."

"Clothes? Pack my clothes? Has everyone lost their minds?" Maggie questioned, her voice nearing hysteria. "What's in that letter? How could you send me off with a stranger to a man who cares nothing about me. He walked out on me, remember? He left me when I needed him."

"Maggie," Sophia took her granddaughter's youthful hand in her own weathered one and patted it gently. "You must be brave, my dear. You must listen to me and do as I say. I am an old woman, and I don't have many years left in this world. God is in this change."

"Don't say that," Maggie interrupted curtly. "God can't possibly care about me, or He'd have kept Garrett Lucas in New Mexico. God has never cared about me, or He would have given me a father. One that would stay and do the job, rather than leave it to someone else to do."

"Maggie, that's not fair. Please hear me out," Sophia pleaded, and Maggie grew frightened. It wasn't at all like her grandmother to take on an air of frailty. Maggie's eyes darted in the direction of Garrett Lucas, but she could see he was fidgeting with his coat button, trying to leave the two women some privacy.

"I don't want you thinking I don't love you anymore. Nor do I wish for you to believe me cruel and heartless in this matter. You're seventeen years old, and your father feels it's time for you to consider marriage and settling down to your own family."

Sophia stopped to see the impact her words were having on Maggie. She could see tears brimming in her granddaughter's eyes and knew her own weren't far behind. "Your father has found a husband for you, Child. He has that privilege and right."

"A husband? I guess I could've guessed he didn't want a daughter. He just wants a son to replace the one he lost." Maggie's bitterness was clear.

"Now, Child, be fair," Sophia implored.

"What would I want with one of Father's old cronies? He probably has some ancient man lined up. I won't do it. I can't!" Maggie sobbed the words. She fell to her knees, hating herself for breaking down in front of Mr. Lucas.

"Child, you must understand. Your father is not a well man. The letter makes this clear. He wishes to leave his estate to you. And," Sophia added most reluctantly, "he wants to have a say in who will share that responsibility with you."

"Let him find someone to give his empire to. I don't want it. I want to stay here with you, Grandmother. I don't want to leave Topeka."

Just then the hall clock chimed two. Maggie turned terror-stricken eyes first to her grandmother, then unwillingly to Garrett Lucas.

Garrett hated being the cause of the fear he saw in Maggie's eyes. She was easier to handle when she was defiant. He wished he could assure her that he was only here as a favor to Jason, but he knew she'd never listen to him. No, it was best that he let the two women work through this together.

"If God loves me so much, why is He allowing this to happen? Better yet, why are you?" Maggie knew her words tortured her grandmother, but she had to make her grandmother see her pain.

"Maggie, I have little choice. I would love to have you here for the remainder of my life, but your father has set his mind."

"He doesn't care about me, Grandmother. It's just his land and his business ventures. Don't you see? If he cared about me, he would have come home to Topeka. He wouldn't have jeopardized my security by forcing me away from all I know and love. He wants a land baron, not a daughter. He's always hated me for what happened to mother!"

"Nonsense, Child. You listen to me and listen well. I was there when your mother died. She struggled to give birth to your brother, but we all knew neither one of them was going to make it." Sophia's eyes clouded with tears.

"Typhoid fever had been fierce in town. Your mother was well into her pregnancy when you came down with the fever yourself. Before I knew what had happened, your mother was sick as well."

Maggie felt tears fall hot upon her cheeks. She buried her face in her grandmother's lap. Sophia gently stroked the long auburn curls. "Your father always blamed himself. He couldn't live with his grief nor with the child that reminded him so much of his wife. You were a constant reminder of what he had lost. I love my son, Maggie. I never faulted him for leaving you in my care. I saw the necessity of it then, just as I see the necessity of this now. God has always been here for us."

"Father left because he blamed me for Mother's death. He hates me, and I don't care!" Maggie exploded.

"That is absurd, Maggie. You didn't give your mother typhoid, and your father didn't blame you then or now." Sophia lifted the letter to fan herself, succumbing to the heat and stress. Her face paled.

"Grandmother!" Maggie cried, reaching out to steady her. Garrett was beside Sophia in a moment.

"Get her some water," he commanded. Maggie raced to the kitchen and returned with a glass.

"It's not very cold," she said apologetically.

"It will be fine, Child," Sophia assured her. "I'm feeling better now. It's just this insufferable heat. If this is any indication of what the rest of the summer will bring, I'm not sure how I'll stand up under it."

"See, you need me," Maggie said pleadingly. Then she whirled to face Garrett. "You can't expect me to leave her here alone!"

Garrett was standing close to Maggie. Close enough she could smell the cologne he wore, musky, yet sweet. He looked down at her with soft eyes and opened his mouth to speak.

"It isn't my decision, Miss Intissar. I'm only doing what I promised your father I'd do."

"I'm fine, Maggie," Sophia insisted.

She did look better, Maggie decided, but the girl feared that neither of them would be able to bear the separation.

"I don't want to leave you." Maggie threw herself to her knees again and hugged her grandmother tightly.

Sophia brushed the damp hair away from Maggie's forehead. "I don't want to see you go. I love you, Child. But you must do this for me." Sophia raised Maggie's face to meet her own. "You must go with Mr. Lucas. Promise me you will go upstairs right now and pack your things."

Suddenly, there was no room for further discussion. Maggie stared intently at her grandmother's wearied face and then looked up at the towering stranger. She lowered her head and with a voice of complete dejection whispered, "Yes, Grandmother."

"And Maggie, remember God will always see you through the storms," Sophia added. "He's there for you Maggie, but you must come willingly. Don't put God off simply because you fear He will desert you. He won't." Sophia had prayed so often that her granddaughter would turn from her bitterness to accept Jesus as her Savior.

Maggie got to her feet and brushed off the skirt of her gown. "I will take my leave now, if I may," she said ignoring Garrett's closeness. Sophia nodded, and Maggie moved from the room.

As Maggie reached the oak staircase, she turned and made the mistake of meeting Garrett's unyielding eyes. Maggie sighed and began to climb the stairs, when a thought came to her. *Lillie! I'll sneak out of my room, down the trellis, and run to Lillie's house.* Maggie hiked her skirts and fairly flew up the remaining stairs. She was safely behind her bedroom door when Sophia Intissar rose slowly to her feet in the parlor below.

"If I know my granddaughter, Mr. Lucas, and I believe I do, I can count on her trying to leave this house without your knowledge. I would suggest you keep your eyes open. We have a staircase in back as well as the one in front."

Garrett nodded. "I understand. I'll keep track of her. You just rest." Garrett turned to leave, but Sophia placed her hand on his arm.

"Please be gentle with her, Mr. Lucas. Life has not always treated her kindly."

"I'd venture a guess it's been rough on all of you. Please don't worry. I'll be a perfect gentleman. I'll do as Jason instructed me, and nothing more than is necessary to fulfill his wishes." With that, Garrett walked out the front door of the Intissar house.

Chapter 2

Maggie gazed around the room. She wondered if she should bother to take anything with her. No. She could always borrow clothes from Lillie. Nervous excitement washed through her body. It would be a pleasure to defeat Garrett Lucas and to show her father once again that she wanted nothing to do with him.

It was odd how days, even weeks, passed when Maggie didn't think of her father. God, on the other hand, could never be outrun.

Putting such uncomfortable thoughts aside, Maggie went to the window. She touched the powder-blue Priscilla curtains and remembered making them with her grandmother. Maggie held the soft folds against her cheek. She thought of how she and Grandmother had gone downtown to pick out the material and wallpaper for their new home in Potwin Place.

Maggie threw open the window. "I won't be forced to give up all that I love. It's just not fair!" she cried out loud. "Father can't force me to leave Grandmother and marry someone I don't know."

There was a light rap at the door. "Maggie, do hurry along, Child. We've only a few minutes before we leave," her grandmother called softly.

"In a minute," Maggie responded. She hurriedly reached out the window to take hold of the trellis. Her skirts were quite cumbersome as she struggled to put her foot out the window. Gingerly, Maggie climbed onto the delicate wood frame sharing space with the climbing roses. The trellis shook vigorously for a few moments, then settled under her weight.

"If he thinks that he can just come in here and take me away, he's got another think coming," Maggie muttered to herself as she fought her skirts and the trellis. "He's got to be twelve kinds of a fool to think I'd go anywhere with—" Her tirade ended abruptly as she was wrenched from the trellis into the arms of Garrett Lucas.

A look of amusement played in Garrett's eyes, and Maggie couldn't help but notice how effortlessly he carried her, squirming and twisting, back to the front door. "You were saying?" he questioned sarcastically.

"Oh, you are insufferable! Put me down!" Maggie said, suddenly finding her voice.

Garrett carried her through the etched glass double doors of her Queen

Anne home. He took the stairs two at a time and didn't stop until he reached the upstairs hallway.

"Which room?" he questioned.

"Put me down! Grandmother!" Maggie yelled.

"Unless you want me to help you pack, I suggest you settle down and do what your grandmother told you to do. I'm going to be watching this house the whole time, so no more tricks. Do you understand?" Garrett's words left Maggie cold. "Do you?"

Maggie nodded slowly.

"Very well," Garrett said as he set Maggie on her feet. "Now get your things together and be quick about it, or I'll come in and help you!" With that he went downstairs and left Maggie to watch after him in total amazement. Who was this man?

Maggie hurried to the sanctuary of her room. There was no more time for memories or escapes. If she couldn't get away from Garrett at home in Topeka, would it be possible to flee while on the train?

Suddenly, a plan began to form. "If Father thinks he's won this round, he's wrong." Maggie said, pulling out a drawer from her writing desk. She dumped the contents onto the desktop. Coins and trinkets spilled out. "I'll show him," Maggie muttered to herself as she counted the money. Finally, thirty dollars and some change was counted out. "I wonder if this is enough to buy a train ticket home," Maggie mused.

Next, she pulled out a piece of writing paper and jotted a note to her best friend, Lillie Johnston. She tried to explain what was happening and that, somehow, she'd be back. She sealed the envelope and left it in the middle of her desk, knowing her grandmother would find it and have it delivered.

Quickly, Maggie pulled off her gingham day dress and took out a green linen traveling suit. The day was too hot for such an outfit, but Maggie knew it would be expected by the matrons of society.

Maggie herself often scoffed at the rules and regulations that the women of Potwin Place had made for themselves. But they were rules that were followed by the genteel of society everywhere, not just those in this upper-class neighborhood.

Maggie pulled on her petticoat, then eyed herself in the mirror. She was only seventeen, not even an adult. Still, many of her friends were already married. Some even had children. She was woman enough she decided, but for what?

She labored with her shirtwaist and the faux lace collar that tied at her neck. Securing the collar with a velvet green ribbon, Maggie turned her attention to the skirt.

Within twenty minutes, Maggie stood at the base of the oak staircase, dressed in her green suit with valise and purse in hand. She was an alluring picture with her long auburn hair put up and a green hat pinned jauntily to one side.

Her appearance was not lost on Garrett. "Let me take that, Miss Intissar," he said as he stepped forward to take the valise from Maggie's hands. Maggie glared at him but said nothing. He took the bag and stepped back.

"You must be stronger than you look. This thing weighs more than a yearling heifer," he drawled.

"I am a great many things more than what I appear to be, Mr. Lucas," Maggie answered, refusing to allow him the upper hand.

"Somehow, Ma'am, that doesn't surprise me." His eyes pierced her soul, and Maggie felt as though she'd just been put in her place.

"Oh good, you're here at last," Sophia said as she entered the room carrying another small bag. "I had Two Moons pack you some things to eat." Sophia referred to her Indian housekeeper who had been with her since she'd been a young girl.

"That isn't necessary, Ma'am," Garrett began. "Mr. Intissar sent along plenty of money for the two of us to eat along the way."

Maggie thought of at least a dozen retorts but kept her tongue in check for a time longer. Once they were on the train, Garrett Lucas would discover just how difficult his trip was going to be.

"I only thought you might need something extra. I suppose it's the mothering instinct in me." Sophia started to discard the bag, but Maggie reached out and took it.

"Nonsense, Grandmother. It was a wise idea," she said gently, while flashing a look at Garrett Lucas that made it clear he'd overstepped his bounds. "One can never tell when the food will be unsatisfactory. Why, Lillie told me just last week the food offered on their trip to Omaha had been appalling."

"Of course, Ma'am. It was very thoughtful of you." Garrett spoke politely, all the while returning Maggie's blazing stare. He raised one dark eyebrow slightly, as if contemplating a further reply, then changed his mind. "I suggest we be on our way. It's already three o'clock."

"Very well, Mr. Lucas." Sophia allowed him to take her arm and lead her to the carriage.

Maggie lingered for a moment, trying to drink in every inch of the house. Standing at the foot of the stairs, she could look into three different rooms. They held comfort and good memories. Suddenly, she wanted to embrace it all, fearing that she'd never see her home again. Why was God punishing her? Hadn't she paid enough?

Maggie choked back tears and steadied her nerves. She'd make it back, she vowed to herself. All the Garrett Lucases and Jason Intissars in the world would not keep her from her home and Grandmother.

"Come along, Maggie." It was Grandmother calling from the carriage.

Maggie stepped onto the porch and shut the door behind her. She turned to find Garrett Lucas at her arm.

"I would suggest, Miss Intissar, that you make this matter as easy on your grandmother as possible." Garrett's voice was deadly serious. "She has done nothing but care for you and love you. You are a spoiled and selfish child." He paused to search her eyes. "I will not allow you to cause her further grief by a display of childishness at the train station."

Maggie's mouth dropped open in shocked surprise. "How dare you—" Her words were cut off by his stern expression.

"I'm not the enemy here, but you are going to get on that train if I have to rope you and tie you to the seat. Everyone, including that sweet, old woman, has danced to your tune long enough. You are now in my care, Miss Magdelena Intissar, and I am quite capable of dealing with you."

Maggie was stunned. She could barely work her legs to walk down the porch steps. It wouldn't be as easy to give Garrett Lucas the slip as she'd hoped. Mutely, Maggie allowed Garrett to lead her along the board walkway to the carriage.

Topeka of 1888 was bustling with life and activity. It was the capital of Kansas and in its own right demanded grandeur and charm. Potwin Place was the high point of residential Topeka, although it desired to become a city in its own right.

Potwin Place homes, while fairly new, were elegant and stately. They were surrounded by well-manicured lawns. Young trees had been planted along the avenues. Maggie was well aware she had lived a privileged life. Now she could only stare longingly as the carriage took her from the place she loved to an uncertain future.

Maggie had always loved the hubbub of the city, but even that simple pleasure was lost on her as she brooded about the future. The carriage passed the large stone church which Sophia insisted her household attend every Sunday. Maggie thought momentarily of God. He was up there somewhere, she decided as she looked into the fluffy clouds. Somewhere up there, but certainly not with her.

Soon, the two-story depot came into sight. Maggie realized the moment of truth was nearing. She toyed with the idea of causing a scene. Maybe there was some way to discredit Mr. Lucas so that her grandmother couldn't possibly send Maggie with him.

Maggie shot a quick glance at Garrett Lucas. He narrowed his eyes slightly as if reading her mind. The look on his face was adamant, his message unmistakable.

"I must say, Mrs. Intissar, you have a lovely city," Garrett observed, breaking the silence that had lasted the duration of the carriage ride.

Sophia roused herself. "Yes, I suppose it is one of the more lovely times to be here. The flowering trees, the honeysuckle and lilacs. Topeka is a sweet smelling town. However, we have some nasty storms. Cyclones, you know." She spoke with a heavy voice, and both Garrett and Maggie knew her mind was far from thoughts of the weather.

"Yes, Ma'am," Garrett replied, "We have them out West, too. Sometimes they come in a series of storms that last all day."

Sophia nodded. "I've seen storms like that. It's always been the thing I've disliked most about our fair state. Of course," she added rather absentmindedly, "if not cyclones, then something else."

Maggie sat in silence, trying to formulate a plan. There'd only be one chance to make it work. She thought of the various junctions and water stops on the Atchison, Topeka, and Santa Fe Rail Road lines. She'd traveled with her grandmother as far as Newton, but beyond that, she was rather uncertain about the route. She'd have to escape before they reached Newton.

The carriage ride came unceremoniously to an end at the depot entrance. Garrett jumped to the ground before the driver could announce their arrival.

"Allow me to help you, Ma'am," Garrett said tenderly, reaching up to take hold of Sophia's waist. "Forgive the familiarity, but I fear this heat might grieve you if I allow you to exert yourself."

"You are very kind, Mr. Lucas. My son has always been a good judge of a man's character. I see his judgment is still sound."

Maggie rolled her eyes, not realizing that Garrett could see her. "Yes, Father is quite knowledgeable about men and horseflesh, cattle and land grants. It's women who seem to escape his understanding," she said sarcastically. She refused to take Garrett's offered hand and nearly fell from the buggy as she tried to dismount.

Garrett flashed her a brief smile and returned his attention to Sophia. The heat was nearly unbearable for the older woman.

"June isn't always this hot. Some years, we're still enjoying cool temperatures at this time. Why by all the means of Kansas, we could be quite chilled tomorrow. We have a saying about the weather here, Mr. Lucas, if you don't like it, wait a day and it'll change," Sophia murmured. She stumbled slightly, leaning heavily against Garrett's offered arm.

"Ma'am, I know you wish to see your granddaughter safely on the train, but the truth is it would be better if your driver took you home. I don't want to worry about you having to make it back to the carriage without help." Garrett's command of the moment went unquestioned. Sophia allowed him to place her back in the buggy.

"Maggie, listen to me," Sophia said leaning down from her seat. "Don't cause Mr. Lucas any trouble. Just do as your father wishes, and perhaps in the fall, I'll come and visit you."

Maggie felt tears on her cheeks. She hated appearing weak in front of Garrett, but perhaps it was what he needed to see. He should understand how miserable he was making her.

"Grandmother, I simply can't bear to leave you." Maggie began to cry. "I don't want to go." She held tightly to her grandmother's arm.

"It will be alright, Child," Sophia murmured, gently stroking Maggie's face. "God sometimes sends adversity to strengthen and teach us. You'll grow stronger from this. Now remember the things you've been taught. Never forget you are loved."

"I'll remember," Maggie promised.

"It's time to go, Miss Intissar," Garrett said softly, extending his arm for Maggie.

"I'll see you soon, Grandmother," Maggie said standing on tiptoe in order to reach her Grandmother's ear. "I'll pray every night that God will bring us together again." She wondered if she had added that last statement more for herself than for her grandmother.

Maggie allowed Garrett to lead her away. As they passed through the depot entrance, she paused to look back. Her grandmother was waving weakly. Maggie returned the wave until Garrett firmly propelled her to the other side of the depot and onto the boarding platform.

Oh, Grandmother, Maggie thought. *Somehow I will return to you. Somehow.*

Chapter 3

"All 'board!" the conductor called as a stern-faced Garrett approached, pulling a willful Maggie behind him.

"Afternoon to you, Mister," the conductor said without breaking his concentration on the pocket watch he held tightly in his hand. "Missus," he added, touching the brim of his blue cap. Maggie stiffened at the comment, causing a smile to play at the corners of Garrett's mouth.

Maggie tried to pull away, but it was no use. Garrett only smiled broadly, and raised a questioning eye from beneath his black Stetson.

"Tickets, please," the conductor requested.

Garrett pulled two tickets from his vest pocket and handed them to the older man.

"Um, I see here you're in number fourteen. That'd be the second car down," the conductor said, motioning to a porter.

"Y'sir," the porter said with a nodding bow of his head.

"These passengers have seats in number fourteen. See to it," the conductor instructed. "And be quick about it. I'm about to call final 'board."

"Y'sir," the porter smiled and offered his assistance. "Do you have bags, Sir?" he questioned Garrett.

"I've already checked them," Garrett answered. "Except for this one. We'll take it with us." Garrett motioned to the carpetbag Sophia had packed. Maggie clutched the bag as if it were all she owned.

"Very good, Sir. Right this way."

Maggie felt herself being pulled along at such a pace that when Garrett stopped, she nearly fell headlong onto the tracks. Garrett steadied her and gently handed her up the steps of the train. Maggie was amazed at how light his touch could be when he wasn't bullying her along.

The porter led them down the narrow train aisle. "Seats twenty-three and twenty-four, right here, Sir," the porter said. "I'll show you to your sleeping compartments this evening."

"Thank you," Garrett replied, handing the man a coin. The porter smiled broadly and nodded his head to the couple.

"Take the window seat, Miss Intissar," Garrett stated matter-of-factly. "I believe the train is about to pull out, and it would do little good to have you sprawled in the aisle."

Maggie stepped meekly to her seat. Garrett, although surprised, said nothing. Instead, he took off his hat and coat and, before sitting, removed his vest as well. Maggie's discomfort became evident as Garrett pulled his necktie off and unbuttoned his shirt collar.

Garrett noticed Maggie's flushed face. She quickly turned away, and he couldn't help but grin. "I'm finished, if that's what you're wondering," he teased. "It'd do you some good to get out of that jacket and open up a button or two yourself."

"I'm fine for the time being," she lied, wishing she could do just as Garrett had suggested. The worst heat of the day was only heightened by the closed, cramped quarters of the train.

"As you wish, but remember we're traveling south. The heat will only get worse once we leave Topeka," Garrett said with a shrug of his shoulders.

His words only reminded Maggie that they were leaving her home. A further reminder sounded loud and clear as the train whistle gave two long blasts. Maggie felt the color drain from her face. It was all she could do to keep from fighting Garrett in an attempt to get off.

The train gave a bit of a jerk, as if it needed help to start moving down the tracks. Finally, it started pulling slowly out of Topeka's Santa Fe Station. Maggie watched as people on the platform waved. One older woman, sending a kiss with her gloved hand, reminded Maggie of her grandmother. Maggie bit her lip to keep from crying, but her eyes held betraying tears.

Long after there was nothing but outlying farms and scenery to look at, Maggie continued to stare out the window. She remembered several years earlier when she had gone with Lillie to see the circus. The two girls had watched the animals get loaded on the train after the final performance. Maggie had felt sorry for the animals in their barred cages. Now, she felt caged.

After nearly fifteen minutes of strained silence, Garrett spoke. "We should talk before this situation gets worse," he began. He leaned back against the padded leather of the seat and crossed his arms behind his head.

Maggie stiffened and moved closer to the window. She was hot and sticky, and the humidity made it nearly impossible to breathe. She wanted to lower the window, but the smoke and cinders from the train's smokestack would only worsen things. Either way, Garrett Lucas was too close, and she wished desperately to put some kind of distance between them. She sighed deeply.

"Did you hear what I said?" Garrett questioned.

"I heard you," Maggie barely whispered the words. "I simply chose not to argue with you."

"I have no intention of arguing with you, Miss Intissar, and begging your pardon, but I believe I will call you by your first name." Garrett's voice told Maggie he'd settle for nothing less.

"Whatever you feel is necessary, Mr. Lucas," Maggie replied with a coolness to her voice that surprised even her. "It is of little consequence what name you call me by."

"Dare I believe you are offering to cooperate with me?" Garrett questioned sarcastically. He turned his body slightly toward Maggie, which only made her more uncomfortable.

A woman with two children occupied the seats across the aisle, and she leaned toward Garrett and Maggie to catch pieces of their conversation. Maggie detested the woman's prying attitude and lowered her voice even more.

"I've already agreed to go with you to wherever it is my father calls home. I don't care what you call me, and I don't care where you take me. Now, what more is there to discuss?" Maggie felt rather proud of her little speech.

"I see. What, may I ask, brought about this change in the wild-eyed child that I had words with earlier?" Garrett questioned, intently studying Maggie for some clue as to what she was planning.

Maggie bit hard on her lower lip, and Garrett smiled, letting Maggie know he was aware he'd hit a nerve.

"You have your father's temper. Are you aware of that?" Garrett asked. Maggie said nothing, but she noticed over Garrett's shoulder that the woman had leaned even farther into the aisle. Garrett turned to see what Maggie was looking at.

"Have you lost something, Ma'am?" Garrett asked the embarrassed woman. The woman shook her head and quickly turned her attention back to her children. Garrett chuckled and continued his analysis of Maggie.

"You have his eyes too." Garrett's voice sounded low and melodic. Maggie felt herself relaxing against her will.

"I suppose one would have to share certain characteristics with one's parent. It isn't necessary to live with a parent to look like one. I also look a great deal like my mother, and she died nine years ago," Maggie said rather stiffly, refusing to fall under Garrett's spell.

"Yes, I know. Your father showed me her picture. She was a beautiful woman, and you are the very image of her."

"Am I mistaken, or have you just complimented me?" Maggie questioned curiously.

"And the lady is intelligent too!" Garrett drawled sardonically.

Maggie could no longer play her part. "You're insufferable!" she huffed and turned back to the window.

"Ah ha! I knew the temper was still there. Don't think that you can set my mind at ease by playing the prim and proper lady. I will not trust you on this trip, and you might as well know my terms right up front," Garrett said firmly.

Maggie stared incredulously as Garrett sat up and reached over to pull her to the edge of her seat.

"Now, off with the jacket before you pass out. And take off that collar," he ordered. He reached out as if to undo the buttons himself.

Maggie noticed the widening eyes of the woman across the aisle. Garrett turned to the woman briefly. "I can't believe you women actually travel comfortably in these getups you call traveling clothes." The woman turned crimson, but Maggie noticed she didn't pull back like before.

"Take it off," Garrett commanded a stunned Maggie.

"I've never been so insulted!" Maggie tried to jerk away, only to find Garrett's firm hands holding her upper arms.

"I'm sure no one has ever dared to cross you, Maggie. But this time, you've met your match. Your father didn't send me without considering the type of person this job required. Now do as I say." Garrett loosened his grip as Maggie obediently began to unbutton her jacket.

"This is totally inappropriate," she muttered under her breath. "I'm a lady, and I demand that you treat me as such."

"Perhaps when you start acting like one, I'll be more inclined to treat you differently. Fashion or no, I can't see having you passed out from heat. I'm truly thinking only of your comfort. Now let me help." Garrett's words were so precise they sounded rehearsed.

Maggie allowed him to help her out of the traveling jacket. She had to admit, at least to herself, it was an immediate improvement. She leaned back and sighed. Why was this happening? Did God hate her so much? Why couldn't she live with her grandmother? Was it because she refused to hear God's calling?

"Now, as I said before, we really should talk." Garrett's voice intruded into Maggie's thoughts. "I know you're feeling badly. I know you don't want to go, and I know that you're afraid."

"I'm not afraid of anything!" Maggie exclaimed, raising her voice slightly. When several of the train passengers joined the nosy woman in turning to see what the commotion was, Maggie immediately stared out the window.

"You were saying," Garrett whispered pressing close to her ear.

"Get away from me," Maggie hissed. "I may have to suffer through your deplorable presence, but I will not have you accosting me."

Garrett laughed loudly, causing people to stare at them once again. The woman across the aisle was thoroughly enjoying the scene.

"Will you be quiet?" Maggie whispered angrily. "I won't have the entire train watching me. One nanny is entirely too many, but now you'd saddle me with a dozen more," she said, waving her arm at the people who stared. Everyone, with the exception of the nosy woman, turned away quickly.

"Look, little girl," Garrett said in the authoritative tone Maggie had grown to hate. "You're spoiled and selfish, and a woman, you're not!"

Maggie felt her face grow red with embarrassment. Garrett Lucas was impossible. It made thoughts of escape seem that much sweeter. She struggled to regain her composure.

"Mr. Lucas," Maggie began when she could trust her voice. "I am tired of your insults and tired of trying to make sense out of this situation. I don't suppose it's possible for you to understand what I'm going through, therefore I don't see any reason to continue this conversation."

"Maybe I understand more than you give me credit for," Garrett answered gently.

"I suppose anything is possible," Maggie said wearily. "But I don't believe you appreciate my position. I am seventeen years old. I've lived all my life in Topeka. What few friends I have are ones I've spent a lifetime making.

"Why, Lillie Johnston from next door has been my companion since I was a very small child. Her father and mine invested in the railroad together. Her parents and mine were good friends. When Lillie's parents decided to build a house in Potwin Place, my grandmother arranged to build there so we could remain close. I was to be in Lillie's wedding later this month. So you see how little you or my father know about me."

"I've learned a great deal about you through your grandmother's letters to your father," Garrett said noting the surprise on Maggie's face.

"I see," Maggie replied, knowing that her grandmother had written long, detailed accounts of their life in Topeka. Maggie decided that by sharing those letters with a stranger, her father had betrayed the family once again.

"I know that, except for times when Lillie prodded you to attend social events, you've lived a cloistered life," Garrett continued, much to Maggie's dismay. "I know that you've refused gentleman callers, telling your grandmother that men were more trouble to deal with than they were worth."

Maggie blushed a deep crimson. "My father had no right to share that with you. In fact, my grandmother had no right to share it with my father. But," she paused, gaining a bit of composure, "I suppose that is all in the past."

"Your father has every right to know about you. He's tried for years to get you down to New Mexico with him. Seems to me that it's you, not him, who refuses to put the past aside. I can't imagine a living soul disliking Jason Intissar, much less hating him the way you do." Garrett's words were like a spike driven into Maggie's heart.

"You have no right to talk to me like that! I demand that you have the porter show me to my sleeping compartment so I might retire for the evening."

"I see. And if I refuse?" Garrett questioned in a cautious tone.

"I can't very well force you, now can I? I am, after all, just a spoiled little girl. But, I am not feeling well, and I am asking you," Maggie continued at nearly a whisper, "to let me go."

Maggie hoped her case sounded believable, but just in case, she quietly held her breath, a trick she and Lillie had learned as young girls. If she held her breath long enough, she'd grow faint. She and Lillie had done this on more than one occasion to get out of school. If Garrett expected childish behavior, then that's what she'd give him.

Garrett eyed her suspiciously. She was incredibly beautiful and looked nothing like the child he'd accused her of being. He liked her spirit, but he had to admit that she didn't look well.

"Alright, Maggie." Garrett agreed and signaled for the porter.

"Sir?" It was the same porter who'd shown them to their seats.

"Please show Miss Intissar to her sleeping compartment. I'm afraid the heat's been difficult for her," Garrett said as he stood and helped Maggie to her feet.

Maggie slowly exhaled but found herself dizzy from her antics. She fell against Garrett's arm. The woman across the aisle gasped loudly, but Garrett ignored her.

"Maggie?" he questioned, quite concerned. Maggie kept her face down and smiled to herself. *Good,* she thought. *Let him worry.*

"I'm so sorry," Maggie said aloud. "I'm afraid I'm feeling worse than I thought."

"Porter, lead the way. I'll bring Miss Intissar," Garrett directed, and the porter headed in the direction of the sleeping car. Garrett pulled Maggie tightly to him. "Lean on me, Maggie. I'll help you."

The fact that Maggie willingly accepted his help caused Garrett great concern. She would never allow him to touch her if she were strong enough to do otherwise. When they reached Maggie's room, Garrett instructed the porter to bring fresh water and a glass.

"I want you to drink this," Garrett said to Maggie as he poured the glass full of water. "Then I want you to undress and get some rest."

Maggie raised an eyebrow this time. "You seem intent on speaking on very familiar terms with me. I'd rather you leave this relationship as unfamiliar as possible. Neither one of us has anything to gain by doing otherwise."

"On the contrary, Maggie. We have a great deal to gain by working through this antagonism—if not for our sakes, then for the sake of your father," Garrett replied as he pushed the glass into Maggie's hand.

Garrett's fingers touched Maggie's hand and sent a searing charge up her arm. She made the mistake of looking into his eyes. They were steely blue, and yet there was something more. They seemed to hold a glint of something that Maggie couldn't quite comprehend.

She pulled away from his hand and the glass of water. "Wha. . .what?" she stammered. "What could this possibly have to do with my father, and why should I care?"

"Because your father has gone to a great deal of trouble for you. He cares very deeply for you, and he wants your happiness," Garrett said, placing the water on the dresser of Maggie's compartment. "And, despite what you may think, his plans for you are better than your own."

Maggie stamped her foot. "My father doesn't even know me, Garrett Lucas! He's making arrangements for me to wed a man I don't know. A man who doesn't know me or what I care about in life."

"Your father knows more about you than you give him credit for, Maggie," Garrett stated as he walked to the door. "And, I might add, so does the man he's chosen to be your husband."

Maggie grew furious at this. "And just how would you know?" she asked, crossing her arms in front of her.

"Because, Maggie," Garrett replied dryly. "I am that man."

Chapter 4

G arrett returned to his seat with the porter close behind him. "Will you be needin' anything else, Sir?" the porter asked in a low voice.

"No, thank you," Garrett replied rather distracted.

"What about your missus, Sir?"

"No. Nothing." Garrett stated firmly.

When the porter had walked away, Garrett punched his fist against his leg.

I never should have told her like that, he thought. He stared out the window at the open expanse of Kansas grasslands flashing by. The train was traveling at nearly seventeen miles an hour.

Garrett closed his eyes and remembered Maggie's expression as he had told her that she was to marry him. Her look of terror had done little to assure him that he was doing the right thing.

Things had seemed much simpler back on Jason Intissar's ranch. His mind flashed back to the day Maggie's portrait had arrived. Jason was intensely proud of his little girl, as he always referred to Maggie, but Garrett had seen a woman behind the little girl's eyes.

"She's a beauty, but wild, like a green-broke mustang," Jason had announced as both men studied the portrait. Maggie had put up quite a fight over the portrait sitting, agreeing to it only after Jason had given his word that she could stay another year with her grandmother.

The promised year had come and gone. Throughout the weeks and months, Jason and Garrett had found themselves paying homage to the portrait. Garrett remembered the day Jason had found him in the library studying his daughter's likeness.

"I've had some time to reflect on matters," Jason had begun. "It seems to me that a ranch the size of mine will need more than a wisp of a girl to run it. I've worked hard to train you in every area of my holdings. Seems only fitting that you reap the reward."

"Meaning?" Garrett had questioned.

"Meaning Maggie. She'll need a strong man. A good man. A Christian man." Garrett had said nothing, afraid to believe what he was hearing. Jason had continued, "I want you to marry Maggie. That is, if what I think I've read in your eyes is true. You do love her, don't you?"

Garrett had found the thought startling, almost unsettling. But he'd known it was true. Everything Garrett had learned about Maggie in her grandmother's letters had filled him with a growing love.

"It won't be easy," Jason had explained. "She has a temper to beat all, and she won't take lightly to my choosing a husband for her."

Garrett had agreed to Jason's plan, certain that, in time, Maggie would come to feel for him the love he already felt for her.

The blast from the train whistle brought Garrett back to reality. Indeed, Maggie hadn't liked the idea of her father choosing either a husband or a home for her.

Garrett could understand Maggie's pain, but not her hatred. From their first encounter when Garrett was only fifteen, Jason had never been anything but kind to him. He had looked past the angry, pain-filled young man and seen potential that Garrett hadn't known existed. There was a kindness about Jason that brought people from the farthest reaches of the New Mexico Territory to seek work or assistance. Having known what it was to be in need, Jason never failed to feed the hungry or help the hurting.

Jason had been successful in a little bit of everything, and Garrett couldn't think of a wealthier man in the territory. Knowing that he was dying, Jason's fondest wish was to leave his empire to the two people he loved most, Maggie and Garrett.

Garrett sighed. "I can't blame her for hating me. Jason and I knew this wasn't going to be love at first sight."

Garrett hated the thought of hurting Maggie, and yet he'd had to create an attitude of uncompromising firmness between them. He'd had to act the ruffian and cad in order to drag her from the care of her beloved grandmother. But Garrett was determined to bring Maggie back to Jason and put an end to her father's continued heartbreak.

Garrett glanced at his watch. Soon they'd be stopping for supper. At least Fred Harvey's restaurants, known as Harvey Houses, were at virtually every major stop on the rail.

Garrett remembered past meals with fond satisfaction. Fred Harvey allowed only the finest foods to be served in his restaurants. So meticulous was Harvey that he had water hauled in steel tank cars to every restaurant. Harvey had announced that this way, no matter where one traveled on the Santa Fe line, the coffee would taste the same. A wise decision, Garrett surmised, knowing the farther west they traveled, the heavier the alkali content in the water.

The car door opened, admitting the conductor. He announced loudly their arrival in Florence, the supper stop. Those who planned to dine in the Harvey House had given their meal choices to the porter back in Emporia. Their selections had been wired ahead and would be waiting, piping hot, for them to eat.

Garrett sighed. As much as he hated the idea of disturbing Maggie, leaving her alone on the train was out of the question. She was likely to run away as she had other times when Jason had sent for her.

Meanwhile, Maggie was pacing in her sleeping compartment, ranting and raging against her father, Garrett, and even God.

"The arrogance! The absurdity! If my father thinks for one minute that I'll allow him to marry me off to the likes of Garrett Lucas, he's out of his mind!" she shouted. She grabbed her glass of water and threw it against the door.

When her tantrum had played itself out, Maggie sat down on the edge of the bed. The entire room was only a few feet across and eight feet long. There was a window, a bowl and pitcher sitting on a tiny dresser, and a small wooden commode. The bed itself was barely wide enough for one person, and Maggie wondered if her feet would hang over the edge.

She sat in silence for a long while and contemplated Garrett's final words. He was to be her husband! "Oh God," she breathed. "Why do You hate me so?"

A clouded memory appeared. Her mother's loving face bent over her in care, then nothing. "You do hate me," Maggie murmured in utter despair.

Maggie caught sight of her grandmother's carpetbag and pulled it close. She felt a lump in her throat as she thought of her grandmother sitting alone in the big Queen Anne house.

"Grandmother, I love you so. Please God, even if You can't forgive me, take care of Grandmother until I can get back to Topeka," Maggie murmured.

Her mind was overwhelmed with the events of the day. It had all happened so fast. Her father had been wise to handle the situation as he had, for she would have gone into hiding if she had she known of his plans.

In his own way, he had probably tried to tell her. Maggie's mind wandered back to an unopened stack of letters collecting dust in the attic back home. She had heard nothing from her father for two years after he left. When at last a letter had arrived, Maggie had refused to read it. Grandmother had been understanding, Maggie remembered, but she had also engaged her granddaughter in discussions about forgiveness and God's overall plan.

"Oh, Grandmother," Maggie sighed.

She opened the bag and removed its contents one by one. There were a dozen or more biscuits, and Maggie knew they'd be the lightest, finest soda biscuits ever made. Next she pulled out several pieces of fruit and a large chunk of cheese that her grandmother had lovingly wrapped in an embroidered tea towel. Maggie reached down deep and touched something quite familiar. She began to sob. It was her grandmother's Bible.

Maggie hugged the Bible to her chest and cried. Her pain grew more intense. She allowed the Bible to fall open. The final verse of the Old Testament loomed prophetically across the page: " 'And he shall turn the heart of the fathers to the children, and the heart of the children to their fathers, lest I come and smite the earth with a curse' " (Malachi 4:6).

"But this can't be right," Maggie said aloud, snapping the book shut. "Grandmother needs me, and I need her. My father hasn't turned his heart to me, and I certainly won't turn mine to him. Will You curse me without considering my side of the matter?"

Just then a knock sounded at the door, and Maggie began to tremble uncontrollably. Was it Garrett? What would she say?

Silently, Maggie placed the food in the carpetbag and set it on the floor. Then she eased down to the mattress, pulled her legs up under her, and feigned sleep. The knock sounded again, then the soft voice of the porter called her name. Finally, there was nothing.

Afraid to move, Maggie succumbed to the weariness that possessed her body and drifted into a fitful sleep. The day's events combined with the heat had been too much.

Maggie dreamed of a field of prairie flowers. Tall Kansas sunflowers waved majestically above the knee-high prairie grass. Bachelor buttons and sweet williams dotted the landscape with vivid purples and blues. She was running and running across the prairie until she could feel her legs ache from the strain. She pushed herself to continue until the pain in her legs became unbearable. Maggie felt herself falling in slow motion. Down she went to the velvety softness of new prairie grass.

Someone was calling her name, and when she opened her eyes, she met the bluest eyes she'd ever known. Garrett Lucas!

Maggie struggled to move away from Garrett, but it was no use. Her legs were badly cramped, and the pain she'd felt in her dream had become a very real sensation.

"Don't touch me!" Maggie winced in pain as she tried to move her legs.

"Stop fighting me. I'm not going to hurt you," Garrett said gently as he tried to help Maggie sit up.

"I don't want your help, and I don't want you here. Why are you here?" she suddenly questioned, forgetting her fear.

"We're in Florence. It's a supper stop. I've only come to wake you up and take you to supper," Garrett reasoned.

Maggie laughed nervously. "Supper? You think that I'm interested in eating? You waltz into my life, take me away from everything I love, tell me I have no choice—no say, and," she paused, drawing a deep breath to steady her nerves, "you top it off by telling me that you—you, Garrett Lucas—are to be my husband. And now you act as if nothing has happened and come to take me to supper?" Maggie tried to pull away from Garrett but found herself pinned against the wall of her compartment.

"I told you to stop fighting me. I'm not going to hurt you. I have the highest respect for your father and for you," said Garrett in a hushed whisper. Maggie could barely hear him above the noise of her own ragged breathing.

Garrett'a face was only a matter of inches from her own. Maggie swallowed hard and felt her face flush. She stopped fighting and matched Garrett's stare with one of her own.

Neither one said a word. Suddenly, Maggie knew her life would never be the same. By some means, her father and Garrett would have their way. What made it worse was that Garrett sensed this understanding in her.

Garrett moved his face closer, and Maggie closed her eyes, certain that he would kiss her. She'd never been kissed before, and part of her wondered what it would feel like.

When nothing happened, Maggie opened her eyes to find Garrett had pulled away. He looked at her with smug satisfaction, and Maggie wanted to disappear. How could he stir such intense feelings that her anger melted away, leaving her helpless to fight him?

"Shall we go to supper?" Garrett drawled, enjoying the upper hand. He helped Maggie to her feet and steadied her as she waited for the blood to return to her legs.

"I suppose I have no other choice," Maggie said soberly. "Lead me where you will, Mr. Lucas."

Chapter 5

Maggie went through the motions of eating dinner. She said very little, even though the food was some of the best she'd ever enjoyed. Maggie had never eaten at a Harvey House. She and her grandmother had always intended to do so but had never gotten to it.

Garrett had ordered the English-style baked veal pie for himself as well as Maggie. Accompanying the veal were fresh vegetables and a selection of salads, one of which was made with lobster brought in from the East.

Maggie wanted to show as little interest as possible, but her curiosity got the best of her once or twice. When the Harvey girl brought out dessert, Maggie nearly moaned.

"I don't know where I could put another bite," Maggie said to the young woman. "Just look at this piece of pie!"

Garrett smiled to himself, happy to see Maggie talking, if only to the Harvey girl.

"It's a quarter slice, Ma'am. That's the way Mister Harvey says it's to be done. He doesn't want his customers leaving the Harvey House hungry." The girl curtsied.

"No chance of that," Garrett joined in good-naturedly. The Harvey girl smiled appreciatively at Garrett, and for some reason, Maggie felt angry.

"If you'll excuse me, Mr. Lucas," Maggie said, getting to her feet. "I will have this young woman show me where I can freshen up."

Garrett's eyes narrowed. They sent Maggie a silent warning, but she merely tossed Garrett a smile over her shoulder and followed the Harvey girl from the room.

"You'll find provisions to wash up at the end of the hall. The rest is out the back door," the Harvey girl pointed. "I've got to return to my station now."

Maggie lingered several minutes at the back door. It would be easy enough to slip from sight, but to where? If she left, Garrett would be right on her trail, and there would be no chance to escape before he found her.

She turned her attention to the pitcher of water on the alcove table. She poured a small amount into the bowl and took a fresh wash cloth from the stack beside the pitcher. Dipping the cloth over and over, Maggie managed to wash away most of the day's grime. Taking a comb from her bag, Maggie tried to put her hair back in order. She'd lost several hairpins.

Convinced that she had done her best, Maggie started back down the hall. As she neared the entrance to the dining room, she noticed a large map of the state. The rail line was clearly outlined and included the many spurs that ran from the main line to a variety of small Kansas towns.

Maggie traced the route. There would be a variety of whistle stops in between, but Newton would offer her the best chance of getting home. A smile played on her lips. "We'll see just how smug Garrett Lucas is when he wakes up in western Kansas and I'm gone," Maggie whispered under her breath.

In the dining room, Garrett was finishing a cup of coffee. His relaxed appearance gave no hint of his inner turmoil. Four times, Garrett had checked on Maggie, making sure she hadn't disappeared. Now as she took her seat across from him once again, he was captivated by the beauty he saw. Although he'd accused her of being a child, it was increasingly clear she was a young woman.

"The train's been delayed," he told Maggie. "We can wait it out here or on board. What's your choice?"

Maggie said nothing, pretending to take sips of tea. Pushing the fine china cup back to its saucer, she forced herself to meet Garrett's eyes.

"It is of little consequence to me, Mr. Lucas. I leave the matter entirely up to you," she said icily. Each word had been carefully chosen and delivered.

"Very well. Let's return to the train." Garrett motioned toward the door. He left a generous tip of thirty cents and helped Maggie from her chair.

Maggie waited patiently while Garrett paid for the meal with money her father had provided. She felt angry at the thought of her father's scheming but said nothing as Garrett lead her back to the train. Outside, the weather had turned chilly, and Maggie was glad she'd worn her heavy traveling suit.

Garrett walked slowly and made small talk about the town of Florence. Maggie feigned interest and even glanced north at the main part of town, but she breathed a sigh of relief when Garrett finally led her back to the train.

"You've been awfully quiet," Garrett drawled, making note of Maggie's sigh. "I don't suppose you'd give up this playacting and talk to me."

Maggie raised an eyebrow and lifted her face to meet Garrett's inquisitive stare. "I don't know what you want me to say, Mr. Lucas. I'm tired and confused, and as a spoiled and selfish child, I can't imagine having anything to say that could be of interest to you."

It was Garrett's turn to sigh. "Maggie, that's not true. First off, I wish you'd call me Garrett."

"First? What next?" Maggie questioned in a sarcastic tone.

"Frankly, I wish you'd sit a spell with me. It's early, and you'll have plenty of time to rest later." Garrett was as polite and considerate as Maggie had ever seen him.

"Very well—Garrett. I will sit with you," Maggie said, trying to put Garrett's mind at ease. It was important to make him believe she'd accepted her fate.

Garrett felt his chest tighten when Maggie said his name. He grinned broadly as he helped her board the train and led her down the aisle to the window seat.

For a moment, Garrett stood admiring Maggie's profile. The lanterns above the aisles threw a mysterious glow. In their gentle light, Maggie looked more a woman than her seventeen years.

Maggie grew uncomfortable under Garrett's detailed scrutiny. "What was it you wanted to discuss, Mr. Lu. . . , Garrett?" Maggie questioned, hoping he'd stop examining her face.

"Maggie, you don't need to be afraid of me," he said softly, taking the seat beside her.

"I'm not. . ." Her words trailed off. There was no sense in lying. "I guess it's just a natural reaction," she finally admitted.

"Of course," Garrett agreed. "I wouldn't expect anything else, but I want to put your mind at ease if I can."

Maggie wished she could freeze the moment in time. The muted light of the train, the star-filled sky beyond the windows, and Garrett Lucas looking at her in a way no other man had ever done.

Garrett closed his brown, calloused hand over her small, soft fingers. Maggie's breath caught in her throat. She tried to will herself to pull her hand away.

"I wish you wouldn't do that," she whispered without daring to look into Garrett's blue eyes.

"Is that the truth, Maggie?" Garrett inquired, daring her to face her feelings. He knew playing upon those feelings might jeopardize the progress that had been made, but human nature urged him on.

Maggie touched her free hand to her forehead. "I can't think clearly when you're close by."

Garrett laughed out loud, causing several of the train passengers to lift their eyes from newspapers and embroidery work. Maggie was grateful their nosey train companion had departed. Garrett gave Maggie's hand a squeeze.

"That's a good sign, Magdelena, *mi querida*." he murmured, so low that Maggie could barely make out the words.

"What does that mean?" she questioned, not certain she wanted an answer.

"I'll tell you later," Garrett grinned. "I don't think you could appreciate it right now."

Maggie spoke out boldly. "A term of endearment, no doubt." The warmth of Garrett's hand seemed to radiate up her arm.

"Would you hate that so very much?" he inquired.

Maggie didn't trust herself to answer. She lowered her face as she felt blood rush to her cheeks.

"I'm sorry," Garrett said. "I shouldn't have pressured you with something so intimate."

"No," Maggie whispered. "You shouldn't have." Silence fell like a heavy blanket between them. Maggie wished Garrett would remove his hand, but he didn't.

"Don't you have any questions about your father?" he asked. He hated to break the moment of intimacy by bringing up Jason's name.

"I suppose I am curious," Maggie said thoughtfully. She pulled her hand from Garrett's, pretending to loosen the lace collar at her neck. What she said was the truth, and it couldn't hurt to listen.

"Good. What would you like to know first?" Garrett questioned her as easily as if they'd been lifelong chums. This feeling of familiarity bothered Maggie.

"Start anywhere. I don't know much at all. Grandmother used to share bits and pieces with me, but she knew how uncomfortable it made me," Maggie replied absentmindedly.

"Why, Maggie? Why did it make you uncomfortable to hear about your father?" Garrett pried, hoping Maggie would answer truthfully.

"Because he'd hurt me so badly," Maggie blurted out. She couldn't help the tears that formed in her eyes. She turned her face to the window, but Garrett reached across, compelling her to face him.

"Sometimes it's necessary to open up a wound, to clean it out and let it heal. Life's like that too, Maggie," he said softly.

Maggie wiped a single tear away as it slid down her cheek. "Some wounds never heal, Garrett."

"They can with God's help. 'My heart is sore pained within me: and the terrors of death are fallen upon me.' That's from Psalms," Garrett offered.

"You know the Bible?" Maggie questioned in disbelief.

"Not as well as I'd like to, but I suppose more than some. I found religion a way of life when I was young. But it wasn't until after I lost my parents that I learned what a relationship with Jesus Christ was about," Garrett answered.

"I didn't know your parents were dead. What happened to them?" Maggie questioned, steering the conversation away from the issue of salvation.

"Their wagon overturned on a mountain road. They were hauling goods back from Santa Fe and never came home. I was twelve at the time."

"How awful," Maggie gasped. "What did you do?"

"I did the only thing I could do," Garrett shrugged. "I mourned their passing and was packed off to Denver to live with an aging aunt."

"You had no other family?" Maggie was suddenly quite interested.

"None. My mother's sister was quite a bit older. She was the only living relative I had in the world. Life out West isn't easy on people," Garrett reflected. "My aunt died two years later, and I took off on my own."

"Where did you meet my father?"

"I'd wandered down to Santa Fe," Garrett said, smiling sadly. "I was nearing my fifteenth birthday and feeling pretty sorry for myself. Here I was, a young man alone in the world. I was just existing, not really living. I felt God had deserted me. That's when your father came on the scene.

"I was sweeping out a livery stable for a man in Santa Fe. He paid me twenty cents a week and let me sleep in the loft. It wasn't much, and I was getting pretty tired of it. My parents and aunt had left me some money, but I couldn't touch it until I turned twenty-one. Since my fifteenth birthday was coming up, I figured I'd take my week's wages and blow it at the saloon.

"I'd never been to a saloon, but I guzzled down as much rotgut as I could buy. I sat there nursing the last few drops in my glass, when it hit my head and stomach at the same time. I made a mad dash for the back door and the alley. That's where I met your pa."

"My father?" Maggie asked surprised.

"He happened to be walking down the alley just then. Most nights he'd walk for hours by himself. You have to remember, he'd just come to this territory. He'd lost your mother and baby son and had had to leave behind a baby daughter. If I had been five minutes later to the alley, I'd have missed him all together."

"What happened?"

"I thought I was dying, but your father helped me, and when it was all over, we shared our troubles. Your father offered me the use of his hotel room, and we fast became friends."

"My father was depressed because of Mother's death, wasn't he?" Maggie asked, picking at imaginary lint on her skirt.

"Not really. Jason, your father that is, said he believed his wife was safely in heaven with your brother. He showed me where the Bible said there'd be no sorrow in heaven, so he knew she was happy. What he couldn't abide was his need to separate his life from yours."

"Me? I was the reason he was so unhappy?" Maggie wanted to change the subject, yet in her heart she wanted to understand the years that had separated her from her father.

"He told me all he wanted to do was work so hard he could go to sleep without seeing your face. He told me how you'd stood at the gate, tears streaming down your face, calling for him over and over," Garrett paused, knowing Maggie was filled with the pain of this memory. He reached his arm around her shoulder and pulled her close.

Maggie allowed Garrett to hold her. She no longer hated her father for leaving her. What else could he have done? She had deserved to be left behind.

After a few minutes, Maggie composed herself and pulled away from the sanctuary of Garrett's strong arms.

"He just kept walking. He never looked back," Maggie began. I ran the length of the fence calling him. I knew he blamed me for my mother's death. I needed so much to know he still loved me, but he said nothing."

"He couldn't, Maggie. Not and still walk away, and if he'd stayed, he knew he'd be forever lost in his remorse and sorrow. It couldn't have been an easy decision," Garrett answered gently. "I can just see you as a little girl, standing there waiting for him by the gate, day after day."

"How did you know?" Maggie's surprised expression matched her tone.

"Your father told me, and I would imagine your grandmother told him. Maybe she thought it'd make him come home. Maybe she thought it would turn him around."

"But it didn't," Maggie said sadly.

"No, it didn't, but there is another reason your father sent for you rather than traveling to Topeka himself," Garrett said in a way that demanded her attention.

"What?" Maggie questioned.

"If you'll recall, your grandmother mentioned your father hasn't been well."

"Yes," Maggie murmured.

"Your father always intended to make things right. He thought if he gave you enough time, you'd outgrow your hatred. But now he doesn't have that luxury."

"Why not?" Maggie asked.

"Because he's dying, Maggie."

"That isn't possible! He's not an old man, and he has plenty of money for doctors and medicine. He can't be dying," Maggie stated in disbelief.

Garrett's eyes softened. "All the money in the world can't buy you a new heart. Jason's heart has worn itself out, and there's no way to make it right again. He's aged rapidly, lost a great deal of weight, and spends most of his days in bed."

Maggie let the news soak in. "How, how long. . ." Maggie couldn't ask the question.

"How long does he have?" Garrett filled in the words.

Maggie nodded.

"Only God knows for sure."

Maggie felt more tired than she'd ever been before. She could no longer deal with her painful past.

"Garrett, I believe I'd like to retire. I'm completely spent."

"I understand. Let me walk you to your sleeper." Garrett stood and offered Maggie his hand. For a moment she hesitated, but her heart reasoned away any objections. She placed her hand in Garrett's and allowed him to lead her down the train aisle.

The lantern in Maggie's sleeping compartment made the room look warm and inviting. She paused in the doorway.

"Good night, Garrett," she said. She tried to think of something else to say, but the intensity of Garrett's stare banished rational thought. Maggie could feel her heart beating in her throat. Garrett was too close, and his hand was still firmly around her arm.

When he leaned down and gently pressed his lips on hers, Maggie went limp. She'd never been kissed by anyone on the lips, until now.

The kiss lasted a heartbeat, but to Maggie it seemed like a lifetime. When Garrett raised his head to speak, Maggie kept her eyes lowered. "Good night," he said before retreating down the narrow train aisle.

Chapter 6

At midnight, the train entered Newton, Kansas. Maggie was jerked awake by raucous laughter and drunken singing. As she struggled to sit up, she remembered Garrett's kiss.

"I've got to get away from here," she said in a hushed whisper. The sound of breaking glass outside drew her attention, and she peeked out from behind the window shade. The depot's large white letters read, "Newton."

Surely, Garrett's asleep at this hour, Maggie thought. *I should leave now.* The girl rushed to find her clothes. She reached into the inner pocket of her jacket and found her money still safe.

The lantern burned very low, and Maggie hurried to the mirror and did her best to pull her hair back. She tied it with the ribbon that had held her lace collar at the neck of her blouse. "It'll have to do," she conceded, not totally satisfied with the results.

Maggie pulled her coat on quietly and grabbed the carpetbag. Gently she edged the door of her sleeping compartment open and checked the hallway for any sign of Garrett. There was none.

As quickly as she could, Maggie maneuvered through the shadowy corridors of the train car. At last she was rewarded with the exit door.

"Well, Miss, if you're getting off here, I'd suggest you hurry. Train's pulling out directly," the conductor told her in his disinterested manner. Maggie prayed that he wouldn't question Garrett's whereabouts.

"Thank you, I will," Maggie replied. "Can you tell me where the nearest hotel is?"

"That whitewashed clapboard over there," the conductor said, eyeing his watch. "Sorry, Ma'am. We're pulling out. Are you staying?"

"Yes," Maggie managed to say. She took a last look at the train. The laughter had died down, and there was just the muffled noise of several other passengers walking away from the railroad station. The conductor returned the steps to the platform of the train and waved his brass lantern to signal the engineer.

As the train groaned and jerked down the tracks, Maggie thought of Garrett. She was almost sorry she'd outfoxed him. She chuckled to herself as she walked toward the hotel.

Maggie found sleeping quarters with only moderate difficulty. As tired as she felt, she would have gladly slept in the barn. The manager had given her a candle, and Maggie didn't bother to inspect the room other than to locate the bed.

She undressed and, with a quick breath, blew out the candle and settled into bed. Maggie thought about all the things Garrett had told her. A part of her wished she could break down the barriers between her father and herself, but Maggie was certain he would never forgive her. Loneliness filled her as she again saw herself as a child. She struggled to remember something, but it passed away quickly in the cloudiness of sleep.

Several hours later, Maggie woke with a start. She couldn't remember where she was. The sun was just starting to shine through the lace curtains of her hotel room window.

Maggie swung her legs over the side of the bed, newly aware of her surroundings. The room wasn't much to look at, but it was clean and safe. The girl shivered from the cold wooden floor as she crossed to the window.

Careful not to reveal that she was dressed only in her camisole and petticoat, Maggie pulled back the curtain. Most of Newton still slept, and she wondered what time it was.

It must be early, she thought to herself. Realizing she was hungry, Maggie placed the carpetbag on the bed and pulled out a soda biscuit. As she began to eat, she remembered the evening before when she'd dined with Garrett in Florence. The heady aroma of the Harvey House food lingered in her mind, making her biscuit seem inadequate.

She also remembered the intimate conversation, Garrett's touch, and their kiss. Maggie shook her head as if to dispel the memory, but it was no use. Dancing blue eyes and a gentle smile were all she could remember. That and the fact that she was supposed to become Garrett Lucas's wife.

Within an hour, Maggie was dressed. Her traveling suit was hopelessly wrinkled, but there was no use worrying about it. She took the carpetbag and headed downstairs.

"Morning, Miss." The same man who'd given her entrance the night before was greeting her as though he'd woken from an undisturbed night. Maggie couldn't help but smile.

"Good morning," she answered politely. Just then, half a dozen children came running through the lobby. They were laughing and playing tag.

"Now children," the man began. "You know the rules about running inside. Go on out if you're going to run." The children stopped long enough to acknowledge their father, and then rushed through the hotel door out onto the street.

"Now, Miss, what can I do for you?" he asked, turning his attention back to Maggie.

"When will the next train for Topeka be through?"

"Well, that's hard to say. Usually, the train you were just on transfers its passengers at Great Bend. Then it comes on back and picks up eastbound passengers," the man told her.

"Usually?" Maggie held her breath.

"They've been having trouble with the Arkansas River. Rains are causing grief with the flood levels. If there's much more rain, the Arkansas is going to be out of its banks, then there won't be any trains through for a spell."

"If it doesn't flood," Maggie began in a hopeful tone, "when will the train be back through?"

"This afternoon."

Maggie bit her lower lip as she thought. Garrett was bound to know she was gone by now. If not, it wouldn't be much longer before he found out. She couldn't risk staying in Newton long enough for Garrett to return on the afternoon train.

"What about a horse? Where could I buy or rent a horse?" Maggie questioned innocently.

"You could check at the livery stable, but I wouldn't get my hopes up. Horses are hard to come by out here. You won't find too many people willing to rid themselves of one. Besides," the man answered, noticing Maggie's attire, "you aren't really dressed for riding."

Maggie tried to smile, but her mind was in a frenzy. If she couldn't get out of Newton within hours, Garrett would find her.

"What about the stage? Will there be a stagecoach or freighters leaving for Topeka today?" Maggie knew she was appearing desperate.

"I don't know what's chasing you, little lady, but the answer is no. Stage isn't due through here for another day," the proprietor said sympathetically. "I'd check with the livery stable first, but I'd say if you're going to leave Newton today, it'll be on foot."

Maggie nodded and thanked the man. She walked to the livery stable, where the livery owner told her there hadn't been a horse available for sale since February.

"Where you want to go, little lady?" a foul-smelling man asked Maggie.

"I'd rather not discuss it," Maggie said, growing increasingly uncomfortable as the man's friends joined him.

"She ain't your type, Jake," one of the man's filthy friends offered. "You're more my type, now ain't you?" The other men laughed and ribbed each other with their elbows.

"You saddle tramps git out. You hear me? Now git!" the livery owner bellowed. When the men begrudgingly walked away, Maggie turned to thank the man.

"I appreciate your help. I don't suppose there's any hope of someone hauling freight out this morning?"

"Nope, I'd know if there was. As far as I know, you're stuck here at least until tomorrow, probably more like next Friday. I don't think the train will get past the Arkansas River crossing."

A discouraged Maggie walked to the Harvey House and sat down for a hot breakfast. Her money was going fast, but if she did have to walk out as the hotel manager had mentioned, she would need proper nourishment.

While eating breakfast, Maggie learned the train she'd been on the night before had already turned back in the direction of Newton. The Harvey girl informed her they expected the train for the lunch meal.

Maggie wondered what she should do. She could try to hide out in Newton or get on the train after Garrett got off. She toyed with several ideas while absentmindedly stuffing food in her mouth. She was surprised to find herself nearly finished with her meal when the Harvey girl appeared at her table to see if she needed anything else.

By eight o'clock, Maggie had decided to walk to Florence. The town was a main hub for the stage, and freight was being hauled out every day. Maggie didn't know how long it would take to walk the thirty miles to Florence, but putting space between Garrett and herself was the only thing that mattered.

After paying for her breakfast, Maggie got directions to the general store and went in search of supplies.

A cheery bell rang on the door of the store as Maggie entered. She was greeted by an elderly woman who eyed every stranger suspiciously.

"Where did you come from?" the woman questioned rudely.

"I'm from Topeka," Maggie answered, hoping her honesty would quell the woman's curiosity.

"Topeka? You came here from Topeka? When?"

"I came in last night, and now I'm getting ready to leave. I have a few things I need, and if you don't mind, I need to hurry," Maggie retorted rather harshly.

"You running from the law, Girl?" the woman continued to pry.

"Absolutely not!" Maggie exclaimed.

Quickly, Maggie located the things she needed for the walk. She was grateful she'd had the sense to wear walking shoes. She located a canteen and some dried fruit and placed them on the counter.

"I figure you must be planning on walking somewhere. I'd be mindful of the weather if I was you," the older woman said, seeming to soften a bit. "My big toe has been aching all night from the chill in the air. I figure a powerful storm is brewing, and we'll be due for rain tonight." Maggie nodded and paid the woman.

"You aren't going to walk far in that outfit are you?" the woman asked, smoothing back a strand of gray hair.

"It'll take me as far as I need to go," Maggie replied and walked out of the store.

Maggie knew following the train tracks would be the wisest thing to do. She also knew it would be the first place Garrett would look for her. She walked several yards before deciding to parallel the tracks as best she could without being seen. The prairie stretched out endlessly before her. Only an occasional stand of trees broke the monotony.

Remembering the old woman's warning, Maggie looked to the skies. Clouds were building to the west. Probably the same storm that had flooded the Arkansas River, Maggie surmised.

For a moment, she thought better of her decision to walk to Florence. She turned to survey Newton once again. Surely, it couldn't be that hard to find a hiding place.

She looked skyward again, and her mind turned to thoughts of God. Where was He in all this? Maggie couldn't help but wonder what God would want her to do. She'd spent so much of her life ignoring God's direction that now she felt ridiculous for her concern.

But maybe God wanted to use something in this to help her find her way. A place where Maggie could finally belong. She sighed. Why would God care about her? After all, she'd done nothing but turn her back on Him. No, Maggie decided, God certainly wouldn't listen to her now.

Calling upon every ounce of courage she possessed, Maggie moved north, away from the tracks. She knew she'd be able to see the telegraph wires from quite a distance, and the added space gave her a slight feeling of security. When Maggie felt confident she was far enough away from the tracks to be hidden by the tall prairie grass, she turned east. Determined to reach Florence as soon as possible, Maggie quickened her steps.

"Soon I'll be back where I belong," Maggie said aloud, trying desperately to bolster her sagging spirits. But in truth, Maggie wasn't sure where she belonged.

Chapter 7

By ten o'clock, Maggie knew leaving Newton had been a mistake. Her feet hurt and her back ached. Sitting down, Maggie took off her shoes and surveyed the terrain around her. It was pretty enough, she thought as she rubbed her blistered feet. The fields were covered with tall, thick prairie grass. In the distance, rolling hills were covered with soft greens and purples.

Returning her shoes to her feet, Maggie stood and brushed the grass from her skirt. If only it were as easy to brush off the emptiness that filled her heart!

The air felt heavy and sticky. The farther Maggie walked, the more desperate she felt.

"But I had to leave," she reasoned aloud. "I couldn't go on with him—with Garrett." Just saying his name reminded her of the tender way he'd kissed her.

Growing up in Topeka, Maggie had avoided both boys her own age and older men who found her prime wife material. It was the age of the mail-order bride, and Maggie couldn't help but laugh out loud as she remembered one particular encounter. Harley T. Smythe, a local bride broker, had come unannounced to the Intissar home.

Maggie could still remember the stunned look on her grandmother's face as Mr. Smythe had explained his intentions of arranging a marriage for the older woman. Sophia had listened patiently, but not without discomfort. When at last Mr. Smythe took a breath, Sophia had interrupted and led him back to the front door.

"Mr. Smythe," Sophia had stated as she fairly pushed him through the portal. "I have no intention of remarrying." With that she closed the door in Harley T. Smythe's astonished face and let out a laugh matching Maggie's.

Maggie felt tears in her eyes. "I love you so much, Grandmother. You were always there for me, and you always made me happy." Maggie continued talking as if her grandmother walked beside her. Somehow it made the miles pass more quickly.

She had walked some distance when the grasslands started giving way to rockier scenery. The rocks were a nuisance, but there was no avoiding them.

Soon, Maggie came to another obstacle. A wide ravine, apparently a dry wash or creek bed, cut deep into the ground. Maggie considered her plight, but within seconds her mind was made up for her. The sound of riders caught her attention.

"Garrett!" The name caught in her throat. Three mounted horses were kicking up a fury of dust in the direction Maggie had just come from.

Without thinking, Maggie started down the edge of the ravine. The rocky gravel gave way, causing her to slide halfway into the small canyon. The ravine was deep and ran for miles either way, with small caves and inlets hidden in the rock walls. As she reached the bottom, Maggie hurried in the direction of the railroad tracks.

She kept straining to hear the sound of hooves. She knew the men must have seen her, and she began to run, tripping over larger rocks. She heard rumbling in the distance. The sky had grown dark. Her side began to hurt and her legs were cramping, but Maggie knew she had to continue running.

The ravine grew deeper and began twisting and turning. Maggie could see where the railroad trestle crossed the ravine. If she could make it to the trestle, she might find a place to hide. She hiked her skirts up higher and put all her strength into running. As she approached the trestle, her eyes darted back and forth. No sanctuary revealed itself.

Quickly, Maggie scurried under the trestle and continued down the ravine. Rain started to pour, and Maggie grew desperate as she heard a horse's whinny. The riders were very close.

" 'Deliver me in Thy righteousness, and cause me to escape: incline Thine ear unto me, and save me.' " She murmured the Psalm, surprised that she had remembered it. She thought about praying, but changed her mind. She never could abide the attitude of calling on God when one was in trouble, only to go one's own way when things went well.

Just when Maggie found it impossible to force herself any farther, an opening in the ravine wall revealed itself. It was scarcely more than a two-foot-wide indention, but Maggie could hug her rain-drenched body against the rock and avoid being seen by the riders above her.

A flash of lightning startled the girl, and she bit her lip to keep from crying out in surprise. The boom of thunder so soon after the lightning let her know the worst of the storm was nearly upon them. The wind picked up, muffling the riders' voices.

"I don't see her, Jake," one of the men called out. "Let's go back to town and out of this mess."

Maggie tensed. It wasn't Garrett after all but the ruffians from the livery stable in Newton. Remembering the look in Jake's eyes caused her to freeze in fear.

"I guess you're right. I'm pert near soaked to the bone already."

Maggie recognized Jake's grizzly voice. Another flash of lightning caused Maggie to jump. Overhead, the horses snorted and stamped.

"Come on. Let's git," Jake called to his companions. "Another day, little lady," he yelled in the direction of the ravine. Maggie shivered at the thought.

The men rode away, but with the storm growing stronger, Maggie stayed against the ravine wall. Thunder continued to boom out answers to lightning, and the sky grew even darker. Maggie noticed water collecting in the ravine bottom.

After another ten minutes, the lightning had lessened but not the rain. The water was nearly to Maggie's ankles, and it continued to rise.

I've got to get out of here, Maggie thought. She began to wade toward the railroad bridge. The weight of her water-drenched skirts threatened to drag her down, but she held her skirts up above her knees and kept wading. She got to the trestle, thankful that the skies had lightened a little.

Maggie rested against one trestle support after another until she'd worked her way out of the ravine. At the top, she rested under the bridge and considered what to do next. The water had risen even higher and resembled a small creek.

Suddenly, Maggie became aware of what a sheltered life she'd led. Someone had always been close at hand to help her out of trouble. While she'd learned many social graces and home skills, she was just as Garrett had said: a spoiled and selfish child.

When the rain let up, Maggie continued her journey toward Florence. The sky was overcast, but the sun was beginning to heat things up. Maggie felt sticky and uncomfortable in her clothes.

The clouds began to build again, and huge thunderheads were lining the horizon to the west. Maggie recognized signs of another storm. She picked up her pace, but because of her blisters, she just as quickly slowed down again.

Tears welled in Maggie's eyes. All she wanted to do was go home, care for her Grandmother Intissar, and be happy. Why would God begrudge her that? But Maggie already knew the answer. God was not making war on her. She was making war on God.

Refusing to deal with the issue of God and her need for Him, Maggie concentrated on each step. "I'm one step closer to Topeka. I'm that much closer to home," she murmured as the soggy ground mushed up around her feet.

The sky grew darker as the squall line neared. Maggie felt even more vulnerable than before. Part of her wanted to sit down on the waterlogged ground and cry, but she knew that she had to find shelter.

Maggie could see very little that constituted a safe haven. Ahead to the north was a small stand of trees. They weren't likely to offer much protection, but perhaps they would buffer the wind. As Maggie pushed forward, she remembered her grandmother's warning about trees and lightning. She knew she was being foolish, but the alternative of open prairie seemed far less appealing.

Maggie barely reached the trees when the first huge raindrops began to fall. The sky had taken on a greenish hue, a sure sign of hail.

The trees offered little cover. The brush around them was laden with dead leaves, grass, and twigs. Maggie chose a spot surrounded on three sides by young trees, hoping that if lightning proved to be a problem, it would strike taller, older trees.

The wind picked up and chilled Maggie to the bone. Rain pelted her from every direction. Maggie hid her face in the carpetbag, refusing to watch the violence around her.

After what seemed hours, the storm played itself out, leaving colder temperatures behind. Maggie began to walk, no longer able to bear the pain and cold of sitting crouched against the trees.

There was little hope of reaching Florence before night, and Maggie began to wonder how she would endure a night on the prairie. If she continued walking after dark, there would be no way of knowing where she was. But if she stopped, she'd have to sleep out in the open.

Maggie walked on in the fading light. Every part of her body was saturated from the rain, and the weight of her clothing was slowing her pace to a near crawl. Finally, as the last bit of light slipped over the horizon, Maggie dropped to her knees in the soggy prairie grass.

The prairie sky filled with stars, and the moon darted in and out from behind clouds. Maggie huddled shivering on the ground below. Her senses were dulled from the cold, and her mind was groggy with sleep. The last thing she remembered was the distant howl of a coyote.

The next morning dawned bright and clear, but the wind was still cold. Typical of Kansas weather, summer didn't guarantee warmth.

Maggie pulled herself to a sitting position and waited for her head to stop spinning. When the dizziness refused to subside, she began to panic. She shook her head and felt blinding pain.

Slowly, she got to her feet and tried to get her bearings. There was no sign of the railroad or the telegraph poles. There was nothing to do but walk in the direction of the rising sun. At least that would put her in an eastward direction.

Minutes worked into hours, and Maggie still had no indication that she was where she ought to be. She strained her eyes to catch some sign of life but saw nothing except hills and rocky fields.

When the sun was nearly overhead, Maggie stopped and ate some of the food from her carpetbag. It satisfied her hunger but did nothing to clear her head. She rested on the grass for a moment, fighting dizziness. Mindful that precious time was escaping, Maggie summoned all her strength in order to push on.

She got on her hands and knees and tried to stand, but immediately fell back to the ground. She tried again and again, but it was no use. Finally, Maggie gave up and let her body slump to the ground.

"I give up God!" she cried to the heavens. "I give up. Whatever it is You want, I accept. I won't fight anymore. If marrying Garrett Lucas and living in the New Mexico Territory are best for me, then so be it. I will not defy Your will any longer. But, please, please help me now. Show me what to do, where to go! Please!"

Maggie was unable to keep her eyes open. She dreamed of warm fires and her grandmother's hot chocolate. She was vaguely aware of a dull ache in her head and chest, but she couldn't rally enough strength to figure out why she hurt so much.

When next she opened her eyes, the sun was just setting on the horizon. Or was it rising? Maggie tried to get some sense of the time of day, but her mind refused to register anything but pain. She coughed until she nearly passed out. The intense cold made her shake violently.

At one point, Maggie opened her eyes and thought she saw people in the distance, but when she squeezed her eyes tight and opened them again, she realized it was just her imagination.

The sky grew dark and the ground grew colder than ever. Maggie's teeth began to chatter uncontrollably. She didn't hear the approaching sound of horse hooves, and she barely felt the hands that gently turned her over and helped her to sit. When she opened her eyes, she could only gasp one word before falling back against the offered support.

"Garrett."

Maggie saw tears in Garrett's eyes as he cradled her in his arms. They couldn't be real, she decided. Nor could the words she heard him saying.

"Maggie, my Maggie. What would I do if I lost you now? Please, God don't let her die!"

No. Those words were only her wishful imagination, Maggie decided as she drifted into sleep.

Chapter 8

I t seemed only moments had passed since Maggie had last opened her eyes. But looking above, she was dumfounded to find mud, thatch, and sod hanging over thin poles. Where was she? Maggie struggled in vain to remember what had happened on the rain-drenched prairie.

Mindless of the pain in her chest, Maggie sat up and began coughing violently. A bearded Garrett Lucas rushed into the room to her side.

"Try to take a sip of water," he said, gently supporting her back while handing her a tin cup. Maggie did as he said and found her cough abated somewhat.

"What happened? Where are we?" Maggie whispered hoarsely. She was puzzled that Garrett wore a beard and his attire had so drastically changed since last she'd seen him on the train.

Garrett went to the small cook stove and returned with the cup.

"Drink this," he instructed.

Maggie took the cup and looked inside. It held a thick black syrup. "What is it?" she questioned skeptically.

"It's medicine to clear out your lungs," Garrett replied, concern hanging thick in his voice.

"Your stomach too, I'd venture to say," Maggie said, trying to lighten his mood.

Garrett laughed at Maggie's words. It was so good to hear her speak, even if to question his actions.

"I'm glad I amuse you, but what in the world has happened? I remember walking out of Newton, and the terrible storms, but after that. . ." Maggie paused trying her best to remember.

"Drink first, and then we'll talk," Garrett said, pointing to the cup. Maggie screwed up her face at the thought of drinking the medicine but did as Garrett instructed. The blend wasn't so bad. Maggie finished it and held the empty cup up as proof.

Garrett set the cup aside and pulled up a crude wooden chair. "Now, I believe we have some things to discuss." His dark brown hair was a bit wild, and the beard made him look older.

Maggie was captivated by the way Garrett looked, but she refused to acknowledge even the slightest admiration. She waited for Garrett to continue.

"I don't know what in the world you were thinking, getting off a train in the middle of the night," Garrett tried unsuccessfully to sound stern. When he looked at Maggie, even in her sickly state, she was all he'd ever wanted. She was beautiful, intelligent, hardworking, and resourceful—although, he would have to teach her a bit more about that last quality.

"I wanted to go home to my grandmother," Maggie offered lamely.

Garrett ignored her remark. "I went to let you know the train was turning back because of the flood waters. I had the porter open your door when you didn't answer, and—" His voice caught. "I felt like dying inside when I saw you were gone."

"Father would have been quite miffed with you, eh?" Maggie teased, still refusing to acknowledge the seriousness of the situation.

"Don't you know how close you came to dying?" Garrett's face contorted painfully.

"I suppose very close."

"You suppose that, do you? Well, if I hadn't come riding up when I did, you wouldn't have lived another hour. You were drenched to the bone and nearly unconscious. I was lucky enough to locate a doctor. He and his wife agreed to let us stay here in their dugout."

"So, this is a dugout?" Maggie murmured while looking around the small room. Everything seemed to touch. What little furniture she could see was poorly put together, not at all what one would expect a doctor to have. The dugout had been dug by hand, some six or eight feet into the earth. The roof rose above the prairie only two or three feet.

"Yes, this is a dugout. But that isn't the issue. Maggie, please promise me you won't run away again. I can't imagine returning to your father or grandmother and explaining that you got yourself killed."

Maggie could sense the genuine concern in Garrett's voice. *Why did he care so much? He hardly knew her.*

"I'm sorry, Garrett. I shouldn't have run, but I was scared. I kept thinking about never seeing Grandmother again. Then I thought about having to face my father and his condemnation. All that along with what it would be like to. . ." Her words faded as she nearly mentioned the idea of becoming Garrett's wife. Embarrassed, Maggie lowered her face.

"I put a great deal of pressure on you," Garrett apologized. "I'm sorry for that. Back in New Mexico, the plan seemed so right."

"I guess sometimes we only seek our own way," Maggie said softly. "I don't think I've ever done as much praying as I have in the last few hours. Not that I really expected God to listen to me."

"Last few hours? How long do you think we've been here, Maggie?"

"I was just going to ask you that."

"Five days," Garrett replied dryly.

"Five?"

"That's right." Garrett leaned back against the chair. "Five days of wondering and waiting. Praying that you'd live but feeling so helpless. That's part of what I wanted to talk to you about."

"I can't believe it's been that long. It seems like just hours ago I was bartering with God for my rescue, and here you are."

"Oh, Maggie. I wish it was that simple. I found you, brought you here, and waited. Doc said he'd done all he could. We took turns watching over you. I told God if He would make you well, I'd never force you to marry me." There. He'd finally said the words.

Maggie burst out laughing, and with the laughter came the cough again.

"Maybe we should wait. Maybe you aren't up to this," Garrett hastily suggested, concerned that she was becoming hysterical.

"No, pl. . .please," Maggie sputtered the words, trying to contain her cough. "Don't take offense. I'm only laughing because I made a similar deal with God myself. I told him I'd do whatever He wanted me to, even if that meant marrying you and living with Father. I said if God would rescue me, I'd stop fighting Him."

"I see," Garrett said thoughtfully, realizing Maggie had said nothing of a commitment to Jesus. "Seems we've both been bartering with God."

"Grandmother would chastise me," Maggie admitted. "She used to say, 'Never offer God anything you aren't ready, willing, and able to give.' "

"And now, Maggie." Garrett's voice was barely audible, "are you ready, willing, and able to follow God's direction for your life?"

"What about you, Garrett Lucas?" Maggie avoided the question.

"It seems to me, God saved us both in spite of ourselves. I don't think we thought too clearly. I'd hate to be rash with any decision, but I did promise God I'd leave you be."

Maggie tried not to show her disappointment. Part of her was starting to like the idea of becoming Mrs. Garrett Lucas.

"I promised God I would do anything, even live with my father and become your wife. I can't break a vow to God," Maggie answered honestly.

"I'd say there's something important to learn from this. We need to seek God's will over our own. He'll guide us, but He can't if we're always trying to lead," Garrett reflected.

"I believe that's true. I guess I'm ready to try harder at trusting Him," Maggie added.

"Even with your life?"

Maggie lowered her eyes and fingered the sheets nervously. "I don't know. I don't want to make that kind of decision lightly, and I don't want to make it simply because I'm scared. I want it to mean more than that."

Garrett nodded. "I wouldn't presume to rush you. You'll make the right choice when God's timing is complete."

"Thank you for understanding," Maggie whispered. "I appreciate that more than you'll ever know."

"I wonder, Maggie," Garrett mused, leaning toward her from the edge of his chair. "I wonder if we could start over."

"Start over? What do you mean?"

"I'd like to be your friend, even if I never become your husband. Although," Garrett added with a wry smile, "I'd like to be that too."

Maggie blushed.

"I believe," she replied after a thoughtful moment, "we could be friends. I will be your friend and I will go to my father's ranch willingly. On that I give you my word."

Garrett gently lifted Maggie's chin. He studied her delicate cheekbones and dainty lips. When he looked into Maggie's eyes, he found a sincerity he hadn't dared to hope for.

"I know it will please your father, and if it means much," Garrett added, "it pleases me."

"Garrett, please don't rush me about my father. I still feel uncomfortable about this whole thing. I won't lie and tell you otherwise. I feel trapped, but I know that going to him is the right thing." Maggie tried to clear the hoarseness in her voice. "I can't pretend I feel anything but pain about the past and my father."

"I understand. I just love Jason so much. He's been like a father to me." Garrett immediately regretted the words.

"I wish he'd been a father to me," Maggie breathed.

"I wish he could have too. Selfishly, I'm glad he left Topeka. I'd be a far worse man if I'd never met him. But because I care for you, I'm sorry he had to leave you."

He cared for her. Maggie warmed at the thought. Refusing to get carried away, Maggie pushed the feeling aside.

"There are a great many things I wish I could change," she finally said, looking up at the sod roof. "But wishing doesn't make it so. It doesn't bring people back to life, or give you a place to belong."

"Maggie, you'll always have a place to belong. You belong to God, but you just don't know it yet. You belong with your father, but you can't get past the mistakes. And," Garrett sighed, "I'd like to think you belong with me."

Maggie offered a gentle smile. "All I can do is try," she replied. "But it's going to take time, and I'll need your understanding."

"I promise to help in whatever way I can." Garrett whispered the words although he wanted to shout in triumph. With God's help, he had broken through the wall of protection Maggie had built around herself. The foundation for friendship had been laid.

An hour later, a white-haired woman came bustling through the door and down the dirt stairs of the dugout. She huffed as she struggled to carry in a basket of vegetables.

"Well, look who's awake," she said, spying Maggie.

Garrett smiled broadly. "We've already had quite a lively conversation. I gave her some medicine and made her stay put."

"I must say, Child, you gave us quite a fright. Doc will be mighty happy to see you've pulled out of it," the woman remarked, stepping to Maggie's bedside.

"Maggie, this is Dottie. She's the doctor's wife," Garrett introduced. "She and Doc have allowed us the pleasure of staying here until you get well enough to travel."

"It's a pleasure to meet you," Maggie said sweetly. "It's so kind of you to let us stay here."

"Ain't nothing at all. I was glad for the company. Doc doesn't always make it home very early, and it gets mighty lonesome out here on the plains. I was glad to have you both, 'specially this one," Dottie nodded toward Garrett. "He's been a Godsend—brings me fresh water for the garden and totes and fetches just about anything else I need."

"If she'd waited, I would have carried in those vegetables too," Garrett added with an admonishing look.

"Weren't that heavy. Didn't see any reason to go bothering you." Dottie waved him off. "Now how about you, Missy. Hungry?"

"I think I am," Maggie replied, realizing she wanted something to eat.

"Good. I was just about to get us some lunch. Broth for you and stew and biscuits for us." The older woman pulled on a clean apron.

Maggie wrinkled her nose. She'd hoped for something more substantial. Nonetheless, she felt very fortunate and cared for. She pushed aside the nagging thought that God had watched over her.

Day after day flew by. As Maggie grew stronger, she spent more time contemplating her life. She also developed a real love for Dottie and Doc. The older man had infinite patience and entertained his patient with humorous stories from his practice.

Maggie enjoyed watching Doc and Dottie as they playfully bantered words. Doc teased Dottie as if she were a young schoolgirl, and Maggie noticed Dottie blushing on more than one occasion. *It must be wonderful to love each other so much after so many years of marriage,* Maggie thought.

Eager to be up and around, Maggie talked Doc into letting her get out of bed at the end of the first week. As the end of the second week neared, she and Garrett began talking about the trip back to Newton.

"With the horse I bought in Newton, we can make it back to town in a matter of hours," Garrett began, as he and Maggie strolled along the outside of the dugout. The sky threatened rain any minute, and Garrett wouldn't allow them a longer walk. "Or Doc could drive us in his buckboard. I thought I could leave him the horse as partial payment for all he and Dottie have done. They don't have a good saddle horse."

Maggie remembered her unsuccessful search for a horse.

"How did you ever find a horse to buy in Newton?"

Garrett's eyes danced with amusement. "I take it you tried and failed?"

"Yes, as a matter of fact, but—" Maggie's words were lost in the rumble of thunder.

"I think we should get inside," Garrett suggested.

"I agree. I've been in one too many storms already," Maggie said, turning toward the dugout steps.

The storm roared across the prairie. The roof of the dugout leaked, and it swayed in the gusty winds. Maggie had to light the lamp twice because of the draft from the storm.

"We'll be lucky if there isn't hail," Garrett stated as he cracked open the door and looked out. "I'm glad Dottie went to town with Doc this morning."

"Do you think it will get much worse?" Maggie asked, paling at the thought.

"I don't know. The rain's letting up some, and the wind is dying down. Maybe the worst is past. I'm going to take a look," Garrett replied and opened the door. "You stay put."

Maggie watched Garrett's booted feet disappear up the stairs. Curious about what was happening, she followed him. He seemed intent on something to the south, and when Maggie made it to the top of the stairs, she found out why. She gasped as she caught sight of a large tornado heading toward them.

"I told you to stay down there!" Garrett yelled, pointing to the dugout.

"Dear God," Maggie breathed her prayer. "Deliver us."

The twister played out its energy on the open prairie, darting from side to side as if in some frenzied dance. Maggie could see bits of dirt and debris flying up in the air as the storm approached. The tornado was enormous, and its path still headed directly toward the dugout.

"Let's take cover," Garrett said.

"Where?" Maggie asked fearfully, running down the stairs in front of him. There were tears in her eyes.

Garrett took everything off the table and pushed it against the wall of the dugout.

"Here. Get under the table." He pulled the mattress and blankets off the bed.

"Take these," he said, thrusting the blankets at Maggie's huddled frame. He crawled under the table and pulled the mattress in with him, securing it around them to shield them from any debris.

"Give me those blankets," he instructed.

Maggie started to hand the blankets over when the roaring of the wind caught her attention. It had started as a dull, constant noise in the background. Now it sounded as if a train were nearly upon them. Maggie caught Garrett's expression and knew instinctively it was the tornado.

Garrett grabbed the blankets and pulled them over their heads. He wrapped his arms around Maggie as the door to the dugout burst open, and the roof began to give way.

Above the roar of the Kansas twister, Garrett began to pray. "Dear Father, protect us from the destruction of this storm and give us shelter in Your watchful care. We pray this in Jesus' name. Amen."

"Amen," Maggie murmured in agreement. Warmth washed over her and her fears abated even though the storm continued to roar. Was this the peace of God that her grandmother had tried so often to explain?

Suddenly, Maggie found it difficult to breathe. It was as if all the air was being sucked out of the room. Her ears popped from the pressure of the storm. But more than anything else, she felt Garrett's strong arms around her.

Chapter 9

The storm completely destroyed the roof of the dugout, but Maggie and Garrett escaped without a scratch. Maggie was amazed by the power of the storm, but even more, she wondered at the power of God to protect them from destruction.

When Doc and Dottie returned to the dugout, Garrett was already repairing the roof and Maggie was clearing debris.

"We were lucky," Doc said as he gave Garrett a hand with the long roof poles. "The twister didn't touch Newton."

"We were blessed here too," an exhausted Garrett answered. "The twister only skirted the edge of the dugout. The barn and smokehouse had some shingles blown off, but the rest of the farm is undamaged."

Maggie and Dottie carried handfuls of sod outside and stopped to appraise the situation.

"Could'a been a lot worse," Dottie said, wiping sweat from her forehead.

"That's just what Garrett was saying, Dot," Doc replied as he secured his end of the support poles.

"I've been through some bad storms before, but usually it was from the comfort of a cellar," Maggie exclaimed, still amazed at the calm, unchanged land around them.

"Well, these dugouts work nearly as well," Doc exclaimed and took the sod and branches that Maggie still held. The four worked until nightfall. After a hearty supper of Dottie's fried potatoes and pork chops, everyone went to bed early.

Days later the dugout was back in order, and Dottie declared it better than ever. Maggie seemed to thrive on the physical work, and Doc declared her completely healed. With that announcement, Garrett determined he and Maggie should move on to Newton and catch the earliest westbound train.

Maggie was sorry to leave Doc and Dottie, but more than that, she was scared to be traveling alone once again with Garrett. It wasn't that his company was unpleasant. It was the pleasure she found in his companionship that worried Maggie. Her fear was clearly reflected in her eyes, and she flinched when Garrett took hold of her arm after he'd finished packing their meager possessions in the buckboard.

"It's going to be alright, Maggie," Garrett whispered as he helped her into the wagon. "Trust me."

Maggie met Garrett's eyes. Excitement surged through her as she realized that this man would one day be her husband. *Trust him?* Maggie questioned her heart. *Was that possible?*

Maggie roused from her thoughts as Garrett and Doc sat down on either side of her. She waved a bittersweet goodbye to Dottie, promising to write. But once the farm was out of sight, Maggie fell back into silence. She thought about the future and wondered about God.

Maybe her grandmother had been right. Maybe Maggie never felt like she belonged because she didn't. She didn't belong to God.

Maggie lost herself in the memory of things her grandmother had told her about salvation. Over many Sunday dinners, the older woman had gently shared the need for Jesus Christ and eternal life.

"One can't outrun or outgrow one's need for Jesus, Maggie," Sophia had reminded her granddaughter. "Oh, people try. They find ways to compensate for the loss of God in their life."

"Such as?" Maggie had questioned.

"Well, look at Lillie." Sophia had referred to Maggie's friend. "There is no need for God in Lillie's life, at least as far as she is concerned. Her money brings everything she thinks she needs."

"Don't be hard on Lillie. She's very precious to me," Maggie had argued with her grandmother.

"Exactly. If you knew Lillie was in danger—the kind of danger that could take her life—and you could show her how to be saved from that perilous end, would you save her?" Maggie remembered the question as if it had been yesterday.

"Of course, Grandmother, you know I'd give my life for Lillie," Maggie had replied, knowing where the conversation was leading.

"Well, Maggie, Jesus has already given His life for Lillie and for you. You are both in risk of an eternal danger that I can never save you from. I can help you to see the need, but only God can deal with your heart, and only Jesus can save you from death."

Maggie chilled at the memory of her grandmother's words. She rubbed her temples. If only there weren't so many things to consider.

Garrett arranged for rooms at the Harvey House in Newton, and Maggie was grateful to find bathing accommodations that didn't require a metal wash pan. She lingered for a long time in the hot water.

"I do believe in God," Maggie reasoned with herself in the tub. "I just don't know about trusting Him with everything. Surely God expects me to take care of myself, especially when I get myself into trouble through carelessness." Just then a flash of pigtails, a bedroom window, and her mother's smile came to mind. Despite her best efforts, Maggie couldn't focus the memory. *What was haunting her?*

After warming the water in the tub twice, Maggie pulled a soft fluffy towel around her and prepared for dinner. She went to a small wardrobe and pulled out a pale blue silk gown, lavishly trimmed with Irish lace and satin ribbons.

Maggie pulled the dress over her head and gently smoothed it out. The Harvey House laundress had done a good job of removing most of the wrinkles. Maggie fastened the tiny buttons up the back of the gown, struggling to secure the last few.

She stood back to survey herself in the mirror, fluffing the slight fullness of the sleeves. Satisfied, Maggie sat down to the task of putting her hair in order. After another fifteen minutes, she was finished. She was just putting her hairbrush and mirror back, when a knock sounded at her door.

"Coming," Maggie called. She opened the door without thinking to ask who it was. She knew it would be Garrett.

Garrett studied her silently and smiled broadly. "I've seen the other women downstairs, and you'll outshine them all."

Maggie blushed, not knowing what to say. She was quite inexperienced at this type of flattery. Garrett seemed to understand and took her by the hand.

"Let's go to dinner. The train passengers have finished and the dining room will be serving supper to the public." Maggie pulled her door shut and allowed Garrett to lead her down the hall.

The dining room was no shoddy affair. People from town seemed to revel in the finery and quality of Fred Harvey's English taste and decorum. The crystal was spotless, the china without cracks or blemishes, and even the fine linen tablecloths were immaculate.

Maggie ate lobster in a rich cream sauce, as well as baby carrots cooked with grated orange peel, greenbeans with red pimentos and almond slivers, and a variety of other things she couldn't even remember. After dinner, Garrett suggested a walk.

"Will you be sorry to meet him?" he asked.

"My father?" Maggie inquired, knowing very well the answer.

"Yes. Will you be sorry to meet him again?"

"Sorry? No, not really sorry. I was sorry he had to go away and sorry we both seemed to cause each other such heartache, but I can't honestly say I'll be sorry to meet him again." Maggie went on to tell Garrett about the last time her father had come to Topeka.

"I stole out the back and ran to Lillie's house. Her parents weren't home, but she was. We went to her upstairs bedroom and spied on my father and grandmother as they looked for me. Part of me wanted to run back to him."

"Why didn't you?" Garrett questioned as he assisted Maggie over a missing portion of boardwalk.

"I don't know," she answered softly. Suddenly she didn't want to talk. They strolled in silence for the remainder of their walk.

When they returned to the hotel, Maggie reached into her purse for the key to her room. Without a word, Garrett took it from her and opened the door. "We'll be leaving quite early. I'll ask one of the Harvey girls to wake you in time for breakfast."

The silence fell between them once again, and Maggie felt the intensity of Garrett's stare. Sounds from the restaurant faded away, and even the commotion of hotel guests at the far end of the hall seemed to be in another world.

Garrett stepped forward, and Maggie knew he would kiss her. She wanted him to, yet she remembered her grandmother's warning about being unequally yoked with unbelievers. Grandmother had spoken of men who might court Maggie, but the truth was Maggie was the unbeliever.

Maggie backed into her room abruptly, leaving a surprised Garrett standing with his arms slightly outstretched.

"Good night, Garrett," Maggie whispered and closed the door.

Maggie leaned hard against the door after locking it. She wondered if Garrett was still on the other side. Her heart pounded and her mind was muddled with conflicting emotions. Maggie prepared for bed and hoped sleep would come quickly.

The train ride to Trinidad, Colorado, passed uneventfully. Summer storms had cleared the air, making temperatures quite bearable. The air also became dryer the farther west they traveled. Maggie loved to study the changing landscape. They had passed from rolling prairie hills to parched lands of sagebrush and juniper.

Maggie knew her feelings for Garrett were growing, and Garrett had made it clear how he felt about her. The confusion came because of her own spiritual battle. Maggie didn't want to deal with God or her father, and on the last day of their train journey, she determined to put them both aside and concentrate on her feelings for Garrett.

When dark hues of purple lined the western horizon, Maggie grew curious. "Are those the mountains?" she asked Garrett in little girl excitement.

"Yes, but this distance doesn't do them justice. Wait until we're closer." Garrett shared Maggie's enthusiasm. The mountains meant they were almost home.

Several hours later, Maggie was rewarded with a pristine and glorious sight. The Rocky Mountains in their summer splendor towered majestically before them.

"I've never seen anything like it in all my life. Just look!" Maggie exclaimed as she lowered the train window. She quickly pulled her head back in, as cinders flew back from the smoke stack, stinging her eyes. She tried to fish her handkerchief out of her bag, but it eluded her.

"Here," Garrett offered. "Look at me and I'll get it." Eyes closed, Maggie obediently turned her face to Garrett and allowed him to work.

"There! Good as new," Garrett proclaimed.

When she opened her eyes, Maggie met Garrett's eyes only inches from her own.

"Thank you," she whispered. Desperate to regain her composure, she added, "Does it always look so grand?"

Garrett laughed softly. "Yes, it always does. I find it hard to believe you've never traveled to the mountains before. I'm surprised your grandmother never took you."

"Grandmother wasn't one for traveling. She liked to stay in Topeka, garden whenever possible, and go to church activities."

"I see," Garrett said thoughtfully. "What about you? What did you like to do?"

"Well, let's see. I liked to go to the picnics our church had down by the river. We'd have at least one a month during the summer. I also enjoyed reading and the parties Grandmother and I went to." Maggie poured out the words easily but continued to look out the window, refusing to miss a moment of the newness that passed by.

As the tracks began to climb the steep grade of Raton Pass, Maggie couldn't help but gasp at the scenery. The mountains rose imposingly on either side, and the evergreens reached for heaven. There was snow on the higher peaks, and wildflowers waved along the tracks.

"We certainly don't have anything like this in Kansas," Maggie said, turning briefly to meet Garrett's eyes.

"That's true," Garrett agreed.

"You must love it a lot," Maggie said thoughtfully.

"Indeed I do. I can only think of one other thing I care more about." Maggie knew Garrett was struggling with his feelings just as she was. They seemed to have an unspoken agreement to leave the subject alone, so Maggie attempted to steer the conversation to safer ground.

"Is my father's ranch this beautiful?"

"Every bit as much and more. It lies in a rich green valley on the other side of the mountains. It's protected on both sides by the Sangre de Cristo range."

"The what?" Maggie questioned, giving Garrett her undivided attention.

"Sangre de Cristo. It means the blood of Christ. Your father said it reminded him of what was important in life. His ranch sits in a deep valley. It's great land for cattle and horses. The Pueblos have a mission not far from the ranch house. Your father set it up for a missionary couple down there. The Pueblos raise fine crops and sheep, and they share portions with your father in exchange for beef," Garrett shared eagerly.

"The Pueblos? Who are they?" Maggie questioned.

"They're Indians. Perfectly harmless," Garrett added at the look of alarm on Maggie's face. "They have a way with irrigation and planting that would make your head spin, and they live in adobe houses like the ranch, only smaller."

"Adobe? I can see I'll have a great deal to learn," Maggie murmured thoughtfully. "We might as well put this time to good use. Tell me about adobe."

"Adobe is an orange clay brick." Garrett was more than happy to teach Maggie about her new life. "The bricks are formed from straw and clay," he continued, "and then allowed to dry in the sun. The adobe is used with a small amount of timber to create a house. Then the workers mud the entire house, filling in the cracks and smoothing over the surface of the walls. The bricks are quite thick and keep the houses well insulated."

"I see, and my father's house is made of such adobe?"

"That's right. It may not seem as refined as your house in Topeka, but it holds a charm all its own."

"And the interior?" Maggie asked, trying to get a mental picture.

"We don't waste much wood out here, and you won't find a lot of it used in the house. There are some hardwood floors and paneling is used on the walls in a couple of rooms, but usually the stone walls are whitewashed. The interior of your father's house is as nice as any I've seen. I think you'll like it."

"I suppose so," Maggie said softly. She remembered her home in Potwin Place, and how she'd helped her grandmother pick out the colors, wallpaper, and furnishings. "I know it will mean a great deal to my father if I do."

"You don't have to put on a show for him, Maggie," Garrett replied. "Your father is a very simple and very compassionate man. He only asks for honesty."

Maggie stared out the window. The train engine was straining to pull the cars through the tunnel at Raton Pass. They were barely moving.

"I think he expects a bit more than that," Maggie finally said.

"But he won't expect you to put on airs. Just be honest with him, Maggie. He'll want it that way."

The day grew quite warm, and in spite of her excitement, Maggie dozed off and on as they drew nearer her new home.

"Wake up Maggie," Garrett was shaking her shoulder. "We're in Springer."

Maggie jumped up quickly. "I must have fallen asleep."

"I'll say," Garrett drawled in mock sarcasm. "Pert near a three hour nap, little lady."

Maggie laughed. The sound warmed Garrett's heart. It was good to be at peace with Maggie, even though the peace was fragile.

"Will my father be here to greet us?" Maggie questioned, realizing she didn't know.

"He'll be back at the ranch, waiting. He'll have sent the wagons for our gear and some other things we've ordered shipped here," Garrett answered as he pulled his black Stetson on. "Of course, most of the shipment was picked up a couple weeks ago due to our little delay to put you back in order."

Maggie felt a twinge of embarrassment for the detainment. She started to say something but was stopped by Garrett's appearance. She'd never seen him in blue jeans before. His white cotton shirt was open at the neck, and his neatly trimmed beard gave him a mysterious air. Garrett had considered shaving his beard before they left the dugout, but Maggie had protested, telling him it gave him character. Not that Garrett Lucas didn't already have plenty of that, Maggie decided.

When they stepped off the train, Garrett was quickly surrounded by men. They laughed and slapped each other on the back, all talking at once for several minutes. Maggie was certain she'd overheard one of them say congratulations. She wondered if they'd betted on whether Garrett would make it back to New Mexico with her.

Garrett turned quickly to motion Maggie to join them. "Maggie, this is Bill. He's one of your father's right-hand men."

Maggie smiled shyly. "It's nice to meet you," she said softly. The man smiled from ear to ear, revealing several missing teeth. His hair, from what Maggie could see as it peeked out from under a grimy hat, was gray fading to white.

"Pleasure's mine, Miss Maggie!"

He seemed so pleased to meet Maggie that she almost didn't catch the name of the next cowboy as Garrett had her meet the entire crew.

"This is Mack, this tall, scraggly looking guy is Cactus Jack, and this old good-for-nothing is Pike." Garrett whirled Maggie around the circle. They all seemed happy to meet her and so genuine in their greetings and best wishes that Maggie felt warmly welcomed.

"Joe and Willy are waiting for us at Five Mile Junction," Bill announced to Garrett.

"Well, it's nearly noon, and I'd imagine if we're going to make Five Mile Junction by night, we'd better get a move on," Garrett announced. It was clear to Maggie from the response of the cowboys that Garrett was in charge.

Maggie tried to take everything in: the countryside, the town, the people. Springer was the county seat, but it was much smaller than Topeka.

She stood to one side watching a hired carriage pull away with a distinguished looking man and woman. The woman was fussing with her ill-fitting traveling clothes, and the bored man was studying the head of his cane. It appeared life was the same all over. Maggie couldn't help but smile to herself.

"Do you need to stop for anything before we get on the road?" Garrett was asking.

"No, I don't think so," Maggie replied, trying to think of anything she might need.

"There's a small trading post north of the ranch. We usually get supplies and anything else we need from there. If you think of something once you get home, let somebody know and we can add it to the list. Someone is always heading over to the post office every few weeks," Garrett explained.

"We'll be that far removed from civilization?" Maggie questioned, not realizing her look of astonishment.

"I never thought of it that way," Garrett answered thoughtfully. "I guess I never needed anything more, so it didn't seem so uncivilized."

"I didn't mean to insult the place," Maggie said apologetically. "I just presumed we'd live near town. I never thought much about my father's place."

Garrett helped Maggie into the wagon and easily jumped in to take a seat beside her.

"Well, you'll have a few days' ride to consider it." With that, Garrett gave the reins a flick and the horses took their place behind Mack's wagon.

The wagon wasn't nearly as comfortable as the train had been, and while the scenery was of intense interest, Maggie's backside was sorely abused from the rocky pathway they called a road.

Two hours later, they stopped to eat. The rest was quite brief, however, and Maggie soon found herself back on the dusty trail headed into the mountains of the Sangre de Cristo.

Maggie was disappointed with the countryside. From the train, the land had seemed greener and less sandy. Up close, it looked like the edge of a desert. Maggie hoped her father's ranch would be different.

As the sun passed behind the mountain peaks and the sky took on a purple hue, Maggie grew quite chilly. As if reading her mind, Garrett halted the wagon long enough to take a blanket out from under the wagon seat.

"Here, this ought to help. We're almost to Five Mile Junction." Garrett helped Maggie pull the blanket around her shoulders.

Little more than a gathering of shacks and corrals, Five Mile Junction looked wonderful to Maggie. After a delicious supper of steak, potatoes, biscuits, and pie, Maggie was shown to a small room. She'd changed into her nightgown and was brushing out her waist-long hair when a knock sounded at the door.

"Yes?"

"It's me, Maggie," Garrett announced. "May I come in?"

"Of course, just one minute," she said as she pulled on her robe. "Alright, come ahead."

Garrett sucked his breath in hard as he caught sight of Maggie illuminated by candle. She was so delicate, yet her strength astounded him. And if all went well, one day she'd be his.

"You're so beautiful," he said in a husky whisper.

Maggie lowered her gaze, refusing to meet his eyes. She could feel a blush coloring her cheeks.

Garrett closed the space between them in two strides. He stood directly in front of Maggie without touching her. Maggie lifted her eyes to meet his. Words seemed inadequate, yet both felt captive to a spell. A spell that needed to be broken.

Garrett took a step back. "This trip is getting rougher all the time." Maggie nodded. "Tomorrow, we've got a lot of ground to cover in a short time. Are you up to it?" Again Maggie nodded, finding it hard to speak.

"Good. I'll have the cook wake you at five."

Garrett took another step back. He wanted so much to hold Maggie in his arms. No one would have to know, no one but them—and God. The thought caused Garrett to remember their future depended on more than physical attraction. He walked to the door and, with one last glance, pulled it shut behind him and breathed a sigh of relief.

Chapter 10

Maggie couldn't remember a rougher ride or a more desolate land. Aside from sagebrush and scrawny trees, Maggie could see nothing to break the monotonous, dusty brown earth. How could her father love this country?

Garrett concentrated on steering the team through the narrow, rocky pass. He was growing painfully aware of Maggie's presence as she bounced back and forth in the wagon seat. He needed a way to distance himself from her long enough for Jason to have a chance to get to know his daughter.

"Is this all there is to it?" Maggie questioned disappointedly as she gazed from side to side.

"What do you mean?" Garrett asked.

"All of this," Maggie said, motioning to the landscape. "I thought you said it was beautiful."

"Your home is beautiful. You'll see. This is just the way we get there," Garrett answered stiffly. The lead teams were slowing to a stop, and Garrett reined back on his team. "Whoa, whoa boys," he called softly.

"Why are we stopping?" Maggie inquired, forgetting the scenery.

"We'll water the horses here. They've had a long, hard haul," Garrett answered rather curtly.

"Garrett?" Maggie said his name, and Garrett swallowed hard. She was charming without being aware of it. Her cheeks were red from the wind, and her hair had come loose and hung in curled wisps around her face.

"Have I done something wrong?" Maggie questioned earnestly. "Is it because I don't like the land?"

Lifting Maggie from the wagon, Garrett looked deep into her sapphire eyes framed by long, sooty lashes. Why did he notice every detail about her? How could she be more beautiful out here than she'd been back in Kansas?

"Wrong? The land?" he whispered hoarsely. "I don't know what you're talking about," he lied and instantly regretted it. His hands lingered around her waist for a moment. Then he turned as if to leave.

"You've hardly said two words to me all day. If I've done something wrong, I have a right to know it." Maggie's words were a little harsher than she'd intended.

Garrett fought to control his emotions. How could he wait a year or more for Maggie to grow up and marry him? What if some other young man swept her heart away before he had a chance to insure that it belonged to him?

"I have to water the horses," Garrett said and walked away.

"Well!" Maggie huffed and turned to go for a walk. She climbed up the rocky ledge and became so winded that she had to sit down and catch her breath. Garrett had warned her about the altitude and how it would take time to get used to.

As she regained normal breathing, Maggie climbed the rock and marveled at the dainty wildflowers that sprinkled the ground around her. From the wagon, she'd been sure this land was devoid of any beauty.

She reached down and picked a frilly yellow flower that matched the gown she was wearing. After fingering the lacy edges of the flower, she tucked it in the lace lining the yoke of her bodice. She loved the feel of the mountain breeze through her hair and pulled loose the ribbon that tied back the bulk of her auburn hair. What a feeling! Perhaps this arid land had something to offer.

As she reached a small rocky ledge, Maggie was rewarded with a splendid view of the Sangre de Cristo. The snowcapped summit of the highest peak glistened and beckoned to her. She almost felt like she was coming home.

"Maggie!" Garrett's voice intruded on her thoughts.

What was bothering him? Maggie worked her way down the rocky path again. "I've done nothing to cause him grief," she muttered to herself as she checked her steps, remembering to walk from side to side as Garrett had taught her.

"Where have you been?" Garrett snapped. His eyes narrowed and grew darker. "I've been looking all over for you!"

"I just took a walk, that's all," Maggie answered calmly. She wasn't going to let Garrett Lucas cause her to lose her temper.

"You make sure somebody knows where you're going before you go heading off somewhere." Maggie bit her lower lip until she tasted blood. Garrett continued to scold her as if she were a child. "This isn't like Topeka. This country is wild and unpredictable."

"It's not alone," Maggie muttered.

"Just what's that supposed to mean?" Garrett questioned. He was already mad at himself for allowing his frustration to distance Maggie.

"It means you've never answered my question, and I don't understand why you're treating me so cruelly." Maggie stood against the sun, her jaw set. "Now are you going to give me an answer?"

Garrett reached out and took Maggie in his arms. He bent his lips to hers and had barely touched them when he pulled back and walked away. A few feet down the path, he turned on his heel, returned to Maggie, and kissed her soundly. Maggie could feel the dampness of his sweat-soaked shirt and the powerful muscles of his protective arms. Suddenly, Garrett pulled himself away and strode back to the team.

Maggie stared at his retreating back. *I guess that's the only answer I'll get*, she thought. *But what an answer.* After a few minutes, she joined Garrett at the wagon and allowed him to help her up.

"Mack's going to drive you," Garrett said and walked away.

Maggie was truly confused. If her company was so unpleasant, why had Garrett kissed her? And if it wasn't because of a distaste for her company, why had he sent Mack to drive the team?

Mack turned out to be a pleasant traveling companion. He was young and energetic like Garrett, but he wasn't Garrett. Mack told Maggie stories about cattle drives and growing up in Texas.

Maggie felt badly that she only half-listened. She was still consumed by questions about Garrett's attitude. She asked Mack why Garrett had requested him to trade wagons, but Mack only shrugged his shoulders and told her he was just following orders.

The day passed quickly, and when evening came, Maggie asked Mack, "Where will we stay the night?"

"Out here under the stars, Miss Maggie," he answered, surprised that she didn't already know.

"Oh, I see," she said, looking around her.

Moments later they stopped for the night. The men quickly unharnessed the horses, rubbing them down and giving them feed and water. Bill made a supper fire while Mack and Cactus Jack unloaded food and water.

Maggie felt totally useless. She didn't know the first thing about camping, and she couldn't find out where Garrett had gone. After about an hour, Bill announced supper was as fit as it was going to get, and the party gathered around the fire to eat.

"Where is Garrett?" Maggie questioned, unable to contain her curiosity.

"He's on the ridge, Miss Maggie," Bill offered the words along with a tin plate of beans and warm spiced apples. "He'll keep the first watch of the night."

"Oh," Maggie whispered. She wondered what he was keeping watch over, but she was too fearful of the answer to ask. Was it animals or people? Perhaps it was the banditos Mack had told her of. Maggie shivered.

"You'd better sit here by the fire, Miss Maggie," Bill directed, motioning her to a blanket. "I'll bring you some biscuits and dried beef to go with that. How 'bout some coffee to wash it all down with?" The older man worried over her like a father.

"No, thank you. Water would be fine."

"Whatever you like, little lady," Bill said and was on the move to bring Maggie her water.

Supper passed quickly, and much to Maggie's surprise, the men went about cleaning up the dishes and leftovers without looking once in Maggie's direction for help. When she offered to dry the plates, Bill waved her off.

It was growing cold when Maggie realized she'd left her shawl in the wagon. She remembered Garrett's earlier rebuke about not announcing her whereabouts and decided she'd better tell Bill where she was headed.

"Bill, I'm going to the wagon to get my shawl."

"Better take some light. There's hardly enough moon to see by tonight," Bill replied, looking up at the starry sky. Maggie nodded.

"Just grab ya some fire." Bill motioned to the campfire and went about his business.

In her seventeen years, Maggie had never had to pull a stick from a fire, and she wasn't sure how to go about it. She stood by the fire, wanting to ask one of the hands for help, but they were busy. She finally gave up and went to the wagon in the dark.

Maggie had just reached the wagon when she heard the lonely howl of a coyote. Maggie thought of her home in Topeka and wondered if her grandmother was lonely. She had Two Moons, but it wouldn't be the same. Grandmother loved conversation, and Two Moons rarely spoke.

There was also Lillie. Maggie missed her badly. It would be fun to share her adventures with Lillie when she got a chance to write.

Maggie carefully placed her foot on a wheel spoke and pulled herself to the top of the wagon. She climbed in back with little effort and was feeling rather proud of herself when she heard a low growling sound somewhere behind her.

She turned to see two greenish yellow eyes staring back at her. Maggie felt a scream in her throat, but it wouldn't release. Motionless, she watched and waited as the growling intensified. Her breath came in quick gasps, and her heart pounded.

"Garrett!" She managed to scream the name, causing the growling to stop for a moment. "Garrett!"

Maggie saw the eyes lunge at the wagon. She heard the impact of the animal as it hit the wooden side and the commotion of the men at the campfire.

Maggie had never been given to fainting, but she had never faced such fear. As she passed into unconsciousness, she heard a single gunshot ring out, then nothing.

"Maggie? Maggie, are you alright?" Garrett called as he held her against his chest. Maggie felt herself floating. Finally, she opened her eyes. Someone had brought a lantern, and she heard Garrett assure the other men she was okay.

"It's alright, Bill. She's not hurt," Garrett announced. "I think that coyote might be rabid or elsewise she got into some loco weed. Better check it out." Bill took the hint and motioned the rest of the ranch hands to follow him.

"Come on, boys. We've got a coyote to skin." Bill continued to talk to his companions as they walked back to camp, but Maggie was only aware of Garrett and the protection she felt.

"I'm beginning to wonder if I'm going to get you to your father alive," Garrett said as he held Maggie.

"I'm sorry. I told Bill where I was going. Honest, I did," Maggie said, struggling to met Garrett's eyes.

"I know, Bill told me. But he also told you to take a light."

"I didn't know how to get the stick out of the fire," Maggie admitted in a defeated voice. "I didn't want to be a bother."

Garrett threw back his head and laughed. "That coyote didn't mind the bother," he finally said. "The fire would've kept him at his distance."

"I didn't know," Maggie said, feeling utterly dejected. How could she know what was expected of her in this new world?

"Oh, *mi querida,* you are a prize," Garrett whispered as he ran a finger along her jaw. "I wish I could go straight to Pastor David and have him marry us."

Maggie sat up rather abruptly. "But I thought you and Father planned for me, I mean us, to marry right away."

Garrett grinned. "I'd like that more than I can say, but that isn't the plan."

"What then?" Maggie questioned.

"You need to get to know your father, and—" He paused for a moment. "You need to do some growing up."

"Growing up? Well, I never. I wouldn't be the first woman to get married at seventeen. Besides, on July 24th I'll be eighteen!" Maggie exclaimed, squaring her shoulders.

"Maggie, you need to learn about life, and you need to be a daughter before you become a wife." Garrett noticed the disappointment in Maggie's expression. "It's funny how just a few weeks ago you were all spit and fire, hating me with your eyes if not your words. Now you can't understand why you can't be my wife. Maggie, have you ever thought of the responsibilities of a wife?"

Maggie blushed deeply. Garrett smiled as if reading her mind.

"I know how to cook, clean, sew, and most everything else a good wife would need to know," Maggie said, avoiding Garrett's eyes. "I hardly see what being a daughter has to do with being a good wife."

"It has a great deal to do with it, Maggie. Why wouldn't you have much to do with gentlemen callers?"

"How dare you delve into my personal life!" Maggie was indignant.

"Don't you think a husband should know such things?" Garrett inquired softly.

"But you aren't my husband, and it doesn't sound like you want to be," Maggie pouted. A spark of hope flared as she wondered if she could entice Garrett to marry her immediately. If she arrived on the ranch as Mrs. Garrett Lucas, perhaps she wouldn't have to deal so intensely with her father.

Garrett looked seriously at Maggie as he turned her to face him. "Magdelena Intissar, you'd better knock off the little girl theatrics and listen up. You will never be the woman you were meant to be as long as you don't reconcile your relationship with your Heavenly Father. You've never accepted Jesus as your Savior, and you'll never be happy without Him. But, just like with your father, that relationship is a personal one. One that I can't interfere with or get for you. You'll have to take it one step at a time, on your own."

Maggie lowered her eyes. "I just don't know if I can, Garrett." Garrett pulled her tightly against him.

"I know you can," he breathed against her soft hair.

"Will you help me?"

Garrett was quiet for a moment. When he spoke, Maggie felt her heart nearly break. "No, I can't. I won't be there."

Maggie tore herself from his grasp. "You won't be there? Then where will you be?" she demanded.

"I'm going away. That way you'll have to deal with your father and with God. I'll be nearby, but I won't be influencing your decisions and actions. You won't be so confused then."

"Just how do you know what I'll be and won't be? Garrett Lucas, I think you're a cruel man. How could you take me away from my home, thrust me into the presence of someone I don't know, and expect me to handle the situation alone?"

"But Maggie, you won't be alone. God will go with you."

"God doesn't appear to have come with me this far," Maggie said, immediately regretting the words.

"Maggie, you don't believe that. I know your words were spoken out of fear, but I'm telling you that you have nothing to fear. Your father adores you. He's missed you every day of your separation. You won't find it hard to span the years, I promise. And as for Jesus—well, He's been standing with open arms all your life."

"Words. Just words," Maggie said, pulling herself to her feet. "I'm in exactly the same position I was years ago: on my own, to stand alone. You probably won't come back." Her voice gave way to a sob.

Garrett was beside her in a flash. "I'll be back. Don't ever doubt it. I'm going to marry you one day, Maggie Intissar, and that is something you can most definitely count on."

Surprising herself and Garrett, Maggie jumped over the side of the wagon and headed toward the campfire light.

"I mean it, Maggie. Don't ever doubt me," Garrett called after her. Maggie kept going.

Taking a blanket Bill offered, she rested on the makeshift bed Bill had prepared from pine needles and blankets. She refused to let the men see her cry, but long after the sounds of heavy breathing and snoring filled the air, another sound joined the night. It was the sound of Maggie's intense, muffled sobs—cries that did not escape Garrett Lucas.

Chapter 11

The next day, Maggie was riding with Bill when they paused at the opening of the valley her father ranched. Maggie stared in awe.

Piñon Canyon, as the ranch was called, stretched for miles. The burnt orange adobe ranch house contrasted sharply with the sturdy green piñon pines, which grew in abundance in the valley. Other, smaller buildings dotted the landscape, and several huge corrals stood in direct angles from the house. Beyond the inner circle of the ranch threaded a wide, silvery stream.

"I can hardly believe it," Maggie said in wonder. "I never would've guessed something so heavenly could be hidden in the middle of the desolation we've been riding through. It's beautiful!"

"That it is, Miss Maggie. I've called it home for nearly twelve years now, and it's always a welcome sight," Bill said enthusiastically.

"Twelve years? But my father has only been in the territory for eight years."

"That's so, but I worked this ranch for the former owner. Course it weren't nothing like what your pa has made of it. It was just a little stomping ground then. I was one of only three hands. Your father keeps over fifty." Bill urged the horses forward with a flick of the reins.

"Fifty? Why does my father need so many people?" Maggie questioned, suddenly wanting to know everything.

"There's enough work for fifty people, so he hired fifty," Bill said in his joking manner. "See, there's a lot more to a ranch than meets the eye. Somebody's got to keep up with the herd's feeding, watering, herding, branding, medicating, and such. Then there's those who keep up the land and the property. Those fences didn't just put themselves up, and they don't stay up without help. Not to mention the house help."

"I get the picture, Bill," Maggie laughed. Then, more seriously, she asked, "What's my father like?"

"I think pretty highly of your pa. He's an honest man, pays a fair wage, and sees to it that no one goes without. He even keeps a mission on the property. It's over that ridge, 'bout twelve miles. He supports the minister and his wife who keep it up for the Pueblos."

"Oh yes, the Indians," Maggie tried to sound intelligent.

"That's right. Your pa looks after everybody."

"But why? Why does he care so much?" Maggie wondered aloud.

"I 'spect it has to do with what your pa is always saying. God was good to him, so he'll just pass it on and be good to others." Bill fell silent, and Maggie didn't ask anything else.

The day passed quickly, and after several stops to rest and water the horses, the travelers were in the valley, making their way down the well-worn path which led to Piñon Canyon.

As they approached the first corral, several brown-skinned cowboys came riding up on horseback. They rode alongside Garrett talking in Spanish and laughing. Some fell back to greet the others and cast glances at Maggie. While she couldn't understand what they said, their smiles and excitement led her to believe she'd passed inspection.

Maggie suddenly grew self-conscious about her appearance. She was wearing the same yellow dress she'd had on for days. She was freckled and sunburned, and her hair hung in a lifeless braid down her back. What would her father think?

Once again, Maggie began to fear her reunion with her father. What if Jason Intissar had love and kindness for everyone except his daughter? What if she still stirred painful memories of her mother? Maggie had been told by her grandmother that she resembled her mother more than ever. What if her father couldn't deal with the haunting image?

In less than a heartbeat, the group halted at the huge stone walkway leading to the double doors of the ranch house. Maggie wanted to run. Her eyes darted around, and she gripped the side of the wagon. The muscles in her chest tightened, making normal breathing impossible.

Just then, Maggie caught Garrett's sympathetic look. He winked at her as Bill helped her from the wagon. The ranch house doors opened, and Jason Intissar burst through.

"Magdelena! You're really here! Oh, my Maggie, my daughter!" Maggie's father embraced her tightly. She could feel his bony thinness.

Jason stepped back to eye his daughter. Maggie said nothing. The feelings she'd buried so long ago, feelings of an eight-year-old girl watching her father walk away, threatened to overwhelm her. She wanted to say something, but her mouth refused to form the words.

"Oh, Maggie. It's really me." Jason laughed, hoping the assurance would help Maggie put aside her worried expression. "I've missed you so much! I can't believe you're finally here." Jason took her hand and twirled her in a circle before him. Maggie felt her body mechanically respond, but her heart was too overwhelmed to allow rational thought.

"You're more beautiful than your painting. Your mama would be proud. You look just like her. My, but how I miss her, *mi querida.*"

"That phrase—what does it mean?" Maggie questioned.

Jason smiled and took hold of her hand, "Desired one, my daughter. Just as you are to me."

Maggie raised an eyebrow, remembering Garrett's use of the phrase but said nothing, noting the sadness in Jason's eyes.

Garrett Lucas broke the spell. "Well, Jason, here she is. I knew it would be worth the effort, didn't you?" Garrett's words were both sincere and mocking. Maggie flashed fiery eyes at him, but Garrett's lazy grin and laughing eyes were too much. She looked away.

"It was worth the effort and the wait. How do I thank you, my dear friend?" Jason exclaimed, turning to grab Garrett's hand with his free one.

"You've already rewarded me by promising me your daughter in marriage," Garrett said casually. He stared intently at Maggie until she could feel herself blush from head to toe.

"Garrett!" Jason cried. Garrett waved his concern away.

"She knows all about it. She's even happy about it. She just doesn't like the waiting," Garrett said, pushing back the brim of his hat. Maggie fumed at the nonchalant way in which Garrett treated their betrothal.

"Is this true, Maggie?" Jason questioned. Maggie was touched by the deep concern in her father's voice. She allowed her eyes to meet his. He was grayer than she'd remembered, and his shoulders seemed more stooped. He wasn't an old man, but the sickness had taken its toll. And, try as she might, Maggie couldn't find a reason to hate her father any longer.

"Maggie, is it true you're willing to marry Garrett?" her father asked pleadingly.

Maggie squared her shoulders and looked first to Garrett. He was actually enjoying this moment. He raised a mocking eyebrow as if to mimic her father's question. Maggie let go of her father's hand. She thought of denying it all, but when she saw the anguish in her father's eyes, she couldn't.

"Yes," she whispered and turned her eyes to the smooth stone beneath her feet.

"Praise God!" her father exclaimed. "I had only hoped to dare that this marriage might take place. Oh, what happy news the two of you have brought me."

Maggie felt defeated and tired. She wanted to get even with Garrett, but she didn't have the energy to fight back.

The warmth of the noon sun was bearing down on them, and Jason motioned them to the house. "Come on. We need to get you out of this heat.

I'll bet you'd like a bath," Jason said, taking hold of Maggie's arm and leading her into the house.

Garrett had been right, as usual. She loved the interior of the ranch as much as she'd loved the outside. Her father had made it warm and cheery with vast amounts of Indian pottery and fresh flowers. Indian blankets woven from coarse wool in intricate and colorful patterns were hanging from the walls.

Jason began showing Maggie first one thing, then another. The dining room was richly warm with wooden floors and dark cherry furniture. Heavy brocade draperies at the large windows blocked out the hot afternoon sun.

Maggie barely heard her father's words as he explained the meaning behind different pieces of furniture. It was all she could do to comprehend that she was in her father's house and Garrett was going to leave.

Finally, Maggie spoke. "Please, could I see it all later? I'm so tired."

"Forgive me, of course. I'm just so anxious for you to feel at home here," Jason said as he paused to embrace Maggie once again. "I love you, my little Maggie. Welcome home."

Maggie felt strange going to bed in the middle of the day, but her father had explained that everyone took a siesta during the heat of the day. She found a bath drawn for her, and once she'd bathed and donned a soft cotton nightgown, she was shown to her bed by Carmalita, the young woman who was to be her maid.

Carmalita was young, perhaps twenty or so, Maggie judged. She was plump and very pretty. Maggie immediately liked her.

"We've looked forward to your arrival, Miss Magdelena." Carmalita spoke perfect English, although her accent betrayed her Mexican heritage.

"Please, just call me Maggie and don't be so formal. I find myself in need of new friends and hope to start with you," Maggie said sincerely.

"I would be most honored to call you friend, Miss—Maggie." Carmalita replied softly. There weren't many women on the ranch, and Maggie was a welcomed change.

"Good. I will rely on you to teach me everything, but first I want to sleep," Maggie yawned and laid back against the softness of down pillows.

"I will wake you for afternoon refreshments," Carmalita replied gently as she closed the door behind her.

Maggie surveyed the room. It looked out of place with the rest of the house. The room was clearly designed with a woman's tastes in mind. The walls were papered in a lavender rose print. Lavender shutters were closed tightly over a window. French doors with lavender ruffled curtains were set in an archway. Maggie wondered where the doors led, but weariness kept her from exploring.

Suddenly, she began to think of Garrett. Did he really mean to leave? And what of her father's contentment as he'd bidden her pleasant dreams? He seemed so genuinely happy to have her home.

Home. Strange that one word should stir so many different feelings. Home had always meant Topeka, yet Maggie felt torn. Coming to this mountainous paradise had been like coming home. How did one explain such feelings?

Maggie shook off the worries of the past few weeks and closed her eyes. She fervently wished she could put Garrett's smiling face from her mind, but it refused to leave. Exhausted, she gave up and slept, oblivious to the conversation taking place in her father's study.

"Garrett, it's so good to have you back," a wearied Jason was exclaiming as he weakly lowered himself to a chair.

"Good to be back, although I wondered at times if we'd make it."

"She was pretty ornery, was she?" Jason laughingly asked.

"She was everything you warned me of, and more. Did you know I had to pull her off a two-story trellis?" Garrett smiled as he remembered the scene and quickly joined Jason's hearty laugh.

"I'm not kidding. Sophia had warned me that Maggie would make a run for it. I figured somebody looking as prim and proper as your daughter would sneak down the back stairs or hide in another room until she could slip out the front, but not Maggie. She hiked up her skirts, all those petticoats and such, and stepped as pretty as you please out her bedroom window and onto the trellis."

Jason alternated between laughing and coughing.

"Maybe I should stop," Garrett said, concerned about Jason's condition. The older man's health had rapidly deteriorated during Garrett's absence.

"No, please. I want to know. I need to hear it all," Jason said, the smile never leaving his face. " 'A merry heart doeth good like a medicine,' the Scripture says. Now continue so my heart can have a good dosing."

Garrett chuckled in spite of his concern. "Well, there she was, picking her way through the roses and lattice work, all the while yelling about the injustice of life. I wouldn't have seen her up there, if I hadn't heard her first. Quite a set of lungs on your daughter, Sir."

Jason fairly howled at this. "Got it from her mother," he gasped.

"I'm sure." Garrett winked and continued. "Anyway, when she got close enough, I reached up and grabbed her."

"She didn't see you?" Jason coughed the words. He hadn't enjoyed himself this much for years.

"No, Sir," Garrett managed while holding his side and laughing. "She doesn't see as much when her mouth is open."

"At any rate," Jason said, trying to compose himself. "You're here. Through all the trials and Maggie's stubbornness, you've managed to bring my daughter back to me. Thank you so much."

"You know how I feel about it, Jason. I love your daughter more than ever." Garrett's declaration nearly moved Jason to tears.

"Strange how quickly a body can pass from hilarity into sober reflection," Jason murmured thoughtfully. "I think I'll follow my advice to Maggie and take a nap. This has taken a lot out of me." Jason struggled to get to his feet, and Garrett offered him a steady hand.

"Sounds like an excellent idea," Garrett agreed. "First though, I'll see to you."

Garrett helped Jason into bed and walked toward the bedroom door. That's when it caught his eye. The life-sized portrait of Maggie hung in regal splendor across from Jason's bed. Garrett paused to study the teasing smile and passionate blue eyes. He wanted to grow old with that smile. Turning to leave, Garrett couldn't resist smiling back.

Chapter 12

Maggie woke several hours later to Carmalita's gentle nudge. She stretched leisurely thinking she hadn't slept so well in weeks.

"You will find Señor, your father, has thoughtfully purchased all the things you will need," Carmalita remarked, opening the doors of a huge mahogany wardrobe.

Maggie gasped. "There are so many clothes!" she said. There were gowns for every occasion possible, as well as some native-style skirts and peasant blouses. Maggie found these particularly interesting.

"Señor thought you might like them," Carmalita offered. "It gets quite warm here, and they are most comfortable."

"I can't imagine it gets much hotter than Kansas. There were days when you scarcely could move from the heat," Maggie said. Could it have only been weeks since she'd been safe in her own room in Topeka?

Maggie found riding outfits with long split skirts, petticoats, and light-weight camisoles. Just when Maggie thought she'd seen everything, Carmalita would open a drawer or pull Maggie along to another chest. Maggie was amazed. She found boots, slippers, gloves, shawls, and things she'd never thought about owning.

"Carmalita, how in the world did my father arrange for these things? How did he know they would fit?"

"Señor had your former dressmaker send your measurements. Then he ordered materials, and I made them into clothing. Of course, I had help and some things we ordered from the catalog."

"I see," Maggie said.

"Come, you must select something. Your father will expect you to join him and Señor Garrett for tea."

"Oh, he will? Perhaps I should decline and show them both they can't anticipate my actions." Carmalita looked puzzled, and Maggie put aside the notion of causing a disturbance at Carmalita's expense.

"I'll wear this," Maggie said, taking a white cotton peasant blouse and colorful skirt. Carmalita smiled broadly at this sign of acceptance.

"Come. I'll show you how to wear them."

Several minutes later, Maggie surveyed her image in the dressing table mirror. "I look so different, almost wild." she observed. Her hair hung down to her waist in auburn waves.

"How would you like to wear your hair?" Carmalita questioned. "I am quite good at dressing hair."

"I think I prefer to leave it down for now. I might as well go completely casual," Maggie murmured.

Carmalita left and returned with Mexican sandals. "These will make your outfit complete," she said, handing the sandals to Maggie.

"They are beautiful. I've never seen anything like them." Maggie sat down while Carmalita showed her how to put them on.

"Oh, they're so comfortable. I love them, Carmalita."

Carmalita smiled more broadly than ever, but mindful of the time, she motioned Maggie to follow. "Come. Your father is waiting."

"And Señor Garrett?" Maggie questioned sarcastically.

"Si. Your *novio* is waiting," Carmalita answered as she guided Maggie down a long hallway.

"My what?" Maggie asked Carmalita in a hushed whisper.

"Your fiancé. Your sweetheart. You are to marry Señor Garrett, is it not so?" Carmalita questioned.

Maggie rolled her eyes and pushed back a long strand of hair. "I suppose everyone knows about this arrangement." It was more a statement than a question, and Carmalita said nothing as she led Maggie down the long corridor.

"Finally!" Jason Intissar exclaimed loudly as Maggie stepped into the room. Garrett turned from the fireplace and swallowed hard. The look on his face told Maggie that her appearance had taken its planned toll. *Good,* Maggie thought. *I hope he realizes what he's throwing away. I am not to be put aside like a child's toy.*

"Child, you're positively radiant. The climate agrees with you. Did Carmalita show you everything?" Maggie's father questioned eagerly. He hugged Maggie warmly.

Maggie wanted to respond to her father's embrace, but caution flooded her heart and she stood perfectly still. If the reaction pained Jason, he said nothing.

"Garrett and I were discussing your trip. I'm so glad you gave up your plans to run away. You could have been killed, Maggie." Jason's words were full of concern. He didn't sound condemning as Maggie had expected.

"I did what I felt I had to do," Maggie said, taking a seat in the woven cane chair that Jason offered her. An uncomfortable stillness blanketed the room.

Jason broke the silence. "Well, you're here now, and I pray you'll be happy. I've done everything I could think of to welcome you and make you comfortable. I know Carmalita showed you the clothes, but there is more than that. I had special furniture made for your room, I've had several geldings made available for your choice of mount, and I've tried to prepare an abundance of reading materials in the library."

"That was quite thoughtful of you, Father. However, it wasn't necessary. While I've never had to live without the things I needed, I am not like most well-to-do women. I can live quite simply if I need to." Maggie lifted her chin in a defiant move her grandmother would have recognized as a warning.

"Maggie, we need to talk. We three," Jason said, motioning toward Garrett. Maggie stared icily in Garrett's direction. "Pray continue, Father," she said with slight sarcasm.

"Stop it, Maggie. Your father deserves better than one of your temper tantrums," an angry Garrett stated. "He's only trying to make it easy on you Now stop acting like a spoiled child."

"You seem rather intent on making an issue of my age. As I've told you before, I will be eighteen in less than three weeks. Most of my friends are married, and some even have children. I am not a child, nor do I act childish. I am, however, running out of patience with this game.

"I am here, Father. Not by my wishes, but by Garrett Lucas's and yours. I am not happy I had to leave Grandmother. She's an old woman, and her health is failing. Now she will live out her days alone, and I resent that." Maggie paused briefly to note the expression of surprise on her father's face.

Maggie didn't want to hurt her father, but overpowering fear was gripping her heart. She didn't want to remember thoughts and feelings that were threatening to surface. Anger seemed the only way to hold them at bay.

"Does my ability to speak for myself surprise you? Did you think I'd come running back for the happy reunion? I don't hate you as I once did." Maggie heard her father gasp and regretted her words. But it was too late.

"Yes, that's right. I did hate you," Maggie said the words to her father, but it was Garrett she was thinking of. Garrett and his plans to desert her just as her father had, just as God had.

"You left me. I had just lost my mother and the baby brother I had yearned for, then you turned and walked away. I was ridiculed as an orphan. The few friends I had pitied my loss and my life. My only hope was in Grandmother. She stood by me and held me when I was afraid. She kept me on the narrow path when I felt sure I would stray." Tears threatened to spill from Maggie's eyes. She could see her father, too, had tears. Garrett, however, remained strangely still.

Maggie softened her voice. "I don't hate you anymore. Garrett told me why you left, and while I suppose Grandmother tried to explain it to me many times, Garrett finally accomplished getting through to me. I won't pretend I'm not fearful of this entire arrangement, and while it's true I have come to accept the idea of marriage to your choice of a husband," she said, waving her hand toward Garrett, "I don't believe the man in question has the same desire."

Garrett's lips curled into a smile. Jason looked first to Garrett, then back to Maggie before both he and Garrett burst into laughter. "Oh, Maggie, you have no idea." Jason's words stung.

"Then why don't you fill me in? Or don't I have a right to know what is to become of me?" Maggie's words were devoid of emotion. Everything inside her went numb.

Jason started to speak, but Garrett raised his hand. "I told you before, Maggie. I fully intend to marry you, but it will be in my own good time and after you've made peace with your father and God."

Jason said nothing, and Maggie noticed he strained to breathe. She didn't want to fight the sick, frail man her father had become.

Maggie turned to face Garrett. "I have spent a lifetime distancing myself from painful relationships. If what you said to me last night was true, then I am about to begin that task once again."

"But, Maggie," Jason interjected. "Garrett loves you. If you can't see that, you're blind. He's trying to tell you that we need to break down the wall between us. It hurts me so much to see you like this, Maggie."

"I can't pretend to be what I'm not. Nor can I conjure feelings that aren't there," Maggie spoke slowly. "I can't forget what happened, and I don't think you can either."

"What are you talking about?" Jason questioned earnestly.

Maggie wasn't sure. More than a feeling, a vague memory filled her mind. It had to be quite terrible, Maggie decided, or her mind would let her remember.

"Never mind," Maggie replied firmly. Something kept her from continuing. "As for you, Garrett Lucas, either you want to marry me or you don't. You have no right to put me off."

Garrett toyed with an Indian pitcher. He smiled slightly as he traced the pattern etched on the pitcher's side. "You mean like you're putting off your father and God?"

Maggie jumped to her feet. "Stop it! I won't tolerate any more of this!" She walked quickly from the room, nearly running by the time she approached the long hallway. She suddenly realized she had no idea where she was going. Tears blinded her, causing her to stumble. Strong hands steadied her, and in a heartbeat, Maggie felt herself held firmly in Garrett Lucas's arms.

"Leave me alone!" she exclaimed in a half sob. She jerked wildly, trying to escape.

"When are you going to give this up? Trust me, I know what I'm doing," Garrett whispered in Maggie's ear.

Maggie went limp against Garrett's chest. "You can't leave me here. I don't know him. I don't know how to live here," Maggie sobbed.

"You'll learn and do so much faster and more thoroughly without me here. Remember, until a few weeks ago, you didn't know me either. Now you're ready to commit your life to me."

"I don't believe you! I don't believe you will come back. You'll be just like him. You'll walk away and keep going." Maggie's words tore at Garrett's heart.

"Hush," he said softly, as he stroked Maggie's hair. "I'm sorry, *mi querida*. I never thought about it that way." Gently he lifted her tearstained face to meet his searching gaze. "I promise, Maggie. I promise you we'll be man and wife one day. I won't leave without returning to claim what is mine. But," he paused, losing himself in the liquid blue of her eyes. "I don't believe you can ever be mine until you resolve your feelings toward your father. I know too we can't be anything to each other until you come to salvation in Jesus."

Maggie pushed away from Garrett's embrace. She squared her shoulders and wiped her eyes. There was a new composure about her, and Garrett showed his surprise.

"When will you leave?" Maggie calmly questioned.

Garrett said nothing for a moment, as if considering her question. Finally, he spoke the word Maggie dreaded. "Tomorrow."

Maggie smoothed the front of her skirt and lifted a stony face. "As you wish. Garrett Lucas, I release you from any commitment you think we might have between us. I'm on my own from this moment. I don't believe in you or my father, and I am beginning to question what possible reason a merciful God could have for all this." She began to walk down the hall when Garrett pulled her back.

"Sorry. It doesn't work that way. I don't release you, Maggie. I don't release you to run away from me and hide in your bedroom. I don't release you to run away from dealing with your father and the pain that is firmly planted between you. And most of all," he spoke with determination, "I don't release you from a reconciliation with God." With that, Garrett turned and walked away.

Maggie stood openmouthed, looking after him. She was still standing there when Carmalita found her. Maggie waved her away. She needed to be alone.

What if Garrett was right? How could she learn to deal with all that stood between her and her father? Maggie suddenly remembered the Bible verse she'd found while on the train: " 'And he shall turn the heart of the fathers to the children, and the heart of the children to their fathers, lest I come and smite the earth with a curse.' "

Was God cursing her by taking Garrett Lucas away? What if something happened to Garrett and he died before being able to return to her? Would God curse her because she had been unwilling to put the past behind and open her heart to her father's love?

Chapter 13

July and August passed in a blur. Maggie's birthday came and went, and even though her father thoughtfully surprised her with gifts, Maggie barely acknowledged the day. Her heart ached. Garrett was gone.

Day after day, Jason approached his daughter, only to be waved off. Occasionally, Maggie had asked her father about Garrett's whereabouts, but Jason had promised not to tell her. His reward was his daughter's stubborn refusal to have anything to do with him. Jason refused to give up, however, and continued to find some small place in his daughter's life.

As September approached, Maggie's emotional state had not improved. She'd taken to riding Thunder every day. The huge Morgan crossbreed was aptly named. He was as black as midnight and stood fifteen hands high.

Everyone on the ranch murmured about the Señor's sad-eyed daughter. Maggie spoke only to Carmalita and her father, and him, only when she had to.

As autumn flooded Piñon Canyon with golds and oranges, Jason began to worry. He wanted to make things right with Maggie before he died, but he couldn't reach through her pain and depression. Daily, he prayed for insight. His health was failing fast, and Jason feared if a reconciliation didn't take place soon, it might not take place at all.

On one particularly hot day, Maggie entered the courtyard where Jason was taking breakfast. She had grown extremely thin, and despite her golden tan from day after day in the sun, she didn't look well. Dark circles around her eyes gave her face a gaunt, inhuman look.

"Maggie, sit here with me," Jason commanded gently.

"I'm not hungry," Maggie said, pulling on her riding gloves. "I'm going to ride Thunder up on the ridge today."

"Maggie, I need you to sit for a moment with me. Surely you can give me. . ." Jason's words gave way to a fit of coughing. Maggie was painfully aware that the frequency of her father's coughing spells was increasing. The doctor had explained her father's lungs were filling with fluid and his heart couldn't work hard enough.

Maggie looked at her father's reddened face. As the coughing began to subside, she took the chair beside her father.

"Thank you, Maggie," Jason whispered. "Thank you for hearing me out."

Maggie said nothing. She allowed Carmalita to pour her some orange juice but waved away her offer of eggs and toast.

"Maggie, you need to take better care of yourself. You must eat. It isn't right." Maggie knew she had a problem. Carmalita had already taken in Maggie's clothes twice.

"Please don't worry," Maggie said. She didn't intend to grieve her father. She was only trying to forget the pain of losing Garrett.

"Maggie, I want you to listen to me. I know we can work this out, and I know you can come to love me again." Jason's voice broke, and Maggie ached at the thought of his pain.

She thought for a moment, then offered, "But I do love you, Father. I don't want you to worry. I do love you, and I know you love me." The words came mechanically and without feeling. It seemed a small price to offer the dying man.

"Maggie, love is so much more than words. I want to spend time with you. I want to know your heart, and I want you to know mine. I have much to teach you about the ranch, and above everything else, I want you to come to know Jesus."

Maggie stiffened. God seemed to hammer her from every direction. Even when she rode Thunder and struggled to forget the image of Garrett's handsome, bearded face, God's words filled her mind. Maggie lowered her face, fearful of facing her father's eyes.

"I know you miss Garrett, I miss him too. He was my right hand, especially after I got sick," Jason continued. "I feel his absence daily, especially with winter coming on and the problems with the banditos in the hills." Jason hadn't intended to mention it to Maggie. He saw her eyes widen slightly.

"Bandits here?" Maggie questioned.

"It's possible. We've found some butchered cows, and several head are missing. It's unlikely that it's the Pueblos. I give them whatever they need through the mission." Maggie nodded.

"Maggie, I can't take back the past. God knows I would if it were possible. We both know, however, it's not." Jason struggled for air.

Maggie felt herself straining with every breath. For the first time she noticed the purplish red color of her father's skin—skin that barely stretched over the bones of his face. Tears formed against Maggie's will.

"I don't know what to think anymore," she whispered. "I don't want to remember the pain of the past, and I don't understand why Garrett doesn't write. Why doesn't he let us know he's okay?" The words came out as whimpers, the fearful whimpers of a small child.

"I don't know, Maggie. I know we'd both feel better if he did, but I do know Garrett Lucas rides with God. Wherever he might be, God is by his side," Jason remarked confidently.

"If God rides with Garrett, maybe that's why He doesn't seem to be here," Maggie replied.

"God not here?" Jason exclaimed. "How can you say such a thing? God is all around us. He's urging your heart to listen. He is calling you to forgive and accept His forgiveness."

"Forgive?" Maggie questioned.

"Yes, forgive. I want you to forgive me for leaving you, Maggie. I want you to forgive me for shutting you out. Do you think it's possible?" Jason asked sincerely.

"I don't think it's a matter of forgiveness, Father," Maggie began slowly. "I can't forget what happened. It changed so many things about me. It made me stronger, more independent, and I suppose more distant.

"I didn't make many friends. I feared they too, would leave me. When Garrett told me he he was going, it was like watching it happen all over. I don't think it's a matter of forgiveness," Maggie said, lifting her eyes to face her father's surprised expression.

"But it is. Maggie, you haven't let go of the past. If you had forgiven me, you could have let Garrett go with his promise of return and believed him. You wouldn't be questioning your Heavenly Father, either."

Maggie thought over her father's words. Could they be true?

"I don't understand," Maggie finally said. "What does this have to do with God?"

"Maggie, your Heavenly Father is more reliable than your earthly one. You can count on God to be there every time, all the time, whenever you call out to Him. Don't harden your heart toward God. He isn't punishing you."

Her father's words seemed so clear, so truthful, yet Maggie hated to allow old feelings to surface. She hated to touch the emotions of the little girl from long ago, and she resented the fact she had to.

"If God loves me so much, why is He allowing me to hurt so badly?" Maggie couldn't hold back the tears. She put her face in her gloved hands and cried. "If God loves me, why did He take my mother and brother away?"

Jason was beside her in a moment, holding her and stroking her hair. There were tears in his eyes as well.

Eight years of pain and anguish poured from Maggie's heart. "He can't possibly love me. It isn't possible. I just know God hates me." Maggie's sobs tore at Jason's heart.

"Oh, Maggie, God does love you. As much as I love you, God loves you much more. We are like the silver and gold ore which runs through the rocks of the mountains. Precious and brilliant but useless without refining. We are being refined for God's purposes. I learned after your mother died that I had to accept God's will for my life and forgive."

Maggie lifted her face. "Forgive me?"

"No, Maggie," Jason whispered. "Forgive myself."

"What do you mean? You hadn't done anything wrong. I was the one who caught the fever, and all because I went to Lillie's house without permission." Maggie's sudden confession brought back her buried memories.

"Lillie's house!" Maggie whispered the words. Lillie's family had had the fever. Maggie remembered the red quarantine flag that had hung on the fence gate and front door of the Johnston house.

"I went to Lillie's house. Remember before Potwin Place, when we lived side by side in town?" Maggie questioned, painfully remembering details that she'd successfully repressed for years.

"I remember," Jason murmured.

"Mother was too busy to play with me. I was willful and spiteful, and I wanted to show her I could take care of myself. Mother told me to stay home. She explained the quarantine, but I didn't care.

"When she went to her room to rest, I went to Lillie's. I slipped in the back door, past their cook, and up the back stairs. Lillie wasn't as sick as her sisters, and I played with her. When I got sick the next day, I knew God hated me. Mother died because of me. She really did! Now I know why God is punishing me!" Maggie's body racked with uncontrollable sobs. "I killed my mother and brother!"

"No, Maggie! Listen to me," Jason said, pulling Maggie to her feet.

"It was all my fault, all my fault!" Maggie wailed hysterically.

It took all the strength Jason had to shake Maggie. "Stop it. Stop it, now! You did not kill your mother, but that mistaken idea has always stood between us, Maggie. Because of it, you thought I blamed you for her death." Maggie regained a bit of her composure, but tears still poured down her face.

"Well, didn't you? Even a little bit?"

"No, because I knew the truth," Jason said sadly.

"What truth?"

"We shared water from the same well as the Johnstons. Our well had caved in nearly three weeks earlier because of the flood. Remember? We had to stay with my mother because the Kaw River had flooded its banks. After the water receded and we returned home, I found that the well was beyond repair."

Maggie wiped her eyes. "I remember the flood. I remember all the mud we had to clean out of the house."

Jason smiled sadly. "You couldn't have caught typhoid overnight from a simple visit to Lillie. You were already exposed through the water we shared. Your mother was sick when you came down with the fever. It wasn't because of the baby that she couldn't continue to care for you through your illness. It was because she was sick herself. Don't you see, Maggie? She didn't get typhoid from you. She was already sick."

A tremendous weight lifted from Maggie's shoulders. "Then God didn't punish me for being disobedient by taking my mother and brother, and. . ." Maggie paused to study her father's face. "You!" she whispered softly.

"No, Maggie. God didn't punish you then, and He's not punishing you now. He's standing with open arms, just as I am."

"Oh, Father. I'm so sorry. Please forgive me!" Maggie threw her arms around her father's neck.

"Maggie, my Maggie, it is I who seek your forgiveness. Can you forgive me?"

"Oh, yes. A hundred times, yes!" They stood for several minutes holding each other. Jason's heart was filled with pure joy. His Maggie was home!

The remainder of the day passed much too quickly. Maggie listened to her father talk of his early days in New Mexico, trips to Colorado in search of gold and silver, and the ranch he'd created.

Maggie, in turn, tried to explain a lifetime of feelings and dreams. She was sharing a memory from her school days when Jason suggested a short walk in the rose garden.

Maggie linked her arms through Jason's and allowed his slow, faltering lead. "Please finish what you were saying," Jason encouraged.

Maggie started to speak, but just then he brought her to the garden. "It's beautiful!" she exclaimed. Her father had created a paradise. The rich, sweet fragrance of roses filled the air.

"How could I have lived here all this time and not known about this?" Maggie wondered aloud.

"Often we have precious things at our fingertips and fail to see them," Jason answered thoughtfully.

Maggie nodded and reached down to touch the velvet softness of a delicate yellow rose. "These are my favorites," she proclaimed, looking at the other roses as if to make certain.

Jason smiled proudly. "I've been experimenting with mixing varieties. This is one of my newer plants."

"What do you call it?"

"God's Hope."

Maggie stiffened slightly. "Father?"

"Yes?" Jason gave his daughter full attention.

"How can I be sure? About God, I mean. How can I be sure I'm saved? Grandmother told me on many, many occasions, but it all seems so distant now."

Jason's heart soared. "It's very simple, Maggie. You ask God to forgive you and He does. You have to trust Him, Maggie. I know your trust doesn't come easily, but it's what faith is all about. Just repent and believe on the name of Jesus. He'll do the rest."

Later that night, Maggie knelt beside her bed for the first time in years.

"Heavenly Father, I know I am a willful and childish young woman. I know, too, that I am the one who's put walls between us. Thank you for letting me see this before it was too late. Please forgive me and help me to seek Your will in my life. I want Jesus to be my Savior, and I want to trust You all the days of my life. In Jesus' name I pray, amen."

As she got up, Maggie wondered, *Am I really saved?* She didn't feel different. Could she do as her father had suggested and trust God?

"If the Bible is true," Maggie said aloud, "and I believe it is, then I must trust. I need faith in God's ability to save me and to bring me new life through His Son. He's offered me a place to belong, but it's up to me to accept."

Maggie walked to the open French doors and looked out into the starlit sky. Garrett was out there somewhere. Would she ever see him again? He'd promised he'd be back for her, but could she believe him?

In the distance, coyotes yipped and howled at the moon. The echo of their mournful cries chilled Maggie.

"Please God," Maggie prayed aloud. "Please bring Garrett back to me."

Chapter 14

Garrett's mood was black and stormy. He stood beside his horse, Alder, using firm brush strokes to rid the animal's coat of clay and mud which had accumulated during their ride. It was the last day of September, and instead of giving routine orders to ready Piñon Canyon for the winter, Garrett was trapped twelve miles away at the mission David and Jenny Monroe had established for the Pueblos.

Alder sensed his master's mood and stood as still as stone. Garrett finished currying his horse, and after knocking most of the mud from his boots, he made his way to David and Jenny's house. The sky started to pour rain as Garrett entered the kitchen. Warmth hit his face in a welcome wave. The smell of tortillas and meat made him recognize how hungry he was.

"Garrett Lucas, you get in here and change those clothes!" Jenny Monroe demanded. Garrett smiled. Jenny was Garrett's junior by at least two or three years, but at times she seemed years older.

"Yes, Ma'am," Garrett drawled lazily and tipped his Stetson.

"Hurry up. Supper will be on shortly." It was all the encouragement Garrett needed.

An hour later, Garrett pushed away from the crude wood table and patted his stomach. "Good grub, Jenny!" he declared, and several little voices mimicked him

"Good grub!"

Jenny Monroe looked down the twelve-foot table into the grateful brown eyes of the orphans she cared for.

"Go on with all of you," she said and stood to clear the table. She turned loving eyes to her husband of five years.

"David, why don't you and Garrett take yourselves to the sitting room, and I'll have Mary and Anna get these kids to bed." Seven little moans echoed down the length of the table, but the children who were old enough to take care of themselves got up from the table and raced upstairs. The older girls, Mary and Anna, tenderly cared for the youngest three.

"Come along, Garrett," David Monroe called. Garrett rose slowly from the table. He was tired and stiff from bringing down strays from the upper ranges.

The sitting room was warm and inviting. Garrett sat down in front of the fire, appreciating its warmth. He watched David Monroe put more wood on the fire. Garrett longed to hear of news from Piñon Canyon, but he waited patiently for David to sit.

"I suppose you'd like to hear the latest," David said, joining Garrett in a chair by the fire.

"You know I would. It was all I could do to wait through dinner. How's Maggie?" Garrett asked anxiously.

"I have a letter. Would you like to read it?" David asked, pulling the envelope from his pocket. Garrett nearly leaped from the chair to take the precious paper from his friend. He scanned the pages with intense interest. At one point David thought he saw tears in Garrett's eyes, but just as quickly his eyes dried.

"She's accepted the past. That's good," Garrett said absently. "And she's accepted Jesus as her Savior. That's even better!" Joy surged through Garrett's heart. Maggie was working through the past with her father, and soon, very soon, he could return to the ranch and marry her.

"David, this is wonderful news! Why didn't you tell me sooner?"

David Monroe chuckled. "Easy, Garrett. There's still a long way to go."

"I know all that, but it's a huge step forward. I mean, if you'd seen her these last few months. She's skin and bones, and the dangerous way she rode the gelding made me want to give up at least a thousand times."

"I told you it wasn't wise to spy on her," David reminded.

"I know, but I couldn't help it. I just had to feel close to her. I've loved her for so long."

David nodded. "I know what you mean. It was a good thing Jenny lived in the same town as the Bible college I attended. I would have gone mad without her."

"Then you understand," Garrett whispered. "David, sometimes, I'm not sure what to make of it. At first I thought it was a silly infatuation. But as I listened to the letters from her grandmother, I drank in every word about Maggie and couldn't wait to meet her," Garrett paused, remembering his anticipation of their first meeting.

"When I finally stood outside her house in Potwin, I wasn't sure I could play my part. I'd already told Jason how I felt, and he couldn't have been happier. But I knew I'd need to convince Maggie, and I wasn't sure I could. Boy, the prayer that went into that one!"

David smiled. "I always believed God was setting you up for something special, Garrett."

"He sure was. When I realized that Maggie was falling for me, I started to panic. There was the matter of her father, and I was even more troubled by the wall she'd built to shut out God. She couldn't see God's love for her. That's why this letter offers the best possible news. Maggie has learned she can count on God."

The two men barely heard the rustling of Jenny's skirts as she brought coffee into the sitting room.

"Here we are," she said in her soft, gentle voice. Garrett had heard that voice comfort heartbroken children and soothe the worried heart of her husband. Jenny Monroe's every action reflected her Savior.

"Thank you, Jenny," Garrett said as he took the offered cup. "David just showed me the letter. Isn't it great news?"

"It certainly is, Garrett. Just what we've prayed for. We must continue to pray, however. You know how hard this time will be." Jenny spoke with authority. Garrett wondered if something in her past gave her special insight.

"I reckon it will be at that," Garrett replied. Truth was, he hadn't considered anything past the contents of the letter.

"I think it would be a good time to drop a note of encouragement, Garrett," David interjected.

"Oh, yes," Jenny agreed, sitting next to her husband. They exchanged a look of tenderness which made Garrett's heart ache.

"You think so?" Garrett asked hopefully. He'd wanted to write Maggie every day, but at the advice of David and Jenny, he'd given Maggie the opportunity to make the right choices on her own.

"Definitely," David began. "She'll need to know you still care, and she'll need to know you've been praying for her—you're still praying for her. Maybe," David added, remembering something Garrett had said earlier, "maybe you should let her know you've never been far away, that you've been watching over her."

"I think that'd be nice, Garrett," Jenny said. "I know a woman's heart likes to hear things like that. Share some encouraging Scripture too. She'll need the Word as she learns to walk in faith."

Garrett got to his feet, nearly spilling his coffee. "I'll do it right now. Do you suppose Lupe could deliver it tomorrow?"

"I'm sure he'd be happy to," David said enthusiastically. "I've got some papers to send to Jason anyway, so the trip will be necessary for both of us."

Jenny placed her hand upon her husband's cheek. "Why don't we leave Garrett to his letter? I would love an evening stroll." The love shone clear in her eyes, and David wrapped an arm around her and pulled her close.

"I'd like that too," he agreed. "If you'll excuse us," David said, rising to his feet. "We have a walk to take."

Garrett watched as they left the room. David and Jenny Monroe shared a deep, abiding love. Garrett dreamed of a love like that with Maggie, and the news he'd just received finally made it possible.

Later that night, after pouring his heart onto three pages of David's personal stationery, Garrett lay in bed staring up at the ceiling. "How much longer, Lord?" he wondered aloud. "How much longer until I can go home?"

He thought about the words he'd written. He'd wanted to explain everything he felt. He kept remembering how Maggie had told him she wouldn't wait for him. How would she feel now that she'd made peace with God and her father?

Long into the night, Garrett tossed and turned. His sleep was fitful, and more than once he woke up drenched in sweat. Morning couldn't come too soon.

∽

Back at Piñon Canyon, Maggie awoke to the warmth of fall sunshine. She stretched slowly and purposefully like a sleek mountain puma.

For a moment, Maggie listened to the morning sounds of the ranch. She smiled at the smell of hot coffee and bacon. Maria was preparing breakfast. After months of near starvation, Maggie felt like making up for lost time.

Quickly, she threw back the covers and went to her vanity. She poured cool water from the pitcher and washed the sleep from her face. Carmalita hadn't arrived to help her dress, but Maggie didn't mind. She went to the wardrobe and pulled out a dusty rose day dress. Just as Maggie was securing the last few buttons, Carmalita knocked and entered the room.

"Señorita Maggie, you should have called for me," Carmalita said, rushing to help Maggie.

"Nonsense. I'm not an invalid, even if I've acted like a sick cow for the last few months." Carmalita looked shocked, and Maggie gave a little laugh. "I'm sorry, Carmalita. I'm really not loco, as Maria would call it. I've finally found peace."

Carmalita began to brush Maggie's thick, auburn hair as Maggie continued to explain. "These past months, I died a little each day, wondering if my harsh words had driven away the man I hoped to marry. I hated myself for hurting my father and for being so ungrateful. But you know, Carmalita," Maggie said, pausing to put her thoughts in just the right words. "The worst part was my alienation from God."

"What do you mean?" Carmalita questioned.

Maggie took hold of Carmalita's hands. "Carmalita, two days ago I gave my heart to Jesus. I'm at peace with God, and now I can truly begin to live."

Carmalita smiled shyly, but with understanding. "That is good, Señorita Maggie. I, too, am a Christian."

"You are!" Maggie exclaimed with positive delight. "How wonderful. We can help each other."

Carmalita seemed happy with the change in her mistress. She finished Maggie's hair quickly and went to tidy up the room.

Maggie whirled in front of the mirror, suddenly very interested in how she looked. The rose colored dress hugged her slim figure, and the gored skirt swept out from her hips and flowed to the floor. The wine trim on the bodice and sleeves made her hair look a deeper, coppery color. Satisfied with her appearance, Maggie joined her father for breakfast.

"My, you're up early, aren't you?" Jason said as Maggie took her place at the table. "And don't you look pretty."

"Thank you, Father."

Maria placed platters of fried potatoes, scrambled eggs, and ham on the table. Maggie helped herself to generous portions of everything.

"What would you like to do today?" Maggie asked her father between bites.

"I'm afraid I'm not up to a great deal." Jason gave a series of hoarse coughs which left him breathless.

"What if we enjoy each other's company here in the house? You can tell me more stories about the years we've missed, and I can tell you some of mine." Maggie tried to hide her concern for her father, but it was evident by the furrow of her brow.

"You mustn't worry, Maggie. I don't fear death. I have found peace with God and with my beloved daughter. I can go home to heaven with a peace I'd only dreamed possible."

"I wish you wouldn't talk about dying, Father. It seems like asking for trouble." Maggie sounded tense and curt. She hated her father referring to his death. She wasn't ready to let go of him.

"Maggie, you can't pretend something isn't going to happen just because you don't like the idea," Jason sighed. "I wish I could stay to see you married and with children of your own. I'd like to watch you and Garrett take over the running of this ranch. But I only asked God to let me live long enough for us to put our differences aside. He's given me that and more. I'd say anything else is added blessings."

"But, Father." Maggie started to protest, but Jason waved his hand.

"Don't blame God or resent His timing. Promise me, Maggie. Promise me you won't allow my death to cause bitterness in your heart."

Maggie looked at her father for a moment. His faded blue eyes were sunk deep into his face. There was a grayish pallor to his skin and frailty to his movements.

"How can I promise a thing like that? I don't want to lose you. It seems like I just found you, and now you'll be taken from me." Maggie said thoughtfully.

"You must trust God, Maggie. In His infinite wisdom, He will work all things together for good. Would you have me stay and suffer like this?"

"No, Father. Never! I didn't mean—"

"I know you never meant it that way," Jason said, taking hold of Maggie's hand. "But you must consider my viewpoint. I'm tired of the weakness, the lack of air, the coughing. It pains me to remember the man I used to be and to see the man I've become."

Her father was right, Maggie realized. It was pure selfishness to want her father to continue living. And for what? Her pleasure? Her need?

"Forgive me, Father. I want the very best for you, and I promise I won't hate God for whatever the best may be. If it means losing you soon, and I pray it doesn't, then I will accept His will. In the meantime, I want to enjoy every moment." Maggie gave her father's hand a squeeze.

"Good. You have no way of knowing the contentment that gives me."

Maggie smiled and felt at peace. She finally had the father she'd longed for, and with him came the security of belonging.

Chapter 15

Before Garrett's letter could be delivered by Lupe, another letter arrived at Piñon Canyon. With it came the news that Sophia Intissar had passed away.

Devastated, Maggie sat in front of the fireplace, watching the dying embers of a late morning fire. Her heart ached and her throat felt painfully tight. She wanted to cry, but the tears wouldn't come.

Maggie couldn't forget the anguished look on her father's face when he'd read the news. Her father had collapsed on the nearest chair and cried bitter, pain-filled tears. When her father's emotions had sent him into paroxysms of coughing, Maggie had called for Miguel to help him to bed. Medication had finally brought her father the relief of sleep.

Several hours had passed, and Maggie couldn't believe how quiet the house had grown. Usually the muffled sounds of Maria singing in the kitchen or Carmalita talking excitedly about her upcoming wedding to Miguel filled the house.

Maggie lifted the letter again. It had been penned more than a week earlier by Lillie Johnston Philips. Lillie had always loved Sophia as her own grandmother. She told Maggie that Sophia had died peacefully in her sleep. Lillie, nearly four months a bride, had helped her parents arrange for the burial services, despite the fact she had discovered she was in a family way.

Maggie smiled at Lillie's reference to the new life she carried. One life ended and another began. And in her father's bedroom, still another life hung in the balance.

Maggie noted that her grandmother had been buried the same day she and her father had resolved their differences. Perhaps her grandmother had sensed an end to the painful past and knew she could go to heaven unhampered by regrets and worries. Maggie smiled at the thought of her grandmother walking the streets of heaven and enjoying the company of many old friends.

"Heavenly Father," Maggie prayed. "I thank You for the years I shared with Grandmother. I'll miss her very much, but I know she's safe and happy, and for now, that seems enough. Please be with Father. He isn't strong enough to bear much more, and I'm not ready to let go of him. Help me to prepare for his passing, and please don't let him suffer. In Jesus' name, amen." When she finished praying, Maggie felt a great peace that gave her the strength to go on.

Later that afternoon, another letter was placed in Maggie's hands. Even though she had never seen Garrett's handwriting before, she knew the letter was from him. Retreating to the privacy of her bedroom, she tore open the envelope. Her heart beat faster as she read his greeting.

> *My beloved Maggie,*
> *A tremendous burden has been lifted. I was just told of your reconciliation with Jason, and your acceptance of Jesus as Savior. I want to shout for joy. I know how you have struggled with God over the years. I know it was never easy to see God as the loving Father He is. Now, however, I desire more than ever to share my life with you and grow together in the love He has given us.*

The letter continued, and Maggie drank in each word. Every sentence was exactly what she'd longed to hear. She read Garrett's words of love and pledges of lifelong devotion. How it thrilled her to see each cherished promise and know without doubt that he loved her. Maggie's one disappointment was Garrett didn't give a specific time when he would return. She folded the letter and tucked it into her skirt pocket to read again later.

Even though it was the beginning of October and the afternoons no longer held the intense heat of summer, Maggie had grown accustomed to siesta. After checking on her father, she decided to stretch out and take a nap.

Nearly two hours later, Carmalita urgently woke Maggie.

"Maggie, Maggie! Come quickly. Your father is very ill." The fear in Carmalita's voice left Maggie shaken. She ran after Carmalita to where Jason Intissar lay vomiting blood.

"Carmalita, what are we going to do?" Maggie cried. She held her father's bony shoulders steady as another spell of coughing began.

"We can send Miguel for the doctor," Carmalita offered.

"Then do it, and tell him to go quickly!" Maggie exclaimed. "And Carmalita. . ."

"Sí?" Carmalita answered, pausing in the doorway.

"You'd better get a couple of ranch hands—men my father is fond of. I'm going to need help until Miguel and the doctor get here."

"Right away," Carmalita replied and quickly left the room.

Maggie turned her attention back to her father. "Father, is the cough passing?"

"I think so. Let me lay back on the pillows." Jason's voice was barely audible.

Maggie eased her father back. Her father seemed oblivious to any comfort the new position offered. He strained for each breath, and Maggie fought the urge to run from the room.

To get her mind off her father's ragged breathing, Maggie began cleaning up the area around his bed. Carmalita returned and took over the cleaning, urging Maggie to care for her father.

Maggie sat stroking her father's balding head. She dipped a cloth in cool water and began to wipe away blood stains from his face.

"We came as quick as we could, Ma'am."

Maggie looked up to find the compassionate eyes of Bill, her father's trusted foreman. Behind him stood a young man she'd never met.

"This here is Mack's little brother, Rob," Bill explained. Maggie offered a brief smile to the shy, sandy-haired young man.

"Thank you both for coming. Father's been taken by quite a bad spell this time. I sent Miguel for the doctor, but I know I'll need help with him before they return," she whispered. Her father's labored breathing became even louder, and Maggie could barely concentrate on what she was saying.

"No problem, Ma'am. I'd give my life for Mr. Jason. He's been a right good boss and friend," Bill said, lowering his eyes to the dusty hem of his jeans. Rob remained silent.

"Bill, I think Father would rest better if we could prop him up. I can't lift him, but if you and Rob could help me, we might get the job done."

"Sure thing, Miss Maggie." Bill's voice held the devoted enthusiasm Maggie needed to hear. Together, the three worked to ease Jason into a more comfortable position.

The hours wore on, and Maggie felt encouraged as her father's breathing became less ragged. She dozed in a chair, and only when the clock chimed midnight did she agree to turn in.

Maggie started to slip into bed fully clothed. There seemed little sense in undressing. What if her father grew suddenly worse? Carmalita would hear nothing of it.

"No one will care if you appear at your father's bedside in your robe. But you need your rest," Carmalita said, taking charge of Maggie as if she were a child.

"But," Maggie started to protest.

"You'll sleep much better in your nightgown, and you'll need all your strength." Carmalita finished pulling Maggie's blood-stained dress over her head and replaced it with a fresh cotton nightgown.

"I'll have Bill wake me if your father wakes up or gets any worse." Carmalita said, blowing out the candle. Maggie wanted to argue, but her mind wouldn't make sense of the situation. Reluctantly, she fell back against her pillow and slept.

The first crimson rays of the late fall sun were peeking over the mountaintops when Maggie woke with a start. Remembering her father, she threw back the covers, pulled on her robe, and raced down the hallway.

When she opened the door, Maggie was surprised to find Dr. Avery leaning over her father. He looked up as Maggie entered the room.

"Good morning, Miss Intissar," he said in his deep, rumbling voice. "I've been here for about an hour."

"I wanted to check. . . I mean, how is he?" Maggie asked in a nervous whisper.

"He's sleeping. I've given him morphine," Dr. Avery informed her.

"Morphine? What's that?" Maggie asked. Finding her courage, she drew closer to her father's bed.

"It's a drug that will take your father's pain away and help him to sleep. Your father is a very sick man, Miss Intissar, but of course you know this."

"Yes, I do. I want the truth, though. Is he going to die? I mean right away, today?" Maggie's voice betrayed the pain of her heart.

"I can't be certain, but I don't look for him to leave this bed again," Dr. Avery said with finality. Maggie's knees weakened. Her face turned ashen as the meaning of the doctor's words sank in.

"I'm sorry, Miss Intissar," the doctor said, helping Maggie to a chair. "You must be strong. You'll not be any good to him this way."

"I know," Maggie whispered. "But it seems so unfair. I just found him, and now I will lose him once more." Dr. Avery turned back to his medical bag.

"I am going to leave enough morphine powder so you can give it to him regularly. He won't be in his right mind while on the medicine, but he won't hurt either," the doctor explained matter-of-factly. "Should I instruct Maria about the dosing?"

"Please, that would be best," Maggie said, recognizing that she herself wouldn't remember any instructions.

"I'll be leaving, then. There's nothing more I can do. I've been with your father through the thick and thin of this illness. We both knew it would come to this. I must tell you, Miss Intissar, your father has faced his illness bravely, always insisting on the truth no matter how bad the news. He's been a good friend, and I will miss him sorely when he's gone." Dr. Avery's rock solid voice broke.

Tears fell unbidden down Maggie's cheeks. What a beautiful memorial to the man who lay dying. "Thank you, Dr. Avery. Thank you for being his friend, and thank you for coming to care for him once more. I'll let you know when it's over." Maggie got to her feet. "Forgive me for not walking with you to the kitchen, but I want to stay with my father."

"I understand, Miss Intissar," Dr. Avery said, turning to leave. "If it's any comfort," he added, "your father won't know what's happening. He won't feel the pain, and he won't strain to breathe."

Maggie gently stroked her father's icy hand. "Thank you. Thank you so much."

Chapter 16

A few days later, Maggie was presented with a problem she'd not anticipated. Bill informed her that the regular supply trip hadn't been made to finish stocking up for the winter.

"I know it's late notice, Ma'am. We should've thought of it a lot sooner, but what with your pa so sick and all, it just slipped my mind," Bill offered apologetically.

"I understand, Bill. I'm just not sure what we should do about it. I don't know anything about running this ranch. My father wanted me to learn and we had great plans, but now it's apparently not to be," Maggie said sadly.

"We've been lucky so far. The snows have stayed put, and we've enjoyed mild weather. But I think it's about to end. My joints have been bothering me somethin' fierce, and that always means a change in the weather," Bill said, rubbing his elbow.

"What should we do?" Maggie asked earnestly. Just then, Carmalita entered the room with hot mugs of coffee.

"Maria thought you'd enjoy this Mexican coffee."

"Mexican coffee?" Maggie questioned, sniffing the contents of her mug.

"Sí, it has cinnamon in it," Carmalita said with a smile. Carmalita smiled a great deal these days because she planned to marry Miguel shortly before Christmas.

"How interesting," Maggie murmured and sipped the coffee. "It's delicious." She cast a bittersweet smile at the dark-eyed servant. Maggie longed for a wedding of her own.

"Maria's Mexican coffee warms a fellow's bones and treats the tongue to a feast," Bill said with enthusiasm.

"Well, I'm afraid despite the good coffee, we still have a big problem. Bill, do you know anything about the book running of the ranch?" Maggie asked the bewildered foreman.

"Not a thing, Miss Maggie. Never had to. Your pa always left it to Garrett, that is, when he didn't take care of it himself."

Maggie sighed. "I wish we had Garrett with us now. I'd gladly let him take over everything."

"I could have Miguel ride out after him," Carmalita suggested.

"What?" Maggie's voice clearly showed her surprise. "You know where Garrett is?"

"Sí," Carmalita answered matter-of-factly. "Your father has kept in touch with him at the Pueblo mission."

"That's our answer, Miss Maggie. If we can get Garrett here, we'll be fixed fine. He'll be knowin' just what to do and when," Bill remarked, handing his mug back to Carmalita. "Now if you'll excuse me, I've got some ranch hands to see to."

"Thank you, Bill. I'll have Miguel go after Garrett immediately," Maggie called out to the retreating figure. She turned to Carmalita. "Send Miguel right away. Have him tell Garrett everything."

"Sí," Carmalita replied and rushed off to locate Miguel.

Maggie went to check on her father. She could hardly contain her excitement. Garrett would be coming home. She smiled to herself. It had been over three months since Garrett had walked out of her life. Even so, Maggie remembered his promise to make her his wife. A shiver ran through her. *Garrett's wife!*

Jason Intissar slept peacefully. The morphine had made him oblivious to everything, but at least he didn't hurt. For that Maggie was grateful.

Absentmindedly, she picked up some knitting she'd left beside her father's bed. It was to be a blanket for Lillie's baby. The thought of her young friend newly married and expecting her first child brought tears to Maggie's eyes. She remembered leaving the note for Lillie before she left Topeka and promising to return in time for the wedding.

Maggie smiled at the memory of the smug, spoiled girl she had been. Spoiled. It was what Garrett had called her, and he'd been quite accurate.

Maggie worked on the blanket and thought of what their meeting would be like. Would she be sitting down to dinner when Garrett came rushing through the door? Perhaps he wouldn't make it until morning. Maggie's mind raced with thoughts. Would he see the change in her, or would he still believe her to be a spoiled child?

Carmalita came in to tend the fire. The late autumn days had grown chilly, and while the adobe ranch house was well insulated with its thick walls, there was an undeniable hint of winter in the air. Bill's joints must have been right about the change in weather.

"Did you send Miguel?" Maggie asked anxiously.

"Sí, he was happy to go. He has missed Señor Lucas, but more I think he wanted to talk to Pastor Monroe. He will marry us," Carmalita replied as she stoked the fire. The wood she added to the cherry red coals ignited immediately, warming the room.

"Are you finished with your wedding dress yet?" Maggie inquired, caught up in Carmalita's excitement.

"Not quite," the girl answered. She went around the room, tidying up anything that seemed out of place.

"Do you need anything else to complete it?" Maggie questioned, thinking she could go with Garrett to get supplies.

"No, I have everything. It's just the waiting that's hard." Maggie nodded in heartfelt agreement with Carmalita's words.

The day stretched into evening, and when Maggie found her legs cramped from hours of sitting, she decided to take a walk. The liquid gold sun dripped lazily between two snow-covered peaks. Golds, pinks, purples, and oranges swirled delicate fingers against the cold gray-blue of the evening sky. It was breathtaking!

Maggie wandered to the corral where Thunder stood stomping at the dirt. He wanted to run as much as Maggie wished to ride. As she approached, he whinnied softly and came to greet her. His nudging muzzle was disappointed to find Maggie's cupped hand held no surprise of sugar or carrots.

"Sorry, Boy. Not this time." Maggie watched the sleek gelding move away to seek out food. She loved him. She loved almost everything about Piñon Canyon Ranch. Strange that she had fought coming here. It was somewhat like coming home. No, it was more. She had come home.

As Maggie walked slowly back to the house, her thoughts again drifted to Garrett. She looked up to the mountains and wondered if he could see her now. But the mountains surrounding Piñon Canyon refused to give up any secrets.

Supper was quiet and lonely. Maggie's slim frame was only starting to fill out again. Carmalita was always trying to get her to eat. Many times, Maria sent tempting treats from the kitchen for "Señor's skinny daughter," as Maria teasingly called Maggie.

Maggie picked at her meal. It wasn't a lack of hunger that kept her pushing the food from one side of the plate to the other. It was the memory of Garrett. Everywhere she looked, she saw laughing blue eyes, and when she was least expecting it, the wind carried the sweet musky scent of his cologne.

Maggie finally gave up on the roasted chicken and went to the library. Carmalita had thoughtfully started a fire in the library's wood stove, and the room beckoned to Maggie. She loved the library.

Maggie picked up a book she'd been trying to read since her father had fallen ill. The book still held little interest, however, and Maggie placed it back on the shelf.

She went to the huge walnut desk that commanded the attention of anyone who entered the room. Her father had ordered the desk made to fit his specifications. Solid walnut, it had been varnished slightly to bring out the dark lines of the wood's natural grain. It was trimmed with brass handles for the four drawers which lined either side and with brass corner plates at the top edges of the desk.

Maggie sat down in the black leather chair she'd seen her father work from. It swallowed her up. Lovingly, Maggie touched the desktop and its contents. These were the papers her father had been working on before becoming ill. How she wished she understood the running of the ranch books. She'd see to it that Garrett taught her all about them. It seemed very important to know every detail of the ranch—how it was run, when they performed certain duties, and why.

Maggie reluctantly made the familiar walk down the long hall to her father's bedroom. Bill was preparing to bed down on the small cot at the foot of the bed. Maggie glanced at the clock on the fireplace mantel, surprised to see it was nearly ten o'clock.

Confident her father was sleeping soundly, Maggie found Carmalita and informed her she was going to bed. Bill would notify them if anything needed their attention.

Maggie smiled when she discovered Carmalita had already prepared a fire in Maggie's bedroom. Maggie warmed herself for a moment, then slipped into a nightgown. She was about to get into bed when she heard a knock at the door. It was Carmalita.

"Come quickly, Maggie. Señor is not good."

Maggie threw on her robe and raced down the hall after Carmalita. Nothing could have prepared Maggie for the sight of her father writhing and crying out in agony. How could this be? Moments ago, he'd rested comfortably.

"What happened, Bill?" Maggie cried as she rushed to her father's side.

"I don't rightly know, Miss Maggie," Bill began. "I was just getting to sleep when he started a thrashin' and moanin'. I'm afeared the medicine ain't doin' its job."

"That doesn't make any sense. We gave him the regular dosage. It's always worked before," Maggie stated in utter confusion. How could she stop her father's intense pain?

"Father, it's Maggie."

For a moment, the older man's eyes opened. They seemed to flash recognition, then they rolled back, their heavy lids closed. Maggie's tears burned hot on her cheeks. *Dear God, how much more can he stand? Why is he allowed to suffer like this?*

Maria arrived with a larger dose of medication, and after Bill, Maggie, and Carmalita were able to hold Jason's thrashing body still, Maria forced the medicine down his throat.

Maggie sat for the next two hours, waiting as her father's pain faded into peaceful sleep. She dozed off and on, and when Bill suggested she make her way back to bed, she didn't argue.

Gratefully, Maggie climbed once again into the warmth and comfort of her own bed. Her eyes refused to stay open, and her mind was clouded with sleep. Her last clear thought was to wonder what was keeping Garrett and Miguel.

Chapter 17

When Garrett and Miguel hadn't shown up by the end of the second day, both Carmalita and Maggie began to worry.

"They should have been here by now," Maggie said, pulling back the curtain and searching for any sign of the two men.

"Sí," Carmalita said softly as she cleared the breakfast dishes.

As the day warmed to an unseasonable temperature, Maggie determined to ride out on Thunder in hopes of meeting the men as they returned. Even Carmalita agreed it was a good plan.

Maggie checked in on her father first. He slept soundly, and Maria was keeping careful watch for any signs of discomfort. There was little need to worry about the addictive effects of the medication. It was clear to everyone that Jason Intissar would soon join his wife in heaven.

Maggie slipped into a dark blue riding skirt. She pulled on her long boots. They almost felt foreign to her. It had been over a week since she'd ridden. She finished dressing and tied her auburn hair at the nape of her neck with a ribbon.

Making her way to the corral, Maggie located Bill and coaxed him into saddling Thunder for her. Bill had been an absolute lifesaver, and Maggie intended to thank him properly when things settled down.

Although Maggie had never been to the mission, she'd paid careful attention to Bill's directions and landmarks. She didn't intend to go very far, but by midday, she'd covered quite a bit of ground. The sun was blazing overhead.

Maggie paused to take a drink from her canteen, grateful that Bill had insisted on her taking it. Thunder whinnied softly.

"It's okay, Boy," Maggie said, recognizing her mount's thirst. "If Bill's directions are right, a water hole lies just ahead."

As Maggie neared the water hole, a hideous odor filled the air. The stench grew unbearable as Maggie approached the water. She could see strange mounds of dirt on the far side of the hole, but as she drew near, Maggie realized they weren't mounds of dirt at all. The ground was littered with partially butchered cattle carcasses.

Maggie felt nauseated, and Thunder whinnied nervously at the sight. The bloated carcasses were not only beside the water hole, but in the water itself, hopelessly fouling the contents for human or animal use.

Maggie's mind whirled. What could it mean? She'd heard the hands speak of rustlers in the area, and there was the ever-present worry of banditos. The renegade band of Mexicans, Indians, and mixed breeds were a constant worry to the outlying ranches. Banditos had families hidden high in the rocky hills, and they were considered a brotherhood of the utmost secrecy.

Maggie knew Maria had family among the banditos, although she never spoke of it to Maggie. Carmalita had whispered the secret to Maggie, telling her it was one reason Piñon Canyon suffered no more loss than an occasional steer.

Surveying the carnage and waste, Maggie grew cold. She pulled Thunder's reins hard and put him into a full gallop. She wanted to get back home, and she pressed Thunder to the limit of his endurance, fully aware of the white foam which spotted the gelding's coat.

After covering half the distance to the ranch, Maggie remembered Thunder's need for water. She reined the huge gelding to a stop and dismounted. Pouring the contents of her canteen into her hat, she placed it under Thunder's nuzzle. Thunder greedily lapped up the water. It seemed such an inadequate offering, but Maggie had no other choice.

Silently, she surveyed the land around her. It was rocky and dry. Climbing back into her well-worn saddle, Maggie felt uncomfortable. Once again she looked around her. The mountains rose majestically, and their snow-capped peaks shown as brilliant halos against the intense blue of the sky. Nothing here should make her uneasy, but remembering the water hole, Maggie decided things weren't as innocent as they appeared. Cautiously, she made her way back to the ranch.

The sun was starting down when Maggie rode into the corral yard. Bill was frantic.

"Where've ya been? I've been worried sick, feared that maybe those banditos got hold of ya. I should'a never let ya go," Bill ranted as he helped Maggie dismount.

"I'm fine, Bill. Really," Maggie said.

"Then what's that tone of voice about?" Bill questioned as he handed Thunder's reins to one of Maria's sons.

"Bill," Maggie began as soon as the boy was out of ear shot. "I found some dead steers at the first water hole."

"What'd ya say?" Bill asked, uncertain his ears had heard right. Maggie started walking toward the house, and Bill realized she meant for him to follow.

"I don't want anyone to overhear me," Maggie offered as a brief explanation. She paused as they neared the house. "I found seven or eight partially butchered steers. They are all around the water hole and some were even dumped in the water itself."

"Banditos!" Bill exclaimed.

"Do you think so?" Maggie asked, feeling sick again as she remembered the sight at the water hole.

"Has to be. Rustlers wouldn't butcher 'em. They'd drive 'em off and sell them. Banditos can't drive the steers up into their hideouts, so they take what they want or need and leave the carcasses."

"If it is banditos, what will they do next?" Maggie wondered aloud.

"Probably nothing right now," Bill answered deep in thought.

"Bill, we've got to get to Garrett and Miguel. Is there someone else we can send to the mission?" Maggie questioned. "I—we need him so much right now," she added, desperation mounting.

"I'll get Mack. If I send him in the morning, they should be back by nightfall." Bill's words offered little comfort, but when the older man's large, weatherworn hand came down on Maggie's, warmth and closeness briefly stilled her fears.

The following morning, Maggie and Bill stood in the yard watching Mack ride away. Maggie offered a silent prayer for Mack's safety and speed. As she turned to go to the house, she noticed Bill's hesitant steps.

"Maybe we should'a sent someone with him," Bill muttered, and Maggie wondered if he was right. Neither one said another word. Maggie nodded slightly, and Bill touched the brim of his dirty white hat as they parted for their respective duties.

The day moved in slow motion. The only positive bit of excitement was her father. Maggie entered the sickroom to find Maria talking in low whispers to her father.

"Father, but how? Oh, Maria, I thought I'd never be able to talk to him again," Maggie cried as she knelt beside the bed of her father. His slightly drugged gaze fell on his daughter.

"Your papa is doing much better," Maria explained, "so I lessened his medication."

"You aren't hurting?" Maggie questioned, taking hold of her father's hand and holding it to her cheek.

"No, not as much." Jason barely whispered the words.

Maggie breathed a sigh of relief. "Father, there is so much I need to talk to you about. I need you so much." Maggie let her tears fall unashamed against her father's hand.

"Don't cry," Jason murmured and, using all his strength, he gave Maggie's hand a slight squeeze.

"Father, I can't lose you now. Please get well," Maggie begged.

Jason shook his head. His eyes were nearly lifeless. Maggie could see the pallor had not changed, and every breath her father drew brought a hideous rattling sound. A death rattle, Maria had called it.

Maggie straightened her shoulders. It was enough that she could share a few more words of endearment. It was enough that she could tell her father of her love one more time. Peace settled over her, and Maggie decided against telling her father about the ranch's needs and Miguel's absence.

"I love you, Papa," Maggie said, smoothing his forehead.

"I love you too," Jason breathed weakly.

"I'm glad you made me come here. I'm thankful to God that you sent Garrett for me. I know it was right for me to put the past behind and to accept your forgiveness and God's." Jason said nothing, but the slight upturning of his mouth told Maggie he was pleased.

Maggie continued to talk even as Jason dozed and the shadows of afternoon fell across the room. The room chilled. Maggie placed a few pieces of kindling in the fireplace and watched with satisfaction as the wood ignited. The room grew comfortable again, and Maggie was just settling down beside her father's bed when Carmalita came in to light the lamps. The worried look on her face reflected the torture she felt at Miguel's absence.

"Don't worry, Carmalita. They'll all be back soon." Maggie tried to offer the words as an encouragement, but Carmalita rushed out of the room sobbing. Maggie started to go after her, but her father's weak voice stopped her.

"Who'll be back, Maggie?"

"Oh Father, don't worry about it. Everything is fine, really it is," Maggie said soothingly. She didn't want her father to worry.

"Where's Garrett? I'd like to see him, Maggie." Jason said, seeming to forget his concern.

"I've sent for him, Father. He'll be here soon."

"You do love him, don't you? I wouldn't force you to marry him. You know that, don't you?" His words required great effort.

"I know, Father. I know," Maggie assured her father.

"You didn't answer me," Jason whispered and coughed. Maggie feared the cough would return and sought to quiet her father.

"Hush now, Father. Please relax or you'll spend all your energy." Maggie gently stroked her father's hand, hoping to quiet him.

"Maggie," Jason struggled to speak. "I. . .have to. . .know." He was gasping for breath and Maggie wondered if she should find Maria. She stood as if to go, but Jason refused to release her hand. "I have to know," he said more firmly.

"Know what, Father?" Maggie asked, confused by her father's sudden strength.

"I have to know if you love him. Do you love Garrett Lucas, as a woman should love a man who'll be her husband?" Jason's eyes were suddenly clear, and Maggie knew he was studying her intently. Perhaps he couldn't die in peace without knowing she'd be happy.

Maggie fell to her knees beside the bed. "Yes, Father. I love Garrett very much. I think I've loved him since I first laid eyes on him in our parlor back in Potwin. If not then, I'm sure I fell in love with him when he caught me in his arms as I was trying to escape down the trellis." It was the first time Maggie had admitted to herself when her love for Garrett had taken root.

Carmalita reentered the room, but Maggie continued to talk unashamedly of her love for Garrett. "Father, you were so wise in choosing such a man for me. I'm sorry I was such a willful and spoiled child. Garrett called me that, you know? Willful and spoiled," Maggie remembered with a laugh. "I was too." A sudden thought caused Maggie to worry, and her concern was reflected on her face.

"What is it, Maggie? There's something more you aren't telling me." Jason's look of alarm caused Maggie to share her fears aloud.

"It's only that I told Garrett to stay away. I told him I wouldn't wait for him. I wasn't very nice, Father."

"Is that all?" Jason sounded relieved. The sudden smile on his face confused Maggie all the more.

"Is that all? Isn't that enough? I love him," Maggie said, lowering her eyes. "What if he doesn't love me anymore?"

Maggie felt firm hands on her shoulders, and Garrett's deep voice stilled all her fears. "There's no chance of that, Maggie Intissar. I will always love you."

"Garrett!" Maggie jumped to her feet and lost herself in his laughing blue eyes. Regardless of what others would think, Maggie threw her arms around Garrett's neck.

Garrett exchanged a smile over Maggie's back with Jason. Both men silently acknowledged the transfer of Maggie's care from Jason to Garrett.

Garrett held Maggie tightly and could hardly contain his happiness. His Maggie loved him.

Maggie pulled herself away, becoming aware for the first time of the man standing behind Garrett. She lowered her eyes and blushed at the thought of this man overhearing her words of endearment.

Garrett's soft chuckle told Maggie he understood her sudden silence. "This is David Monroe, our local preacher."

Maggie raised her eyes and took the hand David offered her.

"I'm pleased to meet you, Miss Intissar."

"Please call me Maggie. I'm pleased to meet you too. My father has nothing but the highest praise for you," Maggie said and turned to her father. "Look who's here, Father. It's Garrett and Pastor Monroe."

Jason nodded ever so slightly.

"I'll agree to call you Maggie, but you must drop the formalities and call me David," the blond man said, smiling broadly at her. Maggie liked him immediately and soon forgot her discomfort.

"Agreed," she declared.

"Maggie, I'd like to speak to you," Garrett said, taking her arm. "In private." Maggie looked first to David, then to her father.

"Father, I need to speak with Garrett. Will you be alright?" she questioned, fearing if she left him for even a moment, something might go wrong.

"I'll be fine. I want to talk to David anyway," Jason assured her. Maggie nodded, wondering if David would offer her father comforting images of eternity in heaven. As she walked into the hallway with Garrett, she strained to hear their words.

"Did you hear me, Maggie?" Garrett questioned in a whispered hush.

"What?" Maggie asked, turning to see a concerned Garrett.

"There's no easy way to tell you this, but Miguel is dead."

Chapter 18

Hrow? Where?" Maggie asked, her mind flooding with questions. "Banditos," Garrett replied. Maggie shivered uncontrollably. She felt cold and dizzy. Concerned, Garrett put an arm gently around her and said, "Come with me to the library and we'll talk."

Maggie tried to make her feet work, but her brain refused to function. She sat where Garrett directed her to sit, not knowing what to say.

Garrett sat across from Maggie and told the story. "Miguel never made it to the mission. When Mack showed up and told me about the butchered steers, I figured there wouldn't be good news about Miguel. We looked for signs of him on the trail, but there was nothing. Then we decided to take a look at the water hole where you found the carcasses. We found Miguel at the bottom of the pond."

"Dear Lord." Maggie breathed the words, and Garrett knew they were a prayer all their own.

"We buried him. We couldn't bring him back here in the shape he was in."

Maggie nodded dumbly. She suddenly realized she had been at the site of Miguel's murder. While she had sat on Thunder, Miguel had lain dead at the bottom of the water hole. The room began to spin.

"I'm so sorry, Maggie," Garrett offered softly. "I know this is difficult. There was no easy way to tell you." Again Maggie nodded and said nothing. Garrett continued talking, but Maggie's mind went to Carmalita.

"Oh, Garrett," she interrupted. "What about Carmalita? Does she know?"

"I told Maria. She said she'd break the news to her," Garrett replied, rubbing the back of his neck.

Garrett was dusty and sweat soaked, but Maggie had never known a more welcome sight. God had sent him back safely to her. She offered a silent prayer of thanksgiving for Garrett's safety, but she couldn't forget Carmalita's sorrow.

Slowly she got to her feet. "I'll have Maria prepare you a bath. I must go to Carmalita." With that Maggie turned and went in search of the two women.

Garrett stared after Maggie for several minutes. He was amazed at the change in her. Where once had been a childish young girl, now stood a woman. A woman who compassionately put her pain aside to tend to the hurts of others. Garrett smiled. His Maggie had grown up.

Maria went to draw a bath for Garrett, but she could offer Maggie little help in locating Carmalita. Maggie looked throughout the ranch house but found no sign of the missing girl. She searched the quiet courtyard without success.

Maggie finally made her way to Carmalita's room. When there was no response to her knock, she quietly opened the bedroom door. A single lantern burned on the night stand, but Carmalita was gone.

Maggie returned to her father's room and found him listening to David Monroe read from the Psalms. Knowing what comfort her father found from the Bible, she decided against disturbing them and went to seek out Garrett.

Garrett sat refreshed behind Jason's large walnut desk. He was dividing his attention between a cup of black coffee and a ledger book when Maggie arrived.

"I can't find Carmalita!" Maggie's voice betrayed the worry she felt. Garrett looked up from the papers.

"Have you looked everywhere?"

Maggie nodded. "I checked the entire house. Oh, Garrett. I'm worried. Miguel was everything to Carmalita. Where could she be?"

Garrett pushed the papers aside and grabbed his coat. "I'll check the barn and the corrals. You stay put. I'll be back shortly."

Maggie paced the room until she was certain she'd worn a hole in the heavy Indian rug. She tried to sit, but her mind was consumed with worry and grief. Just then, Garrett came rushing into the room.

"She took a horse. I've a feeling she's gone to find where we buried Miguel," Garrett announced.

Maggie rushed to where Garrett stood. "But it's dark and growing colder by the minute."

"I've sent a couple hands after her. I felt it was important for me to stay. I hope that's okay with you."

"Oh yes, Garrett. Please don't leave me again." For once, Maggie didn't try to hide her tears. Garrett took her into his strong arms.

"Hush, now. I'm here and I'm not going anywhere—at least not without you," he added softly.

"Señor, Señorita." Maria burst into the room, panting from her hard running.

"What is it, Maria? Have you found Carmalita?" Maggie asked as she rushed to Maria's side.

"I found this," Maria said, holding up a piece of paper.

Garrett took the note from Maria. His eyes narrowed slightly as he read it.

"What is it, Garrett?" Maggie questioned anxiously.

"It says Carmalita knows who killed Miguel. She's gone to avenge Miguel's death," Garrett spoke gravely. "I'll have to go, Maggie. Maria, go find Bill for me, and hurry."

"Sí." Maria was still breathless, but she sped from the room.

"Garrett, you can't go! What if it's a plot? What if they want to kill you?" Maggie cried.

Garrett unlocked the gun cabinet. "I can't expect Carmalita to face banditos on her own. She's probably unarmed, and a lone woman approaching a rowdy bunch like that? Well, I'd rather not say what I'm thinking."

Garrett opened the cabinet and took out a rifle and some cartridges. Maggie crossed the room to his side.

"Please don't go. Send someone else." She was crying. Garrett placed the rifle and cartridges on the table and took Maggie in his arms.

"Shh, don't cry. It's going to be alright. We might even catch up to her before she gets very far." Garrett stroked Maggie's damp cheek, knowing the tears she cried were from love for him.

Maggie lifted her face to Garrett's and looked deep into his eyes. She saw his resolve. "I love you, Garrett," she whispered.

"Maggie, you can't know how I've dreamed of hearing you say that. I've waited a lifetime for you. I love you, and I'm not going to do anything foolish to risk the happiness I know we'll share." With those words, Garrett leaned down and kissed her. It was a long and loving kiss. A kiss that left Maggie flushed and breathless.

"Garrett," Maggie's voice still held the urgency she felt. "Let's pray together before you go."

Garrett smiled. "I can't think of anything more necessary," he answered. Taking down a well-worn Bible from the fireplace mantel, Garrett turned to Psalm 91. " 'He that dwelleth in the secret place of the most High,' " Garrett read, " 'shall abide under the shadow of the Almighty. I will say of the Lord, He is my refuge and my fortress: my God; in Him will I trust. Surely He shall deliver thee from the snare of the fowler, and from the noisome pestilence. He shall cover thee with His feathers, and under His wings shalt though trust: His truth shall be thy shield and buckler.' "

Garrett replaced the Bible and knelt with Maggie. "Father, we seek Your guidance. You know the situation and our need better than we do. We ask that You cover us in Your protection. Protect Carmalita too, Father. She's out there somewhere. We don't know where—but You do. Place a shield of protection around her. In Jesus' name—"

"Wait," Maggie interrupted. "Father, please watch over Garrett. I know I've been a stubborn child in the past, but Garrett has sought Your will for a long, long time. I know he places his trust in You. Sometimes it's hard for me to trust, but I know You love him even more than I do. Please bring him safely back to me. In Jesus' name. Amen."

"Amen," Garrett added and squeezed Maggie's hand. "And to think," he smiled. "I get to share this with you for a lifetime."

Maggie smiled too. "I feel better. Now I can let you go without fearing the worst." Getting to her feet with Garrett's help, Maggie laughed nervously.

"What?" Garrett asked.

"I wish I had a piano."

"A piano?" Garrett responded. "What does that have to do with anything?"

"Back in Topeka, whenever things got bad or I felt lonely, I would pound out my frustrations on the piano. It helped to pass the time, and it soothed my nerves." Maggie smiled and looked around the room. "Father bought me a wardrobe full of clothes, but there isn't a single piano on the ranch." She feigned utter misery.

Garrett laughed and whirled Maggie in a circle. "You shall have the best and finest piano money can buy for a wedding gift from me," he said as he finally let Maggie's feet touch the ground. "Though I haven't the slightest idea how we'll get it here." At this they both laughed.

Bill came rushing into the room, knowing the gravity of the situation from Maria's brief explanation. He was somewhat confused to find Garrett and Maggie laughing. He cleared his throat to gain their attention.

Garrett was the first to sober. "Bill, we've got to go after Carmalita." Maggie grew solemn.

Bill nodded his head. "Maria told me. I've got ten men who'll ride with us."

"Good. Then let's be at it," Garrett replied.

"There's somethin' else you ought to know, Boss."

"What?" Garrett questioned.

"The boys finished a head count on the stock. We're short nearly a hundred steers."

"A hundred? Are you sure?"

Maggie didn't like the tone of Garrett's voice. Something in Bill's statement had signaled more danger, of this she was certain.

"They're sure alright. Herd's been down from the hills for over a week. Them that we didn't sell, we turned loose on the ridge. Since I saw signs of snow, I had the boys bring 'em on down. After we got 'em all corralled, we counted about ninety-eight missing."

"What does this mean, Garrett?" Maggie asked.

"Most likely rustlers," he replied and went to the desk to retrieve the rifle and ammunition.

"Rustlers and banditos? And poor Carmalita out there? Please be careful, Garrett." Maggie's voice quivered as she placed her hand on his arm.

"I will. Keep praying." Then he kissed her and was gone.

Chapter 19

Maggie went silently to her father's room. David was reading the Bible in a gentle, even tone. Silently, Maggie took up her knitting and sat in a chair across the room. The words David recited offered her comfort as no others could.

David sensed something was wrong, but he knew better than to disturb Jason's rest by asking questions.

After an hour, Maggie could no longer sit still. "Excuse me, David, I think we should let Father sleep now." David nodded, sensing the urgency in Maggie's voice.

"Jason," David said. "I'll be in the kitchen trying to talk Maria out of her spectacular custard. If you need me, just give a holler."

"Thank you, David. You've been a comfort, but Maggie's right. Sleep will do me good." Jason's words were hoarse whispers.

"Father, do you need more medication?" Maggie knew it had been several hours since his last dose of morphine.

"No, no. I feel surprisingly better. You run along and fix David up with something to eat. I'm fine, child. Really." Jason raised his hand weakly to flag them on their way. Maggie took hold of it.

"I love you, Father. I'll be close by. You just rest."

Maggie led David to the kitchen, but Maria sent them off to the dining room, promising to serve them her best custard.

"Things aren't as they should be," Maggie began as David helped her with her chair.

"I thought as much, but I didn't want to worry your father. He's perceptive for a sick man."

"A dying man," Maggie murmured.

"Yes, that's true. Hard to believe though," David declared. "I've never met a man who lived life to the degree your father has." David paused as he studied Maggie. It was easy to see why Garrett was drawn to her. "Has your father told you about the mission?"

"A bit here and there. Until a short time ago, we weren't on speaking terms. And I wasn't on listening terms, either. I missed a great deal of time with him because of my stubbornness."

"You can't live your life under a rock of regrets. We all have things we wished we'd done differently. Some things we wish we hadn't done at all, but what's done is done. We seek God's forgiveness, change our ways, and make amends. You're doing a fine job, Maggie. It's clear you've brought him happiness."

Maria entered the room and placed two warm bowls of custard on the table. Moments later, she returned with David's favorite caramel sauce.

"You spoil me, Maria. But I love it." David laughed and ran a hand through his straight blond hair.

"Thank you, Maria. It looks wonderful," Maggie added.

"Don't tell me you've never had Maria's caramel custard?" David asked, a look of disbelief on his face.

"I might have and not remembered. Not much of the past few months registered. I was so angry. I could have eaten about anything and never known."

"Mostly, Señorita didn't eat at all," Maria stated matter-of-factly.

"That's true," Maggie laughed. "Twice, Carmalita had to alter my clothes. Poor Carmalita," Maggie's voice sobered.

"What is it?" David questioned.

"Carmalita took off after the people who killed Miguel. She left a note saying she knew who was responsible. Garrett rounded up some men and took off after her."

"It's awfully cold and dark out there," David began. "But Garrett knows every inch of this land. If anyone can find her, he can. But I'm sure glad I didn't ask about this while we were with your father."

"Yes," Maggie said, tasting the custard. "Maria, this is wonderful!"

"Gracias, I'm glad you like it. I'll be in the kitchen if you need me."

Maggie nodded and continued explaining to David. "On top of everything else, some cattle are missing. It seems the rustlers and banditos are plotting to destroy us."

Just then, Maria came rushing into the room. "Señorita, Señorita! You must come quickly."

"What is it, Maria?" Maggie said as she followed Maria to the kitchen door. David was close behind the women.

Maria opened the door to admit a young Mexican boy. He looked twelve or thirteen, and Maria introduced him as her grandson. "He lives in the mountains," Maria added, admitting to his life with the banditos.

Maggie looked back and forth from Maria to the young boy. "Well? What is it?" Maggie asked, no longer able to contain her concern.

The boy rattled off in Spanish, and while David nodded his understanding, Maggie didn't know what was being said. When the boy finished delivering his message, David interpreted it for Maggie.

"He says his people didn't butcher your cattle. He's been sent here by his parents because they knew his grandmother would protect him," David explained. Then he turned and questioned the boy.

The boy answered hesitantly, but his response satisfied David. "He says the banditos would never harm Señor Jason's hacienda. He's been very good to them, and that is why they've sent word to you. They don't want to be blamed for this."

"How did they find out about it?" Maggie questioned.

"They found the mess at the water hole. They knew someone had made it look like banditos were to blame." David answered. "They wanted to vindicate themselves."

Suddenly, Maggie grew cold. If Carmalita knew the person who had killed Miguel and it wasn't done by banditos, then the murderer had to be someone on the ranch. As if reading Maggie's mind, David instructed Maria to have her grandson stay the night and to lock all the doors and windows.

"David, the killer could be riding with Garrett right now," Maggie sobbed. "I can't lose him." She started for the door, but David held her fast.

"I can't let you go, Maggie. You know that, and you know why. Now come with me, and we'll sit with your father," David said firmly.

"But what of your wife?" Maggie asked. "Will she be safe at the mission?"

David's jaw tightened. "Let's go sit with Jason."

The hours passed, and Maggie struggled to appear at ease in front of her father. David had started reading the Bible once more, and Maggie wondered if he were doing so in part to answer his fear for Jenny.

Jason had fallen into a deep sleep, so David put aside the Bible and stretched his long legs by walking to the bedroom window.

"If you like, I could show you to the guest room," Maggie offered. Her own body was suffering from the tension. She had considered retiring to her room, but she hated to leave David alone.

"No. I think we should stay together," David said, turning to meet Maggie's worried expression.

"Don't worry, Maggie. I've always been overly cautious. It's one of my faults."

Maggie smiled. She knew David was trying to put her at ease. The wind picked up, and a light mist started to fall. Maggie listened to the rain grow heavy, then lighten again. She remembered times in Topeka when she'd sat in her room listening to the rain. She'd loved to snuggle down under the covers of her bed as the rain beat against the window panes. It had always made her feel safe. What she wouldn't give to feel safe now!

Uneasy, Maggie joined the others in fitful sleep. As the first light of dawn crept over the eastern mountains, Maggie and David were jerked awake by thundering horse hooves. Maggie glanced at her father, but he still slept soundly.

David went first to the window, then to the bedroom door. "Stay here," he ordered, and Maggie nodded. For once, she had no thought of disobeying orders.

She went to the window, anxious to see if she could catch sight of the riders. The scene revealed nothing. Maggie twisted her hands together. She paced back and forth at the end of her father's bed.

"Dear God, Garrett has to be alright. You have to keep him safe for me." Suddenly, her prayers sounded selfish. Maggie reconsidered her words. "Father, I know You have a plan for each of us. I can't imagine a plan for me without Garrett by my side, but I trust You. I believe You'll care for Garrett and for me in the best way. I give it over to Your will, Lord." Before Maggie could finish her prayer, voices in the hallway interrupted.

Maggie rushed to the door just as it opened. Garrett stood before her. Seeing that Jason was asleep, Garrett pulled Maggie into the hall and closed the door.

Maggie sobbed as she fell against Garrett's chest. "You're alright!" she whispered between her tears.

"Come with me, Maggie," Garrett said, refusing to let her go. They joined David in the living room. Garrett led Maggie to the high-backed sofa and had her sit beside him.

"Is it—did they?" Maggie couldn't bring herself to ask the questions on her mind. She was shaking from head to toe.

"It's over. At least for now," Garrett said softly, putting his arm around her in support.

"Carmalita?" Maggie dared to ask.

"She'll be staying at the mission while she recovers from all this," Garrett said. Noticing David's anxious expression, he added, "Everything is fine there." David sighed in relief.

"We can talk about this later if you like," Garrett offered.

Maggie nodded, relieved that she wouldn't have to hear the details of what had taken place.

"I think I'll bid Jason good-bye and go home," David announced. "Jenny's bound to be beside herself."

Garrett nodded and added, "I had a couple men stay on until you get there."

A relieved look passed over David's face. "Thanks, Friend."

"I think I owe you thanks as well," Garrett replied. They shared a nod, each acknowledging the other's actions.

For a long time after David had left the living room, Maggie did nothing but allow Garrett to hold her. Silently, she thanked God over and over for bringing Garrett home safely. She praised Him for keeping Jenny and Carmalita safe too.

Just then, David returned. "Maggie," he said. "Your father is asking for you." Maggie dried her tears with her apron and followed David to her father's room.

"I'm here, Father. What can I do for you?" Maggie tried to smile as she knelt beside her father's bed.

Jason Intissar turned his weary blue eyes to the daughter he'd spent a lifetime loving. Behind her stood Garrett, arms folded across his chest, feet planted slightly apart.

"Father?" Maggie's small voice drew Jason's attention. "Is everything alright? Are you in pain?"

"No, Child. I called you here for something else." Jason paused to take a deep breath. "Maggie, I know I'm not going to live much longer. I thank God for these few moments with you, but I'm not a selfish man in respect to life. I've had a good one, and I'm ready to meet my God and your ma."

Jason stopped to draw another ragged breath. His body was seized by a fit of coughing, but to Maggie's surprise the spell lasted only a few moments.

"Father, you need to rest. We can come back later," Maggie said, getting to her feet.

Jason held out his thin hand. "Please wait."

"What is it, Father?"

"I have only one request, Maggie. Just one thing before I die," Jason said in uneven words. "I've already told David about it."

Maggie turned to meet David Monroe's tender eyes. She turned back to her father.

"I know a girl wants things a certain way on her wedding day and you're deserving of that, but I want to see you married, Maggie. I don't have the time for a fancy wedding, and I'm asking a favor of you." Jason's words died off into a barely audible whisper. "I want you to marry Garrett here, today."

Maggie's heart lurched. She worried about hurting Carmalita by marrying so soon after Miguel's death. She also had no idea what Garrett had just been through. Perhaps he wouldn't want to get married right away. But her father's request was appropriate, and Maggie knew he didn't have much time.

Almost fearing the intensity of Garrett's eyes, Maggie turned to find him smiling. She blushed and lowered her eyes. Marriage to Garrett was what she'd dreamed of. It was hard to imagine in a few moments that dream would become reality.

Maggie turned back to her father. "I'd be happy to marry Garrett, right this minute, Father. Dresses, parties, and rooms full of people aren't as important as sharing this moment with you. If it meets with Garrett's approval, David can marry us this very minute."

Jason's face lit up with a huge smile.

"Well, what do you say, Mr. Lucas?" Maggie turned boldly toward Garrett. "Will you marry me?"

Forgetting the terror of the night and his deep concern for Maggie's safety, Garrett relaxed and even managed to laugh. "Are you proposing, Miss Intissar?"

Maggie joined his laughter. "Yes, I believe I am."

"In that case, I accept. But don't go getting any ideas about bossing me around in the future. This here is just a favor to Jason," he drawled, and everyone broke into laughter.

Chapter 20

While Maria was summoned to get Bill and Mack and anyone else who wanted to witness the event, David prepared for the wedding service. Garrett conferred with Jason in hushed whispers, and Maggie was suddenly alone.

She stood at the window, watching the rain. Rain was a bad omen on a wedding day. Maggie tried to remember the old saying. Something about the number of raindrops that fell would be the number of tears the bride would cry.

But, Maggie reminded herself, she didn't believe in bad luck. She believed in God's guidance. The rain was just rain.

"Scared?" Garrett's question was barely audible as he came up behind Maggie.

"A little—I guess," Maggie said. She looked up, slowly meeting Garrett's eyes—eyes so blue and powerful she felt herself grow weak.

"You haven't changed your mind, have you?" Garrett asked seriously.

Maggie's face shot up and her eyes flashed. "Never!"

"Then there's nothing to fear. We look to God for our future. I love you, Magdelena Intissar. I love you with all that I am." A tear slid down Maggie's cheek.

"I love you, Garrett Lucas. I can only pray I will be the wife you need." Maggie murmured. Garrett took her in his arms and held her tightly.

"Whoa, now. We haven't gotten to that part yet," David Monroe called from beside the fireplace. Everyone laughed and the tension broke.

Maggie joined hands with Garrett and stood at the foot of her father's bed. She glanced around the room at the ranch workers who'd become her friends. She only wished her mother and grandmother could have lived to see her wedding.

Maggie looked down at her attire and smiled, thinking how appalled her friend Lillie would have been at the blue calico dress. But Maggie knew Lillie would have liked Garrett.

Once or twice, Maggie gazed over her shoulder to find her father looking on, contentment beaming from his face. This moment was for him.

A few minutes later, David told Garrett he could kiss his bride. Garrett pulled Maggie close. His arms wrapped around her like a warm blanket. Their eyes met, and the promise of new life flashed before them. Then Garrett kissed Maggie deeply while the wedding guests cheered.

Jason held his hands up to Maggie and Garrett. "I've waited a long time for this day. I'm proud to call you son," Jason said, his eyes planted firmly on Garrett. "I'm trusting you to care for my daughter and to keep your family in line with the plans the good Lord has for you. This ranch and all I have is yours. Yours to share with Maggie." Garrett nodded and squeezed his father-in-law's hand.

"And my Maggie," Jason sighed. "How beautiful you are today. I want you to be happy. I want you to enjoy what I've made here, but most of all I want you to keep your heart close to God. I'm so glad I was here when you accepted Jesus as your Savior. I can go on now—knowing you're in God's care and Garrett's."

"Surprise!" Maria exclaimed as she reentered the room. Maggie turned to see that Maria had brought refreshments.

"How wonderful!" Maggie cried, rushing to Maria. "Our own reception."

Garrett joined his wife with a smile. "She's more interested in food than her new husband." Maggie blushed, suddenly aware she'd rushed from Garrett and her father to a tray of pastries.

Garrett laughed all the more at the sight of Maggie's embarrassment. "Well, I just thought it was kind of Maria," Maggie added, giving up at the roar of laughter from everyone.

The ranch hands didn't need second invitations to enjoy the treats. Maria poured steaming cups of Mexican coffee while the hands helped themselves to the tray of goodies.

David joined in the revelry. He had downed his third pastry by the time Maria offered him a cup of coffee. "These are some good eats, Maria. I wish Jenny had the recipe."

"I could write it down for her," Maria offered.

David nodded in appreciation. "You do that, Maria. I'd be much obliged."

Maggie had glanced over at her father once or twice. He was beaming. She was about to ask him if he wanted something to eat when Garrett asked her something.

"I'm sorry. I wasn't listening," Maggie said apologetically.

"I was wondering if you thought this might be too much for your father. Maybe we should herd everybody out of here," Garrett whispered.

Maggie glanced around Garrett to where her father rested. Suddenly, her heart stopped. Color drained from her face, and she pushed past Garrett and ran to her father's bedside.

Jason still bore the smile Maggie had seen earlier, but his lifeless eyes betrayed the secret that he'd passed from one world to the next. Maggie placed his hand against her cheek, patting it gently.

"Father? Father, wake up," she cried, but in her heart she knew her father was dead.

Garrett and David were the only ones who noticed what was taking place. Garrett stood behind Maggie. He gently placed his hands on her shoulders. David moved to the opposite side of the bed and felt for a pulse. There was none.

"He's gone," David murmured softly.

It was only when David closed Jason's eyes that Maggie felt the impact of his words. Maria noticed what David was doing and quickly crossed herself and whispered a prayer. This caught the attention of the three ranch hands.

"He's past the pain now," Bill offered softly. "Mighty sorry to lose him, though. Mighty sorry." Maggie saw tears in Bill's eyes and heard his voice quiver. Bill had cared deeply for her father. Mack and Rob were silent, though Maggie noticed Mack turn to wipe his eyes with his sleeve.

Maggie moved away from Garrett and the bed, watching David tend to her father's body. Everything was moving in slow motion. Bill said something to Garrett, but Maggie couldn't make out the words. She couldn't hear anything over the pounding of her heart. The room began to swim, and desperately, Maggie reached out to steady herself. She saw Garrett look at her, then she collapsed at the foot of her father's bed.

Garrett rushed to lift Maggie in his arms. "Maria, get me a cold cloth."

"Sí, Señor," Maria said as she hastened from the bedroom.

"David, I've got to get her out of here," Garrett called over his shoulder.

"Don't worry about it. Take care of your wife," David answered. *My wife*, Garrett thought. After months of separation, they were finally married.

Garrett was moving toward the west wing of the house when he came across Maria.

"Come with me, Maria. We'll put her in my room."

Maria nodded and brought the basin of water and washcloth she'd gone for. She managed to balance the basin while opening the door for Garrett. He moved across the study that adjoined his bedroom, grateful that he'd left the bedroom door open. Maria followed, watching the tender way Garrett placed Maggie on the bed.

"Give me the cloth," Garrett requested. He placed the cloth across Maggie's forehead and began to pat her hand.

"Maggie, *mi querida*, wake up."

Maria moved forward to loosen the buttons at the neck of Maggie's gown. Maggie stirred slightly, and Garrett gently wiped her face with the damp cloth, hoping the coolness would bring her back to consciousness.

"Father," Maggie moaned softly. With a jerk, her eyes flew open. "No-o-o!" she cried. She struggled to sit up, but Garrett's firm hands held her back.

"Just rest a minute," insisted Garrett.

"Oh, Garrett," Maggie sobbed into her hands. Her body shook uncontrollably, and Garrett held her long after her tears had soaked the front of his shirt. "He can't be dead, Garrett! He can't be."

Maggie pulled back and turned her red, swollen eyes toward Maria. "Maria, please tell me he isn't dead."

But Maria found it hard to speak. She lowered her eyes, her own tears falling freely, and quickly left the room.

Maggie looked back to Garrett whose eyes were also wet with tears. "We'll all miss him," Garrett whispered.

It was then Maggie became aware of Garrett's pain. She steadied herself, studying the weary face of the man who was now her husband. The strain was as great on him as it was on her.

"Oh, Garrett, I'm so sorry. I know how you loved him," Maggie said, her heart filled with aching for the sadness she saw in Garrett's eyes. When tears began to roll down Garrett's cheeks, Maggie held him tightly. Together they shared their sorrow. It was not the wedding day either one would have planned, but their shared pain brought deeper intimacy to their marriage.

Two days later, Maggie joined Garrett beside the grave of her father. In torrential rain, Bill and Mack had taken turns digging the final resting place of their boss and friend. Maria had prepared Jason's body with David Monroe's help.

Garrett had finalized arrangements for the last of the winter supplies to be brought in. He'd also handed the rustlers who had murdered Miguel over to the law.

Maggie had been horrified to learn that the rustlers' leader was Cactus Jack, her father's own ranch hand. Knowing her father was growing sicker and Garrett was nowhere around, Cactus Jack had figured they'd have a good chance of stealing lots of cattle.

The plan might have worked, but Carmalita had overheard pieces of a conversation between Cactus Jack and Miguel. Cactus Jack had wanted Miguel to join his operation, and when he'd refused, Cactus Jack had threatened his life.

With God's help, Garrett had been able to locate Carmalita before she'd found Cactus Jack and his men. Garrett had seen her safely to the mission and then turned his sights on collecting both his cattle and the rustlers responsible for their disappearance.

"It's time, Maggie," she heard Garrett saying. Maggie nodded somberly.

She was grateful so many people were taking care of her. Everyone had pitched in. Maggie hadn't needed to lift a finger to help with the funeral or the ranch.

As she stood in the rain, watching little rivers run down the side of the dirt mound that would soon cover her father's casket, Maggie shivered. Garrett quickly placed his coat around Maggie's shoulders. Maggie turned her eyes briefly to meet those of her husband.

Suddenly, she felt out of place. Garrett had his duties. Bill, Mack, and Maria all had their jobs. But Maggie's days of caring for her father were over, and she had nothing to do. Now that Carmalita was staying at the mission, Maggie didn't even have her to talk to.

Maggie glanced at the western ridge. She'd given up hope of Carmalita coming to the funeral. In this wet weather, the twelve mile ride to the ranch would be miserable for the heartiest ranch hand. Silently, Maggie chided herself for expecting Carmalita to put aside her grief over Miguel to attend the funeral.

Just as Maggie tried to concentrate on David's words, Carmalita came into view. Motionless, she looked down from the crest of a ridge, then nudged her horse to the valley and across to the ranch. She sat proudly, almost regally, in the saddle. David's words fell silent as all eyes turned to watch the stately procession. When Carmalita approached the graveside, Maggie left Garrett's side and went to her.

Pain and sorrow clouded Carmalita's face. "This," Carmalita said as she revealed a small pine wreath, "is for Señor."

Maggie reached up and took the gift. Dark green branches were intricately woven with red braided calico. Maggie appreciated the honor being paid to her father.

"Gracias, Carmalita," Maggie whispered, knowing further conversation would be meaningless. Maggie walked to the grave and lovingly placed the wreath upon her father's casket. Then she glanced back toward Carmalita. Carmalita nodded and started her horse back toward the mission.

"I'll miss her," Maggie whispered.

"We all will," Garrett said as he put his arm around his wife.

Maggie tried to focus on the words David had chosen to comfort those gathered for her father's funeral. " 'I am the resurrection, and the life: he that believeth in me, though he were dead, yet shall he live: And whosoever liveth and believeth in me shall never die,' " David quoted with love and assurance.

Maggie knew the words were true. Her father's death wasn't disturbing her as much as the feeling of being displaced. When David finished speaking,

Maggie excused herself and moved to the house. Maria followed closely behind.

"Would you like some coffee or tea, Señora?" she asked in her thick accent.

"Thank you, Maria. I think I would like some coffee. I didn't sleep well last night," Maggie replied gratefully.

"Where will you take it?" questioned Maria as she shook the rain from her coat.

"Bring it to my room," Maggie began and then thought better of returning to her old bedroom. "No, please bring it to my father's room. I'd like some time alone." Maria nodded and left for the kitchen.

Maggie shook the rain from her coat and hung it to dry. She went to a small chest of drawers in the pantry and pulled out a fresh apron. During her father's illness, she had needed an apron's large, roomy pockets to carry a variety of things, but as Maggie tied the strings into a bow, she questioned her action.

I don't know why I'm putting on an apron, Maggie thought. *There's no one to nurse and nothing to do. I'm not needed.* Maggie walked to her father's room and sat in the rocking chair.

Maria had thoughtfully started a crackling fire that was warming the cool, damp air. Sitting opposite her portrait, Maggie studied the youthful image of herself. She remembered with sadness the hours she'd spent sitting for the portrait so her father would let her stay in Topeka.

Maria arrived with the coffee, but knowing Maggie wanted solitude, she did nothing more than pour a cup and leave.

Maggie sipped the dark liquid, enjoying the warmth that spread through her body. So many relationships had come to an end, but what of the gains? She had a new husband, but she wasn't sure what she was supposed to do with him.

Dear God, please help me to know my place and to find contentment in it. I feel so confused right now, Maggie prayed. *I want to belong, but with so many people I loved now gone, I don't know where to start. Please guide me, Lord. Teach me how to be a good wife.*

Garrett entered the room.

"Mind if I join you?" he drawled. Maggie could tell he was trying to be lighthearted.

"No, not really. At first I wanted to be alone, but not now," Maggie replied. Calm was beginning to spread through her soul, and Maggie knew her Heavenly Father was giving her peace.

"I'm glad," Garrett said, sounding old. "I need you." Maggie's eyes widened.

"You need me? Whatever for?" she questioned curiously.

"How can you ask?" Garrett inquired as he took a chair.

"Well, I have to confess I was feeling unnecessary. I don't know anything about the running of this ranch, and you have it all under control anyway. I'm not needed in the house—Maria manages nicely by herself. Winter is here, so there's little I can do outdoors. Even if I could go outside, what would I do?" Maggie asked.

She paused, studying the details of her father's now-familiar room. "When Father was alive, when he needed me to care for him, I knew I had a place to belong. I had a purpose."

"You think you have no purpose now?" Garrett questioned, contemplating Maggie's words.

"Yes," she admitted. "I suppose that sounds foolish, but there it is. I'm eighteen years old, and I feel so stupid. I don't know the first thing about being a rancher's wife. For that matter, I don't know much about anything."

"Come here, Maggie," Garrett ordered and motioned her with his finger. "Right now. Come here."

Maggie tilted her head and studied her husband. Setting her coffee aside, she walked slowly to where Garrett sat. When she stood beside him, Maggie could see tears in his eyes.

Garrett reached up and pulled Maggie to his lap. "I want you to listen, and listen good. Do you understand?" he questioned in a stern voice.

Maggie nodded. She could feel the warmth of his arms around her. It felt good to be held.

"A long time ago, I asked God to send me a wife. A helpmate, just like Eve was intended for Adam. I knew I wouldn't enjoy going through life without a companion. I never cared enough for my own company, I guess," he said with a little grin. Maggie smiled slightly.

"Fact is, I always saw myself with a woman by my side and children of my own. Family is mighty important to me, Maggie, especially because I lost mine at such an early age." Again Maggie nodded, but said nothing.

"God answered my prayer by sending you, and I praise Him daily for such a blessing. But I know nothing about being a husband except what the Bible tells me. By watching my own pa and yours, I saw what a father's heart was like. I learned to have the mind of a businessman and rancher. But I didn't learn anything about the heart of a husband. I'm starting from scratch, just like you."

Maggie's heart swelled at the deep love Garrett felt for her. She did belong. She belonged to God as His eternal child, and God had also blessed her with a husband—a husband who prayed for her. Maggie thanked God she belonged to Garrett.

"I understand," Maggie said with wonder. "It doesn't matter that I don't know the first thing about ranching or being a wife. What matters is I belong—we belong—to God and to each other."

Garrett held Maggie tightly and gazed steadily into her eyes. "That's all that matters, Maggie," he said with certainty.

"I love you, Garrett Lucas," Maggie whispered softly.

"And I love you, Maggie Lucas."

Outside, the rain poured harder than ever. Thunder echoed in the distance. But inside, two hearts had found shelter in the shadow of the Most High, a place to belong.

Perfect Love

Chapter 1

Lillie Philips placed a final hairpin in her honey blond hair and sat back to study her work. Yes, it would be perfect. Lillie felt a special pride in her appearance, especially now that she and her beloved husband, Jason, were expecting their first child.

Her hand went lovingly to her stomach. A slight curve was starting to form—enough to let her know Jason, Jr., was really there. She smiled at how adamant Jason was that this baby would be a son. "Of course it will be a son," Lillie thought aloud. "The Philipses always get what they want."

At eighteen, Lillie Philips was the envy of many women in her home-town of Topeka, Kansas. She was considered one of Topeka's most beautiful women, with finely chiseled features that resembled a china doll. She had lived a spoiled and pampered life and enjoyed all the things money could buy. While other people put their faith and future in dreams and lofty aspirations, Lillie Philips had already come into her era of prosperity.

Lillie reached down and picked up an ornately framed picture of her best friend, Maggie Intissar. "No," she thought aloud. "Maggie Lucas."

She and Maggie had shared many secrets and girlhood hopes together. When Maggie had lost her mother and brother in death and her father had deserted her to her grandmother's care, Lillie had helped Maggie through the pain. They were nearly inseparable, and when Lillie's family had chosen to build a home in the newly developed Potwin Place, Maggie's grandmother had agreed to have a home built next door so Maggie and Lillie could continue to grow up together.

Lillie could scarcely believe that over seven months had passed since Maggie had been whisked away to her father's ranch in New Mexico by the dashing, mysterious Garrett Lucas.

Although Lillie knew Maggie had hated her father at one time, she was happy Maggie had come to love him before his death. At least Maggie wouldn't have to carry that burden through life.

Lillie was grateful too, Maggie wouldn't have to be alone anymore. She was now Garrett Lucas's wife, and judging from the letters she sent to Lillie, Maggie was most content with the way her life had turned out.

Lillie smiled lovingly at the tintype. "Oh, Maggie," she sighed in content-ment, "I can only hope that you're as happy as I am."

Hearing a carriage below on the cobblestone drive, Lillie forgot the picture and went quickly to the large cheval glass. She smoothed the lines of her blue, watered-silk, day dress that matched her eyes. It was the third gown she'd had on that day, and within the hour she'd dress again for dinner. Lillie couldn't get enough of rich, beautiful clothes and finery. She twirled in front of the mirror, making certain every inch of the gown fell perfectly into place.

When she heard Jason's voice in the vestibule, Lillie quickly pinched her cheeks and fluffed the leg-of-mutton sleeves, lavishly created from expensive French lace. Finally satisfied with her appearance, Lillie descended the stairs in grand fashion to greet her husband.

Jason stood at the entryway table studying the day's mail. He lifted his gaze momentarily to catch sight of Lillie. Her beauty never failed to make him catch his breath.

The mail was quickly discarded as Lillie's satin-slippered feet reached the final step. Jason swept her into his arms and kissed her.

"Good evening, Wife," he murmured affectionately.

"And good evening to you my beloved husband."

"Umm," Jason sighed against his wife's perfumed neck. "I've missed you today." Lillie relished the attention. It was hard to believe they'd been married for nearly six months.

"Why don't we take our supper upstairs," Jason suggested.

Lillie felt shivers run down her spine. How she loved this romantic man! "I think it's a wonderful idea. I'll tell Cookie, and you go ahead upstairs." Jason smiled but refused to unhand Lillie.

"I need just one more kiss to see me through." Before Lillie could protest, Jason planted his lips firmly on hers.

"Perhaps," Lillie said, pulling away breathless from her husband's kiss, "we should forget supper and spend the evening curled up together in front of the fire."

Jason laughed heartily and set Lillie at arm's length. "Nonsense woman! I've worked a hard day at the law firm. In fact, I'll have you know you're looking at a full partner in the law firm of Canton, Meiers, Johnston, and Philips.

"Oh Jason!" Lillie exclaimed. "Why didn't you tell me sooner? This is wonderful news. It's exactly what we'd hoped for. I'm so proud of you!" Lillie threw her arms around Jason's neck and hugged him tightly.

For the first time, Jason seemed to become aware of Lillie's rounding figure. His hand went to her still slender form and lovingly rested on the slight swelling. "I see my son is getting bigger each day."

"My daughter, you mean," Lillie couldn't help but tease.

"If you dare to have a daughter, my dear wife, I'm afraid I shall have to put you from the house!" With that Jason laughed good-naturedly, as did Lillie. Life was good, and they both knew how fortunate they'd been to be born to wealth and security.

An hour later, the housekeeper appeared at Jason and Lillie's bedroom suite. She entered the sitting room carrying an overflowing tray of Cookie's finest culinary treats.

"Thank you very much, Mrs. Gregory," Lillie stated in a refined manner. "You may put it there," she motioned to the doily covered, Queen Anne table that stood beside the door.

Mrs. Gregory nodded and placed the tray on the table. "Will you be requiring my services for anything else, Ma'am?" she requested in a formal, sedate fashion.

"I think not, Mrs. G.," Jason said as he emerged from the bedroom. "Lillie and I are celebrating, and we can do quite well on our own."

Mrs. Gregory gave a stiff nod and took her leave.

"Now, my dear," Jason said with a mischievous grin. "I think it's time you take down your hair and change into something more appropriate."

Lillie raised an eyebrow in mocking shock. "Why Jason Philips, are you trying to romance me?"

Jason laughed aloud. "Trying? No. Succeeding? Yes. Now do you need my help?"

Lillie laughed softly. "No, no. I'll be back in a minute. You see to our supper."

～

Several days later, Lillie thought back to that evening as nearly the most perfect one of her marriage. Jason had looked so handsome, and he'd been so attentive. Then, of course, there was the promotion and the excitement of planning what they would do with the extra money that would soon be coming their way.

To match everything else, Lillie felt the baby move for the first time. Even Jason, Jr., wanted to be an important part of the celebration, Lillie remembered fondly. She was so anxious to have her baby and give him every benefit that life could afford. Her son, Lillie decided, would have the world at his feet; she'd see to that.

Lillie tapped her pen impatiently as she tried to keep her mind on the task at hand. She needed to decide which parties she and Jason would attend for the upcoming Christmas season and which they would decline.

She would have loved to attend them all, but that would be impossible. Not only were several of the galas being held on the same night, but propriety required Lillie limit her public appearances.

In her growing condition, she felt it would be the height of bad taste to make her presence too obvious. Many people, especially the women, would talk behind her back for making any appearance at all, but Lillie was not about to miss the Christmas social season.

Several hours later, Lillie sat with a stack of rejected invitations in one pile, acceptable events in another, and personalized, perfumed responses in yet another. Deciding to take a nap, Lillie rang a bell for Stanford, their household butler.

At Stanford's appearance, Lillie handed him her responses. "Would you see to it these get posted. I'm going to take a short rest."

"Very good, Madam," Stanford said with a bow.

Lillie found the warmth of her downy quilts a comfort as she snuggled down deep into their folds. Outside, she could hear the wind blowing unmercifully against the window pane. It made a sad moaning sound leaving Lillie lonely as she faded into sleep.

Lillie knew she was dreaming, but she felt a dread and fear she'd never before known. She found herself in a small room. It was dark, and the air was stale and tainted by something foul. She struggled to find a way out of the room, and yet no aid to escape would show itself to her. Where was she?

The dream continued despite Lillie's fight to wake up. She was walking down a long corridor, and at a distance, a single candle was burning. As Lillie made her way to the candle, a draft blew out the flame. All at once, Lillie felt as if something cold and evil was upon her. She started to run, but the presence followed close behind her. Suddenly, Lillie could feel its cold, icy breath on her neck.

With a start, Lillie sat straight up in bed. She'd never been one to have nightmares. Where had all those depressing images come from? She tried to laugh the dream off as the result of something she'd eaten, but in her heart, Lillie was troubled. She considered sharing her troubled thoughts with Jason but decided against it. Jason had been acting strained lately, and she didn't want to burden him further. Still, the dream was disturbing.

When Jason arrived home, Lillie was downstairs waiting to greet him at the door. When he entered the house, Lillie immediately perceived something was troubling her young husband.

As Stanford took Jason's snow-covered outer coat, Lillie pulled her husband along with her to the front sitting room. A warm, cheery fire was blazing, and Lillie led Jason to a chair in front of it.

Jason refused, however, and took a seat instead on the red velvet sofa, pulling Lillie to sit beside him.

"But I was going to rub your neck," Lillie protested.

"It'll wait. Please sit with me," Jason said thoughtfully.

"What is it, Jason? You haven't seemed quite yourself since your promotion."

"That's what I want to talk about, Lillie. Do you know who Mr. Canton is?"

"He's the senior partner of the law firm, isn't he?"

"That's right. He had a long talk with me the day he promoted me." Lillie listened patiently as Jason continued. "I know this will sound strange, but Lillie, he wanted to talk to me about God."

"God?" Lillie questioned curiously. "What ever would God have to do with your promotion?"

"That's what I wondered, but the fact was, Mr. Canton said he was worried about me," Jason stated rather blankly.

"Worried about you? But whatever for? You perform your job admirably. You've earned recognition through your work with the Santa Fe Railroad," Lillie argued. "Why, Colonel Holliday said—"

"Yes, yes, Mr. Canton knows all about that," Jason interrupted. "Surprisingly, he knows a great deal about me."

"Then what is this about you and God?" Lillie questioned again.

"Mr. Canton told me money could buy certain things in life, but it couldn't buy you life. Then he went on to explain God was the only One who could make life worth living," Jason answered.

"How did he propose God could do this?" Lillie inquired sarcastically.

"Now, Lil, just listen for a minute. Mr. Canton made a lot of sense that day. He made so much sense I went back and talked to him again today."

Lillie moved away in shocked dismay. "Jason Philips, whatever on earth possessed you to do such a thing?"

"Because I realized some of what he said made sense. There is an emptiness inside me. I hadn't thought about it much because every time I started to ponder the void, I'd find something else with which to occupy myself," Jason said, reaching his hand out to Lillie.

Lillie surprised both of them by pulling away. "Jason, don't tell me you've found religion." She studied Jason's face. He paled slightly and a look of pain crossed his brow.

"I might as well be straight with you. I asked Mr. Canton how a person should go about having the special kind of relationship with God he'd told me about. He told me I needed to repent of my sins and ask Jesus Christ to be my Savior."

"And?" Lillie interrupted.

"And I did it. I asked Jesus into my heart. I'm a Christian now, Lillie."

"Oh, it's just that simple is it?" Lillie said with a hint of anger. "What kind of price tag comes with it?"

"What do you mean, Lillie?"

"Just how much of our hard-earned money is now designated to go to God?"

"It hasn't got anything to do with money, Lillie. It has to do with your soul and where you'll spend eternity. It has to do with realizing we are sinful and without Jesus Christ, we can't hope to buy our way into heaven. I've accepted this way of life, Lillie. I'm not going to change my mind," Jason added softly.

Nothing could have shocked Lillie any more than Jason's announcement. She sat back against the sofa looking much like she'd had the wind knocked out of her.

When she could think rationally again, she questioned, "How does this affect us?"

Jason smiled. "That's what I wanted to talk to you about. Lillie, you need Jesus, too."

"I don't need religion, Jason Philips. Religion is for the poor in purse and poor in spirit. The two go hand in hand; they always have."

It was Jason's turn to look shocked. "Why Lillie Philips, what a snob you've become."

Lillie turned an indignant crimson. "How dare you! You've changed all our plans with one stroke of divine genius, and you call me names?" She stood up abruptly and started to walk from the room.

Jason was beside her in a flash. His wavy blond hair fell over one eye as he reached out to pull Lillie into his arms. "I didn't mean it, Lillie. It's just you sounded so, so different." Lillie refused to look at him, so Jason lifted her face with his hand.

"I love you, Lillie. That hasn't changed." Lillie softened at his sad, boyish face. Jason was clearly suffering.

"I know you love me, Jason. But I don't think I can play second fiddle to God. That's not part of the dream we shared when you proposed. I don't mind if you have religion—after all we do attend church every Sunday—but please don't preach at me," Lillie said in a controlled, emotionless voice.

"I didn't mean to preach. I just got caught up in the moment. Finding God has been the best thing that's ever happened to me," Jason expressed enthusiastically.

"You used to say that about me," Lillie said stiffly as she pulled away from her husband. "Many wives have to contend with another woman, but I have to compete with God. Now I wonder, Jason Philips, which one of us do you think will win?"

Without waiting for an answer, Lillie swept from the room with the taffeta skirts of her evening gown rustling mockingly behind her.

Chapter 2

L illie passed through the next few days hostile and wounded. She barely spoke to Jason, and the loss was painfully evident in both of their lives. Every time her hand fell to her to stomach, Lillie felt like crying. How could things have gotten so far out of hand?

The things that normally cheered Lillie now had little effect. The Christmas tree had been put up in the front sitting room, and Lillie had gone Christmas shopping twice. Both times she'd come home with the carriage full of Christmas purchases, but the aching and loneliness wouldn't leave her. The place in her heart she'd reserved for Jason and their love seemed void of life.

The more Lillie tried to pretend everything was alright, the worse things got. Jason was clearly in pain, and part of Lillie wanted to comfort him and tell him she would try his God. The other part of her was furious with both Jason and God for daring to change her plans and dreams.

On the Friday before Christmas, Lillie dressed with special care for the biggest gala of the Christmas season. The Cyrus Hollidays were throwing a party and had invited all of Topeka's elite. Lillie had nearly burst with pride at being included for such an occasion.

Lillie studied her appearance in the mirror. She'd had her figure corsetted as tightly as she dared. As a result, her stately hourglass figure showed little sign of her condition. Lillie admired the white velvet ball gown she'd had specially made for the Hollidays' party.

Mrs. Gibson, her regular seamstress, had outdone herself, Lillie decided. The gown was generously designed with seventeen yards of the whitest velvet available. Mrs. Gibson had added red velvet ribbons to trim the skirt, bodice, and long, fitted sleeves. The bodice, though lower than Lillie would have liked, was lavishly trimmed in handmade Chantilly lace.

Turning ever so slightly, Lillie could admire the fashionable bustle bedecked in its trimmings. A huge red velvet bow lay across the top of the bustle and fell gracefully into the lavish folds of the gown. There had never been such a gown in all Kansas, Lillie decided self-confidently.

Noting the time, Lillie quickly secured a strand of pearls at her throat. Grabbing her matching velvet handbag, she made her way downstairs.

Jason was waiting in his study, and when Lillie appeared in the doorway he felt as if he'd been knocked down by a runaway train.

"Lillie, you are, without a doubt, the most beautiful woman in the world." His voice was deep and husky. Lillie maintained an aloofness that sent cold chills through Jason.

"Are you ready?" she questioned, knowing full well he was. His own richly cut, black dinner jacket had a small snip of holly and ivy as a boutonniere. Jason was always thinking of clever things that way. Lillie hated to admit that her first impulse had been to throw herself into his arms.

"I'm ready, but there is something I'd like to give you before we leave," Jason said softly as he crossed the room to stand before Lillie.

"Give me?" Lillie questioned, knowing her abominable behavior of the last few days had not merited any generosity.

"I wasn't sure if you'd like it, but I hope you do. It's my peace offering."

Lillie took the small box. Obviously jewelry, she judged. She opened the box and gasped. A diamond and ruby necklace with accompanying earrings lay glittering up at her.

"Oh, Jason, how wonderful!" Lillie said as she lifted the necklace up to catch the light. "Help me put it on," she requested as she undid the clasp on her pearls.

Jason smiled sadly. "It's nice to know I can still do something to please you," he answered as he secured the necklace. Lillie immediately took pity on him.

"Oh, Jason," she fairly purred. "I'm sorry for the way I've acted. I didn't know what to think. I thought maybe you would stop loving me."

Jason pulled Lillie into his arms. "I could never stop loving you. You are an important part of my life." He bent his head to kiss her, and when Lillie didn't stiffen or pull away, Jason kissed her long and passionately.

Lillie's arms went around her husband's neck. How she had missed him and his kisses. She vowed then and there to put aside her differences and be a loving wife to Jason.

At the sound of Stanford clearing his throat, Jason released Lillie with a gleam of sheer ecstacy in his expression.

"Yes, Stanford?" Jason asked nonchalantly. Lillie took this opportunity to replace her earrings with the diamond and ruby ones. She was admiring the effect in the mirror when she overheard the butler speak.

"Sir, it's begun to sleet. I've taken the liberty of bringing the carriage to the side entrance."

"Very good, Stanford," Jason replied and turned to assist Lillie.

Jason handed Lillie into the carriage and climbed up beside her. After tucking a blanket around them both, he tapped on the carriage top to signal the driver that they were ready.

"You know, Lillie, I've been thinking that after the baby comes, perhaps we could take a trip to Chicago. I know there are some things for the house you've been wanting to buy. What do you think?"

Lillie could barely see her husband's face in the shadows of the carriage, but she could tell he was smiling. "What a wonderful idea, Jason. Is this another Christmas present?"

"In a way. I thought you might like to do something different after our son's birth. I know from here on out you'll be rather confined, and I wanted to give you something to look forward to in the spring besides croquet."

Lillie laughed at Jason's reference to her favorite lawn game. "Well you most certainly have," she said and leaned over to kiss Jason's cheek. The carriage jostled her, however, and she found herself thrown against his shoulder instead.

"Jones?" Jason called out the window to the driver as the carriage again lurched to the right. "What's wrong?"

"Ice, Sir. My apologies but I'm doing everything I can."

A sickening cold penetrated Lillie's bones. There was something about the darkness and the cold that reminded her of the nightmare she'd had. She tried to shake off the feeling as she braced herself against the rocking of the carriage, but it wouldn't leave. The stab of her tightly laced, whalebone corset, made her cry out.

"Are you alright?" Jason questioned, pulling Lillie close to keep her from bouncing around the inside of the carriage.

"I am now," Lillie whispered. "Please just hold me."

Lillie relished Jason's embrace, but her uneasiness continued to mount. She could hear the driver fighting the horses.

"Lillie, did you hear me? Should we turn back? I mean, I'd hate to miss the party, but your welfare is more important to me." Jason's tone betrayed his concern.

Lillie straightened up in surprise. "No! I don't want to miss the Hollidays' party. I could miss all the other festivities, but not this one."

The carriage again slid sideways and Jason grabbed the side with his free hand. "I don't know. I think we should go home." The clatter of the carriage wheels on wood, made Jason realize they'd reached one of two creek crossings that lay between their home and the Holliday residence.

Lillie patted Jason's hand. "See, Silly, we're nearly there. That was the first of the Twin Bridges. The second should be just ahead, then we're only a few blocks away."

"Yes, I know," Jason said, but he didn't sound reassured.

Lillie and Jason startled at the sound of the horses' nervous whinnies. The driver was urging the animals forward, but something had frightened the thoroughbreds. The carriage pitched forward, sliding sharply to the left, then to the right.

The horses sounded again, but this time in a desperate cry. As the carriage began to cross the second of the two bridges, the horses faltered and stopped. The driver got down from the carriage to pull the animals across the bridge. The unexpected movement beside the horses startled them, and they tried first to rear up, and then to back away from the driver.

Lillie panicked when she heard the first sickening sound of wood breaking. Jason was reaching for the door when the carriage pushed through the wooden railing and the back wheel slid off the bridge.

"Just sit still, Lillie," Jason ordered.

For several minutes nothing seemed to happen. After that, however, everything happened at once. Lillie was gripping the side of the carriage, her heart pounding with fear. Choking back tears, Lillie recognized her nightmare.

Jason was calling out to Jones and opening the carriage door when the back end of the carriage went off the bridge. The bottom of the carriage hit with a loud thud that sent Jason to the floor, half in the carriage, half out. Lillie reached forward to help her husband.

"Jason, give me your hand," she tried to sound calm, but her words resembled hysteria.

Jason was dazed for a moment, then reached back to take Lillie's offered hand. Thinking better of it, however, he waved her away. The horses were fighting the pull of the carriage against their harnesses, while Jones was still working to get them to pull forward.

"Lillie, listen to me," Jason began. "We've got to get out of here. I want you to move slowly to the other side of the carriage. Can you do that?"

Lillie nodded. "I think so." Her voice sounded much calmer. "Jason," she continued, "I love you. Please tell me everything will be alright."

The carriage lurched again. They were losing ground fast. The body of the carriage slipped farther backward. They were now at such an angle that Lillie could see the surface of the bridge through the carriage door window.

"Lillie," Jason reached for his wife. How could he tell her of the fear in his heart? How could he explain the imminent danger they were in? "Lillie, will you pray with me?"

"Pray?" Lillie gasped the question. "Pray at a time like this. Jason we've got to get out of here or we'll go over the side with the carriage."

Jason's face was barely illuminated by the faint glow of street lights. Lillie saw anguish fill his eyes. Suddenly, she felt the carriage move, and she knew they were going over the edge.

"I love you, Lillie," were the last words Jason spoke.

"Jason!" Lillie screamed. Then amidst the noise of screaming horses and splintering wood, Lillie's head hit something hard, and she lost consciousness.

Lillie was lost in her nightmare again. She felt the bone-chilling cold and knew the darkness would never turn to light. She thought several times someone was calling to her. Other times she heard crying. Where was she and why couldn't she make herself wake up? Lillie felt frightened for the first time in her life.

Lillie forced herself to open her eyes. The room was dark, except for a ribbon of light that came in through the partially opened door.

Lillie tried to sit up but was stopped by a sharp stab of pain. "Help me!" she screamed. "Somebody help me, please!" She was nearly hysterical when a nurse entered the room.

"There, there," the woman said, patting Lillie's hand and pushing the hair back from her face.

"Where am I? What's wrong with me?" Lillie sobbed.

"You're in the hospital. Don't you remember the accident?"

The accident? Yes, Lillie did remember. The whole ugly scene passed before her eyes again. The carriage, Jason's sad smile. Jason!

"Where's my husband? Where is Jason?" Lillie questioned the nurse.

The woman paled slightly and moved to pour Lillie a drink of water. "I think you'd better rest for a few moments. I need to get the doctor."

Lillie refused the water and grabbed the woman's hand. "Where is my husband?" She longed for the answer, yet in her heart she knew the news was not good.

"I'm sorry, Miss." The woman was nearly in tears. "Your husband was killed in the accident."

Lillie heard someone screaming, then realized she was making the noise. She raged against the bed that held her captive and, blind to the pain, tried to sit up. "I want Jason! I want my husband!"

Just then another nurse entered the room with a doctor closely behind her. "What's all this commotion?" the doctor bellowed, and Lillie immediately calmed.

"Where's my husband? That woman said he's dead. Please tell me she's lying!" Lillie begged the doctor.

"Just relax and lie back. I need to examine you. Do you realize how long you've been unconscious?" The doctor acted as though he'd not heard Lillie's questions. He worked quickly to take Lillie's mind off her fears.

"I. . .I don't know," Lillie stammered. "It seems like just yesterday."

"Well, you gave us quite a fright. We weren't sure you'd ever wake up again," the doctor answered. "Now just follow my finger with your eyes. No, don't move your head."

Lillie did as he asked, but her mind wouldn't let the questions be dismissed. "How long have I been unconscious?"

"Two weeks. Today is New Year's Day."

"New Year's? But it was the week before Christmas. Jason and I. . ." Lillie's words trailed off. "Jason is dead?"

"I'm sorry," the doctor whispered, and Lillie could see the emotion in his eyes.

"How?" she whispered the question.

"He died instantly in the accident," the doctor replied and added, "He didn't suffer."

Lillie felt tears stream down her face. Her hand went to her abdomen as it had so often after learning of her condition. There was no rounding, and Lillie knew she'd lost her child.

"My baby is gone," she announced as if the doctor and his nurses would find this news.

"Yes," the doctor said softly. Lillie saw tears in the eyes of the nurses.

"I'd like to be alone," she said, turning her face away. The doctor nodded and ushered the nurses from the room.

Chapter 3

Two months later, Lillie sat in the parlor of her parent's Potwin Place home. They had brought her there from the hospital, and she'd taken residence in her old bedroom on the third floor. She was awaiting a meeting with her in-laws and the lawyer that handled the family business.

It was the first time Lillie had agreed to see anyone outside of her family, and she was very nervous about the meeting. She smoothed her unadorned black dress and sighed. She had gained over thirty pounds in the last months and although unhappy about it, Lillie had done nothing to prevent it. She'd taken on a lifestyle of solitary hours with boxes of chocolates at her fingertips.

At the sound of voices in the hallway, Lillie stiffened.

"Lillie, they're here." Grace Johnston looked more haggard than Lillie could remember. Lillie nodded to her mother and moved to the window seat.

Grace stepped away from the door and returned with their guests.

"Lillie, dear." It was Gladys Philips. She swept across the room and noted the lack of color in Lillie's face and the added weight. "Jason wouldn't want you to suffer so." Lillie nodded. She knew it was true but had no response to offer.

Her father-in-law, John Philips, stood behind his wife. He smiled slightly, reminding Lillie of Jason's sad little smiles. Why did she have to hurt like this? Why couldn't she have died, too?

The other man cleared his voice. All eyes turned to greet Stanley Canton. Lillie acknowledged him with a nod but said nothing.

"We might as well get to the business at hand," Mr. Canton was beginning. He greeted Lillie's father who had just entered the room and taken a seat by Grace. John and Gladys Philips also took their seats and awaited Mr. Canton's announcement.

"Mrs. Philips," Mr. Canton spoke to Lillie with genuine kindness in his voice. "Your husband was a dear friend and colleague. I extend my deepest sympathies to you."

"Thank you," Lillie answered mechanically.

"To make this as short and painless as possible," Mr. Canton continued, "you're a wealthy young woman, Mrs. Philips. Jason's will entitles you to everything. An account has been set up in your name at the bank, and funds will be transferred there for your use. If there is anything I can do for you, please feel free to call upon me."

All eyes were on her, and Lillie suddenly longed for the sanctuary of her bedroom. She knew she was expected to say something, but what was there to say?

Seeing her hesitation, Mr. Canton tried to offer what he felt would be comfort. "Mrs. Philips, your husband and baby are safely in heaven. You will see them again."

Sudden rage filled Lillie. Standing to her feet, she lashed out at her husband's friend. "I'll have no part of a God Who would rob a woman of her husband and child. A God Who cares not one whit for the pain I am suffering and the devastation I shall have to go through life experiencing."

Lillie ignored the gasps of surprise from Gladys. She knew her in-laws were Christians and held God's will in the highest esteem.

"This shouldn't surprise anyone. It's you who surprise me. How you can all sit there so calm, so resigned! Well, I'm not resigned. I shall never give myself over to the will of an unmerciful God. If Jason's God wants Jason and our baby, then so be it. But He'll not have my gracious consent, nor my heart!" With that, Lillie walked from the room and ran up the stairs to her bedroom.

She threw herself, breathless, across the bed and cried tears of anger and sorrow. She heard someone enter the room, and when her mother pulled her into her arms, Lillie allowed it.

"Lillie, you're so distraught. Is there anything I can do to help?" Her mother's voice was soothing. Lillie felt as if she were a little girl again. How she wished she could be a child once more!

"Oh, Mother, I hurt so much. I can scarcely breathe for the pain that binds me. How can I live without him? How can I wake up in the morning and know I'll never hear his laughter again, never hear his voice, nor feel his touch?" Lillie's tears flowed freely, while Grace Johnston continued to hold her daughter. "And, my baby. My dear, sweet little baby." The heart wrenching sobs were almost more than Grace could stand.

"Go ahead Lillie, just get it all out. All the pain and bitterness," Lillie's mother stroked her daughter's hair.

"What am I to do, Mother?" Lillie questioned, trying to dry her face.

Grace Johnston looked deep into her daughter's red-rimmed eyes. She wanted so much to help her child. An idea came to her. "Lillie, you need a place to heal. I think you should go and stay with Maggie for a time. She loves you so much and has offered several times to have you recuperate at her ranch."

Lillie thought the matter over for a moment. Perhaps her mother was right. Maggie's letters had told of a glorious mountain valley where her father had built a cattle empire. Maggie made the place sound nearly perfect. Maybe she should go, Lillie reasoned. Perhaps the drier climate would offer a welcomed change from the damp, cold of Topeka's spring weather.

"Yes, Mother. I think it would be a wonderful idea," Lillie finally answered.

"Good. I'll speak with your father and have him make all the arrangements," Grace said as she stood. "Now, you start packing. And Lillie," she paused at the doorway. "I think it might be nice if you took something other than black. Jason wouldn't want you to mourn. Forget about society. No one at Maggie's ranch is going to care."

"I'll think about it, Mother."

By the second week in April, Lillie was in the private train car of a man her family fondly called Uncle William. The man, in truth, was William Strong, president of the Atchison, Topeka, and Santa Fe Railroad.

Lillie had grown up knowing Uncle William as intimately as she had any family member, even though he had no blood tie to her family. When William Strong learned Lillie was to travel to New Mexico, he wouldn't hear of her doing it any other way than by his private car.

Once the train was well out of Topeka, Lillie removed her black hat and veil. She smoothed back her blond hair and sat back against the plush velvet seat.

She was traveling in grand style thanks to Uncle William. From the floor to the chair railing, the sitting room of the train car was richly paneled in walnut. Above this was a red velvet, *fleur-de-lis*-patterned wallpaper, with a tiny gold ribbon running vertically.

Lillie sat in silence trying to take in her surroundings. She glanced down at her plump figure and sighed. The worse she felt about her appearance, the more she ate. It was like trying to fill a void that couldn't be filled. She'd packed four boxes of bonbons to bring with her on the trip to Maggie's.

When night fell, Lillie went into the bedroom. Pulling the black bombazine dress over her head, she quickly replaced it with a flowing, white flannel nightgown, and for a moment, the contrast seemed strangely significant. Black and white; good and evil; dead and alive.

She thought for a time of Jason and his words about God. Then the words Mr. Canton had shared came back to haunt her. God had taken all that she loved. How could she love Him after that? Why should she? She had enough money to do whatever she wanted. She didn't need anything or anyone, especially God.

The gentle rocking of the train lulled Lillie to sleep, and for once, the nightmare didn't wake her up screaming. Instead, she found herself in pleasant memories of Jason and their baby. When she awoke, she ached at the reality that those memories were only a dream. Lillie hugged her knees to her chest and cried.

The solitude of the private car had its drawbacks, and Lillie soon discovered with other people around she hadn't been given to thinking constantly about her pain.

She walked around the room, gingerly testing her balance against the rocking and swaying of the train car. After she dressed, Lillie went to the mirror and grimaced at her reflection. Her face was puffy and blotched from crying. It nearly made her want to put the veiled hat back on.

Instead, Lillie looked out the windows and was surprised to find the train slowing to a stop. She went from one side of the car to the other and finding nothing but rolling prairie, Lillie began to fear train robbers or something worse.

She jumped in nervous surprise when a loud pounding sounded at her car door. Suspiciously she opened it and found the train conductor standing before her.

"Pardon me, Ma'am, but we have an emergency," he said doffing his cap in respect.

"What is it you expect me to do about it?" Lillie questioned rather rudely.

"There's a young woman in the train car up ahead. She's about to give birth, and the young doctor helping her needs a place to deliver her child."

Lillie felt as if a knife had been plunged into her heart. Her child would have been due this month, a point she had struggled to forget. How dare God do this to her? How could He be so heartless as to force her to face it all again?

"I'm sorry, you can't use my car," Lillie said and fairly pushed the conductor back through the doorway. She slammed the door in his face and put her face in her hands.

Lillie had just taken a seat when the door flew open with a loud crash. Filling the door was a handsome, blond man who painfully reminded Lillie of Jason. He was furious, and his eyes burned holes into Lillie.

"How dare you deny someone the right to proper care! You have more than enough space here, and we would only be here long enough to get to the next town. What kind of heartless woman are you?"

Lillie felt bile in her throat. She felt her face turn crimson under the man's merciless scrutiny. "I. . .I," she stammered to say something, to fight back, but no words would come.

"I don't care what you think or what you say, because I have instructed several men to bring that woman here. I shall bind you to your chair if you object, but she will deliver her baby here!" With that he turned and motioned the others to enter the room.

Lillie sat frozen to her chair. She watched as the young doctor cleared the table and had the woman placed on it. Her car had become a flurry of activities, all amidst the cries and screams of the young woman.

Watching the woman's swollen abdomen heave with each contraction, Lillie could no longer remain. She rushed from the car into the prairie fields. She ran and ran, until her breath refused to come. She was mindless of her steps and had no idea where she was. Gasping, Lillie fell to the ground. The springtime smells of rich dirt and new wheat assaulted Lillie's nose.

It didn't matter that she was face down in the dirt. Lillie no longer cared. She cried and cried until she felt certain she could cry no more, but the tears refused to abate. She had no idea how long she lay there, but all at once someone was lifting her.

She opened her eyes to find the concerned blue gray eyes of the angry doctor. He was cradling her against his chest and hushing her tears. Lillie relaxed despite wanting nothing of his comfort.

When her breathing was less ragged and the tears had been wiped from her eyes, Lillie looked up as if to question the stranger who held her.

"I'm Dr. Monroe. Dr. Daniel Monroe," he said as if anticipating her question. "I'm sorry to have treated you so harshly. I can see you're in mourning."

Lillie found herself touched by his concern. It was the first time since Jason's death she'd felt anything but the pain and numbness that had haunted her every waking moment.

"I'm Lillie Phil. . ." She choked on the word. "I'm Lillie, Dr. Monroe," she finally offered.

"Call me Daniel." His words were gentle, almost tender.

Lillie stiffened slightly. She didn't desire that kind of familiarity, but it seemed quite awkward calling him Dr. Monroe. Maybe she wouldn't have to call him by any name at all. "How is your patient—your patients?" Lillie questioned.

A frown crossed Daniel's face and anger again filled his eyes. "They're dead."

Lillie felt her chest tighten. The young mother and her child were dead. Dead! Dead! Dead! The word reverberated through Lillie's mind.

She struggled to draw a deep breath. It was like that moment in the hospital when she had to face up to losing Jason and their baby. Why was this happening again?

"You don't look at all well, Lillie," Daniel said, noticing the woman in his arms had paled considerably. "I think I'd better get you back to the train so you can lie down."

Lillie nodded and allowed Daniel to lead her back to the train. Looking around her for the first time, Lillie realized they were quite a distance from the train and the ground around them was rough and uneven. Taking a step gingerly, Lillie nearly tripped as what looked like solid ground gave way to dust. She grimaced when Daniel's hand tightened upon her arm, but she said nothing.

When Daniel and Lillie entered the private car, the conductor quickly joined them. "We've made arrangements for the woman and her baby. I'm sorry, but I need to get this train back on schedule."

Daniel nodded. "I'm going to stay with this young woman. She's not feeling well and needs my attention." Lillie started to protest, but she was too tired. She was very faint.

"Thanks, Doc," the conductor was saying. "Thanks for all you did. That little gal gave it all she had."

"Yes, she did," Daniel said, and Lillie noticed how his voice was void of feeling. What manner of man was this Dr. Daniel Monroe?

Proprieties seemed unimportant, and as the train was once again underway, Lillie tolerated Daniel's attentions. She watched him curiously. He was about six inches taller than she, and the way his sandy blond hair fell over one eye reminded her of Jason. After taking Lillie's pulse and temperature, Daniel ordered her to lie down and take a nap. To his surprise, Lillie didn't argue.

As Daniel took hold of Lillie's waist to steady her walk, he saw the pained expression in her eyes. His touch was grieving her. "Your husband?" he questioned, and Lillie knew he referred to her mourning.

"Yes. We were in a carriage accident," Lillie murmured. It suddenly seemed important to explain her earlier harshness. "I also lost my baby. He would have been born this month."

It was now Daniel's face that held the pained expression. He felt the old anger returning. He stopped beside the bedroom compartment door. "I am so sorry, Lillie. How calloused you must have thought me. How stupid I am."

Lillie was amazed at the fury he seemed to vent upon himself. "You had no way of knowing," she whispered.

"There seems to be a great deal I don't know," Daniel said and his ominous tone caused Lillie to take a step back. "Otherwise, that woman and her child wouldn't have died!" Then he left, closing the bedroom door behind him.

Chapter 4

Lillie slept soundly for several hours, but as if on cue, the nightmares started again. She tossed from one side of the bed to the other in a vain search for comfort. She saw the same shadows and felt the same numbing cold. She was searching down a long corridor for her crying baby. When at last she came to a door where the crying sounded loudest, she tried the knob. It was unmovable. Lillie cried softly as she listened to the baby cry.

Suddenly, the dream changed. She was standing beside the young pregnant woman who'd died in her train car. The woman was crying out to Lillie for help, but as Lillie reached out the figure changed and it was Jason's face she saw.

"Lillie, wake up!" Lillie felt herself being roused into consciousness. She opened her eyes to see steely blue eyes staring down at her.

"Oh, Jason, I had the most terrible dream," she reached out to hold tightly to the man she thought was her husband.

"Lillie, it's Daniel." The words cut her as surely as if they'd been a knife. The nightmare had been true.

Suddenly, Lillie pushed back as though she'd touched a red hot iron. "What are you doing here?"

"You were crying and screaming," Daniel tried to answer in a soothing tone.

"And?" Lillie refused to be comforted.

Daniel stood up and narrowed his eyes, "And I ran in from the sitting room to help you." he said indignantly and went from the room.

Lillie, fully clothed, followed him into the sitting room of the train car. She immediately went for a box of candy and sat down at the same table where Dr. Monroe's patient had died. The table had been cleaned, and the cloth and flowers replaced. Like everything else in Lillie's life, it appeared untouched by the loss.

Unaware Daniel watched her, Lillie opened the box and began to eat chocolate after chocolate. She stared out into the darkness beyond her window. The only light in the compartment was that of a low burning lamp.

"You're going to make yourself sick," Daniel said as he took the seat across from Lillie.

"It's none of your concern," Lillie answered rudely.

"I see."

"I'm glad you do," Lillie replied. "I certainly don't need you telling me what to do."

"You must have been quite thin," he said with a mocking tone and added, "not so long ago."

"You're a very rude man to discuss a woman's figure, and how would you know whether I was fat or thin?" Lillie questioned.

"I figure at the rate you're eating those candies, you must have been thin. Otherwise you'd be much heavier now." Daniel's tone held amusement, and Lillie felt herself turn crimson at the words.

"You are, without a doubt, the rudest man I've ever met. If you're as poor a doctor as you are a gentleman, no wonder your patients die."

The words hit their mark, for Lillie saw a dark scowl cross Daniel's face. For several minutes no one said anything, and Lillie began to regret the tactless way she'd handled her embarrassment.

"I'm sorry. You are of course only speaking as a physician, and I am allowing my recent pain to affect my manners," Lillie apologized, not understanding why she felt the need to.

Daniel remained quiet. Lillie believed him to be contemplating the young woman who'd died in childbirth. It must be difficult to be a doctor and see death everyday, she thought.

In his mind, Daniel saw an angelic face contorted with pain. The young woman in his memories was slowly dying. Dying by trying to give life to a child: his child. His young wife hadn't lived, despite his efforts to deliver their baby. Their child had never been born, having gone to the grave with Katie Monroe.

Daniel shook off the memory and tried to concentrate on the face before him. "You are, of course, right," he said with more sadness to his voice than Lillie had ever heard from another human being. "I suppose I'm not much of a doctor. However, I do know you are trying to eat away your grief, and it won't work. You're a fine looking woman, Lillie. Why let this continue?"

Getting to her feet, Lillie steadied her nerves with a deep breath. "I think it would be to both our benefits if you were to take your place with the other passengers. I'd like you to leave my train car at the next stop."

"Why wait?" Daniel questioned angrily, as he got to his feet and crossed the room. He pulled open the door and stepped out onto the boarding platform. With one fluid motion, he crossed the railings between the two cars and stood on the platform of the car that joined Lillie's private car to the rest of the train.

"I am sorry to have brought you more pain, Mrs. . . ." He paused, waiting for Lillie to respond. Lillie stood in shock. The noise of the train wheels and the grinding and pitching of the cars filled the room.

"Well, Lillie," he said in a rather sarcastic tone, "I bid you farewell. Enjoy your chocolates." With that, Daniel Monroe opened the door to the adjoining car and entered, slamming the door behind him.

Several hours later, Lillie stood thinking at the door of the car. Her curiosity drew her out onto the platform of the train car. The morning sun was starting to rise on the prairie horizon. The sky was filled with glorious red ribbons of color against the violet hue of dawn. *Red sky in the morning, sailor take warning,* Lillie thought.

She walked closer to the edge of the railing. Watching the ground pass beneath the train's couplings, Lillie gave serious thought to jumping off the train. She wanted to die. There was nothing left to live for. All that she loved was gone, and now she was making her way to her best friend, who was newly married and no doubt, very happy. How could she bear being surrounded by Maggie's joy?

Clacky, clack. Clacky, clack. The noise was hypnotic. Lillie gripped the rail tightly, searching her heart for a reason to go on. There was none.

In the connecting car, Daniel had just removed his coat and was turning in his seat when his eye got a glimpse of Lillie moving toward the rail.

He watched her stand there. She was watching the ground race past her, and Daniel knew she was making a choice between life and death. He wouldn't allow her to choose death. He moved down the aisle and stood, hand on the door, ready to leap across the expanse and pull her back from the clutches of death if necessary.

Something inside him ached for this woman. She was so young, obviously well-to-do, and probably used to having everything her way. But somewhere along the way, she'd been told no, and her loss was more than she could bear. For reasons beyond his understanding, Daniel wanted to hold her and comfort her. It took all of his willpower to remain hidden behind the door.

Lillie stood for a long time. She thought about her life. What should she do? Death beckoned her, but something held her back. She thought of something Jason had once told her. She tried to remember each word, but all that came to mind was Jason had tried to show her a verse in the Bible.

The spell of the rails was broken, and Lillie went back into the train car and searched for Uncle William's Bible. She knew the highly religious William Strong would have a Bible somewhere on his private train car.

Daniel breathed a sigh of relief as he watched Lillie hurry into her car. The decision to live had been made, at least for the time being. He couldn't explain why it seemed important to him, but it was. Taking his seat, Daniel dozed off and on, blending memories of his long departed Katie with those of the mysterious woman whom he only knew as Lillie.

Lillie's search finally turned up a well-worn copy of the Bible. Thumbing through the many pages, Lillie finally recognized the Gospel of Luke as the one Jason had tried to share. Despair filled her as she realized she would have to read every verse in the Gospel of Luke to find Jason's verse.

After flipping several pages, Lillie's eyes fell upon Luke 12:19-21: " 'And I will say to my soul, Soul, thou hast much goods laid up for many years; take thine ease, eat, drink, and be merry. But God said unto him, Thou fool, this night thy soul shall be required of thee: then whose shall those things be, which thou hast provided? So is he that layeth up treasure for himself, and is not rich toward God.' " Lillie slammed the Bible shut.

Her body trembled from head to toe. How could Jason love such a God? Lillie's rage toward God began to build. Did God kill Jason because he hadn't given enough money to the church? Was this the reason she'd lost all that she loved?

Lillie paced the room despite the rocking of the car. What kind of God would take the life of an industrious young man simply because he didn't give enough money to the church? Lillie vowed never again to read the Bible. She replaced the book where she'd found it and went to bed.

It was well past noon when Lillie awoke. The train was strangely silent, and the rocking had stilled. She got up and washed her face. Looking at the wrinkled black dress, Lillie went to where her other gowns were hanging. At her mother's encouragement, Lillie had brought several dresses that hadn't been dyed black for mourning.

She ran a hand over the dark blue calico day dress her mother had recently made for her. Lillie frowned, knowing the reason for the new dresses had been her recent weight gain. Still, when Lillie thought of Jason she knew her mother was right. Jason would hate her wearing black. Even before he had become a Christian, he had detested the practice of months, even years, of mourning being practiced by young, vibrant people who deserved to go on living.

Lillie stared at the clothes for a few more minutes and made a decision. She would no longer wear widow's weeds. She would burn all the black clothing or at least throw it from the train as soon as they were traveling again.

She took a seat by the window, watching with disinterest the passing life of the small town. In a short time, the train was on its way, and only then did the thought cross Lillie's mind: She'd never notified Maggie she was coming.

Lillie tried to think if her mother had said anything about sending

Maggie a letter or telegram, and she soon realized nothing had been said about such things.

After she considered her plight for a few moments, Lillie was shocked to find herself thinking back on Daniel Monroe. She remembered his boyish smile and sandy hair. His hair was wavy, where Jason's had been straight, but it was nearly the same color. It's only because he reminds me of Jason, Lillie thought. It's Jason, I really miss. It's his comforting I want.

Lillie felt guilty because of her thoughts of Daniel. Jason had only been gone a little more than three months. How could she be so callous as to give Dr. Monroe more than a fleeting thought?

"I'm a terrible person," Lillie said aloud. "I didn't deserve Jason, and that's why he's gone." Even in speaking the words, Lillie didn't believe them. It didn't make sense to think that way, and it wasn't the least bit comforting.

She rubbed her temples for a moment and realized she still hadn't pinned up her hair. She let her hand run down the length of her long blond hair and cried. Jason had loved her hair. He was ever after her to let it down. She had thought him such a bother when he pulled at her hairpins, but she fervently wished he were here to play his troublesome game once more.

Without thinking, Lillie went to her sewing bag and pulled out her embroidery shears. Mindless that she'd never had a haircut in her life, Lillie began to cut her hair. She had to leave Jason's memory behind or go mad. She had to forget the past and every detail of her life before this moment.

Snip. . .snip. . .snip. The scissors found their mark, and within moments, Lillie was surrounded by a pile of honey-blond hair. She went to her bed compartment and studied her reflection in the mirror. Her hair fell in a blunt cut, just to the shoulders. It made her face seem thinner. Taking the scissors once more, Lillie deliberated her appearance and cut a framing edge of bangs to fall just above her eyebrows. Satisfied she looked nothing like Jason's Lillie, she went back to the main compartment and gathered up the discarded hair.

When she opened the door to her car, Lillie was surprised at how dry the air seemed. Funny, she hadn't noticed it before. She stood holding her hair in her hands for a moment. "Jason," she whispered to the passing scenery, "I'll never love anyone again, but I can't think of you anymore." She took a handful of the hair and allowed the wind to catch it. Lillie watched as her hair drifted into the nearby field of sage grass. "Good-bye, Beloved."

"And my precious baby." Lillie forced herself to say the words. "I would have loved you so dearly, but instead I must live without you. Good-bye, little angel," she said and cast the remaining golden hair to the wind.

It was a turning point, Lillie knew. She went back into the car and pulled down all the black dresses she'd brought with her. "No more mourning," she said as she returned to the train platform and threw the dresses into the open prairie field. She nearly laughed aloud to imagine someone coming along and finding long strands of blond hair and then black bombazine gowns.

The crisp, dry air felt good on her face, and Lillie shook out her shoulder length hair, running a hand through the strands just to get the feel of it. She felt freer than she had in months. "Good-bye, Lillie Philips," she whispered to the air. "From now on I'll just be Lillie."

From the adjoining car, Daniel watched quizzically at the performance that had taken place on the coupling platform. He was stunned to find Lillie had cut her hair, although he had to admit he liked the new look. It was in total confusion that he watched her throw her clothes from the train, but Daniel knew what it was to say good-bye to the past.

Maybe Lillie had decided life was worth living after all, he thought. Maybe her performance signaled an end to her self-imposed destruction.

Daniel tried to think of his destination instead of Lillie, but the delicate face continued to haunt him. Who was she and why did he seem to care so much?

Chapter 5

Maggie Lucas pulled back on the reins of her favorite horse. "Whoa, Thunder." She paused on the ridge high above Piñon Canyon Ranch. Below, she could see her husband, Garrett, working with several other men. They were mending fence. There were many things about ranch life her husband loved, but mending fences wasn't one of them.

Thunder whinnied softly, bringing the attention of the men to the ridge. Garrett wiped the sweat from his forehead and squinted against the bright April sunlight. When he spied Maggie on the ridge, he smiled.

"I think it's time for me to ride ahead and see if there are any more spots we need to patch," Garrett said with a grin to his hardworking foreman.

"Sure, ride off and leave us with the dirty work," Mack Reynolds feigned the complaint. The fact was this was the happiest he'd seen his boss in years. When Maggie's father had passed away the October before, Mack had worried Garrett would sink into depression. He knew Garrett had lived long enough with Jason Intissar to consider him a father in every way that counted. But marriage to Maggie had left Garrett too preoccupied to grieve for long.

Mack turned to make a comment to Garrett, but his boss was already astride his horse, Alder, and headed towards his young wife.

"Well, you certainly took your sweet time getting here," Maggie said laughingly as Garrett reined up beside her.

"Come here," Garrett motioned with his index finger.

Maggie smiled broadly, "Make me." With that she kicked her heels into Thunder's side and left Garrett in the dust.

After months of riding this ridge, Maggie knew every rut and boulder. She steered Thunder away from dangerous places, even though Thunder too, was well aware of the hazards. Maggie leaned flat against Thunder's neck as she heard Alder's thundering approach.

Garrett came up beside her and plucked Maggie easily from Thunder's back into his arms. He slowed Alder's pace and pulled Maggie tightly against him.

"Umm," Garrett whispered against her ear. "You smell wonderful."

"I've been baking bread. You're just hungry." Maggie smiled, put her arms around her husband's neck, and added, "But if you don't catch up with Thunder, you'll have no lunch."

"Maybe I'll just feast on you," Garrett whispered and nipped playfully at Maggie's neck. She squealed in laughing delight and shifted her weight, nearly sending them sideways off Alder.

"I think I'd better catch up with Thunder," Garrett laughed.

After Maggie was safely back on her horse, Garrett led her to a secluded oasis. "Oh Garrett, this is a beautiful spot. How come I've never found it?" Maggie asked as she slid down from her horse.

"It's a secret place reserved for people in love. Unless you're in love, you just can't find it," Garrett replied, taking the saddlebags from Maggie's horse.

"Then how come you knew about it for so long?" Maggie teased.

Garrett dropped the saddlebags and pulled Maggie into his arms. "Because, Magdelena Intissar Lucas, I've loved you since I first laid eyes on your father's portrait of you. That sassy, spitfire of a girl broke my heart so I could love no other." With that, Garrett bent down and kissed Maggie long and passionately.

"I feel so blessed," she whispered as she walked with Garrett to a stand of tall cottonwood trees.

They spent most of the afternoon laughing and talking. They were still newlyweds as far as Maggie was concerned, having only been married for six months. It was upon that very reflection Garrett suddenly brightened.

"Maggie, you know what I owe you?"

Maggie stared in bewilderment. "What could you possibly owe me?"

"A honeymoon. We never got away after the wedding. Of course, what with your pa's death," Garrett paused remembering how Maggie's father had pleaded with them to wed before his death. He'd died while they were still celebrating their wedding vows, and while his passing had saddened them, Maggie and Garrett both knew Jason Intissar was in heaven.

Maggie nodded, but said nothing. Garrett continued, "Then winter set in, and we couldn't leave the valley."

"But that wasn't so bad," Maggie interrupted and leaned against Garrett. His arms went around her and pulled her close.

"I'm serious, Maggie. I want to take you on a honeymoon. Where would you like to go?"

"But Garrett, you yourself said we're coming up on one of the busiest times for the ranch. The birthings and brandings, fence mendings, herds to be moved. . . ." Garrett put his finger on Maggie's lips.

"Hush," he said tenderly. "I can trust Mack to hire as many men as he needs. I'll send him to Springer to get the men he requires, but I am taking you away. Just you and me."

"Alright," Maggie said, pushing away from Garrett's chest. "Where shall we go?"

"How do you feel about camping outdoors for several weeks? The place is really special, nothing like you've ever seen before." Maggie could hear the excitement in Garrett's voice.

"Sounds wonderful. When do we leave?" she answered enthusiastically.

"How about the end of the week?" Garrett questioned.

"That soon? Do you really think we could?" Maggie was starting to feel the excitement.

"I don't know why not. I'll talk to Mack when we get back to the ranch. In the meantime, Mrs. Lucas, come here and let me kiss you again." Maggie laughed and fell eagerly into her husband's arms. How good God was to her; how very good.

A shadowy veil lowered over the happiness in Maggie's heart. Lillie Johnston Philips, her best friend, was mourning the loss of her husband and baby. It seemed heartless to be this happy. Lillie was hundreds of miles away in Topeka, and Maggie was here with her brand new marriage.

Garrett sensed the change in Maggie's mood. "What is it?"

"I was just thinking about Lillie."

"You mustn't worry, Maggie," Garrett said sympathetically.

"I know, but I'd feel better if I could talk with her," Maggie said solemnly.

"You've done all you can, Maggie. You've extended our hospitality and told her she'd be welcome to come and stay with us as long as she wants. There's nothing more to be done. Now I want you to stop worrying and start planning for our trip," Garrett said firmly but with a smile. Maggie nodded, knowing he was right.

At the end of the week, Maggie happily joined Garrett in the corral. She mounted her horse and followed her husband west across the valley of Piñon Canyon Ranch. It was Garrett's plan to spend the night at the Pueblo Mission which Maggie's father had financed for Pastor David and Jenny Monroe.

They covered the twelve miles in a slow, deliberate manner, and Maggie enjoyed the crisp mountain air, despite the cool temperatures. The world was waking up from a long, silent sleep. Brilliant green shoots of range grass covered their way, as well as the regional spring flowers, Indian paintbrush, and gilia. Maggie breathed in deeply as if in doing so she could absorb all the sights and sounds of the land.

As they approached the two-story, adobe mission, Maggie's excitement increased. She hadn't seen Jenny Monroe since Christmas, and because Jenny was the only English-speaking woman in the area close to Maggie's age, Maggie missed her company.

Jenny and David came out into the yard to greet their friends. Behind Jenny and David trailed several shy, brown-skinned, Pueblo orphans.

"Garrett! Maggie!" Jenny was calling. "I didn't dare allow myself to get too excited until I actually saw you. Come on in and relax."

David waved from his wife's side. "Good to see you both," he added to Jenny's greeting.

That evening, Maggie worked with Jenny in the kitchen, while Garrett and David saw to the livestock.

"It's so good to have this time with you, Jenny," Maggie began.

"I know exactly what you mean," Jenny Monroe said with a sigh. "I was telling David not long after we received your letter about Lillie's accident that I wished I could be with you to offer any comfort I could. How is Lillie doing?"

Maggie's countenance changed, and her eyes betrayed the pain in her heart. "I wish I knew. Lillie hasn't written since her dismissal from the hospital. Her mother sent me two letters to keep me informed. She told me Lillie was grief stricken and not at all herself."

"That's a pity. It must be hard to lose a husband at such a young age. That's one grief I never hope to know about," Jenny said compassionately.

"Me either," Maggie said thoughtfully. "Nor the grief of losing a child."

Jenny grimaced.

"What is it, Jenny? Did I say something wrong?" Maggie questioned.

Jenny shook her head, but Maggie saw sadness in her eyes. Maggie stilled Jenny's bustlings with a hand upon her arm. "What is it, Jenny?"

"I'm sorry, Maggie." Jenny wiped her hands on her apron. "I guess Lillie's grief is one I can relate to after all. Come with me." Jenny walked out the kitchen door. Maggie followed obediently, until they'd walked well past the vegetable garden and several yards behind the house.

Jenny stopped before three, roughly hewn crosses. "My children," Jenny said in a soft, reflective manner. "They were too weak to live," she added.

Maggie felt a tightening in her chest. "Oh, Jenny," she said, near to tears. It was hard to imagine waiting and hoping for a baby, only to lose it.

Jenny touched Maggie's sleeve. "Don't be sad, Maggie. I've mourned enough for both of us. They're with God. I know that much and comfort myself in the thought. Besides," she said, taking Maggie's hand in her own, "God's given me the orphaned Indian children."

Maggie fell silent for a few moments. She thought of the three small graves that held the earthly remains of Jenny's children. Her heart went out to her friend.

When Maggie finally spoke, there was fear as well as sadness in her voice. "I don't think I could bear it."

Jenny smiled. She, too, had thought herself unable to deal with the painful loss.

"God knows what we can and can't bear, Maggie. I don't have any answers for the whys, but I do know He is good to stand beside His own. Your Lillie must find comfort in that, too."

Maggie shook her head. "No, God is not a comfort to Lillie. She believes Him responsible for taking away her family. She is at war with God in a worse way than I was. Her mother wrote me to say Lillie won't even tolerate going to church with the family. She stays in her room, secluded from the rest of the world."

"Poor thing," Jenny murmured "We must pray for her, Maggie. Remember, 'Where two or three are gathered together in my name.'" Jenny Monroe's conviction in God's power was strong. "He will change Lillie's heart, Maggie, but we must continue to pray for her."

"If I hadn't gone through my own transformation with God, I would have thought it impossible to change Lillie's mind. Now, however," Maggie said with a new hope, "I know what God is capable of. I've seen firsthand how He can change a life. I want so much for Lillie to come to know God and to love Him as much as I do."

"Then have faith, Maggie. Have faith and let God do the rest. He doesn't always work as fast as we'd like Him to, but He's always got things under control. Even in this," Jenny said, sweeping her hand past the three graves, "He was in control. I don't believe God killed my children, but I believe He allowed their passing. From it He has added blessings to me in mercy and compassion I might never have learned otherwise."

"I hope one day you'll get to meet, Lillie. I know you'd be able to help her deal with her grief," Maggie said thoughtfully.

"'I can do all things through Christ which strengtheneth me,'" Jenny quoted from Philippians. "It's never us, Maggie, but Christ in us. He is the One who gets us through, and He's the One who will see Lillie through."

Seeing the last slivers of pale lemon sun slip behind the snow-crested mountain peak, Jenny remembered her supper on the stove. "Oh my, we best get back to the kitchen, or there won't be anything but burnt roast for supper."

David and Garrett walked toward the house, the aroma of supper heavy in the air. "Have you heard from him lately?" David questioned Garrett.

"I presume you mean your brother," Garrett replied as he stopped at the well to wash his hands and face. "The answer's no. I haven't heard from Daniel in months."

"I wish he would put the past behind him and come home," David said with a sadness that touched Garrett's heart. He, too, wished that his good friend would come back to the territory.

"We have to have hope, David," Garrett said as he put his hand on David's back.

"Yes, hope and faith in God to bring back the prodigal son," David sighed.

"Don't worry," Garrett reminded him, "God has worked with more stubborn people than your brother."

"I suppose you're right."

"I know I am. I was one of those more stubborn people." At Garrett's words, both men laughed, but the sadness was still shared between them. It was hard to wait for the lost to come home.

～

Springer, New Mexico, had proved to be anything but what Lillie had anticipated. She had envisioned leaving the train to find herself safely upon Lucas soil. When she learned the ranch was several days' ride west, she fell into despair and disappointment.

She'd left word around town that she needed a ride to Piñon Canyon Ranch, but so far there had been no takers. Letting out a heavy sigh, Lillie threw herself across the iron-framed bed.

"What am I to do if nobody comes for me?" she questioned to the air.

When a knock sounded on her door, Lillie jumped from the bed. "Yes, who is it?" she called.

"It's your landlady." The hotel keeper's wife insisted on calling herself that. Lillie immediately unlocked and opened the door.

"What can I do for you?" Lillie questioned suspiciously.

"There's somebody in the lobby who wants to see you. A cowboy from the Piñon Canyon Ranch. You wanna see him or not?" The rotund woman moved from foot to foot as if nervously pacing in place.

"Of course I'll see him. Tell him I'll be right down," Lillie ordered and then saw the look of stubborn pride on the other woman's face. "Please," she added thinking it better to pacify her landlady. The woman nodded and disappeared down the hallway.

Lillie returned to her room and checked her hair and dress. She had chosen a simple calico print of dark blues and browns she'd recently purchased in Springer. She grimaced as she thought of the reason for the new purchase. Her own clothes were growing tight again. Lillie pulled a dark brown shawl around her shoulders and went downstairs to greet her visitor.

"I'm Lillie," she said as she walked into the lobby. Mack Reynolds stood up and extended his hand.

"I'm Mack. Mack Reynolds," he added his last name as if to give his cowboy image more credibility. He could see this city woman was eyeing him warily. "I know you don't know me, but I'm Maggie and Garrett's foreman."

"I see," Lillie answered as if contemplating the job. "And you and Maggie are friends?"

"We sure are. I have the highest regards for Maggie Lucas."

"Well," Lillie said with a bit of hesitation in her voice, "I suppose I have no choice but to trust you."

Mack gave another broad smile. "You won't be sorry. I suppose you're wondering how I knew about you coming here."

"Well, no, not really. I did post a letter to the ranch a couple of days ago. I presumed you had received my note."

Mack laughed heartily. "I imagine your letter is in one of the packs of mail I have on my wagon to take back with me to the ranch. We don't get our mail too regularly. Although they are hoping to put a post office in Bandelero one of these days."

"Bandelero?"

"That's right. We're in the process of creating a new town. It's really on Lucas land, but Maggie and Garrett decided it would be in everybody's best interest to develop a trading post closer to home. Bandelero is expanding pretty quicklike, and now we're waiting for the post office to be approved."

"I see," Lillie replied, not completely sure she did see at all. It was going to be difficult to adjust her thinking to the less-civilized world she'd thrown herself into. "Then how did you know I would be arriving in Springer?" Lillie finally questioned.

"Your mother sent a letter. The trouble is, Maggie and Garrett have gone away on a little trip. I expect them back in a few days, but when I saw your mother's letter marked *urgent,* I took the liberty of checking it out. She mentioned when you'd be arriving, and since I had to come to Springer to hire men for the roundup, I figured I could pick you up as well."

"How considerate of you," Lillie replied, meaning every word. She was thankful her mother had had the sense to send a letter to Maggie.

"I have only one problem, Mrs. Philips." Mack paused for a moment, noticing Lillie's frown. "Would you rather I call you Lillie?"

"I. . .well. . . ," Lillie stammered before answering. "Yes. I do prefer it. Sometimes hearing myself called by my married name serves to be a painful reminder of what I've lost." She had no desire to explain her train transformation.

"I understand," Mack replied seriously. "The problem is we're set to leave this afternoon. Can you be ready that quickly?"

Lillie gave a surprising laugh. "I was ready to leave here the day I arrived. I'll have my things waiting in the lobby whenever you need me to."

Mack smiled. "Great. I'll be back for you in two hours."

"I shall look forward to it," Lillie acknowledged.

Chapter 6

The trip to Piñon Canyon was rough, but uneventful. Lillie had never camped outdoors and found it frightening, but without a hotel or boardinghouse along the many miles of mountain terrain, there was nothing else to do. After nearly a week of being jostled back and forth, they arrived at Maggie and Garrett's ranch.

"It's beautiful!" Lillie exclaimed. "I had no idea. Maggie told me about the ranch and she'd said it was breathtaking, but her letters didn't do it justice."

Mack agreed. "I could never call any place else home."

"I can understand why," Lillie replied.

As they approached the adobe ranch house, Mack began to explain a few things about the house. "You'll be the only woman in the house until Maggie comes home. Maria, our cook, took off to spend some time with her family. Besides, Maggie's come to enjoy caring for the house herself."

"Really?" Lillie questioned. She couldn't imagine enjoying the tasks and chores a large house would demand. The thought of learning to cook had never interested Lillie.

"Why sure," Mack said with a lopsided grin. "She's a pretty fair cook too." It was almost as if he'd read Lillie's mind. "Of course," Mack went on, "it wasn't always so. Maria had to throw out a few batches while teaching her how to make tortillas."

"Tortillas?" Lillie questioned, wondering at the strange sounding word.

"It's what we use a lot in place of bread. Course, Maggie makes good bread, as well. But tortillas are nice for a change. They're round like a dish and thin. You can make 'em out of flour or corn, and then you fry 'em up and eat 'em."

"Sounds interesting," Lillie admitted. She was beginning to realize she was quite hungry, and the talk of food wasn't helping one bit.

"I might add," Mack continued, "we have a friend of Garrett's staying with us. He just arrived the other day." Mack reined back on the horses and brought the wagon to a stop. "I don't suppose he'll be any bother to you. I'll just set you up in Maggie's old room, and he'll be clear down the other end of the hall. You probably won't even see much of him."

"I really don't mind, Mack," Lillie answered honestly. "I think I've been alone too long, anyway. Having you to talk to has opened my eyes to that, not to mention all the things I've learned about New Mexico."

"I'm glad," Mack said as he threw the reins to another cowboy. "Let me help you down, and I'll get you settled inside."

Lillie allowed Mack to usher her into Maggie's home. It seemed strange Lillie would learn all about it from a ranch hand rather than from Maggie. She listened half-heartedly to Mack explain where she could find things she might need. Mack was just explaining she should feel free to scout out the kitchen, when a familiar voice sounded behind them.

"Garrett? Is that you?" Mack questioned.

Lillie whirled around to find herself face to face with Daniel Monroe. "You!" she exclaimed in complete surprise.

Daniel raised a mocking eyebrow, enjoying Lillie's discomfort before answering simply, "Me."

Lillie felt the color rise to her cheeks as Mack explained he was just showing Lillie to the kitchen.

"Well, that's one place I'm certain Lillie will want to know the where-abouts of," Daniel said sarcastically.

"You are a complete beast," Lillie said, stomping her foot. "Why don't you leave me alone and mind your own business?"

Mack was bewildered by the entire encounter. "I take it you two know each other?" he questioned.

"Why, yes. Lillie and I met on the train, Mack. If I'd realized she was coming to Piñon Canyon, I'd have offered her a ride on the back of my horse," Daniel remarked. The glint in his eye and the ever-so-mocking tone to his voice caused Lillie to speak.

"But then that would have placed too much weight on the poor animal." She thought she was delivering his comeuppance, but Daniel, true to form, had the final word.

"Yes, you're right, Lillie. I don't think poor old Scout would have been able to endure both the extra weight and the mountain roads." With that, Daniel started to move down the hallway, chuckling to himself as he did. "I fix a superb supper, Lillie. I do hope you'll join me, as we'll be the only ones here."

"I'd rather starve," Lillie yelled after him. Her remark only invoked more laughter from Daniel, and a deeply puzzled expression on the face of Mack.

"I am sorry, Mack. Dr. Monroe isn't very pleasant company for me. I would go elsewhere if I could, but since there's no where else to go, I will simply stay in my room as much as possible." Mack nodded his head.

"Now," Lillie continued, "I believe you were going to show me to my room."

"Sure thing, Lillie," Mack said and led Lillie down the hall.

~

When the last hint of sunlight faded behind the mountain peaks, Lillie lit the lamp in her room and began to pace the floor. She was starving, yet hadn't she told Daniel she'd rather do that than endure his company?

There wasn't a moment she didn't remember Daniel's hurtful remarks. Why did he have to goad her so? She'd been rude to him; that much was true. But had she truly earned the disrespect and cruelty he seemed intent on giving?

Lillie tried to busy herself by arranging her clothes in the wardrobe and cleaning up from the long, dusty trip. She washed her hair for the first time since she'd cut it and found it a much simpler task. As her hair dried, Lillie noticed the slightest wave to it's baby fine texture. She decided to leave it down, enjoying the feel of it as it bounced against her shoulders. She then donned a white shirtwaist and dark burgundy skirt and sat down to work at her cross-stitch.

By nine o'clock, Lillie could no longer stand the hunger pains. She'd done everything possible to ignore them, but it was useless. A person was entitled to eat three meals a day; even Dr. Daniel Monroe would have to agree with that.

Lillie cautiously opened her bedroom door and peeked down the hall. Hadn't Mack told her Daniel's room was at the end of the hall? Seeing no one about, Lillie gingerly stepped into the hallway and walked silently to the kitchen.

A lamp burned on the small kitchen table, and Lillie picked it up and went to the stove. Someone had left a covered dish on the back edge, and Lillie lifted the towel to find a wonderful dinner. A thick slice of ham made Lillie's mouth water and there was a good-sized portion of fried potatoes as well.

"I saved it for you," Daniel's voice called from the doorway.

"I thought you'd gone to bed," Lillie replied. She was trying hard to keep her feelings in check.

"No," Daniel shrugged, "I was waiting to see how long it took you to come out here for something to eat."

"Why do you find such pleasure in hurting me?" Lillie questioned him against her will. "I hardly see what I've done to deserve such severity."

Daniel's expression softened a bit.

"I'm sorry, Lillie," Daniel offered. "I hadn't intended on hurting your feelings. It just grieves me to see a woman with your kind of looks deprive herself of a healthy body."

Lillie couldn't begin to tell Daniel how much it grieved her to be in the shape she was, but it was like a snowball rolling downhill, picking up more

164

snow as it went. Once the weight started coming on, she ate even more.

"I don't see where that gives you the right to insult me. Suggestions are one thing. They tend to be more compassionate and helpful. Insults just make me mad," Lillie answered honestly.

"I've a feeling you've had plenty of pity and compassion. That's the bad thing about mourning. You can very easily be pitied and sympathized into a depressive stupor. Maybe if someone had the nerve to stand up to you, like I'm doing, you'd see the situation for what it is and take better care of yourself."

Lillie's rage returned. She'd tried very hard to deal with Daniel's words as evenly and calmly as possible, but he wasn't making it at all easy. "I don't know why you've chosen to appoint yourself my keeper, but I don't need your help, so please leave me alone."

"Yes, I can see you're doing a great job," Daniel remarked sarcastically.

Lillie could take no more. Reaching down to the stove beside her, she picked up the cast iron skillet and in blind fury plunged at Daniel.

The move took Daniel by surprise, but not so much he didn't have a good time with the furious woman before him. He took off running and laughing which only caused Lillie to become more incensed.

Mindless to what she was doing, Lillie's only desire was to vent her frustration. Months of anger at herself and everyone else came pouring out as she chased Daniel from room to room. His laughter egged her on, and his sarcastic barbs gave her added energy.

With the skillet raised high above her head, Lillie picked up her skirts and ran in earnest, thinking only of planting the iron pan fully against Daniel's skull.

Just as Daniel ran past the front entry door, Maggie and Garrett Lucas returned from their honeymoon.

"Daniel?" Garrett said in amazement at the laughing man who was dodging blows from a plump, blond woman.

"Lillie?" Maggie breathed and looked up to Garrett.

"Lillie?" Garrett questioned Maggie.

Maggie nodded her head in acknowledgement while Lillie continued to strike out at Daniel. Regaining her wits from the shock of seeing Lillie, Maggie called out to her.

"Lillie! Lillie! Stop this at once!"

Daniel was laughing so hard it became infectious, and Garrett started to snicker too.

"Don't you dare," Maggie said, turning a stern look on her husband. Garrett only laughed harder.

"Lillie, did you hear me?" Maggie called out, taking a step forward.

"Please, Ma'am," Daniel called between his hysterical laughter, "don't stop her. It's the most exercise she's had in months."

At this, Lillie threw the skillet. Daniel easily dodged the missile, but then Lillie threw herself at him as well. She was beating his chest and trying to bite his hand as he took hold of her arms.

"No fair biting, Lillie, unless I get to bite back," Daniel said as he sobered somewhat.

Garrett was still laughing, and Maggie stood with her hands on her hips. "Will somebody tell me what's going on here? This is my house you're fighting in. And will you stop laughing!" Maggie said as she took hold of her husband's shoulders and gave him a light shaking.

Garrett lifted her high in the air and smiled. "I think you were more manageable on the trail. Maybe we should go back to the mountains."

Maggie started to kick her booted feet in protest. "Put me down, Garrett. Lillie needs me."

Garrett glanced past his wife to where Daniel had Lillie pinned against his chest and laughed. "I don't think Lillie knows what she's up against. I've wrestled with Daniel Monroe before," he said as he put Maggie back on the ground, "and he's a hard man to beat."

Maggie rolled her eyes. "A lot of help you are!" She turned to go to Lillie, but Garrett held her fast. "I think we'd better let them work this out themselves."

"Maggie, don't you leave me here with this monster!" Lillie called out, as Garrett began dragging Maggie down the hallway.

"Garrett, stop! She needs me," Maggie protested, but to no avail.

Lillie gave up on Maggie as her friend disappeared behind the dining room door. She tried to free herself, but became acutely aware of the man restraining her.

Daniel had wrapped one arm around Lillie's waist and the other across her shoulders. She tried to kick him, but her feet became tangled in her skirts and nearly sent them both onto the floor.

"If you would kindly stop fighting me, I'll let you go," Daniel whispered against Lillie's ear. He could smell the sweetness of her hair and, despite her added weight, Daniel liked the feel of Lillie in his arms.

The revelation came to him like a flash of lightning, and he suddenly released his grip. Lillie bolted from his arms and ran with all her might to her bedroom. She was ashamed to find herself crying by the time she reached the door and was barely aware Daniel had followed her and was now pounding on her locked door.

She threw herself across the bed and cried. The pain in her throat seemed to constrict normal breathing, and Lillie struggled to catch her breath. She was hysterical, wheezing and gasping. She'd never cried this hard, not even after the doctor had told her Jason was dead.

Lillie began to feel lightheaded and struggled to sit up in order to get her breath. It didn't help. The more shallowly and rapidly she breathed, the worse she felt. Just then the door flew open and Daniel was at her side.

"Shhh," he whispered as he held her. "Just take deep breaths." Lillie's strained breathing slowed, though the tears still fell silently.

"Look, Lillie, I'm sorry. I'll stop with the remarks about your weight. Truce?" Daniel asked earnestly. He hated causing her such pain. What had started out as good-natured teasing had turned quite ugly, and he regretted that he was responsible.

Lillie looked up into Daniel's eyes. They were steely blue and looked as if they could see into her soul. "Alright," she said and swallowed hard "Truce."

"You rest now, and I'll go get Maggie," Daniel said as he got up to leave. Lillie nodded and watched him walk out the door.

Outside, Daniel sighed and leaned back against the cool stone wall. He couldn't get one thought out of his mind: the thought of Lillie in his arms. How good it had felt to touch another human being, especially one as beautiful as Lillie. And she was beautiful, Daniel knew. Despite the added weight and her anger, Lillie was nearly charming him out of his memories.

Daniel felt a tremor of excitement course through his blood. It both grieved him and thrilled him. He knew forever mourning his Katie's death would never bring her back.

But now, another image filled his mind. Lillie. The scent of her hair and the softness of its fine texture against his face. Desperate to shake the memory, he went in search of Maggie.

Chapter 7

Maggie sat cooling her heels in the dining room while Garrett tried to ease her worries.

"Look, Maggie, I know Daniel. We can trust him to work out whatever problem he and Lillie are having. She'll be just fine with him," Garrett said as he rubbed his wife's shoulders. Maggie was nervously twisting a piece of the fine linen tablecloth.

"I hope so," Maggie answered. She was still in shock from finding Lillie at the ranch. "I wish she'd told me she was coming. I begged her for months to come stay with us, but I never expected her to show up without any word."

Garrett reached down and pulled Maggie into his arms. "Don't worry, my beloved," he said and placed a light kiss on her forehead.

"I hate to interrupt," a voice called from the doorway, "but Lillie wants to see you." It was Daniel.

Maggie looked up curiously at the tall, sandy-haired man. He seemed harmless enough. "What in the world was all that about?" Maggie questioned.

"Maybe it would be better for Lillie to explain. She's waiting in her room," Daniel answered. "In the meantime," he continued, "I'm Dr. Daniel Monroe, but I hope you'll call me Daniel." He extended his hand to Maggie and smiled broadly.

Maggie turned to take his hand while Garrett stood with his arm firmly fixed around her waist. "I'm Maggie, Garrett's wife."

Daniel nodded. "I would've known you without the introduction. Garrett used to write me long letters extolling all your virtues."

Maggie laughed as she cast a sidelong glance at her husband. "Those letters couldn't have been all that long."

"On the contrary," Daniel began, but Garrett quickly interrupted.

"I think you'd better go to Lillie," Garrett said as he nudged Maggie in the direction of the door. "As for you," he said taking Daniel by the arm, "we have quite a bit to catch up on."

"Very well," Daniel said with a shrug of his shoulders and a smile for Maggie. "I can always tell her about it later."

Maggie laughed at the look of discomfort on her husband's face. "I shall look forward to it, Daniel. I hope you'll be staying with us for a while." With that, Maggie took off in search of Lillie.

Making her way down the hallway, Maggie was pleased to see Mack had put Lillie in her old room. Maggie rather missed the quaintness of the bedroom her father had designed for her.

Lillie was sitting on the edge of the bed when Maggie walked into the room. "Maggie!" she exclaimed as she rushed into her friend's arms.

"I can't believe you're really here, Lillie. Why didn't you write and tell me?"

"I'm sorry, Maggie. It was very rude of me to arrive unannounced. Mother suggested the change of scenery, and she knew how dearly I missed you. Please forgive me for not announcing myself first," Lillie said as she pulled away from Maggie's embrace.

Maggie took a good look at her friend, and frowned. "Hard to believe isn't it?" Lillie sighed the question. "This time last year I was enjoying engagement parties, and you and I were planning my wedding. Now this," she said with a sweep of her arm across her body.

Maggie was grateful Lillie had made reference to the past. She had struggled to think of a way to tell Lillie how sorry she was for Jason's death. "Lillie, I'm so sorry about Jason and the baby. I wish there were words to express my pain for you. Are you able to talk about it?"

Lillie shook her head. "Not really. I vowed to put that part of my life behind me."

"Is that wise?" Maggie questioned.

"I don't know, Maggie. All I know is I very nearly threw myself off the train on the way down here. I don't want to feel like that again, and if that means forgetting about Jason and the baby, then that's what I have to do."

"Lillie, why don't we go out into the courtyard," Maggie suggested. "We can sit and have a good long talk, and I'll get us some refreshments." Then noticing the lateness of the hour for the first time, Maggie added, "Unless of course you're too tired. We could always wait and talk tomorrow."

"No," Lillie replied. "I'd like to spend some time with you. I've missed our long talks."

"Me too," Maggie said with a beckoning arm. "Come on. I'll get us something to eat and have Garrett light the courtyard lanterns."

"Alright. Just don't let Daniel see that you're feeding me. He thinks I should starve rather than gain more weight," Lillie commented snidely as she followed Maggie into the hallway.

Later when they were seated in the cobblestone courtyard, Maggie asked Lillie to elaborate on her argument with Daniel. "Was it the issue of eating that caused the fight I witnessed?" Maggie questioned as she poured hot coffee for Lillie and herself.

"That and his rudeness," Lillie answered. "I'd simply had all I could take of Dr. Monroe's sarcasm." She reached down to put a liberal amount of sugar and cream in her coffee.

"Why don't you tell me about it," Maggie suggested. "How did you and Daniel meet?"

Lillie grimaced. "Daniel needed my train car to deliver a baby," Lillie began. "I refused when the conductor asked me. Maggie, I just couldn't handle the idea of a woman delivering a baby before my eyes; especially when my own baby would have been due about the same time."

"Of course you couldn't," Maggie sympathized.

"Daniel wouldn't take no for an answer and knocked down my door." Lillie reached out and took one of the thick slices of bread Maggie offered. "It was a nightmare, Maggie. All of it. Jason had started to change," Lillie continued. "I was quite harsh with him about the changes, but we managed to make up before the accident."

"I'm certain that no matter what the problems between you and Jason, he knew you loved him. You mustn't be so hard on yourself, Lillie."

Lillie put down her empty cup and shifted her weight. "After the accident, I started eating and eating. I wanted so much to numb my mind to the pain. I wanted to forget my grief, and. . ." Lillie's words fell away.

"And?" Maggie encouraged her to continue.

"And I didn't want to look anything like the woman Jason loved. I didn't want to be any part of that woman, that life." Lillie got up and paced back and forth.

"Is that why you cut your hair, Lillie?"

"Yes, although I must say, that's the only change I don't mind," Lillie admitted. "Maggie, I hate myself. I hate looking this way. I hate feeling this way. I get up in the morning, hoping against hope it's all been nothing more than a bad dream, but, of course, it's quite real. I just can't bear it at times. Will the pain ever go away?"

Maggie smiled sadly. "I think so. I know I still miss my father, but the pain isn't near what it was a month ago or two months before that. It isn't that I don't love him as much as I did before he died, it just doesn't hurt as much now. Of course, my loss was much different than yours. You lost a husband and a child," Maggie said, noticing Lillie's frown. "I think the sooner you face up to that loss and go on, the better you'll be."

"I'm trying, Maggie. I wanted to change my appearance, but not like this," Lillie said, near to tears. "Daniel never misses an opportunity to make some comment about it. That's why I was so angry. I came out to get some supper, and he was there to make fun of me."

Maggie frowned. "How cruel. I shall have to speak to our Dr. Monroe about his manners."

"You don't need to, Maggie. We have a truce of sorts. At least that's what he promised."

"So you will stay with us for awhile, in spite of Daniel's presence?" Maggie questioned.

"I'll stay as long as you want me," Lillie said with a sad smile.

"Then you'll never go home," Maggie replied earnestly, "because I shall want you here always."

Days later, Maggie and Lillie had fallen into a routine of rising early to talk and bake. Maggie was teaching Lillie how to make bread, and Lillie was trying to work through her bitter emotions.

"Lillie," Maggie began one morning, "do you still enjoy riding?"

"I suppose I would, but with this additional weight, I'm not sure the horse would."

"Nonsense," Maggie rebuked matter-of-factly. "Garrett and Daniel out-weigh you many times over, and they've been enjoying daily rides. I think we should spend some time outdoors. You'd be surprised what the fresh mountain air will do for you, and the exercise will make you feel alive again."

"I'm not certain I want to feel alive," Lillie said as she kneaded a lump of dough. "I really don't have any reason to live."

"Lillie, you have many reasons to live," Maggie said as she placed her hand lightly on Lillie's arm. "Please don't give up."

Lillie sighed. "I came here in hopes of finding a place to heal; even a way to heal. But Maggie I just don't feel good about anything. I'm numb."

"Lillie, God will see you through this. He can give you the answers you're looking for."

Lillie stiffened noticeably and moved away from her friend. "Don't talk to me about God, Maggie. I don't need religion, and I don't need God. I have plenty of money to buy what I need, and I can go anywhere in the world; so if you insist on preaching at me, I'll leave."

Maggie was stunned. Her mouth dropped open in surprise. Lillie's anger and bitterness toward God seemed so overwhelming. Maggie dared to force the issue. "Lillie, what is this all about?"

Lillie left the bread on the floured board and wiped her hands on the white apron Maggie had lent her. "Jason got religion before he died. It was the reason we were fighting. I just know God took Jason away from me, and the baby as well, because I was angry Jason had become a Christian. Maggie, I want no part of a God that would do a thing like that."

"Lillie, God didn't kill Jason, and He certainly didn't kill your baby.

Things often happen in life because of our disobedience or sinfulness, but I don't believe God would take the life of your husband and child just to prove a point."

"Maggie, you never used to care what God thought. You were angry at Him yourself, and I never preached at you when you couldn't see a reason to believe in Him. I expect no less from you."

"But, Lillie," Maggie tried to reason, "you're miserable because of your loss. I'm trying to tell you there is a way for you to see your husband and baby again."

Lillie reached out and in a flash of anger slapped Maggie across the face. "How dare you!"

Tears filled Maggie's eyes. This wasn't the Lillie with whom she'd spent years of companionship. This wasn't the Lillie she'd longed to return home to see. Maggie stared at Lillie for a moment longer before answering. "I dare because it's true," she whispered.

Lillie's temper abated a bit. "I'm sorry, Maggie," she said without emotion. "Maybe I should pack my things and leave."

Maggie stepped forward, and took hold of Lillie's shoulders. "You can run if you like, Lillie. You can leave me and never allow me the pleasure of our friendship again. But you will never outrun God. Now I propose we settle our differences and enjoy a nice long visit, but that's only my desire. If it isn't yours, then I understand."

Tears formed in Lillie's eyes. "It's my desire too, Maggie. I do want to stay. I can't abide the thought of losing your friendship, nor can I live with the idea of returning to Topeka. At least not yet."

"Good," Maggie said and gave Lillie's shoulders a squeeze. "Then I won't preach at you any more. However, I wish you would allow me to help you in another way."

Maggie noticed Lillie's eyes narrow slightly. When Lillie didn't make any move to disagree, Maggie continued.

"I know you're miserable with yourself. I remember how much you prided yourself on your figure, and I want to help you lose the weight you've gained. I want to help you regain your health. Then, if and when you return to Topeka, you'll have no reason to be distressed with your physical state."

Lillie breathed a sigh of relief. "I'd be very happy to have your help, Maggie. I've really made a mess of myself, haven't I?"

Maggie laughed and dropped her hold on Lillie. "Not at all. Now what do you say we go for a ride? This bread has to rise anyway."

Chapter 8

Garrett was having every bit as much trouble with the stubborn Dr. Monroe as Maggie was having with Lillie. Daniel and Garrett had a past that went back several years, but even their longtime friendship couldn't break down the strained wall Daniel had erected.

"I'm glad you finally came back," Garrett said as he and Daniel settled down to breakfast.

Maggie and Lillie walked into the room before Daniel could reply. "Garrett, Lillie and I are going riding," Maggie announced as she pulled on her riding gloves.

"Not without a kiss, you aren't," Garrett said, taking hold of Maggie's gloved hand.

"I wouldn't dream of it," Maggie said joyfully and bent down to receive her husband's kiss.

Maggie and Garrett missed the pained look on Lillie's face, but Daniel didn't. He struggled with the feeling of wanting to comfort her. She was standing close enough to touch, yet Daniel held fast, not wanting to cause her more heartache.

"Please be careful," Garrett said, breaking the spell Daniel found himself under.

"Of course we will," Maggie said and smiled. "I'm anxious to show Lillie the ranch, so don't worry about us. I've packed some dried fruit and cheese. Don't look for us until late."

Daniel lowered his face to keep from showing Lillie the smile that brightened his face. Maggie had told him Lillie had put herself in Maggie's care in order to lose weight. Daniel told himself it was his doctor's observant eye, and not his interest in Lillie Philips, that caused him to believe she was well on her way to recovering her trim waistline.

Once Maggie and Lillie were out of the house, Garrett passed Daniel a platter with two large fried steaks on it. "One nice thing about ranch life is the beef is no farther away than your back door."

"I must say, your choice of breakfast food is different from my usual fare," Daniel replied and helped himself to one of the steaks.

"You work hard out here, and a hearty breakfast is always called for.

Even Maggie eats a great deal more than she used to," Garrett laughed and passed Daniel a heaping bowl of scrambled eggs.

"She's definitely working wonders with Lillie," Daniel said, trying to sound nonchalant.

"You kind of like her, don't you?" Garrett questioned between bites.

"I'd rather not discuss it," Daniel answered, leaving Garrett to realize the subject was closed.

"Well then, maybe you'd be interested in knowing David and Jenny have missed you. They'll be happy to see you. Have you let them know you're here?"

"No and I don't intend to," Daniel said sternly. "I didn't come back to the territory to get a sermon, so I'd just as soon avoid my brother."

"But he really cares about you, Daniel. He was asking me a couple of weeks ago if I'd heard from you and how you were doing. You can't fault the man for caring about his only brother," Garrett reasoned.

Daniel dropped his fork to his plate. "My family business is just that, my business. I don't intend to be harassed by you or anyone else. I only returned because. . . ," Daniel paused for a moment, "because, I can't get this place out of my mind. It's in my blood. I thought when Katie died I'd never want to see this place again, but I was wrong. Images of the mountains, the smell of the piñon pines, the way the air stays fresh and crisp well into the summer heat— I couldn't forget it." Daniel looked away. It had been over six years since he'd been in New Mexico, yet in many ways he'd never left at all.

"You know me better than to believe I'm sticking my nose in your affairs. I just thought you might care," Garrett replied, completely annoyed with his friend.

"I do care, Garrett, but not the way you think I should. So maybe we'd better forget about it," Daniel said and continued to eat his meal in silence.

"Well, let's see. That's two subjects we can't discuss. Do you have a list of any others?" Garrett drawled sarcastically.

"Don't go getting on your high horse with me, Garrett. I've got some problems, we both know that. What I don't need is for you to pass judgment on me. I don't need to have to answer to you or anyone else."

"Not even God?"

"Especially not God," Daniel retorted. He was having difficulty keeping his anger in check.

"So what do you want to talk about?" Garrett inquired.

"Actually," Daniel began, "there is something I want to talk to you about."

"And what's that?" Garrett questioned curiously.

"I've been considering opening up an office in Bandelero," Daniel replied as he pushed the cleaned plate back and poured himself another cup of coffee.

"Dan, that's great news. We got word a month or so ago our regular doctor was leaving the area. His wife can't abide the solitary life, and they're returning to St. Louis," Garrett said as he joined Daniel in a second cup of coffee.

"So you think folks would accept me into the community? Most of them don't know me from before," Daniel said with some reserve. "And, to be quite honest, after losing Katie, I've never had the same confidence in my abilities. I'm really not certain I'd be the asset you seem to think I'd be."

"Nonsense," Garrett said trying to dispel Daniel's lack of self-confidence. "You have the schooling, the training, and the heart. I know you'd be welcomed with open arms."

"There's still the element of being a stranger to most of these people," Daniel argued.

"But you are David's brother, and around here that will count for a great deal. People hold your brother in high esteem," Garrett offered. He'd hoped the words would make Daniel realize how beneficial David could be in helping him get established in Bandelero.

"No doubt they do," Daniel said sarcastically. "I don't need to concern David with my plans."

"He'll hear about them," Garrett replied.

"Hearing about them and being a part of them are two different things. I don't need his help," Daniel insisted, and Garrett realized they were once again at a critical impasse.

"Alright, Daniel, we'll leave David out of this. What did you have in mind?" Garrett questioned as he pushed away from the table.

"I have some plans in my room. Why don't I get them, and we can discuss the matter in detail," Daniel offered.

Hours later, Daniel and Garrett were still pouring over Daniel's plans. "In time, I hope to add onto this office space and make it a small hospital."

"In time? Why wait?" Garrett asked as he studied the blueprints.

"Buildings cost money, and so do the supplies necessary to make a true hospital," Daniel replied. "I've only saved enough to build the office and examining room. I figured I could put a bed in the office and live there as well."

"What if I joined you as a partner?" Garrett questioned, and Daniel's face broke into a smile.

"Are you serious?" Daniel questioned enthusiastically. Suddenly, he could see all his dreams coming true.

"I wouldn't have said it if I weren't serious," Garrett replied. "I have plenty of money. What I didn't inherit from my own folks, Maggie and I inherited from her father. Then there's the amount I've saved up over the last few years and the profits from the ranch. I'm more than capable of helping you achieve your goals and benefiting the community at the same time. So what do you say? Partners?"

Daniel slapped his hand into Garrett's outstretched one. "Partners," he said with gladness.

The moment of joy was dispelled as Maggie came bursting through the door with David Monroe close behind.

"Look who I found!" Maggie exclaimed. "Daniel, it's your brother, and he didn't know you were here."

David's eager face revealed his desire to reach out to his brother. Daniel, however, fixed a scowl to his face, and his steel blue eyes darkened in anger.

Garrett pulled Maggie aside. "Where's Lillie?" he asked.

"She offered to take the horses to the barn. Why?" Maggie questioned, as she realized the tension between Daniel and David. "What's wrong, Garrett?"

"Come on, let's make sure Lillie doesn't need our help."

Daniel refused to speak. He was too angry. If he'd never had to deal with David again, it would have been too soon.

"Dan, I wondered if I'd ever see you again," David said as he stepped forward to embrace his brother.

"You've seen me," Daniel said in a stilted voice. "Now, if you'll excuse me. . ."

"Please stay, Daniel. Can't we talk?"

"No," Daniel said as he turned to leave the room. "We can't."

Harbored back in his room, Daniel sat down in a red leather chair. He was fuming at being forced to meet David head-on. It wasn't Maggie's fault, he realized, but she had brought him back to the house. Garrett must never have explained his differences with David. It would be like Garrett to keep things to himself, but in this case, Daniel wished Garrett had told Maggie of his estrangement from his brother.

Unable to sit still, Daniel began to pace the room. It was a large room with whitewashed adobe walls and a dome-shaped wood stove in one corner. There was a massive four-poster bed with several layers of richly woven Indian blankets to ward off the cold of night, and a large oak wardrobe, which held all of Daniel's worldly belongings. The money he'd managed to save was sitting in his valise.

Daniel looked around the room and felt alien to everything in it. There weren't any memories here, and outside of the Indian pottery and blankets to remind him of the New Mexico home he'd once shared with David, there was nothing here that spoke of home.

Daniel pounded his fists against the adobe wall until they were scuffed and bleeding. Why did he have to feel this anger? Why did the rage continue? Wasn't six years of torment enough?

Having spent his energy at the wall, Daniel sat back down in the leather chair. Leaning over the desk, he put his face in his hands. "Oh, Katie," he whispered aloud, "how ashamed you must be of me."

Daniel thought of the petite young woman he'd married so many years ago. The delicate, young blond had lied to him and to David about her age, so it wasn't until after they were married that Daniel learned that his wife was only sixteen years old. In many ways, Katie Monroe had been wise beyond her years.

She had been suited to Daniel, who was finishing up his residency in a major Kansas City hospital, and before Daniel had realized what had happened, he had proposed and they were married. Daniel smiled when he remembered Katie's willingness to learn new things; she had wanted to act as his nurse and had offered to go to school for training. Daniel couldn't have asked for more in a wife.

Then they'd found themselves in the uncivilized West, and Katie was pregnant. Neither of them felt any concern because Daniel was, after all, a doctor. It wasn't important they be in a big town or organized community. They had each other and that was enough. At least it was supposed to have been.

Daniel sighed. Things had been so different then. He'd shared David's faith in God, believed the words of the Bible that God's love was everlasting and His mercies were new each day. That had been before Katie died.

The baby had refused to be born, and David and Jenny had come to offer support and prayers. Daniel labored with his young wife, struggling to help her deliver their baby, but nothing worked. Daniel begged David to plead with God for Katie's life, as well as the life of their unborn child. David had agreed to pray, but for God's will, not for Daniel's dictated request.

Katie had died, and it was God's will. Daniel decided then and there to turn his face from God and from his brother. How could he accept that the will of a merciful God had been to claim the life of his wife and child? Why would a loving God leave him alone and take the only woman he would ever care about?

Lillie's face came to mind, and Daniel grimaced. Guilt-ridden, he pressed his hands against the sides of his head. Was it possible he cared more about Lillie than he was willing to admit? In many ways, Lillie and he shared a common bond, but what was the purpose of that bond?

So many questions surged through his mind. Maybe returning to New Mexico had been the wrong thing. If he hadn't come, he would never have met Lillie.

For a moment, Daniel allowed the picture of Lillie to permeate his thoughts. She was a good woman, and she was working so hard to improve herself and get back into the routine of living. She deserved better than what he could give her. She was used to the fine life and the big city. Surely she would never be interested in considering him as a lifelong companion.

Where had that come from? Daniel wondered. One minute he was thinking about his beloved Katie, and the next minute it was Lillie.

Tormented by the vision of both women, Daniel was further disturbed by the memory of David's face. David had come with such hope and enthusiasm. He had come to bury the past and embrace the future with his older brother, and Daniel had sent him away empty handed.

The look on David's face haunted Daniel. How could he have caused his own brother such pain? The truth be told, he'd wanted to hug David the minute he'd walked into the room. He'd missed his little brother and the closeness they'd shared for so many years.

Daniel tried to ignore the hurt he felt inside. There was no way he could deal with David. To put aside his differences with David meant coming to terms with God, and that was something Daniel Monroe was not inclined to do.

Chapter 9

September 1889 was a glorious and bountiful time of harvest. The Pueblo Indians had come to Piñon Canyon to trade agricultural products and sheep for beef and horses. Garrett was happy to oblige them as the small garden Maggie and Lillie had cared for throughout the summer wasn't large enough to feed the ranch through the winter months.

Grain sacks provided by the ranch were filled with a variety of corn. Then the Indians brought in several baskets of apples, squash, and pumpkins. Garrett praised the Indians for their wealth of crops. More than one visitor credited the bounty to the Blue Corn Clan and their summer corn dance, as well as to the Cloud People who were always credited for good corn crops. Garrett didn't contradict them but added a simple statement: "God has been very good to us, hasn't He?"

Lillie got her first lessons in canning from Maggie and Maria, Maggie's cook. She seemed to take to the laborious task in a way that surprised even Maggie. Standing over the outdoor caldron one afternoon, Lillie was amazed to discover she was actually enjoying herself.

Lillie knew her happiness was multifaceted. Glancing down at her trim and tiny waist, she wanted to pinch herself to make certain she wasn't dreaming. The weight loss was real, however, and Lillie felt as if a burden of more than flesh had been lifted.

When Daniel and Garrett rode into the yard, Maggie immediately handed her canning duties over to Maria and went to seek out the men. She noticed how Lillie watched Daniel, and wondered if she was developing feelings for the older man.

Garrett was already busy with one of the ranch hands, but Maggie didn't mind. She wanted to talk to Daniel. Making her way into the barn, she found the doctor caring for his horse.

"Daniel, I wonder if you have some time for me," Maggie said as she came up behind him.

"I've always got time for you, Maggie. Where would you like to talk?" Daniel questioned with a smile. He seemed much happier these days, and Maggie was more than a little aware of his interest in Lillie.

"Well, talking is only part of what I have in mind," Maggie began, rather embarrassed by the situation. She followed him to the corral and opened the gate for him. "I need to see you as a patient."

"Is something wrong?" Daniel questioned, and the concern in his voice touched Maggie. He took the rope from the bay's neck and gave him a light smack on the rump. The horse moved quickly across the corral and Maggie waited while Daniel secured the gate. He tossed the rope over the fence post and questioned Maggie again. "Are you sick?"

"No, not really. At least I don't think so." Maggie smiled, then leaned forward to whisper, "I think I'm expecting." Her face lit up at the thought of the child she hoped was growing inside.

A grin played at the corners of Daniel's lips. "Does Garrett know?"

"No. I didn't want to get his hopes up until I was sure. You know how much he wants children," Maggie said softly.

Daniel put his arm around Maggie as they walked toward the house.

"I don't know what you two are up to, but I see red when another man has his arm around my gal," Garrett called good-naturedly from where he stood talking to a ranch hand.

"Too bad!" Daniel called over his shoulder. "You can wait your turn. Right now, the lady prefers my company."

Maggie knew Garrett would wonder about her silence, so she turned to ease his mind. "Daniel is going to show me what type of bandages he needs for the hospital. Lillie and I are going to roll him a whole wagon full."

"I guess I can't stand in the way of medicine." Garrett laughed and waved them off.

After a brief examination, Daniel gave Maggie the news she'd hoped for. "You are definitely pregnant," he said with a smile. "I'd say you can expect this young'un around the third week of January."

"Oh, Daniel," Maggie said, excitement coloring her voice. "I'm so happy, and I know Garrett will be too. My only worry is Lillie."

"Lillie?" Daniel questioned. "Has she been feeling ill?"

"No, but you know how hard it is for her to think about her baby. I wonder what learning about this baby will do to her. I'd hate to be the cause for Lillie's pain, but I'm so happy I'd feel untrue to Garrett and myself if I handled it any other way," Maggie said thoughtfully.

"Of course you would, and Lillie wouldn't expect it any other way," Daniel said solemnly. "She may have difficulty with the announcement, but there's another four and a half months to get adjusted to the idea."

"I suppose you're right. I guess I'd better just put it in God's hands and trust Him to take care of Lillie. He's given me a wonderful gift, and I'm not going to pretend I'm not happy when I'm thrilled," Maggie said as she got to her feet. "Now if you'll excuse me, I have some news to tell my husband."

"I can well imagine what his reaction will be," Daniel said with a grin. "There'll be no way for him to get that black Stetson on that head of his, once it commences swelling with pride."

Maggie laughed and surprised Daniel with a hug. "I'm so glad we have you here, Daniel. I used to worry about what it would be like if I did have a baby out here without medical facilities, but with you here at the ranch, or at least as close as Bandelero, I know I'll be just fine. I'm so blessed that God brought you to us."

Daniel frowned over Maggie's shoulder. It wasn't her reference to God as much as his self-doubt that bothered him. Maggie was certain he'd be her deliverance in birthing the baby, but Daniel wasn't that convinced. He reminded himself silently that at the last two deliveries he'd attended, both mothers and babies had lost their lives.

Maggie turned to leave, not realizing Daniel's dilemma, but turned back briefly to question him again. "What kind of bandages will you be wanting Lillie and me to roll for you? I don't want to lie to Garrett."

Daniel's mind was still focused on his concerns for the blue-eyed woman that so innocently stood before him, willing to place her trust and life in his hands. She didn't look old enough to be married, Daniel mused, but then, neither had Katie.

Daniel took down a rolled bandage and handed it to Maggie. "About four inches wide, and the length can vary." His words were rather stiff, and Maggie mistook his tone for professionalism.

"Sounds simple enough," she replied. Then she added, "Are you coming along to hear Garrett's reaction?"

"No, you go on. I didn't get enough of a ride earlier, and I think I'm going to go back out. Would you mind telling Garrett, in case he wonders?" Daniel requested.

"Not at all, Daniel," Maggie said and left Daniel with a smile.

"So, are you done rolling bandages?" Garrett teased as he met Maggie coming down the hallway.

"Yes, as a matter of fact, I am," Maggie said with smile.

Garrett wrapped his arms around Maggie's waist and grimaced. "I think you took the weight off Lillie and put it on yourself. You know if you get too fat, I'll have to send you away," Garrett joked, and Maggie lifted questioning eyes to her husband's face.

"You wouldn't love me if I were fat?"

Garrett's face looked puzzled for a moment before he said, "Mrs. Lucas, I would love you if you were twice this size."

"Well, that's good," Maggie said with a teasing smile forming on her lips, "because I intend to get twice this size."

Garrett laughed out loud, still not understanding her meaning. "I don't think so, Mrs. Lucas. I'll lock you in your room first, then we'll see how fat you get without a cupboard to raid ten times a day."

Maggie sighed, but the teasing was still in her voice. "As long as you let Daniel come see me, say in about four-and-a-half months," she whispered.

"Why, so you can roll more bandages?" Maggie's teasing suddenly seemed to make sense to Garrett. "Wait a minute," he said and set Maggie at arm's length. He closely scrutinized her figure and her flushed face. "Are you telling me you're, we—"

"That's right," Maggie laughed. "We're having a baby."

"I can't believe it," Garrett said laughing as he whirled Maggie in a circle.

"Well believe it. Daniel says it's true. You were right. We were up to more than just bandages," Maggie teased. "Now put me down before you make me dizzy."

Garrett gently placed Maggie back on the ground and kissed her soundly on the lips. "You've certainly made my day, Magdelena," he whispered using her full name.

"What's going on?" Lillie asked as she came out of her bedroom dressed in riding clothes.

Garrett squeezed Maggie's shoulders. "Hasn't Maggie told you? I figured I was the last one to know."

"Told me what?" Lillie asked innocently, and Maggie jabbed Garrett in the side. She'd hoped to tell Lillie when they were alone.

"Maggie's having a baby," Garrett announced, still not realizing Maggie's discomfort was founded in fear of Lillie's reaction.

"That's wonderful, Maggie," Lillie managed to say, but the words were mechanical and Maggie knew her friend was in serious pain.

"I wanted to tell you later when we could talk alone," Maggie said as she stepped forward to take Lillie's hand.

Lillie surprised them all by backing away. "I'm going for a ride. I'd like to be alone. I'm sure you understand." With that Lillie ran down the hallway.

"What was that all about?" Garrett asked his worried wife.

"I knew she wouldn't be able to handle it," Maggie said and started to cry. Garrett finally understood and took Maggie in his arms.

"Shhh," he whispered against Maggie's copper hair. "God will care for Lillie. Come on, we'll pray for her together."

~

Lillie barked out the commands for a horse and flew into the saddle before the cinch was tightened. She went blazing across the yard and headed toward the mountains. The memories of Jason and the baby barely surfaced through the anger and sorrow that filled her heart.

She's having a baby, she's having a baby! The words echoed in Lillie's ears. Her hat flew off her head and went in the opposite direction of her galloping steed. Lillie urged the horse faster and faster until the scenery was a blur.

In the back of her mind, Lillie became conscious of a voice. Someone calling her name. She turned slightly in the saddle to find a mounted Daniel, riding in a fury to catch up with her.

Lillie kicked the horse's flanks unmercifully and nearly lost control of the reins as the gelding picked up speed. There was no way on earth she was going to deal with Dr. Monroe and any of his wisdom.

Ignoring Daniel as he cut across the field to head her off, Lillie glanced up in time to see a barbed wire fence directly in front of her. Lillie had been riding since she was very young and jumping fences was certainly nothing new to her. She leaned down on the neck of her horse and raised up slightly to hug her body against the gelding. This should have been enough to signal the horse she was prepared for the jump, but it didn't work. Instead, the poor gelding, having never been required to jump fences, came to a complete stop at the edge of the barbed wire.

Lillie fought to keep her hold, but it was no use. Momentum threw her over the horse's head and into the razor-edged barbed wire.

Lillie's scream split the silence. Daniel was nearly a minute behind her, and when he managed to get to the fence, Lillie was thrashing wildly in the tangled broken fence.

"Lillie, stop moving," Daniel ordered as he came to her. "Did you hear me?"

"Get it off me. It's cutting me," Lillie said as she pushed at the wire with her bloodied hands. Her skirts were hopelessly intertwined with the wire, and Daniel knew the more Lillie thrashed, the worse things would be.

"Lillie, if you don't stop it, you're going to hurt yourself even more." Daniel reached out and took Lillie's hands in his own. She was crying, and her tears broke Daniel's heart in two.

"It hurts," Lillie sobbed, but she tried not to fight the wire.

"I know," he said softly. "Now, I want you to remain perfectly still while I see if I can't get you lose. Do you understand?

"Yes," Lillie whimpered.

Daniel tried to untangle the wire gently, but some of it was embedded in the cloth of Lillie's riding skirt. "I'm going to have to cut some of your skirt," Daniel said as he reached for his pocket knife.

As Daniel cut away the bloodied cloth of her skirt, Lillie could see she was far from out of danger. The calves of her legs had been protected by her riding boots, but her knees and lower thighs had no such protection.

"Lillie, you're losing quite a bit of blood." Daniel's face was grave as he continued to work at freeing her. "I've got to get the bleeding to stop." Lillie nodded as she passed into unconsciousness.

When she woke up, Lillie was surprised to find herself back at the ranch house in Daniel's examining room.

"I see you're back among the living," Daniel said as he brought a tray of instruments and supplies.

"What are you going to do?" Lillie questioned fearfully.

"I'm going to clean the wounds on your legs, then I'm going to stitch the ones that need it," he said never taking his eyes from the concoction he was mixing.

"Stitch them? You mean with a needle?" Lillie questioned, swallowing hard. She wished she'd stayed unconscious.

"I don't know of another way," Daniel replied sternly. He was completely in charge, and his years of professional training were making themselves evident in his exacting actions.

"I don't think so," Lillie said as she tried to scoot up the table. She was mortified to find her legs were exposed, while a sheet covered her lap.

"I don't remember giving you a choice," Daniel said as he looked up to see the fear in Lillie's eyes. "Relax, Lillie. I'm not going to hurt you. I have medication that will numb the pain. If I don't stitch the wounds, they'll start bleeding again."

"I don't want this," Lillie said as she pulled away.

Lillie cried out in pain as she struggled to move. Her legs felt like they were on fire, and for the first time she noticed the ugly red gashes that scarred her thighs and knees.

"Lillie, don't move," Daniel said as he placed his hand on her calf. The action stilled Lillie immediately, but not for the reasons intended. Daniel's touch caused her mind to flood with confusing emotions.

Daniel stood fixed with his hand on her leg, and Lillie began to tremble as she looked into his eyes. He recognized the change in Lillie and remained silent. He reached up and touched her cheek as lightly as a feather. When she didn't grimace or pull back, Daniel allowed his hand to travel the length of her jaw.

Lillie couldn't explain the feelings inside her. She wanted to fight Daniel, to tell him not to touch her, but her mouth wouldn't make the words. Her eyes remained fixed to his, and when he lowered his mouth to hers, Lillie didn't fight. Instead, she found herself clinging to Daniel's neck as if he were offering her a lifeline.

The kiss lasted only a moment, but when Daniel pulled away, Lillie saw none of the teasing or sarcasm she knew him well capable of. She was inundated with varying emotions. She felt guilty for having allowed Daniel to kiss her, but she also had enjoyed it. How could she do that to Jason? He'd been the love of her life, and she had sworn to love no other. The words of her marriage vows came back to haunt her: Till death do us part.

Lillie realized she wasn't bound to Jason by anything earthly, but in her heart she'd thought it impossible to ever love again. Lillie glanced at the door to avoid Daniel's eyes.

"If you're thinking of running away, it won't do you any good," he said to break the tension. His mind cried out at the betrayal of his long dead, Katie. But was it betrayal? he wondered.

"I don't want any more pain," Lillie said, with two-fold meaning.

"I know," Daniel said softly. "That's why I mixed this up. It'll take away the pain in your legs. I promise it you're still in pain after drinking this, I won't touch your legs."

Lillie looked suspiciously at Daniel, then at the glass he held. "I don't know," she began, but Daniel was already lifting the glass to her lips.

"Just drink it, Lillie. Then while we wait you can tell me why you were riding that horse like a crazed fool."

" 'Thou fool, this night thy soul shall be required of thee.' " The words of Luke came back to haunt Lillie's thoughts. Fear filled her eyes as she felt warmth spread through her body. She gripped Daniel's arm.

"Am I going to die?" The words were out of her mouth before Lillie realized what she'd said.

Daniel sensed the anguish and fear. He reached out and pulled Lillie into his arms and cradled her gently. "Of course not, Lillie."

"I was a fool, Daniel. I couldn't bear the news that Maggie was with child. I was so selfish in my own pain, but I had to get away from here. I couldn't stand it." Lillie thought her words sounded slurred.

"I know. I know," Daniel reassured. "I have my own reasons for fearing Maggie's condition," he said honestly.

Lillie's eyes opened wide, in childlike amazement. "You do?" The question was barely whispered.

"I lost my wife in childbirth, the baby too. I was their only medical help, and although I'd had the finest university training, I couldn't save them." Daniel's pain was clear.

"You know then," Lillie murmured. "You know about the nightmares and the pain."

"Yes," he said as he stroked her hair.

"Daniel, I must be dying. I can't stay awake," Lillie said sadly, but the fear was no longer in her voice. Before he could reply, Lillie spoke again. "Daniel, do you think God hates me?"

"No," Daniel said in a stilted tone.

"I think He does, Daniel," Lillie said as her eyelids fought the heaviness. "I blamed Him for everything, and I know He hates me. That's why I'm dying."

"Hush, Lillie you are not dying. I just gave you a sleeping powder."

"You hate me too, don't you?" Lillie struggled to ask the question before finally slipping into unconsciousness.

"Nothing could be further from the truth, Lillie. Nothing."

Chapter 10

B ut I don't want to stay in bed any more," Lillie announced to Daniel. "If I let you get up, you'll just run around and tear open those stitches. Be patient, and I'll take the stitches out in another few days."

"If the stitches are coming out in a few days anyway, why can't I get up?" Lillie demanded.

"Because I'm the doctor and I said no." With that Daniel left the room, passing Garrett in the doorway as he left.

"She's not to get out of that bed, and if she tells you otherwise, she's lying," Daniel told Garrett.

Garrett laughed. "Is she being that bad?"

"Worse. I wouldn't go in there unless you're prepared for a battle. Boredom has made her mean."

Garrett glanced past Daniel, where Lillie sat with an indignant look on her face. "I see what you mean. I'll be careful." Daniel shrugged his shoulders and walked down the hall.

"How are you feeling, Lillie?" Garrett questioned as he took a seat in the chair beside Lillie's bed.

"I'm tired of being in this bed," Lillie answered. "Daniel still won't let me get up. It isn't fair."

"Life's not fair, Lillie. Nobody promised it would be. Jesus said we'd have trials and tribulation," Garrett said, trying hard to find a way to talk to Lillie about God. Maggie's concerns for her best friend had quickly become Garrett's concerns as well.

"Then why try?" Lillie asked.

"What's the alternative? We can give up and spend our time in misery and discomfort, but that's not what God has in mind."

"How do you know? Maybe God doesn't like us or maybe He's mad because we've done something we shouldn't. Churches are always telling us what sinners we are," Lillie said.

"We are sinners," Garrett began. "That much is true. But God gave us a way to be forgiven. Jesus came to this earth and died for those sins."

"Surely He died for his friends and family, or for the people of his time. I can't believe He died for those who hadn't been born."

187

"But that's what's so special about it, Lillie. He did die for you. A long time ago, Jesus looked down through history and saw you and me, Maggie, Daniel, and everyone else, and He knew we couldn't make it alone."

"But I feel alone," Lillie admitted sadly.

"I know you do, Lillie. That's because you don't have Jesus. None of us ever belongs until we repent of our sins and belong to Him. None of us heals until we let Him take control of our wounds."

"How can you be sure God cares? How can you know whether He's listening to you or not?" Lillie questioned.

Garrett smiled knowingly. What Christian hadn't asked these same questions? Of course there were those fortunate few who found faith and trust in God an easy thing.

"It's a matter of faith, Lillie. When you finally come to terms with the truth about Jesus Christ, nothing else matters. The pain, the fears, the denial—none of it matters anymore. It all falls away like the Scripture says. The old is passed away, and we become new creatures in Christ."

"Do you believe that, Garrett?"

"I sure do, Lillie. I believe it enough to stake my life on it," Garrett answered with firm assurance.

"I must say you've given me a great deal to consider," Lillie said thoughtfully. "If you don't mind, I'd like to take a nap now."

"Sure, Lillie." Garrett got up to leave, then turned to add, "Lillie, just remember there's nothing so bad God can't forgive it and forget it."

"How can anyone forget something like the wrongs in our life?"

"That's the joy of the God we serve, Lillie. The Bible says He takes our sins and casts them into the sea of forgetfulness and remembers them no more. Now you try to get some rest, and I'll send Maggie to check up on you in an hour or two."

While Garrett had worked to show Lillie the plan of salvation, Maggie had sought out Daniel in order to ease his mind about her condition.

"Is something wrong? Are you feeling alright?" Daniel questioned as he joined Maggie in the courtyard.

"I'm fine, Daniel. I wanted to talk to you."

Daniel's worry still furrowed his brow. "I don't mean to cause you any distress, but in all honesty I'm not sure I'm up to this challenge," he said as he settled into a cushioned, wrought-iron chair. "I was thinking of leaving when Lillie had her accident."

"Daniel, no!" Maggie exclaimed. "You can't leave."

"I don't intend to, Maggie. I considered it long and hard, though."

"And?"

"And I've never been the kind of man who could run from a challenge. I pray I can do justice to your faith in me."

"Daniel, you're a fine doctor. I have the utmost confidence in you," Maggie said sincerely. "I'm so thankful you're here."

Daniel studied Maggie's face for a moment. She was radiant in her expectancy. Daniel remembered another radiant face, so petite and lovely, but that had been a lifetime ago.

"And I'm grateful for your confidence, Maggie. I can see why Garrett loves you so. Thank you for believing in me," Daniel said with a smile. In his mind, however, was the fervent hope he could come to be as certain of his abilities as Maggie was.

~

Nearly a month had passed since Lillie's accident. She traced the pattern of the barbed wire scars and frowned. Once her beauty had been unmarred and she'd been so very proud of it. Now it seemed rather unimportant. Lying in bed all those days had given Lillie time to consider her life.

Beauty was so fleeting. One minute her body had been youthful, unscarred, innocent in nearly every way, then she'd almost lost her life in the carriage accident. Scars had formed from that day on, and they only seemed to grow deeper. Scars upon scars.

Lillie pulled on two layers of petticoats to ward off the dampness of the October rain. She was grateful for the clothing Maggie had lent her and eagerly went to the closet to find something warm.

After pulling on a dark blue, wool dress, Lillie began to brush out her hair. She stared for a moment at the image in the mirror. Her hair now fell to the middle of her back. Funny, she thought, after cutting her hair she'd actually liked the unconventional shortness of it. She brushed her hair over and over until it gleamed from the attention, then braided it down the back and tied it with a blue ribbon.

After this was accomplished, Lillie secured the buttons that lined her sleeves from the wrist to the elbow. She'd always hated tedious tasks like these, but now it seemed with each button, Lillie grew keenly aware of the chore. How often in life had she avoided seemingly tedious tasks simply because somebody else was at hand to do them for her?

Lillie sat down to pull on her high-topped boots. With each turn of the button hook, Lillie realized she'd missed out on many things in life. So much of her life had been consumed with material items and the value of those things. She laughed out loud when she thought that just a year ago she'd have found it offensive to be solely dependent upon a hand-me-down wardrobe. How different her life had become! Lillie finished with her shoes and went to stoke the fire in the kitchen stove.

"You're up awfully early," Daniel said from the shadows of the kitchen. He sat nursing a cup of coffee in the darkness.

"I wanted to build the fire up for breakfast, but I see you've already taken care of that," Lillie said rather shyly. Ever since Daniel had treated her wounded legs, Lillie felt extremely uncomfortable whenever she was alone with him. Lillie knew, however, it hadn't been the touch of his hands on her legs, as much as the shared kiss that made her ill at ease. Ignoring her troublesome feelings, Lillie pulled a white apron from the cupboard and tied it securely around her tiny waist.

"Have you eaten yet?" Lillie asked as she turned up the lamp. Her eyes met Daniel's for a moment. Daniel's steely blue eyes narrowed slightly as if contemplating Lillie's pale blue ones.

Lillie resisted the urge to reach out and touch the sandy hair that still looked slightly rumpled from sleep. Daniel wore a white, cotton shirt open at the neck, and Lillie could see he'd rolled the sleeves up as if to prepare for some job. Lillie wanted to say something to break the spell, but instead, she turned away from Daniel's intense stare and went to the larder in search of bacon.

When Garrett and Maggie joined them, Lillie had already prepared bacon, fried potatoes, scrambled eggs, and biscuits.

"It sure smells good in here," Garrett drawled as he helped Maggie to a seat. Her well-rounded figure spoke of how close she was to giving birth.

"I'll say," Maggie added with enthusiasm. "I could eat a horse."

Daniel and Garrett laughed at this as Lillie placed a platter of food in front of Maggie. "There's no need to resort to horseflesh," Lillie said with a grin. "I don't think the baby would care for that near as well as he would for this."

"You never know," Maggie teased. "After all this is a Lucas baby."

"Just what is that supposed to mean?" Garrett questioned with a twinkle in his eye.

"Well, I—" Maggie's words fell silent at the shouting voices that came from the yard outside.

"What in world is going on?" Lillie said as she moved toward the kitchen.

"Stay here," Garrett instructed and motioned for Daniel to join him. "We'll check it out."

"Garrett, be careful," Maggie said with great concern for her husband.

Lillie put her arm around Maggie and gave her a reassuring hug. "We'll wait right here."

Garrett and Daniel soon returned, and the expression on their faces left the women without doubt something serious was wrong.

"It's the Indian village. The Pueblos have a measles epidemic on their hands," Garrett said as he sat down beside his wife. "Daniel, you might as well eat breakfast first. You won't be able to do much good on an empty stomach."

"I suppose you're right," Daniel said as he sat down and picked up a biscuit.

"Let's join hands and pray," Garrett suggested and took hold of his wife's hand. "Father, we come to You to ask Your blessings and mercies," Garrett prayed. "I want to ask a particular blessing of wisdom upon Daniel as he prepares to work with Your children, the Pueblo. In James 1:5 you tell us 'If any of you lack wisdom, let him ask of God, that giveth to all men liberally.' Father, we need that wisdom now to deal with this measles epidemic and to keep it from spreading any farther. Amen."

"Amen," Maggie whispered.

For a moment an uncomfortable silence fell upon the four. Lillie refused to look up from her plate, and Daniel seemed preoccupied with the task at hand.

"You'll need some help," Garrett said as he dug into the plateful of food.

"I hadn't thought of that, but you're right. I suppose you're too busy to go, and Maggie certainly can't go," Daniel stated.

"Why don't you ask Jenny," Maggie suggested. "David and Jenny know most of the people. I'm sure she'd be more than happy to help you."

"No," Daniel said firmly and dismissed any possibility of argument.

Maggie heard the bitterness and anger in Daniel's voice and decided to drop the matter.

"Why can't I go and help?" Lillie suddenly questioned. "I've had the measles, and I'm healthy and strong."

"I don't think so, Lillie," Daniel said, thinking of her life of ease and comfort. "I don't think you could keep up with the work."

"I have a great deal of determination, Dr. Monroe," Lillie said rather slighted. "I can do most anything I set my mind to. Tell me what to do, and you'll see I'm made out of stronger stuff than you give me credit for."

"I think Lillie's right," Maggie affirmed. "She could be a great asset to you."

Daniel glanced curiously from Maggie to Lillie, and finally to Garrett. At Garrett's nod, Daniel shrugged his shoulders.

"Alright, Lillie can go along," Daniel answered the questioning looks of his three friends. "But I'm warning you, Lillie, it won't be easy and it won't be pretty. There will be a great deal of death and pain. Are you sure you're up to this?"

Ordinarily, Lillie would have raged at anyone questioning her abilities, but she knew Daniel understood what she'd been through. "I need to do this, Daniel." Her voice was soft, almost inaudible. How could she explain to the trio before her that she needed to do something unselfish and necessary. All her life, Lillie had been a lovely ornament, a lovely, useless ornament.

One look at her face, and Daniel nodded. "I understand, Lillie. Can you be ready to leave in ten minutes?"

"Of course," Lillie said as she got up from the table. "I'll go pack."

Chapter 11

Lillie had never worked so hard in all her life. She was scarcely done with one patient when Daniel whisked her away to help with someone else.

Yellow Butterfly, a young Pueblo girl who'd once lived with David and Jenny Monroe, showed Lillie how to draw water from the river and carry it in the handmade pottery on top of her head. Lillie had to laugh amidst the gravity of the situation at her initial failed attempts.

As she made yet another trip back from the icy river, Lillie felt she would never see an end to the suffering and dying. She knelt beside an elderly Indian woman and began to bathe her feverish body with water. The woman's body was dotted from head to toe with telltale red spots.

The woman moaned and tried to speak, but Lillie hushed her with what little Tiwa dialect she'd learned from the Tanoan language the Pueblo spoke.

Lillie spoke the words of reassurance over and over, but they paled in comparison to the effect her touch had on the old woman. Lillie gently stroked the graying hair of the woman as a mother would her child. The woman became quiet under Lillie's hand.

"Lillie!" It was Daniel calling her name from outside the adobe pueblo.

"I'm in here, Daniel," Lillie called as she left the old woman's side, the pot of water securely in hand.

"Are you holding up alright?" Daniel questioned, exhaustion in his voice.

"I'm fine, but I think you'd better go back to the pueblo and get some sleep. If I need you, I'll wake you up," Lillie offered.

Daniel shook his head. "It isn't even noon yet."

"That hardly matters when you've been up all night," Lillie said sympathetically. "I promise I'll come get you if I need you."

Daniel pushed his hair back from his eyes, and for once the action didn't remind Lillie of her dead husband. "Alright. I'll take a short nap, but you wake me by two o'clock."

"I think I can manage that," Lillie said with a slight smile. The truth was she could manage it, but she seriously doubted she'd disturb Daniel once he got to sleep.

The afternoon sun had only warmed things marginally. Lillie had been so busy with her work she hadn't noticed the hour, and with the first evening stars appearing in the sky, it was colder than ever.

With most of the sick resting peacefully, Lillie went to work alongside several Pueblo women who were washing out clothing and bedding. She stood over a caldron of boiling water, relishing the heat from the fire beneath it.

"Doctor Woman, come now," a young Indian girl said as she tugged at Lillie's skirt.

"What's wrong?" Lillie asked.

"Brother's sick. Bring medicine for baby. Come. Come now." The girl's urgency pushed Lillie into action.

Lillie followed the girl, whose long black hair flew out from behind her as the Indian blanket she used for a coat fell away. Lillie had taken to using a blanket of her own for warmth, but she'd forgotten to grab it. She regretted her forgetfulness and was grateful to see the young girl race inside one of the nearby adobe buildings.

The interior was dimly lit as Lillie stepped inside. The pueblos were always poorly lit, but those that housed the sick remained dark for the sake of eyes made sensitive to light by the measles. As Lillie's eyes adjusted, she could see a young mother holding her baby in his cradle board.

"You make my baby well, Doctor Woman?" The woman asked the question with hopeful eyes, as well as with her words.

"May I hold the baby?" Lillie questioned and motioned to the woman her meaning. "I'll need to take him out."

"Yes, yes. Hold baby," the woman mimicked the words. "Hold baby. Make well." The mother began to undo the fastenings that held her small son in his cradle board.

Lillie took the infant in her arms. The child's body was limp and burning up with fever.

"I must take him to the doctor," Lillie said as she took a blanket that hung on a nearby chair.

"Cries-At-Dawn go with you. You tell Doctor, make baby well," the mother said and motioned her young daughter to follow Lillie.

Lillie cradled the baby to her chest and raced through the village. She and Daniel shared a three-room pueblo with the *t'aikabede,* the Pueblo tribal leader, at the opposite end of the village.

Cries-At-Dawn was at Lillie's heels as she entered the pueblo and called for Daniel. She hurried to the room where Daniel was jumping, fully clothed from the makeshift bed where he'd slept.

"Bring him here," Daniel instructed.

Lillie came forward and handed the infant to Daniel, while Cries-At-Dawn looked on from the doorway. Daniel examined the infant briefly and shook his head. "I'm afraid he's gone."

The color drained from Lillie's face. She reached one hand out to the adobe wall to steady herself, while the other hand went to her mouth.

Daniel looked up to see Lillie's reaction. "Lillie, are you alright?" He wrapped the baby and handed him to Cries-At-Dawn. Daniel spoke in Tiwa to the girl. She cried softly as she held her brother close. He felt a certain responsibility to go with the child, but he knew Lillie needed him more.

Daniel returned to the room where Lillie still stood against the wall. Grief had muted her, and the passing of the child in her arms was too much to comprehend.

Daniel pulled blankets from his bed and put one around Lillie's shoulders and the other around his own. Lillie offered no resistance as he led her from the house and down a worn pathway through the village.

Lillie felt numb from the death of the baby. She scarcely felt the cold night air as the blanket slipped from her shoulders. Daniel paused long enough to pull the blanket back around Lillie before moving from the path and into the canopy veil of pine and juniper trees.

Emerging from the trees, Lillie caught the sound of a waterfall. It awakened her mind from it's sorrowful hauntings and brought her back to the present.

"Where are we?" Lillie questioned softly, afraid to break the melodic ripplings that engulfed everything around her.

"This is Sacred Lake. The Pueblo hold this place in the highest esteem. They believe their strength and wisdom comes from here." Daniel moved along a rocky pathway that led them ever upward toward the sound of the water.

"But I don't see any lake," Lillie said as she strained in all directions to catch a glimpse of the water.

"You will," Daniel said as he reached back and took Lillie's hand. "Come on."

Lillie caught her breath in wonder when they reached the trail's end. The waterfall plummeted in splendor before them, and the moonlight glimmered as a thousand twinkling lights wherever it touched the icy crystals of frozen water.

"I thought you'd like it," Daniel said with a smile.

"I've never known anything more beautiful," Lillie said in complete honesty.

The water made a lyrical roar as it fell some seventy feet into Sacred Lake. Against the moon, the falls looked like a glimmering black ribbon as it twisted and cascaded toward the bottom. Sacred Lake stood out amidst the pillars of pine and reminded Lillie of black onyx.

"I had to share this with you. The *t'aikabede* told me of this place. He said he came here often to offer up prayers to the Cloud People and the Corn Mother for a bountiful harvest. He said this place had special healing powers and his people come here to bring cornmeal offerings for the blessings they seek."

"You've certainly learned a great deal about this place," Lillie said absentmindedly.

"I think this entire experience has taught me things about myself. Things I'd let myself forget or ignore," Daniel remarked.

Lillie suddenly realized Daniel was still holding her hand. His hand felt warm and strong against hers, and she felt guilty for never wanting Daniel to let go.

"Tell me about your wife," Lillie said without understanding why.

Daniel smiled and the faraway look in his eyes left Lillie little doubt of the deep love he felt for his long-departed wife.

"Katie was a lot like you," Daniel began. "She was delicate and petite, yet she had strength in her I don't think she knew about. She was kind, loving, and gentle with nearly every living soul. However," Daniel paused and a grin spread across his face, "she had a temper and a stubborn streak that could match yours any day."

Lillie laughed out loud at this. "So you think I'm temperamental and stubborn. Is that it?"

"I don't just think it; I know it. Stubbornness has caused both of us a great deal of grief. Don't you agree?"

"I've always been used to having my own way," Lillie said thoughtfully. "However, my determination has often seen me through difficult times. Times I might not otherwise have found my way through."

"Like when you lost your husband?" Daniel dared the question.

"Yes," she whispered. "I felt Jason's death was my fault. I couldn't abide the fact that he'd given his life to God, when he'd promised to share it with me. I didn't understand a person could do both. I didn't see in time, to really set Jason's mind at ease."

"When Katie died, I blamed God, as well as myself. She put such trust in my abilities, and when she knew I couldn't save her, she died with words of love for me. The last thing she said was she loved me," Daniel uttered the words as a bittersweet eulogy.

Lillie said nothing for several moments. When she did speak, tears dampened her eyes. "I've never understood why God would allow things to happen as He did. It was easy to blame God for the pain because all my life

I'd heard how much I'd wronged Him and how far from the mark of perfection I was in His eyes." Lillie paused for a moment remembering the words Garrett had shared with her when she'd been recuperating from her fall. "I'm beginning to see maybe Garrett was right. Life happens. It isn't always what we hope it will be, and it isn't always what we need it to be. But God is always in it. Somehow I need to trust more and question less."

"That's very wise, Lillie. My brother David would say you've come to an understanding of faith." Daniel's words echoed in his own mind. David had tried so patiently and lovingly to bring Daniel back to God, and now a woman who barely had hope enough to consider God's promises was guiding him back to an understanding of where he'd gone wrong. "Faith is the hard part. You want to believe, you pray to believe, then when things fall down around you—sometimes you can't believe. That's where faith takes over and let's you believe even when the rest of the world says you're crazy."

"Do you think faith will get you through the bad times?" Lillie asked innocently.

Daniel gazed deeply into Lillie's huge, blue saucer eyes. He reached his hand up to touch her windblown cheek. "Yes, Lillie. I do believe that. I didn't realize until now that I still did. But faith is absolutely all I've had with me these years. Faith the pain would go away, faith my confidence would return, and even faith God would send me another companion."

Lillie thought of Jason, but the memory had dimmed with time. Was it wrong to imagine that perhaps Daniel's faith had brought him to her? Was it wrong to hope that God had planned their meeting all along?

"David tried to help me after Katie passed away," Daniel added. "But I blamed him because he'd led me to salvation and to trust in God. I blamed David for Katie's death because he prayed for her and told me God could make things right. When Katie died, David told me God must have other plans for my life and Katie had only been a short, special part of those plans. I hated him for saying that, Lillie. I hated my own brother for the comfort he tried to give me. I felt his God had taken my Katie and my unborn child; therefore I hated both God and David."

"I know," Lillie breathed. "I felt the same about Jason and his God. I couldn't bear being replaced in Jason's life by a faceless image I knew nothing about."

Daniel nodded his head in understanding. His hand continued to stroke Lillie's cheek as he contemplated her words.

Lillie found her free hand voluntarily going up to her face to hold Daniel's hand against her cheek. How she longed to be held. "Please," she whispered in the stillness that surrounded them, "please hold me."

Daniel didn't need to be asked more than once. He pulled Lillie against him and held her tightly. It wasn't Katie he thought of, and for the first time since his wife's death, it wasn't Katie he wanted to hold. It was Lillie.

Lillie clung to Daniel as though she were taking her very life's blood from the embrace. She felt a strengthening and a peace of mind she'd not known herself capable of.

An owl hooted from the tall pines overhead, breaking the spell of silence that shrouded them. Lillie pulled away slightly, just enough to see Daniel's face. His expression was one of peace and something else Lillie didn't understand.

"What is it?" she asked as she reached up to touch his hair.

"I just asked God to forgive me for being so stubborn," Daniel said and the joy in his voice was evident with each word. "Lillie, I'm free again. Free from the past and the pain. Free from blaming God and my brother. I know it sounds incredible, but faith is exactly what has been missing in my life. Until now I could never put a name to it."

"How do you know God will listen? How do you know you're forgiven?" Lillie questioned.

Daniel took Lillie's face in his hands, and his blanket dropped unheeded to the ground. "I know because He promised He would in the Bible. I chose to ignore Him and trust circumstances and emotions rather than His promises. But one thing I know now is God's peace is never conditional upon my surroundings or the events in my life. God's peace is always with me. Jesus promised it, and my faith in it will sustain me through any circumstance."

"How I wish I could be as certain as you are," Lillie replied as she contemplated Daniel's declaration.

"I'm going to pray God will send you that peace, Lillie. I'm going to pray, too, that you will be able to free yourself from the past and look to a new future."

Daniel's words seemed to hint of something more. Could he mean a future with him? Before Lillie could ask Daniel what he meant, he kissed her, silencing all her questions.

Chapter 12

With Christmas only a week away, Lillie and Daniel packed the last remnants of their supplies and said good-bye to the *t'aikabede*. The Pueblos were well on their way to recovering from the measles epidemic, although the fresh mounds of dirt revealed the losses the tribe had sustained.

The entire village turned out to wave good-bye to Doctor and Doctor Woman, as Lillie had come to be called. She enjoyed helping the Pueblo people and was giving serious consideration to becoming a nurse.

A half-day's ride east took Daniel and Lillie to the home of David and Jenny Monroe. Before Daniel and Lillie had ridden into view, David and Jenny stood at the fence post, shocked and surprised.

"You must be Lillie," Jenny said as she took Lillie in hand. "I feel I know you. Maggie has shared so many wonderful things about you." Lillie was dumbfounded by the bubbling and vivacious Jenny Monroe.

As Daniel watched Lillie disappear, he was greeted with a hearty bear hug from his younger brother.

"Dan," David said near to tears. "I thank God you've come home."

"Yes, indeed," Daniel said in agreement. "I've come home to God and to you. Can you forgive me for the past, little brother?"

"Don't you already know the answer to that?" David questioned with a laugh. "I've prayed long and hard for this moment. Jenny too. I'm sorry to say, she had more faith about it happening than I did."

"I didn't give you a reason to have much faith, but the issue of faith is what brought me to a spirit of willingness," Daniel said honestly as he put his arm around his brother.

They were two of a kind—tall, lean, and tan. Yet there were subtle differences in the two men. Daniel had always been the prankster of the two, and it showed in the laugh lines that edged his eyes. David had always been more serious. It was this seriousness and need to understand the deep secrets of God that led David into the ministry. Yet for all their differences, they were brothers.

Jenny swept Lillie into the house and had managed to put a cup of hot coffee in Lillie's hands before she knew what had happened.

"All I can say is it's wonderful to have you both here," David announced as he and Daniel joined them at the table. He motioned for Daniel to sit between him and Lillie and smiled broadly as Daniel accepted the offered chair. Jenny put out a pot of coffee and a large platter of cookies.

"I'd like to offer a word of thanks," David said as he took hold of Jenny's hand, "that is, if no one has any objections."

"Not as far as I'm concerned," Daniel replied as he took David's offered hand. Daniel extended his other hand to Lillie.

Lillie felt her heart quicken as she reached out for Daniel's hand. She hoped her eyes didn't betray her emotions.

Daniel might not have noticed Lillie's face, but Jenny did. She took Lillie's free hand and gave it a heartfelt squeeze. When Lillie cast a glance at Jenny, the loving warmth in Jenny's eyes was apparent.

"Let's pray," David said softly, and all four bowed their heads. "Father, today we offer thanksgiving for answered prayer. You told us that the Good Shepherd leaves the ninety-nine to search for the one lost sheep. Today you have sought and found the lost and brought him safely back into the fold. For this Lord, we praise and honor You; giving You the glory forever and ever. Amen."

Lillie looked up to find Jenny and David had tears in their eyes. Further inspection revealed Daniel too had dampness on his cheeks. Lillie felt as if she were an outsider.

For the rest of the day, Lillie considered the encounter at the Monroe kitchen table. She was confused and empty, wanting to understand what the others knew yet fearing it at the same time. She was sitting alone in the bedroom Jenny had given her when a knock sounded on the door.

"Lillie, it's me, Jenny. May I come in?"

"Of course, Jenny."

Jenny opened the door only a crack. "If this is a bad time I can come back later."

"No. Please stay," Lillie said as she got up and opened the door wide.

"Would you like to go for a walk? I know it's kind of cold outside, but I need to take care of some things in the barn," Jenny said with an openness Lillie couldn't ignore.

"I'd love to," Lillie admitted. "I must admit I was growing rather bored with myself. Too much time to think and all. Does that make any sense?"

"It makes perfect sense," Jenny said kindly. "Come on."

The crisp December wind stung Lillie's face and eyes. She pulled her cape closer and wished she'd thought to add one of the warmer Indian blankets.

"This is a much colder winter than most," Jenny said as she led Lillie away from the house. "I can't abide it when it turns so bitterly cold. Was it this cold in Kansas?"

"Colder. In Kansas the cold is so often accompanied by rain or very wet snow. You can never get warm or dry," Lillie said, and her mind flashed back to the cold dampness of her nightmare. Funny, she hadn't noticed when the dreams had stopped plaguing her.

The barn was adobe like the house. Inside, Lillie was amazed at how warm and comfortable it was. Jenny also kept a root cellar in the barn and stored many of her provisions. After filling her basket with jars of canned vegetables and meat, Jenny suggested they take a different way back to the house.

"I know I'm getting rather personal, but I couldn't help noticing the way you reacted when Dan touched you. I was hoping that maybe God threw you two together for companionship. Is that too painful to discuss with me?" Jenny asked honestly.

Lillie stared at the ground as she answered. "I don't know that painful is the right word. I find myself confused more than anything."

"Why not talk with a friend then?" Jenny suggested.

"I guess I would like to talk to someone," Lillie admitted. "I don't want to burden Maggie, not with her baby coming so soon. I wouldn't want to do anything to jeopardize that child arriving safely into the world."

"Maggie told me about your husband's and baby's deaths," Jenny said as she took hold of Lillie's arm. "You still pine for them, don't you?"

Lillie lifted her face to meet Jenny's compassionate eyes. "Yes, more than you'll ever know."

"I understand quite well, Lillie. I lost three babies myself."

Lillie gasped unable to hide her shock. "Three? How did you make it?"

"It wasn't easy, even with my confidence and faith in God. I was hurt and angry. When I lost my first baby, I stepped back and said, 'It's the will of God. I can accept this.' The second time, I was more devastated than the first. I was so certain nothing could go wrong because the worst had already happened. I was wrong. Things got worse. I wanted to rant and rave at God. I couldn't understand why He would let something like this happen. I wish I could say my faith got me through, but God's compassion took over and numbed my pain, giving me a chance to work through the grief."

"Then what happened?" Lillie questioned, wanting and needing to know how this young woman had sustained her soul through these crises.

"My last baby was due about this time two years ago. Things had gone fairly well, and I was starting to feel confident again. I went into labor, gladly suffering the pain in order to have the child I longed for. I gave birth to a son. He lived only a few hours. I don't know why he died. He looked healthy and strong, but I guess it wasn't meant to be. After that, there wasn't one shred of pride or arrogance left in me. I knew God was preparing my heart for something, but I couldn't figure out what I could possibly learn by losing my children."

Jenny's words echoed in Lillie's mind. Was God trying to prepare Lillie's heart for something as well?

"How could you still trust God after all that?" Lillie asked.

"How could I not? What other alternative did I have?" Jenny replied. "To turn away would mean disregarding all I knew to be true simply because I didn't get my own way. Committing to God means more than trusting Him for the good in life. It means trusting Him in the darkest valleys of life as well."

"I think I understand," Lillie answered. Garrett's words blended with Daniel's and Jenny's were helping her make more sense out of the things Jason had tried to share with her before he died.

"Just remember, Lillie. God doesn't leave you in the dark. He doesn't forsake you and allow you to wander blindly. If you seek Him, He'll lead you back to the light."

"It's so much to take in," Lillie said as she pulled her cloak tight. The wind buffeted both women until their cheeks were rosy and tender.

Jenny laughed heartily as they made their way back to the house. "That's true, Lillie. But it has been my experience to find God faithful at every turn. I don't have my own children with me, but look at the family I have by way of the Pueblos. There are eight children living with us at this time. Sometimes there are more, sometimes less, but always there is someone in need. God sent these children to me because He knew we needed each other. I think that's why you and Daniel found each other as well."

"I never thought of it that way. I saw Daniel as a nuisance at first. He ridiculed my overeating and made fun of my weight. Then he seemed to pop up wherever I went and that truly annoyed me," Lillie stated firmly, then added, "at first."

"Why do you suppose it annoyed you so much?"

Lillie laughed. "I've often asked myself the same question. I'm still not sure I know, but he doesn't bother me near as much as he used to."

Jenny smiled. "I've noticed."

Lillie looked shocked. "I didn't mean anything by it. I mean my husband hasn't even been gone a year. I don't have a right to have feelings for anyone else."

"And why not?" Jenny's tone sounded indignant. "Because society says so, or because your heart says so?"

"I suppose because of society. Saying that bothers me more than you'll ever know. I feel guilty because I seldom think of Jason at all." Lillie's words were full of sadness. "I try to remember things, but the memories are clouded and vague. Then I feel guilty for not being able to remember."

"Lillie you mustn't feel guilty. You aren't under any obligation to your husband. That ended at the grave. Forgetting helps to buffer the loss and allows you to heal. You won't ever forget him totally. Just like Daniel will always remember Katie."

"Do you think it's alright then?" Lillie dared to ask the question that had haunted her heart for weeks. "Do you think it's alright to care about Daniel?"

The two women stopped at the kitchen door, noticing through the window Daniel and David sat talking at the kitchen table. "I think it's more than alright, Lillie. I think it's what God has intended all along. I think it's His way of healing you both."

~

Lillie thought about Jenny's words long after she'd dressed for bed that night. One thing seemed clear: happiness had little to do with material things or a full social calendar.

Lillie had lived quite simply in the Indian village, and mission life could certainly not compare to that which she'd known back in Topeka. Yet, Lillie was certain she'd never felt more at peace. If only she could work through her feelings about God. She wanted to believe the things everyone had told her. She knew Daniel was much happier since he'd made his peace with God.

Snuggling deeper into the layers of blankets, Lillie thought of Jenny Monroe's contented look as she had shared with Lillie about her life at the mission. Jenny mothered the Indian children as if they were her own, and Lillie knew the children loved Jenny in return. If God had given Jenny peace of mind after losing three babies, surely He could give Lillie peace of mind after losing just one. Lillie comforted herself with the thought as she fell into a much needed sleep.

Jenny was already busy with the children when Lillie came down for breakfast. Jenny was combing hair and dressing little bodies, all the while laughing and singing with the children. "You go ahead and get some breakfast. We have our routine, and we'll be just fine," Jenny called out to Lillie.

Lillie suppressed a giggle at the sight of the wiggling toddlers who seemed to mess up their hair as soon as Jenny had combed it. She was still laughing to herself as she entered the kitchen to find Daniel eating breakfast.

"You certainly look happy," Daniel said as he got up to offer Lillie a seat.

"I actually feel happy," Lillie said as she took the offered chair.

Daniel silently appraised the trim, blond woman. It was useless to deny the feelings he had for her. Just the scent of her perfume took his mind back to the first time he'd met her. She had been so angry and vulnerable.

Daniel took his seat at the table and wondered silently if Lillie could ever care for him as much as he cared for her.

"Whatever are you smiling about?" Lillie asked with a grin. The morning happiness at the mission was contagious.

Daniel stared at her with a quizzical look. Should he say something? He toyed with the idea for only a moment before deciding against saying anything that might scare Lillie off. Instead, he shrugged his shoulders and passed Lillie a platter full of biscuits.

In the other room, the musical laughter of children rang throughout the house. "They're certainly a lively bunch," Lillie commented as she helped herself to some bacon. "Jenny's a lucky woman."

"Why do you say that?" Daniel asked.

Lillie put her fork down and stared thoughtfully for a moment. "I guess because she has a mate and children and a home." Lillie's honesty surprised them both.

"Is that what you want out of life, Lillie?"

Lillie met Daniel's stare. She lost herself for a moment in his eyes. Could she tell him how she felt? Should she?

Lillie trembled from the intensity of the moment. Her heartbeat quickened as she confronted the truth. "I never used to think it would be enough. I wanted the money, the parties, and all the beautiful things that went with that lifestyle." She barely whispered the words loud enough to be heard.

"And now?" Daniel questioned, the urgency in his voice clear. He reached out and placed his hand on top of Lillie's. He could feel her tremble beneath his touch.

Lillie swallowed hard and looked down at the large, well-manicured hand that covered hers. The hand of a doctor, the hand of the most intriguing man she'd ever known. "It would be enough," Lillie answered and quickly removed her hand from beneath Daniel's.

Daniel started to say something, but Jenny came bursting into the room. "I hope you found enough to eat," Jenny said as she scrutinized the food on the table.

"We did, and it was wonderful," Lillie said as she concentrated on her plate to avoid Daniel's eyes.

"I'm glad you liked it. Daniel tells me you two will have to be leaving this morning. Are you sure you can't stay longer?" Jenny asked as she cleared the empty dishes from the table.

Lillie hadn't realized Daniel planned for them to leave so soon, but there was nothing to be gained by arguing. "I'd love to stay, but Maggie only has a month or so until the baby's due. I need to be there for her," Lillie replied as she finished her breakfast.

"Of course," Jenny said with a sad smile Lillie understood full well. As happy as they both were for Maggie, there was the bittersweet reminder of the little ones they had lost. "I wish I could come and help, but as you know I have my hands full. Why, just trying to school the older children is a full-time job. But Maggie's in good hands. She has you and our good Dr. Dan. She'll be just fine."

Daniel remained silent. The reminder of Maggie's upcoming delivery was an unwelcome thought. He'd managed to make things right between himself and God, and David as well, but he still doubted his ability to care properly for Maggie and her unborn child.

"Did you hear me, Daniel?" Jenny said as she gave his shoulder a light shake.

"I'm sorry," Daniel said as he looked into Jenny's warm eyes.

"I told you not to make a stranger of yourself again. Bandelero isn't all that far from here, and rumor has it you're building an office and infirmary. So remember how to get here and bring Lillie back as soon as Maggie can spare her."

"I'll do that," Daniel promised. "But now, if Lillie is finished with her breakfast, we'll need to be getting back to the ranch."

Half an hour later, Lillie was bidding Jenny good-bye. "Don't forget what I told you, Lillie. God puts folks together for a reason."

"I'll remember," Lillie said with a smile and cast a glance toward Daniel who waited with the reins to her horse.

"I always know I'm in trouble when women share secrets and smiles," Daniel said as Lillie came toward him to accept his help into the saddle.

The cold leather creaked as Lillie settled into the seat. She gave Jenny a look of amusement, and Jenny laughed as David came to stand beside her.

"If I didn't know better," David said from the ground, "I'd say you ladies were up to something."

Daniel stepped into the stirrup and threw his leg over, landing square in the seat of his saddle. "And just what makes you think you know better, little brother? I'm convinced these ladies are up to something, but as of yet I'm not convinced it's to my detriment; so for the time being I'm going to wait them out."

Chapter 13

H urry, Lillie. Garrett and Daniel will be back with the tree any minute," Maggie called from the front sitting room. She put a hand to the small of her back and tried to rub away the soreness. She knew the action would achieve very little relief, but it had become such a habit she continued to do it.

Lillie finally came down the hall carrying a small wooden crate. "Is this the right box?"

Maggie glanced up and smiled. "That's it. Don't you remember? These are the Christmas tree ornaments from my grandmother's house. You shipped them to me not long after she died."

Lillie placed the box on the lamp table and removed the lid. "Yes, I remember now," she said as she held up one of the delicate glass ornaments.

Maggie came and stood beside her friend. "I'm so glad you're here, Lillie. I've wanted to tell you so, but I didn't want to upset you. I want you to be comfortable and happy," Maggie said, placing her hand on Lillie's arm. "Are you alright? What with the baby coming and it being just last year. . ." Maggie's voice fell silent.

Lillie put the ornament back in the box and turned to hug Maggie. "I'm fine. I don't know if it's God's grace like Jenny said, or just time and healing, but I've grown quite comfortable here. I just hope I haven't worn out my welcome. At least Daniel's been spending most of his time in Bandelero getting the hospital set up."

"Shame on you, Lillie, for even thinking such a thing. This is your home for as long as you want it to be. I speak for myself as well as for Garrett. He told me just the other day his mind was put at ease knowing there'd be another woman in the house. Ever since Maria left for Santa Fe to care for her sick mother, Garrett's been a nervous wreck. He couldn't wait for you and Daniel to get back."

The sound of the wagon signaled the return of the men. Maggie moved toward the door, but Lillie put a hand on her shoulder. "Stay put. There is nothing you can do to help carry that tree in. I'll help them, and you just boss the rest of us around."

Maggie frowned. "I'm not an invalid," she called out to Lillie's retreating form. "I don't see any reason to sit here like some kind of ornament!" She might not be able to help with the tree, but there was certainly no reason she couldn't make them a batch of cocoa.

Maggie made her way to the kitchen and began gathering the things she'd need. The milk was easy enough, as were the sugar and vanilla. It was the cocoa that eluded Maggie.

"Now where in the world did I put it?" Maggie muttered as she tore through the cupboards. After searching through all the lower shelves, Maggie had no alternative but to climb up on a chair to search the top shelf.

This ought to get me into a great deal of trouble if Garrett catches me, Maggie thought. Nonetheless, she hiked up her skirts and struggled to balance her weight enough to get up on the chair.

In the front room, Garrett and Daniel eased the freshly cut pine tree into a metal bucket of sand and dirt. Lillie had helped guide the base of the trunk into the bucket and turned to ask Maggie's opinion of whether the tree was straight or not when she noticed Maggie wasn't even in the room.

"Where's Maggie?" Lillie asked Garrett.

"I don't know. I just know she's not manhandling this tree like she'd like to, so I'm hoping she's staying out of trouble." The words were barely out of Garrett's mouth when a loud crash from the kitchen caused him to drop the tree and go in search of it's source.

Garrett first noticed the jar of peaches that had shattered in streaks of orange across the floor. Then he noticed his wife standing on the chair, looking surprised. "Magdelena Lucas! What in the world do you think you're doing?" Garrett questioned as he lifted Maggie into his arms and off the chair.

"I was going to make us some cocoa. I wanted to add something nice to our party. Now put me down, I have a mess to clean up," Maggie insisted, but Garrett held her all the more tightly.

"I'll clean it up myself, and you're going to sit down and behave yourself," Garrett said as he turned to take Maggie back to the sitting room. Lillie and Daniel stood in the doorway shaking their heads.

"Lillie, make Garrett put me down. Come help me," Maggie called out.

"No chance of that," Lillie replied as Garrett disappeared from the hallway. "I seem to recall asking you for help once upon a time when I was being held captive," Lillie's teasing voice made Daniel laugh.

"I don't think you minded the captivity as much as you claimed," he said as Lillie went to retrieve the mop.

"Oh? You think you know everything don't you?" Lillie said trying to sound quite solemn.

"I think I know you pretty well," Daniel retorted.

She paused by the stove for a moment and the merriment of the moment got the best of her. She picked up the same cast iron skillet she'd once chased after Daniel with. Turning to meet his amused stare, Lillie smiled.

"There seems to be some unsettled business between us, I recall."

Daniel stepped forward, undaunted by the skillet. "And what would that be?" he questioned as he closed the distance between them. Reaching out, Daniel easily pinned Lillie's arms to her side.

Lillie's upturned face feigned a pout. Her eyes were still laughing, however, and Daniel enjoyed the familiarity between them. Freeing one of Lillie's arms, Daniel reached down and took the skillet from her hand. Placing it on the stove, Daniel turned back to Lillie and pulled her into his arms.

They stood face to face for a moment, and Lillie trembled in anticipation that Daniel would kiss her. Ever so gently, his lips met hers, leaving Lillie breathless from the touch. Jason never entered her thoughts.

The pleasure of the moment was almost too much to deal with. Lillie thought her heart would burst from the overwhelming pounding. When Daniel dared the liberty of kissing her twice, Lillie pushed weakly at his chest.

"Stop, I can't breathe," she whispered.

"Maybe you need a doctor," he murmured.

"I can't clean up that mess if you don't let me go," Lillie insisted. Her cheeks grew flushed from the intensity of Daniel's nearness.

"No, I don't suppose you can," he said, refusing to give up his hold.

"What is it exactly that you want?" Lillie questioned teasingly.

"That's simple," Daniel said as he lowered his lips. "I want you."

Lillie felt her mind race at Daniel's reply. He wanted her, but what did that mean? She needed to know, but Daniel didn't seem to be of a mind to continue their conversation. Finally, Lillie gathered her strength and broke free of the embrace.

Her eyes betrayed her willingness, making it clear to Daniel he could easily possess her. But something in her resolve to put distance between them caused Daniel to refrain from pulling her back against him.

"I'll help you clean up," Daniel offered.

"No, I think I'd like a few minutes alone to gather my wits," Lillie said as she reached down to retrieve the pieces of broken glass. "Why don't you go see to Maggie?"

"Alright," Daniel said with a shrug of his shoulders. "But you'd best treat me well, or you won't be getting any Christmas present from me."

Lillie looked up in shock, but Daniel had already left the room. *Christmas present?* she thought. *Why didn't I think to get him a Christmas present?*

The thought of Daniel giving her a gift when she had nothing to offer in return grieved Lillie. After wiping away the last traces of peach juice, she joined the others to help with the Christmas tree, her mind still contemplating a gift for Daniel.

Maggie was sitting quite properly on the high-backed, red velvet sofa, while Garrett and Daniel took instructions from her as to where she wanted things placed on the tree. Lillie laughed and called her friend Queen Victoria.

The mood remained lighthearted and jovial while Daniel, Garrett, and Lillie finished dressing the tree. When the last candle had been attached to the pine boughs, Garrett took on the task of lighting each one.

"It's beautiful," Maggie declared.

"What did you expect?" Garrett asked as he came to take the seat beside Maggie. "I happen to be an expert at decorating Christmas trees."

"Is there anything you aren't an expert at?" Maggie questioned sardonically.

Garrett considered the question for a moment, then said with a laugh, "I can't think of a thing at the moment."

"Then you and Daniel should make a fine pair," Lillie quipped. "He thinks he knows it all too."

Daniel leaned back against the whitewashed adobe wall and crossed his arms against his chest. He'd long ago traded in his city-styled suits for a more casual look, and Lillie was quite taken with the lean, attractive Dr. Monroe.

"This is a much happier Christmas than last year," Maggie said as she handed Garrett the family Bible. "I wasn't sure I could ever enjoy Christmas quite as much as I used to, but you've all made this year special. I don't think it would have been near as much fun without you."

"We have a great deal to be thankful for," Garrett replied as he took the Bible. "Good friends, a new doctor for the territory, a baby on the way, and prosperity. We have much, indeed, to thank God for."

Lillie grew sober in the wake of Maggie's and Garrett's reflection. A shadow from the past crossed her brow, and turning from the others, Lillie pretended to busy herself with putting away the crates that had housed the tree ornaments.

"Don't worry about those, Lillie. Garrett is going to read the Christmas story," Maggie said and beckoned Lillie with her hand. "Come sit over here by the fire."

Lillie did as Maggie bade, but she couldn't get the spirit of the season the others had.

" 'And it came to pass in those days, that there went out a decree from Caesar Augustus, that all the world should be taxed.' " Garrett continued reading from the second chapter of Luke, but Lillie had difficulty focusing on the words. Why couldn't she have the same peace as the others?

" ' And she brought forth her firstborn son, and wrapped him in swaddling clothes, and laid him in a manager; because there was no room for them in the inn.' "

Lillie shifted uncomfortably. She glanced up to find Daniel watching her. His expression was compassionate, and his eyes displayed a gentleness that touched her soul.

" 'For unto you is born this day in the city of David a Saviour, which is Christ the Lord.' "

The words pounded in Lillie's head. A Savior? Her Savior? Could it be possible Jesus Christ came to earth as a baby in order to save her soul from eternal damnation?

" ' And suddenly there was with the angel a multitude of the heavenly host praising God, and saying, Glory to God in the highest, and on earth peace, good will toward men.' " Garrett's deep voice read on, but Lillie could no longer stand her own discomfort. Without a word, she got up and left the house.

The cold night air cut into Lillie's face. She was glad for the warmth of her long-sleeved wool dress. Looking up into the black, moonless night, Lillie could count hundreds of stars. She thought of the star that led the wise men to find the baby that would save them from their sins.

"How could it be You would love me enough to send Your only child to give me eternal life?" Lillie asked toward the sky, not knowing how else to speak to God.

The wind echoed in the pines, but no other answer came to Lillie's questioning heart. "Why can't I remember his face?" Lillie questioned. "Jason's only been dead a year, but when I close my eyes it isn't his face I see. It isn't his arms I feel around me. Why is that, God?" Lillie asked earnestly. "And while I'm asking questions, what am I suppose to do about all this?"

The question surprised Lillie, but she suddenly remembered Garrett's words about salvation. He'd told her she needed to repent of her sins. Well, she certainly felt the need to do that. The hatred and anger she'd carried around hadn't offered her any comfort.

"I may be doing this all wrong, God, but the truth is I'm sorry for the way I've been acting," Lillie began as she hugged her arms to her body. "Garrett told me You'd forgive me if I asked You to and if I was genuinely sorry, so if that's true, then I guess You just forgave me."

Lillie paused as she tried to remember what else Garrett and the others had shared with her. "I guess the rest is a matter of faith. Maggie said You know everything, so You must know how hard trusting is for me. But the way I look at it," Lillie added, "I don't have any reason not to believe. If seeing is believing, then watching Jenny and David, as well as Maggie, Garrett, and Daniel, has surely convinced me there is something worthwhile in putting my trust in You. I want eternal life, God. I want to put the past behind me and know I have a future home in heaven. So if it's alright with You," Lillie said with tears in her eyes, "I'd like for You to consider me Your child."

The wind picked up until it made a low moaning sound as it filtered through the buildings of the ranch. Lillie lifted her face to the sky and, though the cold was numbing her skin, her heart began to thaw.

"I hope I did the right thing," Lillie murmured.

She jumped at the warmth of the Indian blanket Daniel wrapped around her, pulling her inside its folds with her back against his chest. "You did the right thing," he whispered against her hair.

For several moments, neither Lillie nor Daniel moved. Lillie felt at peace for the first time in her life. Even as a little girl, she'd only felt comfortable when she knew she could control the outcome of her circumstances. This was different, however, and Lillie readily handed control of her life to the Savior Who'd come as a baby on that Christmas morn so long ago.

Lillie also relished the strong arms that held her so tightly. She leaned back against the well-muscled chest and sighed. Daniel had helped her in so many ways. He'd taken her mind off her selfish pain and put it into a positive direction. Daniel had been a source of healing for Lillie, and she felt the need to thank God for sending him into her life.

"Thank you, God," Lillie whispered.

Chapter 14

January arrived in unexpected fierceness. Piñon Canyon and the surrounding area usually enjoyed moderate temperatures even in the winter, but not that year. The first blizzard arrived shortly after Christmas, and two more followed close on its heels.

When David managed to get word to Garrett, it was to tell him the mission had been inundated with new arrivals. Many of the Pueblo people were seeking shelter from the fierce winter weather, and the mission was unable to handle the numbers without additional supplies.

"I hate to leave the ranch with Maggie so near to having the baby, but David said several of the Indian children may have pneumonia," Daniel said as he and Garrett readied a wagon full of supplies.

"The baby isn't due for three weeks by your calculations. I don't think God brought us this far, just to let us down now," Garrett said as he tightened the tarp rope. "I think it's important we help David and Jenny."

"Aren't you at all worried about leaving Maggie?" Daniel questioned.

Garrett pulled up the collar of his fleece-lined overcoat. "I've put Maggie in God's hands, Daniel. If I take her back now, it'd be like saying God can't handle the job. He's proven His ability enough for me to trust His promises," Garrett said with confidence. "Besides, Lillie's here and she won't let Maggie get away with anything." Both of the men laughed and went in search of a cup of hot coffee before embarking on the long drive to the mission.

Mack appeared at the kitchen door just as Garrett and Daniel were going inside.

"We're all ready, Garrett," he said with a glance to the western ridge and added, "Looks like a powerful snow to the west. Are you sure you want to try this today?"

"I don't think we have much choice. We're going to tell the ladies good-bye and grab a cup of coffee, and we'll be ready to go," Garrett said as he followed Daniel into the house. "You want to join us?"

"Naw, I've had a gut full of coffee. I'll go wait with the wagons," Mack said and moved out across the yard.

The warmth of the adobe house invited the men to linger, but duty urged them out into the cold.

"I wish you didn't have to go," Maggie finally broke down and said.

Garrett gently brushed his finger along her jawline, then let his hand cup her chin. "I'll be back before you know it, so you just sit here and mind my child."

Maggie moved uncomfortably and allowed Garrett to help her to her feet. "I promise I'll be good," she said with a smile.

"No more cocoa?" Garrett grinned and kissed her on the forehead.

"No more cocoa," Maggie said as she relished the warmth of Garrett's embrace.

Daniel was already at the back door, giving Lillie last minute instructions. "If anything happens, anything at all, you send someone for me right away."

"Don't worry. I remember everything you told me, and I won't waste any time if Maggie needs you," Lillie said as she stood gently fingering the oval locket Daniel had given her for Christmas.

Daniel smiled as he did any time he noticed her wearing it. Lillie looked every bit the prim and proper lady with her starched, high-necked shirtwaist and lavender plaid skirt. The necklace fell in stately grace to hang just below her collar.

Lillie had gifted Daniel with a picture of herself and felt it paled in comparison to his gift. Daniel, however, thought nothing of the kind and kept the picture in his pocket.

"Please be careful," Lillie suddenly whispered.

"Don't worry. We'll be back before you know it," Daniel said.

Lillie had hoped Daniel would kiss her good-bye, but Garrett appeared in the doorway and they were on their way, leaving Lillie to watch as they rode out of sight.

By noon, two inches of new snow covered the ground, with more coming down in huge downy flakes. Lillie occupied herself with baking and cleaning, stopping from time to time to visit with Maggie, who'd spent most of the day in the library.

"How do you feel?" Lillie asked as she looked up from the potato she was peeling to find Maggie in the kitchen doorway.

"I wish I could say wonderful, but that would be a lie," Maggie answered as she poured herself a glass of water and took a seat across from Lillie at the table.

"It won't be much longer," Lillie offered in encouragement. "The time will pass before you know it, then you'll be so happy enjoying that new baby you will have forgotten all about the trouble of getting it here."

"I know you're right, but it feels more like a herd inside me than a baby," Maggie said with a sigh and got to her feet. "I think I'll get this baby a piece of milk toast."

"Maybe you should graze on some corn," Lillie joked and added. "Either way, you stay here, and I'll get some bread from the pantry." Lillie quickly crossed the room to the open pantry door.

Maggie laughed, but her amusement was short-lived. Doubling over, Maggie cried out in pain. "Lillie, I think it's the baby!"

Lillie came rushing back, the color drained from her face as she sized up the situation. Maggie tried to support herself by holding onto the table.

"Maybe you got up too fast," Lillie suggested.

Maggie straightened up and tried to smile. "I don't think so, Lillie."

"I suppose we'll know soon enough," Lillie replied in a worried tone. Daniel and Garrett wouldn't be home for hours, and a gnawing fear was beginning to fill Lillie's mind.

Maggie noticed the deep frown etched on the face of her best friend. "Don't worry, Lillie. Daniel said it would take quite awhile for the baby to be born. Send a rider after the men, and we'll be fine."

Lillie's expression softened a bit. "I'm sorry. I didn't mean to worry. Here I am a nervous wreck when you're the one having the baby." Lillie tried to laugh, but the sound remained muffled in her throat.

"I suppose I should go to bed," Maggie said as she moved gingerly across the room.

Lillie was at her side in a heartbeat. "You'd better lean on me in case another pain comes." Maggie nodded and allowed Lillie to help her to her room.

"Where are your nightgowns?" Lillie questioned as she helped Maggie to sit on the edge of her bed.

"In the bottom drawer," Maggie said and pointed toward the large mahogany dresser.

"I'll get one for you, and while you undress, I'll send for the men," Lillie said as she brought Maggie the nightgown. "Will you be alright until I get back?"

"I'll be fine," Maggie said, trying to sound convincing.

Lillie managed to locate a man who assured her he'd send someone after Daniel and Garrett. On her way back to the house, Lillie grabbed an armful of wood for the fireplace in Maggie's room. There was so much to do, and the thought that Daniel might not make it back in time haunted Lillie throughout her duties.

Despite her fears, Lillie began to gather the things she was certain they would need for the birth of Maggie's baby.

"Lillie! Come quickly!" Maggie called from her bed.

Lillie made her way to the bedroom only to find Maggie sitting on the edge of her bed, drenching wet.

"My water broke," Maggie said, fear thick in her voice. "Lillie, the baby is coming much quicker than Daniel said it would!"

Lillie tried to remain calm. She knew it was important to put Maggie's fears at rest. "Can you make it to your dressing room if I help you?" Lillie questioned. "I'll change the bedding and bring you a dry nightgown."

"I don't know," Maggie grimaced as she tried to stand.

Maggie got to her feet and put her arm around Lillie's neck. Lillie put her arm around Maggie's waist and helped her to a chair.

"Wait here, and I'll bring you something dry," Lillie said, going back to the dresser to retrieve the promised nightgown. "Are you alright, Maggie?" she called from the bedroom.

"Yes," Maggie answered weakly. Despair filled her heart Where were Daniel and Garrett? She wanted so badly for them to be at her side that when Lillie came to her with the gown, she made a request.

"Please, Lillie. Pray with me," Maggie begged. "I'm afraid."

Lillie hugged her friend closely. Praying aloud was something she felt quite uncertain about, but Lillie reasoned it would put her own mind at ease as well.

"Of course I will, Maggie. Just remember, I'm not very good at it," Lillie said as she took hold of Maggie's hand. "Dear God, we need help. I'm asking for a miracle that would bring Daniel and Garrett back to the ranch. I'm asking, too, that until they return You'd show me what to do and how to help Maggie. Amen."

Maggie smiled. It was the first time she'd heard Lillie pray. "You did a great job, Lillie. Thank you."

Lillie patted Maggie's hand. "Let me help you change. Then we need to get you back into bed." Maggie nodded and allowed Lillie to slip the wet gown over her head and replace it with a dry one.

With Maggie safely back in bed, Lillie continued her search for the things she thought Daniel might need for the baby's birth. The time away from Maggie gave Lillie a few moments of painful reflection. She remembered the first time she'd felt her own baby move within her. Without thinking, Lillie's hand went to her stomach. How she longed for the baby that had once been there.

Lillie felt the wetness on her cheek before she realized she was crying. It was difficult to face the past with any kind of assurance the future would hold something better. She knew her life was now different. No, she thought, not just different. Her life had truly improved since she'd accepted Christ as her Savior.

But did that mean life would be less painful? It didn't mean that for Daniel, Lillie thought as she wiped away a tear.

She gathered up several baby blankets that Maggie had lovingly embroidered for her coming child. Lillie felt alone. She gently traced the stitching that outlined a fat puppy and sobbed quietly.

"God, Maggie told me my baby is in heaven with You. I'm glad he's not alone like me," Lillie said as her tears fell onto the blanket. "But God, if You really care about me, if You really do forgive me for the way I acted toward You, please, please take away this pain." Suddenly, Lillie felt compelled to find a Bible.

Not wanting to upset Maggie with her tears, Lillie went to the library. The family Bible rested on a hand-tatted doily atop a small oak table. She went to the table and reached out, almost fearful of touching the worn pages.

She opened the Bible and gasped as the pages fell to the same place in Luke that had upset her so deeply on the train. Lillie forced herself to look past the ominous warning to the verses below that. When she caught sight of the word *lilies,* she read the words aloud.

" 'Consider the lilies how they grow: they toil not, they spin not; and yet I say unto you, that Solomon in all his glory was not arrayed like one of these.' " Lillie was not sure of the meaning of the words in Luke twelve, so she read on. " ' If then God so clothe the grass, which is to day in the field, and to morrow is cast into the oven; how much more will He clothe you, O ye of little faith?' "

Hadn't Daniel said faith was the key? Lillie considered the words and the burden of her heart grew lighter. She had to have the faith that God would do the things He had promised. If He was willing to provide for the simple needs of clothing and food, surely God would provide for the deep needs of her pain-filled heart.

Lillie's eyes fell to the thirty-fourth verse and she smiled. " ' For where your treasure is, there will your heart be also.' " Her treasure was in heaven not only because her departed loved ones were there, but even more so because her God reigned there. Her God! It felt good to claim God as her own.

Making her way back to Maggie, Lillie had new confidence. God was with her, and nothing else mattered.

～

Garrett stared in amazement at the parade of people before him. The wagons had been barely three hours away from the ranch when David Monroe had appeared with at least twenty Pueblo men and women behind him.

"What are you doing here?" Garrett questioned as David approached his wagon. Daniel had come from one of the other wagons to echo Garrett's question.

"Yeah, what are you doing out here in the snow with all these people?" Daniel asked as he gave his brother a hearty embrace.

"I woke up at dawn and the Lord put it upon my heart that I needed to gather as many people as possible and meet you on the trail. I don't really know why, but the feeling was so strong I couldn't ignore it," David replied. "We even brought the horses to pack the supplies back to the mission."

"There's really no need for that," Garrett argued. "After all, the wagons are already packed, and we're well on our way."

"No," David insisted. "It may seem illogical to everyone else, but I know God intends for us to pack these supplies back to the mission by ourselves. Don't ask me why, but I am confident of God's instruction. He always has a purpose for everything He does.

"What about the children you were worried might have pneumonia?" Daniel questioned.

"Fit as fiddles," David said with a shrug. "God works wonders and apparently this time He intends for you to be back at the ranch."

"Well, at least take the wagons. I can't see repacking everything onto the horses. You can return the wagons when the snow clears," Garrett suggested.

"That sounds like a wise idea. Why don't we set up a shelter and have some lunch. After that we'd both be wise to be on our way," David said and then turned to instruct several men to erect the tent he'd brought with them.

Half an hour later, the tent was up and the ground inside was swept free of snow. Garrett and Daniel sat with David and the others to enjoy hot coffee and fried ham and tortillas.

"This coffee sure hits the spot," Daniel said as he poured himself another cup. Several Pueblo women entered the tent with still more food, and David motioned them to bring it to where he, Garrett, and Daniel sat.

The sound of a lone rider drew everyone's attention to the opening in the tent. The snow-covered rider rushed into the tent and glanced around, looking for Daniel and Garrett.

Garrett got to his feet, knowing his ranch hand wouldn't have come so far without a reason. "Joe? Is that you?" he called to the rider.

"It sure is, Boss. I never expected to find you so soon. Figured I'd have to ride all the way to the mission. You and Doc need to get back to the ranch. Miss Maggie's gonna have her baby."

Daniel tensed and David put a hand on his shoulder. Garrett cast a fearful look at David, then Daniel. "But you said the baby wasn't due for weeks. Does this mean something's wrong?"

Daniel wished he could ease Garrett's fear, but reminders of his inadequacies and failings were creating grave concerns in his mind.

"Of course nothing is wrong," David said encouragingly and motioned to one of the Pueblo men. "The doctor is needed at the ranch house. Will you please saddle two horses? You may use my saddle for one of the pack horses, as I'll be driving one of the wagons back to the mission."

"You can use my tack, but my horse is pretty tuckered," Joe offered. "I'll stay on and help get the wagons to the mission, if that's okay with you, Garrett."

"I'd appreciate that, Joe. Come on, Daniel, we'd better hurry."

Daniel's face betrayed his concern. Could he be of value to Maggie and Garrett, or would this be like the other times? Would he have to face his best friend with the death of his wife and child, or would God bless his efforts by allowing both Maggie and the baby to be healthy and safe?

David sensed his brother's misgivings. "Daniel, you're going to do just fine. I think it'd be nice if we share a prayer before you go."

"I think that makes a heap more sense than worrying," Garrett agreed and pulled off his black Stetson. Daniel nodded and bowed his head, knowing his strength came from God. The offered prayer was like crutches to a lame man, bolstering him in spirit and confidence.

When David finished, Garrett lifted his face in a broad grin. Gone were the worry and concern. "God knew where we'd need to be in order to help Maggie and Lillie," Garrett said to Daniel. "He sent David on his way long before we even knew we needed him." At this David nodded, suddenly fitting all the pieces together. Garrett continued, "Since God planned this thing out so far in advance, I'd be an ungrateful fool to worry. Come on, Daniel. I want to be there when my child is born."

Chapter 15

With every contraction, it became more and more apparent Maggie's labor was progressing faster than Lillie had anticipated. With every pain, Lillie sought ways to ease Maggie's suffering. Ever in the back of Lillie's mind was the possibility something could be wrong. She prayed fervently that Daniel would arrive and relieve her of the responsibility that demanded life and death decisions.

Lillie wiped Maggie's sweat-soaked brow. "Would you like a sip of water?"

Maggie shook her head. Her hair was spread out across the pillow, hopelessly tangled from her thrashing. She prayed that the ordeal would soon be over, but she feared it might never end. Exhaustion was quickly overtaking her.

"Lillie," Maggie barely breathed the word. "Has there been any word of Garrett and Daniel?"

"Not yet, but don't worry. I'm sure they'll be here soon. I've prayed about the matter and I have great faith God will help us," Lillie replied.

Maggie had to smile in spite of the fact another contraction was overtaking her. "Oh, Lillie, this time is different," Maggie moaned. "I think the baby is coming now!"

Lillie bit her lip and pulled back the covers. She couldn't suppress a gasp. Maggie began to cry out and Lillie did the only thing she could; she prepared to deliver her best friend's baby.

While Lillie prepared blankets for the baby's birth, she prayed repeatedly. "Please God, send Daniel, I need him." She hadn't realized she was praying out loud until a hand fell upon her shoulder.

"I'm here, Lillie." Daniel hadn't even pulled off his snow-covered coat.

"Thank God!" Lillie said, and tears formed in her eyes. Her hands were trembling as she helped Daniel pull off his coat.

"Don't cry, Lillie. Everything is going to be alright," Daniel whispered.

Garrett was already by Maggie's side, soothing her with his words and smoothing back the tangled hair that fell across her face. He tried to remain calm, but the sight of his wife in such agony prompted him to question Daniel.

"Can't we do anything to help her?"

Daniel smiled and finished washing his hands. Lillie handed him a towel and waited for further instructions.

"Maggie's about to have all the help she needs. As soon as this child is born, the pain will go away. As far as I can tell," Daniel said as he examined Maggie, "that's going to be in just a few more minutes."

Lillie worked well with Daniel. Her fears were laid aside as he performed with confident ease. At two minutes before six that evening, Maggie gave birth to her baby.

"It's a girl!" Daniel said as he handed the crying infant to Lillie. "Clean her up, Lillie. Do just like I told you, clear her mouth and get her warmed up."

Lillie's tears fell on the tiny, wrinkled baby. Taking a warm, wet cloth, Lillie gently cleaned the baby's face, laughing at the baby's impressive amount of coppery hair that looked exactly like Maggie's. As Lillie dressed the baby, brilliant blue eyes cried up at her in protest.

"Hush, little one. I'm your Aunt Lillie, and I'm going to get you ready to meet your momma and papa."

"What will you call her?" Daniel asked the proud parents.

"I thought it might be nice if we named her after our mothers," Garrett replied. "Daughtry for Maggie's mother and Ann for mine."

"Daughtry Ann Lucas," Maggie tried the words. "I like it very much."

Lillie brought the baby to Maggie and Garrett and placed her in Maggie's arms. "Daughtry Ann, meet your momma and papa," Lillie said with joy in her voice. Her eyes still betrayed her tears, but they were tears of happiness.

"Oh, Garrett, she's beautiful!" Maggie exclaimed.

"She ought to be," Garrett said and planted a kiss on Maggie's forehead. "She looks just like her mother."

Maggie's face was angelic in her joy. She lifted her face to meet Garrett's eyes and the love she felt was evident. Daughtry began to fuss as if protesting the absence of her mother's attention.

"I image this little one is hungry," Daniel said as he helped Lillie clean the room. "I think maybe Lillie and I should leave you three alone. Maggie, if you have any trouble at all, send Garrett for me."

"I'm sure we'll be fine," Maggie said as she ran her finger along the velvety cheek of her new daughter.

" 'I will praise thee; for I am fearfully and wonderfully made: marvelous are Thy works; and that my soul knoweth right well,' " Garrett quoted as he touched the fluffy silk of Daughtry's hair.

"That's beautiful, Garrett," Lillie said as she started to follow Daniel from the room. "Where is that from?"

"Psalm 139, verse fourteen. The whole chapter is beautiful, Lillie. I think you'd like it."

"Thank you, Garrett. I'll look into it later." With that, Lillie walked down the long west wing of the ranch house. She felt an urgency in her heart to find Daniel.

She nearly ran the rest of the way to the library, then to the sitting room before finally locating him. When she burst through the doorway, Lillie halted, abruptly taking hold of a nearby chair to steady herself.

Daniel looked up from where he stood staring out the window at the snowy night. He smiled a reassuring smile and it was all Lillie needed. She threw herself across the room and into Daniel's waiting arms.

Tears fell in heated intensity against Daniel's shirt. "I didn't think you'd get here in time. I was so scared," Lillie sobbed. "I kept thinking, what if something is wrong, or what if I don't do something right. Oh, Daniel, I prayed and prayed you'd get here in time."

"Shh." Daniel held Lillie tightly. "Hush. I'm here now."

"But, Daniel, it could have been so awful," Lillie said as she pulled away from his embrace.

"But it wasn't," Daniel said as he reached out and cupped her tear-streaked face. "God heard our prayers, Lillie. He heard them and answered them. Maggie is fine and the baby is fine. You did a good job, Lillie. You'd make a first-rate nurse."

Lillie reached up to wipe away her tears, but Daniel pushed her hand aside. He leaned down and gently began to kiss the tears that dampened her cheeks until his lips found his way to her mouth.

When he pulled his face away from hers, Lillie could see he was looking at her with new intensity. Could it be more than mere concern, she wondered? Could it be love? Did she want it to be love?

"Lillie, you amaze me," Daniel whispered.

"Why is that?" Lillie questioned.

"You're like a fine china doll. So petite and delicate. You looked so fragile the first time I met you; I was certain you would break under the misery that followed you."

"I would have never imagined you cared. After all, I was quite unsightly," Lillie remembered.

"You have never been unsightly, Lillie. If you had been three times that size, you would have still been a beautiful woman," Daniel said honestly. "The weight never worried me as much as the depression."

Lillie pulled away from Daniel and walked across the room. She felt the need to forget the past and distance herself from it, yet there was a need to speak of it.

"I wanted to die," Lillie said. "I thought about throwing myself off of the train."

"I know," Daniel said as he came to stand a few feet away.

Lillie whirled around. "You knew? How?" she questioned.

Daniel remembered the scene as if it had been the day before. "I was on the other side of the door. I saw you standing there, and I knew you were contemplating your death."

Lillie let the knowledge soak in. "And what would you have done if I'd, if I'd. . . ?" Lillie couldn't seem to form the words.

"I'd have been out the door in a flash and taken you in hand," Daniel whispered. "I would never have allowed you to die. Why do you think I goaded you so much?"

"I presumed because I disgusted you," Lillie answered honestly.

"Never!" Daniel exclaimed. "Nothing could be farther from the truth. I had to give you something to fight for. You'd given up on life, so I had to find the one thing that would affect you strongly enough to fight back."

"My vanity?" Lillie smiled. "How obviously vain I must have appeared."

Daniel grinned. "You were quite the grand lady."

"Well, it worked. I don't think I've ever been angrier in my life," Lillie admitted.

"I know," Daniel said with some regret. "I never wanted you to hate me."

"That's good," Lillie murmured, "because I never did. I hated myself and I hated God, or at least I thought I did, but I've never hated you."

"I'm glad you accepted God's place in your life," Daniel said as he watched Lillie intently. "Then again, I'm glad God helped me to find my way back. I think God's been good to both of us."

"That's true," Lillie agreed. She clasped her hands tightly. "I never thought I'd come to understand, but today especially, I've never felt closer to God. I feel absolutely glorious," Lillie exclaimed while glancing toward the darkened window. With a smile she turned to Daniel, "I want to feel the snow on my face," she laughed as she went to the door.

The moon tried desperately to peek out from behind the veil of gray snow clouds. When the moonlight reflected on the snow-covered ground, it sparkled and shimmered like cut crystal. Tiny white flakes were still falling and Lillie raised her arms up in the air as if to receive each one individually.

"You'll catch your death out here," Daniel said as he leaned against the door frame.

"I don't care," Lillie said as she pulled the pins from her hair. "It's glorious and I just want to enjoy the wonder of it all." She whirled 'round and 'round in a circle until Daniel's hands fell upon her waist and he began to waltz with her in the snow.

When they finally came to a stop, Daniel was the first to speak. "God was so good to send you to me, Lillie."

Lillie swallowed hard. "Do you really believe that, Daniel?"

"More than ever," Daniel said in a hushed whisper. "God sent you to me, Lillie, and I don't intend to let you get away."

Lillie's eyes grew wide. "And what does that mean?"

Daniel roared a heartfelt laugh. "It means everything, Lillie. Absolutely everything."

Lillie had hoped for a clearer answer, maybe even some declaration of love. Before she could question Daniel further, however, she began to shiver.

"Come on, we're going in," Daniel said as he pulled Lillie back toward the door.

"But I don't want to," Lillie argued. "I want to remember this night forever. The baby and Maggie; Garrett's proud face; and. . ." Lillie paused, unable to continue.

"And?" Daniel questioned, his laughing eyes still sparkling from the pleasure of having had Lillie in his arms.

Lillie hesitated. Dare she share her heart? What did she know of her heart? There was a time when she thought she understood perfectly well. A time when things seemed much clearer and more easily planned out. But that was then. She cast a sideways glance at Daniel's face and lowered her eyes quickly.

"And?" Daniel pushed her for an answer as he placed his hand on her shoulder.

"And you," Lillie whispered, but it wasn't enough for Daniel. He needed to know more before he could be sure of his own feelings. He reached out and took hold of Lillie's arm, forcing her to turn and face him.

"What about me?"

Lillie felt her breath quicken. "I'm not sure what you mean."

A smile played on Daniel's lips. "I think you know exactly what I mean, Lillie. I want you to admit what you're feeling for me."

Lillie pulled loose and backed up against the door. "What I'm feeling for you?" she whispered. "Isn't that rather presumptuous?"

"I don't think so," Daniel said and leaned forward to kiss Lillie.

"Oh no you don't," Lillie said as she easily ducked his embrace and reached for the door handle.

"Alright for now, Lillie," Daniel laughed. "But you can't ignore it forever, and sooner or later you'll have to be honest with yourself—if not with me."

Lillie opened the door and looked over her shoulder. "Perhaps," she said with a hint of smile, "but not tonight."

Chapter 16

In the days that followed Daughtry's birth, Lillie tended both Maggie and the baby with loving care. It was more than her desire to attend to their needs; the care she provided seemed to satisfy something in Lillie's heart.

Lillie took her instructions daily from Daniel, who himself was quite wrapped up in the finishing of his office and small hospital in Bandelero. She listened intently as he told her what things she should watch for, paid careful attention as he showed her how to do certain things, and in general enjoyed the companionship of working with him on a daily basis.

In the back of Lillie's mind was the nagging reminder that in a week, maybe less, Daniel would move his things to Bandelero. She didn't like to think of spending her days without his company, but she wasn't certain what she should do about it.

"You're awfully quiet today," Maggie said from where she sat propped up in bed.

Lillie, who was tidying the room, stopped what she was doing and sighed. "I guess I have a great deal on my mind. I'd hoped to keep from burdening you with it."

"But we used to tell each other everything," Maggie said as she patted the side of the bed. "Why not sit down and talk to me?"

"I'd like to, but. . . ," Lillie hesitated. "Maggie things are different now. We aren't the children we were when you left Topeka. A lifetime and then some has passed between us, and I'm not sure we'll ever have back what we had as young girls."

Maggie smiled. "I know we've changed, but I think for the most part it has been for the better. We've endured a lot, that much is true, but I don't think for one minute we've lost the ability to remain close. Granted, Garrett is my usual confidant in most things. But there will always be things that are just between you and me. Things Garrett would never care to intrude upon."

"I feel like an intruder at times," Lillie said as she came to sit beside her friend. "You have Garrett and now Daughtry, and I wouldn't wish it any other way. God knows I thought my sun rose and set by Jason and the baby we planned." Lillie's voice sounded void of emotion, but inside she was still tender from the loss. Lillie reached out and took hold of Maggie's hand. "I would never want anything but your happiness. You must know that."

"I do," Maggie said as she placed her free hand on top of Lillie's. "You need to realize though, you are an important part of that happiness. I don't think I could have made it through these past months without you. Especially with the amount of time Garrett has spent away from the house helping see to Daniel's building project."

At the reminder of Daniel's inevitable departure, Lillie frowned. Maggie patted her hand. "You don't have to let him get away."

"I know," Lillie said in a resigned tone. How could she explain to Maggie that it seemed impossible to sort out her feelings for the elusive Dr. Monroe?

Daniel had told her the night Daughtry was born that sooner or later she'd have to come to terms with how she felt about him. He seemed so sure of himself, yet he wouldn't reveal more than a hint of what he was feeling for her.

A warning flashed across Lillie's mind: Don't get too close. Don't care too much. But it was becoming more certain in Lillie's heart that the warning had come too late.

At the sound of Daughtry's fussing, Lillie went to the cradle and brought the tiny girl to her mother. Maggie's eager arms reached out for her daughter. What a blessing this baby had been! Even Lillie was able to take joy in her arrival.

"I'd better get back to work," Lillie said as she ran her fingers over Daughtry's fluffy hair. She wondered if she would ever have a child to call her own.

Then the day that Lillie had been dreading arrived. Daniel announced at breakfast he was taking the last of his things and would be permanently in residence in his office in Bandelero. Without thinking, Lillie offered to help him pack up the remaining medical supplies.

Daniel readily accepted her offer and managed a bit of good-natured teasing as he and Lillie made their way to his examining room. "Seems like just yesterday I was stitching up your legs."

"In a rather deceitful manner, I might add," Lillie replied. She'd tried to forget what had passed between them that day, but she knew things had changed between her and Daniel after that episode.

"It wasn't intended as deceit," Daniel said with a flashing smile. "Cunning, artful, and skillful—but not deceitful. I fell back on an old method I used with frightened children."

"Oh? Didn't you think I knew well enough to let you take care of the problem?" Lillie questioned, knowing she'd had no intention of allowing

Daniel to stitch her wounds.

"Who's kidding whom? You never would have remained still if I hadn't put you to sleep. It was all a matter of needed control," Daniel said good-naturedly. He sensed the teasing in Lillie's voice.

"Yes. You needed to be in control, and I wouldn't allow you."

"You still won't," Daniel said in absolute seriousness. Lillie couldn't bear the intensity of his stare.

"I've truly enjoyed helping you," Lillie said rather shyly as she went back to work. "I think I might go back East and become a nurse."

"Why go away? Everything you need to know, you can learn from me," Daniel replied. Lillie wondered if there was hidden meaning in his words.

"But I need formal training to be a nurse," Lillie protested.

"Out here, no one is going to care. The people are going to be grateful they have someone to tend to their ailments. That's not to say I wouldn't be the strictest of taskmasters. I happen to believe in thorough training for anyone in the medical field. But," Daniel said as he paused from packing his instruments, "I have confidence you would learn quickly. I know how devoted you can be."

Lillie considered his words as she worked. She couldn't shake the fear that gripped her heart. What if Daniel left and she never saw him again? She knew that wasn't what she wanted, and yet what could she do or say to keep him close by?

Garrett came in to help take the crates to the wagon, and Lillie could only stand aside and watch as the two men worked together. She moved around the room that had been Daniel's office for nearly as long as she'd been at the ranch. Every time she'd been in this room, it had been Daniel Monroe, the doctor, who had occupied her attention. Outside of this room, however, it had been Daniel Monroe, the man, who had filled her every thought.

Lillie stood alone, staring at the barren room when Garrett came for the last crate. He took note of the sullen look on Lillie's face and smiled.

"If I didn't know better, I'd think you'd just lost your best friend," Garrett said as he picked up the crate. "But I know Maggie is doing just fine and is sitting in our bedroom nursing Daughtry at this very minute."

Lillie tried to smile, but the look was short-lived. She turned and acted as though she were double checking the drawers of the desk Daniel had used.

"Why don't you tell him how you feel?" Garrett finally questioned. He put the crate back on the floor and pushed his Stetson back on his head. "I mean, that is the reason you're moping around here, isn't it?"

Lillie's head snapped up. Garrett's face wasn't mocking or sarcastic, rather it was compassionate, almost pained. Garrett really cared about her in a brotherly fashion, and Lillie was quite fond of his boyish charm and kindness.

"I don't know," Lillie lied and then thought better of it. "No, that's not exactly true," she added.

"I know it isn't," Garrett said softly. "So why not face up to how you feel."

"Because I'm not sure it's real," Lillie blurted out. She turned away from Garrett and bit her lip. Her hands were twisting the material of her starched, white apron when Garrett turned her to face him.

"Lillie," he said taking her hands in his. "I'm not usually one to give advice and I certainly hate to presume upon feelings, but what have you got to lose? I know you care about Daniel. Why not tell him?"

"I guess because I'm so unsure of myself."

"Then why not pray about it?" Garrett asked.

"I'm pretty new at the Christian life, Garrett. I don't always do things the way you do," Lillie admitted.

"Prayer is the first thing we ought to think to do. I must say, though, I'm not always as good at it as I'd like to be. All I can say is this: God listens and He answers."

"What if the answer is no?" Lillie questioned.

"Well Lillie, that's a chance we all take, but isn't it better that a thing be what the Lord desires?"

Lillie nodded her head. "I suppose you're right. I'm so afraid, though," she said in a voice so childlike Garrett could almost forget she was nearly twenty years old.

" 'There is no fear in love; but perfect love casteth out fear,' " Garrett quoted from 1 John 4.

"But what if it isn't perfect love?" Lillie asked.

Garrett smiled and squeezed Lillie's hands. "Perfect love is God's love, Lillie. That verse tells us we don't need to fear anything as long as we're a part of God's love. God wants only the very best for His children and therefore we don't need to fear the results. If God's answer is no, it's going to be that way for a very good reason. He's a loving Father, Lillie. Just as I would keep Daughtry from going near a hot stove so she wouldn't get burned, God often tells us no for our protection. It wouldn't be any different if the answer was yes. Trust God, Lillie. Give it over to Him in prayer and trust Him for the answer."

Lillie looked into Garrett's sympathetic eyes and found a good friend in this man her best friend had married. "I'll pray about it, Garrett. But what if God doesn't answer in time?"

"He always answers in time, Lillie. You need to have faith He will. I would suggest in the meantime you go tell Daniel good-bye. Maybe it won't be as bad as you think." Lillie nodded, and after Garrett picked up the crate again, she followed him out to the wagon.

"Well, Daniel," Garrett said as he hoisted the crate into the back of the wagon, "this is the last of it." His breath made a steamy cloud in the cold, January air.

Lillie hung back as Daniel embraced Garrett and thanked him for his help. "I could never have gotten this far without you. You've been a blessing and a good friend, Garrett. I'm looking forward to our partnership."

Garrett hugged his friend and patted him heartily on the back. "We're the fortunate ones, Dan." Garrett took a step back and with the slightest nod of his head, indicated Lillie's presence. "I think I'll get back in the house. It's a mite cold out here for me. Besides, I have a family to tend to."

Daniel nodded and asked, "You'll be by in a day or two, won't you?"

Garrett smiled. "You can rest assured I will be by as often as I can spare the time. I like to know where my money is going. Besides, if I don't spread the good word about you, nobody will want you tending them."

Daniel laughed. "You just do that. Oh, and Garrett," Daniel paused, "tell my favorite new mother to behave herself and take good care of that baby. She'll be in good hands with you and Lillie."

Lillie grimaced at the reference. She didn't want Daniel thinking of her as Maggie's nursemaid. She stepped forward, grateful she'd thought to put on her woolen coat before following Garrett outside.

"I'll tell, Maggie," Garrett promised and winked at Lillie as he passed her and went into the house.

Daniel leaned back against the wagon and crossed his arms against the warmth of his heavy overcoat. He silently studied Lillie, wanting desperately to tell her what he was feeling, but wondering if it would make a difference.

Lillie moved closer until she stood within a few feet of Daniel. "I wanted to ask you about your offer."

Daniel raised a questioning eyebrow. "What exactly did you have in mind?"

"Would you really consider training me as a nurse?"

"I told you I would," Daniel replied casually.

Lillie lowered her face. He wasn't making this easy at all. "What would I have to do?" Lillie asked, then quickly added, "to become a nurse."

"I suppose first of all you'd have to spend most of your time with me."

"So, I'd need to move to Bandelero?" Lillie questioned.

"It would help," Daniel replied. He watched Lillie for some indication of what she thought of the idea, but with her face lowered, it was impossible to read her expression.

"But Bandelero is barely a town. I mean, there's no hotel or boardinghouse.

It would be difficult to make a move without a place to stay." Lillie lifted her face slowly, almost fearfully. She was afraid to face Daniel's eyes. He seemed so capable of reading her that it made Lillie feel nervous and guarded.

Daniel wanted to reach out and take Lillie in his arms, but his mind kept his heart at bay. There was no sense in trying to force Lillie to make a decision based on feelings. Feelings were great for the moment, but lifetimes couldn't be successfully built on feelings.

"There's plenty of room at my place," Daniel finally said. "What with the extra hospital rooms we have for patients and all. You'd be welcome to stay with me." His look was so intense Lillie wanted to look away. She couldn't.

"I don't think that'd be appropriate even by western standards," Lillie replied softly.

"I suppose under the circumstances it might be unsuitable, but there is a way to rectify that," Daniel said as he shifted his weight and knocked snow from one boot against the other.

Lillie's sapphire eyes grew wide. "What exactly did you have in mind?" Lillie questioned with trembling lips.

"You could marry me, Lillie," Daniel said in a low whisper.

Lillie felt her legs go weak. She wished desperately she could steady herself, but there was nothing to take hold of. She looked past Daniel to the snow-covered mountains, trying to calm her nerves. Had he really proposed?

Daniel stepped forward and held Lillie's arms. "Look at me, Lillie," he demanded and Lillie quickly obeyed. "You must know how I feel. I've cared for you for a very long time," he said as he reached up to smooth back a strand of honey-blond hair the wind had blown loose. "I can honestly say I've cared about you from the first moment I laid eyes on you."

"Cared about me?" Lillie questioned. Was that the same as love, she wondered.

"I've never really been good with words, Lillie. I know what I'm feeling though," Daniel said in a determined manner. "I also know what I want out of life, and I know I want you to be my wife."

Lillie frowned. He still hadn't said he loved her. Truthfully, Daniel had never once mentioned love. Maybe he couldn't love her. Maybe he'd given all his love to Katie. Lillie tried to reason away her doubts. She'd lost Jason, but she was able to love again or at least she thought she was.

Daniel noted the frown on Lillie's face. His heart tightened in fear. Had he misunderstood her feelings for him? Had he rushed her too soon with thoughts of marriage? He'd been a widower for six years, but for Lillie it'd barely been a year since she'd lost her husband. Maybe she wasn't ready for this. Maybe she'd never be ready to love him the way he loved her.

Daniel dropped his hands and shoved them into his pockets. "I'm sorry, Lillie. I didn't mean to upset you. I just thought maybe you might want the same thing I did. Look, I need to get on over to Bandelero. You think about what I said. Who knows? Maybe you'll change your mind." Daniel stepped up into the wagon. He wanted to kiss her good-bye, but he forced himself to pick up the wagon reins. "You know where to find me."

Lillie looked up in sheer panic. Her brow was furrowed with lines that betrayed her concern, but she couldn't make herself say the words that would stop Daniel from leaving.

The wind picked up, stinging Lillie's cheeks as it hit the tears that fell upon her face.

"Good-bye, Lillie," Daniel said, then with a flick of the reins, headed the wagon down the drive.

Lillie wanted to run after him, to call out to him to stop, but she remained fixed to the spot where she stood. She felt a tight pain in her throat as a quiet sob escaped her mouth. He was leaving her!

As the wagon moved out of sight, Lillie ran through the snow to the corral fence. She hiked up her skirt and climbed up on the first post to better see the departing wagon. For the first time in her life, a prayer came automatically to her lips: "Dear God, please tell me what to do!"

Chapter 17

The rest of the day, Lillie moved as if in a trance. She couldn't make herself focus on the tasks at hand and managed to burn the bread she'd counted on having with supper. Hastily, she put another batch to rise, but she still couldn't take her mind off Daniel and the proposal of marriage he'd offered.

Why wasn't this simple? Even if Daniel didn't love her, he was good to her and he clearly enjoyed being with her. Lillie tried to rationalize away the need for a committed love.

It would be enough to be with someone who acted loving, wouldn't it? Lillie let her mind wander to all the times she'd spent alone with Daniel. She enjoyed talking with him; that was no secret. She thrilled to his knowledge, savored his teaching of medical treatments, and worked well with him at any task. Hadn't she proven to herself they were compatible?

When Lillie heard Garrett leave the house, she crept down the west corridor to see if Maggie was awake.

Maggie was propped up, reading a book when Lillie peeked her head inside the room. Maggie smiled and motioned Lillie in.

"I've been hoping you'd come by," Maggie said with genuine affection. "Come tell me everything that happened between you and Daniel."

Lillie's face betrayed the turmoil in her heart. It had never been possible to hide her concerns from Maggie. "I'm not sure I know where to start."

"Did you tell Daniel how you felt about him?" Maggie questioned as she put the book aside.

"I tried, but no," Lillie said as she wrung her hands. "I couldn't get the words out."

"So, what did you say?" Maggie asked softly as she reached out to still Lillie's hands.

"I told him I wanted to become a nurse. Of course, he already knew that from our earlier conversation. He offered to teach me rather than have me go away to school."

"That seems promising, Lillie. You'd have to spend a great deal of time with him in order to be trained," Maggie said excitedly. "That couldn't hurt your chances of opening Daniel's eyes to how important you are to him."

231

"Do you really think I'm important to him?" Lillie asked innocently. "I know I could be useful, but I want more than that."

"I think you already mean more than that to Daniel Monroe," Maggie said with a smile. "I've seen the way he looks at you, Lillie. I'm not blind to the ways of love."

"Why do you say love? Do you think Daniel loves me?" There, Lillie thought to herself, the question was finally out in the open.

"Do you want him to love you?"

Lillie got up and began to pace. "I've asked myself the same question. I think back to Jason and the baby and I wonder. Do I have it in me to love again? Do I want someone to love me? The only thing I know for sure is I'm not sure of anything."

Maggie laughed. "Sounds to me like the rantings of a woman in love. There's nothing like falling in love to cloud a person's judgment."

Lillie stopped and looked at Maggie. "He asked me to marry him, Maggie."

Maggie's face lit up. Her expression was pure joy. "That's wonderful! So what is this all about? He wants to marry you! How can you stand there so calmly asking me if I think he loves you. Isn't it obvious?"

"I don't know. He never said the words. He told me he cared, but he never said, 'Lillie, I love you.' "

"Words are easy to say. What do his actions tell you?" Maggie questioned seriously.

Lillie thought for a moment before answering. "The second time I laid eyes on Daniel Monroe, he was holding me in his arms while I cried. There I was, sprawled face down in a plowed Kansas field, crying my eyes out and hating everything and everyone around me. He found me, held me, and stayed with me until I was spent. Then he helped me back to the train and stayed with me for awhile. I wanted to hate him for not being Jason, but I couldn't." Lillie became quiet as she thought of other times when Daniel's actions had spoken quite loudly.

Maggie waited silently, feeling Lillie needed to say more. She could see that Lillie was wrestling with herself, so Maggie offered an unspoken prayer for her friend.

"So many times, Daniel has helped me. Even when he was making comments about my weight, it was for my own good. He told me that much."

"What did he say about that?" Maggie asked softly.

"He told me he knew I'd given up on life, that I wouldn't fight for it. He felt he had to do something to motivate me to live," Lillie answered honestly.

Suddenly, her thoughts took her in a different direction and she sat back down beside Maggie. "It's only been a year, Maggie. Just a short, lonely year since Jason died. Am I being disloyal to contemplate remarrying?"

"Only you can answer that. I will say this much. I knew Jason Philips very well. You know he was named for my father, don't you?" Lillie nodded and Maggie continued, "Our families were close when my mother was still alive. Of course, I stayed a good friend to Jason long after she was gone, and I feel I knew him fairly well."

"I know you did," Lillie agreed. "Jason always said you were his best friend after me."

"Remember when you were jealous of the times he would come and talk to me about you?" Maggie reminded Lillie.

Lillie smiled. "Sometimes I'd just as soon forget my acts of irrational stupidity."

Maggie laughed. "I'm setting the stage so to speak. Jason wouldn't want you to mourn him. He's in heaven and perfectly content. Life goes on for you, Lillie, and only you can tell what your heart is comfortable with. If you aren't past mourning Jason, then maybe it is best to forget about Daniel for the time being." Lillie nodded somberly. "However," Maggie continued, "I don't think that is the problem."

"You don't?" Lillie questioned, surprised by Maggie's words.

"No, I don't," Maggie stated firmly. "I think you're afraid to love Daniel, and I think you're afraid to accept his love."

Lillie nodded slowly. "I think you're right, but what should I do about it?"

Maggie took hold of Lillie's hand, "God will show you what to do. Just trust Him and have faith He'll guide you."

Lillie nodded "I know you're right. Thank you, Maggie. I'll always love you. You allowed me to come here to heal my heartache, and through your family, I've learned about God's love for me. You've given me a precious gift, Maggie."

"No, Lillie," Maggie said as she hugged Lillie. "It was God's precious gift." Lillie nodded.

"Do you need anything before I go to my room?"

"Just for you to be happy and whole," Maggie answered.

Lillie spent most of the evening alone in prayer. She wanted to open her mind and heart to whatever direction God had for her.

Lillie contemplated her life since Daniel had become a part of it. She remembered with a smile the day she'd arrived at Piñon Canyon only to find Daniel already in residence. She was quite surprised to realize a part of her had been happy, actually relieved to find him there. At least she had known something about him, unlike Mack and the other ranch hands. There was some consolation in familiarity.

Her mind drifted over the last few months. So much had happened. Through all of it, Lillie realized she'd come to depend on Daniel. It wasn't just the physical attraction or her fascination with medicine. It was Lillie's desire to be Daniel's companion.

Lillie drifted into sleep remembering the little things about Daniel that haunted her every waking thought. The way his eyes were lined from laughter, the way his hands were well-manicured and skilled, and the way he looked at her when he was about to kiss her. These were the images that danced in Lillie's head while she dreamed of dancing in the snow with a laughing, life-loving man. A man she was destined to marry.

Lillie woke with a start. It was the middle of the night and she felt ravenous. Realizing she'd missed supper, Lillie crept quietly to the kitchen. She was suddenly engulfed in memories of Daniel and the night she'd chased him with the frying pan. She couldn't suppress a giggle as she fingered the skillet.

She found some bread. Probably the same she'd left to rise and forgotten all about. Some homemaker she was turning out to be! Thankful someone had thought to bake it, Lillie took a slice, as well as the lamp that sat on the stove, and sat down at the kitchen table.

Lillie ate in the shadowy veil of the dimly lit kitchen. She thought of conversations with Garrett, Maggie, and Daniel. Long after she'd finished her bread, Lillie was still focused on one intimate moment with Daniel. It was after they'd waltzed in the snow; the night Daughtry had been born.

"Sooner or later," Daniel had said, "you'll have to be honest with yourself—if not with me."

Lillie tightly hugged her arms to her body. The vacancy that flooded her heart was filled with only one thought. Daniel!

"I love you, Daniel Monroe," Lillie whispered. The revelation made her smile. She did love Daniel, and something inside her heart told her he must love her too.

The howl of wind outside caused the shutters to knock against the adobe house. The sound had always caused Lillie to shiver, but not that night. She was flooded with the warmth of contentment and happiness. She knew her heart belonged to someone else.

"Jason," Lillie whispered into the darkness, "I loved you once, and you'll always have a part of my heart no one else could ever have. But now," Lillie said with a deep restoring breath, "now, I'm ready to let you go." Lillie knew her heart and soul were once again mended, healed from the pain and suffering of the past.

With a new vitality, she made her way to her bed and went to sleep. In the morning she intended to find Daniel, but for the time being, it was enough to know he was nearby.

The following morning was to be Maggie's first full day out of bed. When Lillie appeared bright and early, dressed in her warmest riding clothes, Maggie laughed.

"Let me guess where you're headed," Maggie said as Lillie took a seat at the same table where she'd bid Jason goodbye the night before; the same table where she'd come to terms with her love for Daniel.

"I'm going to marry Daniel," Lillie said with more joy on her face than Maggie had seen since her arrival to Piñon Canyon.

Maggie smoothed the apron that covered her brown woolen dress. "I knew you'd come to your senses," she teased. "What took you so long?"

"I guess some of us are more stubborn by nature than others," Lillie said with a laugh.

Just then Garrett walked into the room and noticed Maggie. For a moment his face grew sober, then a smile began to form at the corners of his mouth. "Mrs. Lucas, you are without a doubt more beautiful with each passing day. I am a fortunate man. Now come here and kiss me like a proper wife."

Maggie put her hands on her hips and winked at Lillie. "You were mentioning stubborn natures," she said as she turned her gaze to Garrett. "I happen to be twice as stubborn as you, Lillie. If Mr. Lucas wants his kiss, he'll have to come get it."

Garrett raised a single eyebrow before turning on his heel to leave the room.

"Oh, alright," Maggie said as she rushed toward his retreating back, "I could never beat out Garrett when it came to tenacious behavior."

Lillie laughed as Garrett turned on his heel and pulled Maggie into his arms. "It's good to see someone can control her," Lillie said as she got to her feet. "I doubt Dr. Monroe will have as easy a time with me as you've had with Maggie, however."

Garrett rolled his eyes. "God help Daniel!" was all he would say before firmly kissing Maggie on the lips.

"Isn't it wonderful, Garrett?" Maggie questioned as she pulled away from his embrace. "Lillie has decided to accept Daniel's marriage proposal."

"I will upon one condition," Lillie said as she pulled on her warm riding gloves.

"And what condition is that?" Garrett questioned.

"I'll only marry Daniel if he truly loves me. I don't want him only to care about me or want me for a nurse. I need him to love me, and I need to hear him tell me," Lillie said somberly.

"I don't think that will be a problem," Garrett said with a smile. "Are you riding into Bandelero right now?"

"Yes," Lillie replied. "I've packed a couple of bags I can take with me on the horse, that is if you'll lend me one."

"I'll do you one better than that," Garrett said as he released Maggie. "If Maggie doesn't mind, I'll ride with you to Bandelero. Just to make sure you get there safely."

"Of course I don't mind," Maggie said wistfully. "I just wish I could go too."

"I appreciate the offer, Garrett, but I wish you'd do something else for me, or at least send someone else to do it."

"Name it, Lillie."

"I want someone to ride over and get David. I intend to marry Daniel today, as long as you're right and he does love me," Lillie replied.

Garrett and Maggie both laughed. "After watching those two love-struck ninnies running around this ranch, trying to avoid each other," Maggie stated, "I don't know how anyone could doubt that they love each other."

"I tell you what, Lillie," Garrett said as he went to the stove and poured himself a cup of coffee. "As soon as I down this, I'll ride with you. The turn to go to the mission is about a mile from Bandelero. You can go on into town and make sure you still want to marry that man, and I'll go after David and Jenny. If I know anything about Jenny Monroe, she certainly won't want to miss her brother-in-law's wedding."

"It's a deal," Lillie answered, the excitement in her voice contagious.

Maggie embraced her friend warmly, unashamed of the tears that fell. "I'm so happy for you, Lillie. I know God has special plans for you and Daniel."

Chapter 18

Daniel moved through the stark cleanliness of his new office. The desk he'd ordered, as well as the medical examination table and cabinets for supplies, had arrived days before, and thanks to the extra help Garrett had recruited, they'd been properly installed. Now the room looked the part of being a doctor's office.

For months, supplies had arrived on a regular basis, and Daniel took mental inventory as he checked the drawers and cabinets to insure they held the proper contents.

He moved to the large back room. Here, four small beds lined the walls on either side of a large aisle. It wasn't all that fancy, Daniel knew, but it would serve its intended purpose should someone from town or the neighboring area need an appendix removed or some other surgery.

For the first time since before Maggie's baby had been born, Daniel faced his medical future with confidence and a note of excitement. It was his personal life that was defeating him. He knew all the offices in the world were meaningless without Lillie.

Making his way to the adjoining four rooms that formed his new house, Daniel wanted to cringe at the emptiness. The rooms were full with enough furniture and the regular household necessities; Garrett and Maggie had seen to this. But it wasn't a home, and Daniel's heart ached for it to be one.

He walked through the large sitting room. This was the room that adjoined his office. It was designed to make it convenient to hear anyone who might come knocking on his office door during his off hours. Daniel had to smile at that thought. A country doctor usually didn't have too many hours he could call his own. Since word had spread of his arrival, he'd already tended to several minor and one or two not-so-minor ailments.

Nonetheless, Daniel tried to concentrate on the fact God wasn't done with him. Daniel prayed God wasn't done with Lillie, either.

Daniel stirred up the dying fire in the sitting room fireplace until the roaring blaze took the damp chill from the room. He admired the pillows Maggie had embroidered for his sofa and smiled at the curtains he knew Maggie and Lillie had worked on together.

Moving from the room, Daniel passed into the smaller sitting room. This one was designed for privacy. A large wood stove had been used in place of another fireplace. Daniel hadn't bothered to spend much time in this more intimate room. He'd agreed to have it made a part of the house when he'd thought Lillie might consent to marry him. He tried to remind himself there was still hope, but his heart wasn't convinced.

Off from the sitting room was a small hallway in which Daniel could either turn left and go into the kitchen and dining area, or right and go into the bedroom. He'd spent the night in the huge, four-poster bed Garrett had given him. Of course, many of the things in the house were gifts from someone. Most of them seemed to come through Garrett, however, and Daniel couldn't have been more grateful for God sending him such a friend and business partner.

If God would only send him a more intimate partner. If only God would answer his prayer and send him Lillie!

Refusing to be defeated by the situation, Daniel started praying: "God, You know how much I need her. You know how much I love her. I felt certain You were directing me to her and You wanted me to marry her. If that's the truth, if that's really what I understood, then Lord, please open Lillie's heart to love me too."

The knock at the office door sounded through the empty house and startled Daniel from his prayer. "No doubt a sore throat or fever to ease my miseries," Daniel said and laughed to himself.

He finished tucking in the tail of his white cambric shirt as he made his way back through the house and opened the office door. He froze in place as his eyes met the sapphire blue of Lillie's quizzical stare.

She stood before him, silent. Suddenly, Daniel noticed the bag in her hand. He reached out and took it from her and set it inside the office.

"There's another one on the horse," Lillie said matter-of-factly as she walked past him into the office.

She was taking off her bonnet when Daniel finally found his voice. "I must say, I'm surprised to see you. What have you brought me? Goodies from the kitchen? Surely not more bandages!" Daniel was trying desperately to keep the atmosphere tolerable.

"No. No bandages," Lillie said as she placed her bonnet on the desk and proceeded to remove her coat.

"Then what?" Daniel questioned.

"Clothes," Lillie said simply. She smoothed the wrinkled shirtwaist that she'd worn and reached up to pull her hair free from the pins that had held it within her bonnet's bounds. By this action, Lillie was making a clear statement she'd come home.

"Clothes?" Daniel questioned, almost afraid to go further. "For me?"

"Not exactly," Lillie whispered. "They're mine."

"I see," Daniel said and slowly closed the office door. "And just what are your intentions, Lillie."

Lillie leaned back against his desk and smiled. This time she wouldn't make it easy on him. Hadn't he tortured her enough times? "My intentions are to become a nurse," Lillie answered. "You told me you could teach me everything I would need to know."

"I must say, I didn't expect you to have an answer so quickly," Daniel stated in a serious manner. "Have you forgotten the price of my training?"

Lillie smiled coyly. "I haven't forgotten a single thing you said to me, Dr. Daniel Monroe. I'm ready to pay the price."

Daniel stared in disbelief. It was what he'd prayed for, so why should it surprise him?

"You're ready to say yes?" Daniel questioned as he moved toward Lillie. He stopped short of taking hold of her and fought to keep his mind clear so he could concentrate on her answer.

"That depends on the question," Lillie whispered. She matched his bold stare and reached up to trace the outline of his stubble-covered chin. She could feel him tremble as he took hold of her hand to still its movement.

"Don't toy with me, Lillie. This is serious business."

Lillie laughed. "I think you'll see how serious I am when your brother gets here. That is, if you still want to get married. I do seem to remember being asked to marry you. Is the offer still good?" Lillie questioned in a businesslike manner, trying her best not to give way to her desire to embrace Daniel with all her strength.

Daniel seemed to catch on to her game. He took hold of both of her hands and pulled them to his lips. "I don't need another business partner. I have Garrett for that. What I do need is a wife. But more importantly, I need you, Lillie."

Lillie sighed and moved closer to Daniel. He still hadn't told her he loved her, and Lillie knew she needed to know how he felt. She'd still marry him, confident he would grow to love her, but it was important to know where she stood with him. How could she get him to tell her without coming right out and asking?

As if on cue, Daniel began to speak. "I have to say something, and I want some honest answers from you in return. Will you do that much for me?"

Lillie lifted her face to meet Daniel's. "Of course." Her words were soft and sweet.

"Come with me," Daniel said as he led Lillie to the sofa in the large sitting room. The fire still blazed on the grate and Lillie couldn't resist warming her hands before joining Daniel on the sofa.

"Lillie," Daniel began. "I don't want you to rush into this. I can wait for you if I have to. I don't want you to feel forced into a relationship you don't want, just because of what I said to you in the past. I would still find a way to train you as a nurse if that was what you wanted." He paused and a certain sadness was evident in his voice. "Even if you didn't want to marry me."

Lillie nodded. "Go on," she encouraged.

"I've been a widower for six years, but you've only been a widow for just over a year. We haven't known each other all that long either, and I don't want you thinking you have to marry me out of obligation."

"Obligation?" Lillie questioned. Nothing could be farther from her mind, but she let Daniel continue.

"I think it would be easy to take advantage of your vulnerability, Lillie. I don't want to do that. I don't want you that way, because. . ." Daniel grew uncomfortable and fell silent.

"Because?" Lillie prodded.

"Because I love you, Lillie!"

Lillie wanted to shout and sing, but instead she tried to remain calm. She steadied her nerves and held her voice in check as she replied, "I see."

"I do love you, Lillie. I have for a very long time. Ever since losing Katie, I became a hard man. I didn't want to feel anything inside, that's why I pushed God away. God makes a person take inventory of what's inside his soul, and I didn't want to have to deal with that. But then," Daniel paused with a smile. "He got to me in the only area I was vulnerable. He sent you. Lillie, I don't know what you're feeling right now, but since you're here, I know you must feel something. I pray that in time you'll come to love me as much as I love you." Daniel's tone was pleading, but still Lillie refused to give in.

"I'm afraid that's quite impossible," Lillie said with her face lowered to keep from smiling.

"Impossible?" he questioned and Lillie could no longer bear his misery.

"Yes," she said as she came to him. "It would be impossible to come to love you, because I already do love you, Daniel Monroe. I love you with all my heart."

Daniel's fears fell away and a smile replaced the worried, heartbroken look on his face. "Are you sure, Lillie?"

"Sure enough to spend the rest of my life loving you. Sure enough to work beside you and to have your children," Lillie said confidently. "And Daniel, I do want to have children. Please say you want them too!"

Daniel crushed Lillie to him and held her so tightly she thought she might snap in two. "I'd love to have a dozen children with you, Lillie. You'll make a wonderful mother and an even better wife. I knew God had sent you for a reason."

"Oh, He had a special reason, alright," Lillie said as she looked up into the eyes of the man she'd soon marry. "He sent me to a place to heal from my hurt and suffering, then He sent me His love and forgiveness so I might enjoy eternity in heaven. But He didn't leave me simply hoping and waiting for the end of time. He sent you. He sent you to heal me and to love me, and for that, I am most grateful."

"I love you, Lillie," Daniel said as he lowered his lips to kiss her.

Lillie melted against him and felt her heartbeat quicken as it always did whenever Daniel kissed her. How good God was to see her need when she couldn't see it for herself. How like God to bless her in spite of her denying Him.

"Thank you, Father," Lillie prayed as Daniel held her close. She thought of the future with Daniel and smiled without fear at the thought of it. "Perfect love casts out fear," Lillie remembered. God had taken her fear and replaced it with love. Perfect love.

Tender Journeys

*Dedicated to my mother, Jeanine.
Her dream for me never died.*

Chapter 1

1884

J enny Oberling made her way through the rain, struggling to keep her shawl from falling into the mud as she fought against the wind and the large wicker basket she balanced on her head.

Dampness had permeated every part of her body until she could no longer control the chattering of her teeth. How good it would feel if she could make her way home into her mother's waiting arms. But Jenny's mother had been dead a little over six years, thanks to the Apaches.

There was no one, Jenny thought as she battled the storm. Because of the Indians, her family was dead and there would never again be warmth or love for Jenny Oberling.

~

Across town, David Monroe kicked the mud off his boots and deposited his rain-drenched coat on a peg inside the door. He was soaked from the deluge of water, which even now continued to fall.

He worked quickly to get a fire going in the small wood stove, grateful for shelter away from the damp, September air. Settling down to warm his hands, he smiled to himself. Despite the rain and mud, he was happy.

At twenty-two, the soon-to-be-pastor was eagerly anticipating his new work. He was learning to minister to the Indians of the Southwest, a mission he felt strongly God called him to.

"I see you made it without floating away," observed an older man as he entered through a door opposite the one David had used.

"Didn't think I would," David replied with a grin. "When you said it was going to rain a bit, I didn't think I had anything to worry about. You should have told me it would be in proportion to Noah and the flood."

The older man laughed heartily and set a plate of hot food in front of his apprentice. "This is what they call a gully washer. Those little gullies that crisscross the trails can quickly become raging rivers in a rain like this."

"I can believe it," David said as he dug in and ate.

"So, what do you think of our little town?"

"Well, I tell you, Ed. When I came here after weeks on the trail, I thought

Santa Fe was the prettiest place I'd ever laid eyes on," David said, pausing to let his bread soak in the thick beef stew.

"And now?"

"Now," David said as he wrinkled his brow, "I'm certain of it. Of course the company I've kept has helped me fit in. But in this rain, I'm surprised the adobe doesn't melt and wash away."

Ed Clements laughingly agreed. After twelve years of being a widower, the aging pastor was enjoying David's companionship.

"Santa Fe is like a graceful, aging woman," Ed mused. "Of course, everything looks a little drab in the rain, but once the storm passes, you'll see."

"Oh, I don't need to wait," David said, thinking back on the hours he'd spent walking through the city. "The old Spanish missions are incredible, so regal and stately. Even the cemeteries are beautiful."

"It's hard to imagine them being here for centuries. The Spanish were very dedicated to the quest of winning the Indians to their faith. The missions were built to stay, and stay they have," Pastor Ed said as he reflected on the city.

"It seems to me the entire city was dedicated to mission work," David remarked. "The churches are everywhere, and those that aren't still standing have left plenty of relics behind to remind folks of their passing."

"You must understand," Ed added, "that even the city name, La Villa Real de Santa Fe de San Francisco de Asis, means the Royal City of the Holy Faith of St. Francis of Assisi. Lucky for us, they call it Santa Fe."

"I'm amazed at the people, and the devotion to their beliefs," David said as he finished his lunch. "Although I've noticed some people have more dedication to ceremony and icons than toward anything else."

"Oh, there are always some who want to be part of something simply to belong. Most people take their religion quite seriously, however. The Indians have many spirits they honor. They're often like the Greeks and Romans of Paul's day."

"How so?" David questioned.

"Well, some tribes don't have a problem in accepting yet another spirit to honor. The white man's God is powerful. They've seen many examples of white man's success and can only conclude his God must be capable of great things. Others, however, won't listen to a word you say. You present the Bible to them and it means nothing because it's a white man's book. It makes mission work here quite challenging."

"I never thought of it that way," David said as he considered the older man's words.

"When you preach before your own people, they readily accept the Bible as the Word of God. Even the hardest heart doesn't mock the Word, at least not very often. But when you sit down to speak with the Indians, it isn't just the language barrier that frustrates your efforts; it's the cultural barriers as well. You hold up the Bible and tell them it's the one truth they must accept, and they look at you like you're loco."

David nodded, "I guess that's only fair. We think them strange to worship creation rather than the Creator."

"That's right," Ed agreed. "What seems strange to us, we must turn around and see in relationship to what we preach. The Bible is simply a book of words they can't read or understand. The stories aren't part of their past, and the need for a Savior is not part of their ancestral beliefs."

"Then how do you get them to accept the need for Christ?" David asked.

"Ah ha," Ed said with a smile, "that's where we must lean on God. You must never forget, David, that you work with a partner. Never, never try to rush God. He works in His time and in His way. You must live the life and learn what the Indian ways mean to them. You must understand the Indian as well as you understand yourself, in fact, even better. If you know their needs, fears, and hopes, then you can better minister to their hearts."

"Makes a heap of sense to me."

"How about some pie? Mama Rosita brought me two big apple pies," Ed announced and left the room without waiting for David's reply.

Pushing his dinner plate away, David readily accepted the offer of dessert as Ed brought two huge pieces of pie to the table.

"I'll be making some calls this afternoon," Ed said between bites. "I was wondering if you would do me a favor."

"Name it," David answered quickly. He was eager to repay the old family friend who'd opened his church and home to David's studies.

"Well," Ed began, "if you don't have too much studying to do, I'd appreciate a hand in getting some polish on the pews. I've let things go without attention for much too long. Sometimes one of the congregation offers a hand, but with roundups and harvest, people are inclined to do their own work."

"I'd be happy to help. I've nearly finished my reading. One thing about college—whether it was back home or here—professors are fond of giving you plenty to read."

Pastor Ed smiled at his young friend. "It should come as no surprise that you'll spend a good percentage of your pastoring time reading and studying. While God inspires, we can't retire! That's my motto. People think a pastor sits around waiting for a heavenly messenger to hand over a weekly sermon. It just doesn't happen that way. Oh, there are times," Ed admitted as he pushed away from the table, "it seems as if an idea comes in a flash, but in truth I have found everything in my life is God's inspiration for His service."

David listened intently. This was one of the best things about sharing a home with Ed Clements. "They don't teach you that from a text book," David laughed.

"No indeed," Ed agreed. "I'll show you where the rags and polish are and then I'd best be on my way. I told old Mrs. Putterman I'd come and visit her today, and I surely don't want to disappoint that dear saint."

David had worked on the pews for over an hour when he heard the vestibule doors open. Thinking it too early for Ed to be returning, David called out, "Hello! I'm in here."

Clasping a basket in front of her, a young woman peered through the doorway into the sanctuary. Her dark brown hair was plastered to her face and back, acknowledgment that the rain had not yet let up.

"Can I help you?" David asked as he came forward. "You must be soaked. I have a fire going in the back room. Why don't you leave your basket by the door and come warm up?"

"I. . .don't. . .want. . ." The young woman's teeth chattered so she could scarcely speak. "To be a bother," she finally managed to say.

"No bother at all," David said as he motioned her to follow. Leading the way to the back room, David pulled out a chair and set it directly in front of the wood stove.

"This ought to get you warmed up," he said with a smile and added, "I'm David Monroe, and you are?"

"Jenny," she replied. "Jenny Oberling."

"It's nice to meet you, Jenny. I'm new here and don't know too many people. Pastor Ed and I are good friends though. We go way back, and he's agreed to take me in and help me ease into the ministry."

"You're a pastor?" Jenny questioned doubtfully. The man before her looked too young, too handsome, and not at all like the other pastors she'd known.

As if reading her mind, David laughed. "Everybody's got to start somewhere."

Jenny smiled only for a moment. "I didn't mean anything by it," she whispered.

"I know." David wished he could put her at ease. "What brings you to the church today? Anything I might be able to help with?"

"I don't know," Jenny answered honestly. "I was on my way home, and I felt compelled to come inside. Guess it was the rain and the cold."

"You sure about that?" David questioned. Swinging a chair around backwards, he straddled it and sat down to look Jenny in the eyes. And oh, what eyes! David said nothing for a moment as he lost himself in their rich brown depths.

Jenny grew uncomfortable and lowered her face. "I'm not sure about anything. I guess that's the trouble."

"Is that why you came here?"

"I guess," Jenny said with a shrug. "I know a lot of people who put store in prayer and such. I guess I thought it might not do any harm to check it out."

"Would you like to wait for Pastor Ed, or are you comfortable enough to sit here and talk with me?"

Jenny stared openly at David for what seemed an eternity. He had beautiful blue eyes and golden blond hair that liked to fall across his face at an angle. He seemed friendly enough, kind enough, but could she explain her heart to him?

David felt nervous as he waited for her answer. It reminded him of the first time he'd asked a girl to a barn dance. She'd made him wait for an answer, too.

Jenny noticed his discomfort and took pity on him. "I guess we can talk. Only I really don't know what about. I don't know why I'm here, and I don't know what to say."

David smiled and leaned forward against the back of the chair. "We can sit here and say nothing if you prefer it that way."

Jenny removed her wet shawl and smoothed her hair away from her face. "Are you sure I'm not taking you away from something else?"

"Just polishing pews, and that can certainly wait. Why don't I get us some coffee?" David offered as he got up and took the shawl from Jenny. He draped it across another chair and took some cups from the cupboard.

"I'd like that," Jenny said, starting to relax a bit. In the back of her mind was the knowledge she should be going home, but in her heart, an interest had been sparked she'd not expected.

David left to get the coffee, and Jenny took the opportunity to study the room for a minute. The whitewashed walls were unadorned and the furniture simple, yet the room was warm and inviting.

"Here we go," David announced. He poured coffee into each of the mugs and handed one to Jenny.

Jenny took a drink, grateful for the warmth that spread through her body. "Umm, it's good," she said, warming her hands around the cup.

"Now why don't you tell me what you were doing out in this rain?" David prompted as he took his seat and unknowingly lost his heart.

Chapter 2

Jenny looked down at the cup, rather than face David's intense blue eyes. "I was delivering laundry. I take in washing to help pay my way."

"Pay your way?" David questioned with a frown.

"I was orphaned about six years ago. My parents were killed by the Indians in 1878."

"What happened?" David asked as though they both had all the time in the world.

Jenny's brow furrowed momentarily. "We were part of a wagon train traveling on the Santa Fe Trail. It was about this time of year—I remember because after the heat of Kansas in August, we were grateful for the cool September nights. Pa was anxious to get to Santa Fe. He'd heard stories about cheap land and glorious views. Every day he would tell us about the kind of ranch we'd have and what kind of house we'd live in. In reality, he didn't have any idea what life down here would be like."

"Sounds like a man with big dreams," David said with a grin.

"He sure was," Jenny admitted and shared David's smile. Her young heart skipped a beat at the nearness of David's broad-shouldered frame. Jenny wondered if he, too, were a man with big dreams.

"Where did the attack come?" David asked, breaking the silence.

"We were three, maybe four, days out from Santa Fe. Everyone was excited about the trip coming to an end. I remember my mother talking about what it would feel like to take a bath in a real tub again." David smiled and Jenny continued.

"I had two older brothers, and they started talking about helping Pa with the land and how they were going to find wild horses and break them to ride. Me, I just wanted the journey to be over. Day after day it was the same thing," Jenny remembered. "I was tired of sleeping under the wagon. Do you know how tedious it is to smell dirt and sage night after night?"

"Yup," David laughed, remembering his long journey to Santa Fe. "I haven't been here long enough yet to forget that."

Jenny returned the laugh. "I've been here a lot longer than you, and I still can't forget." Her voice drifted off as if she were transported back to that distant time. "I remember listening to my parents talk long into the night. It made me feel safe, knowing they were just above me. I could hear my mother's sweet voice as she'd question my pa about Santa Fe. Night after night, he'd tell her everything he'd read or heard about the territory. He loved her so much, he never tired of telling her."

"They must have loved you a great deal too," David said as he placed his coffee cup on the table. "More coffee?"

Jenny shook her head, "No thanks. I still have some left. I'm much warmer now, and I'm sure the rain has let up some. I'm sorry I've taken up so much of your time."

"You haven't done a thing I didn't invite you to do. I'd really like it if you'd tell me the rest of the story. That is, if you feel like it."

"The Apaches struck our camp at dawn," Jenny said matter-of-factly. "I remember coming fully awake out of a deep sleep and knowing something was wrong. My mother was crying, and my pa was talking in whispers to my brothers. I was made to stay with some of the other children while our parents fought for our lives."

Jenny's voice revealed the pain that held her heart hostage. "I never saw my parents alive again. The Indians burned the wagons, stole our horses, and killed most everyone. A handful of children and old women were all that remained when the cavalry finally arrived."

"How awful for you," David sympathized, not knowing what else to say. He'd never known anyone who'd endured something as heinous as what Jenny had described. When he was taught to deal with grief, his teachers forgot to mention that pain and suffering touched the innocent lives of children, leaving wounds that seemingly never healed.

Jenny looked beyond David's face and stared blankly at the whitewashed wall behind him. She could still see the death and destruction the Apaches left in place of living, breathing souls.

David felt desperate to get Jenny's mind off the attack. "So where do you live now?" he asked.

Jenny forced herself to concentrate on David's voice. Taking a deep breath as if to cleanse the memory, she answered, "I live just down the street with Natty Morgan. She was one of the women who lived through the attack. She took me in and told me as long as I earned my keep, I could stay on."

"Earn your keep? You were a child. You're still hardly more than a child," David said and immediately regretted the words, knowing they sounded pompous.

"I'll be seventeen on New Year's Day," Jenny exclaimed angrily, "and I haven't been a child since the day of the raid."

David noted the emotion in her voice. "You must hold a great anger for Apaches."

It was a simple statement, but Jenny nearly dropped her coffee when David spoke the words. "I hate them. I hate all Indians. They are vile, hideous people who have no souls!"

A heavy silence fell between them as David silently prayed for God's direction in how to minister to the hurting girl.

"Tell me about Mrs. Morgan," David suggested, changing the subject.

"Natty?" Jenny questioned without really expecting an answer. "Natty Morgan is a hard, determined woman. She knows the price of everything and the value of nothing. As far as Natty is concerned, everything is a commodity to be bought, sold, or worked. She has her own ideas about life, and none of them are very encouraging."

"She must be hard to live with," David offered.

"Yes and no. I think the hardest thing to live with is the negative attitude. She's a pessimist by nature, always seeing the bad and expecting the worse. But as long as you do what she wants and don't cost her too much time or money, she's content to leave you be. Though," Jenny said and paused thoughtfully, "I wouldn't want to cross her. She used to run a brothel in Texas, and rumor has it she never needed a strong man to handle the customers when things got out of hand."

"I see," David said, startled by Jenny's casual reference to a house of ill-repute.

"So you do the laundry, and Mrs. Morgan does what?" David finally questioned.

"As little as possible," Jenny laughed. "I think she's used to being taken care of. But the laundry makes us good money and I don't mind."

"But what about school?" David questioned.

"School? I've had some schooling. Enough to learn to read and write. And I can do sums and figures, too. Ma used to work with me on the trail."

"Do you like to read? I have a lot of books, and you're welcome to borrow them anytime."

"I'm not sure I'd ever have time, but it's awfully kind of you to offer," Jenny replied gratefully. He barely knew her and yet he treated her as though she were some long lost friend.

"Do you go to church?" David questioned, wondering if he could interest Jenny in coming to hear him speak on Sunday.

"No. Natty's always seen it as a waste of time. She sleeps through the morning while I work. As much as Natty hates working with dirty clothes, I never have to worry about her hanging around me much, so it's kind of peaceful. Besides, it gives me time to think."

"Think about what?" David asked gently. Jenny seemed so fragile, and David was afraid the wrong question might cause her to bolt and run.

"I think mostly about my parents and my brothers," Jenny added.

"You must miss them a lot."

Jenny nodded and took a sip of the coffee. "It used to be I'd be doing something and I was certain I heard my mother calling me. I'd get up and start to go to her, then remember she was gone." The sadness in her voice made her sound years younger.

"Sometimes I remember our last morning. I can smell the smoke and hear the screaming. Almost every night it's the same thing."

"Nightmares?" David questioned.

"Uh huh." Jenny nodded. Thunder cracked outside and she shuddered.

"You're safe here," David said softly. He longed to put a supportive arm around the girl and drive away her fears.

Jenny gave him a sad smile. "Maybe so, but I can't stay here forever."

"You can have safety and peace no matter where you go," David said determined to share the way of salvation with Jenny. "God's peace is something nobody can take from you. It's the kind of security you can count on no matter where you live or go."

"My mother believed in God. She was a Christian and read the Bible to us every night," Jenny whispered. She finished the coffee and put the cup on the table. "I really should go."

"Why?"

"Natty will be expecting me, and soon it'll be time to get supper on." Jenny realized her words sounded like an excuse.

"Will you come back, maybe even come for church on Sunday?" David asked softly as he reached out and put his hand over Jenny's. "I'd like to be your friend and maybe introduce you to a friend of mine."

"I'll think about it," she said and pulled her hand away. Getting to her feet, Jenny retrieved her shawl and allowed David to help her with it.

"You're welcome to stop by here any time you like," David said as he opened the back door. "In fact, I'd like it very much if you would. I'd like to get to know the city better, and since you've been here five years, maybe you could show me around."

"Maybe," Jenny whispered. The rain had abated, but the sky still looked heavy and dark with low hanging clouds. "I'd best go before it starts in again," she said as she hurried through the door.

As Jenny made her way down the street, she couldn't stop thinking about David Monroe. Something about him had seemed so different, so kind. He seemed to genuinely care about her, and that was something Jenny hadn't enjoyed since the death of her parents.

He wanted her to come back on Sunday. Jenny wondered if he'd be giving the sermon. As she entered Natty's house, Jenny was caught up in dreams of sitting in the congregation, listening to David.

She was just hanging her shawl up when Natty's grating voice sounded from the front room. "Where have you been?"

Jenny went to a drawer and took out a brush. "I was delivering clothes."

Natty came through the doorway, fussing with the button on her well-worn black skirt. "You shouldn't have taken so long. Just look at yourself."

Jenny glanced down at her wet clothes and then looked up at the gray-haired woman. Natty was biting her lower lip in concentration, struggling to secure the button at the waist of her skirt.

"Let me help," Jenny offered. Natty didn't argue as Jenny pushed her pudgy hands aside and took hold of the skirt.

"You'll have to suck in," Jenny said and pulled the skirt together. "There, it's buttoned."

"Well, it's about time. Look, I'm going out, so you needn't fix supper and waste heating the stove. There are biscuits left over from breakfast, and I'm sure you can make a meal on them," Natty said and pulled on a waist jacket. "I won't be back until late."

Jenny waited until Natty was gone to heave a sigh and sit down. No doubt Natty was headed out to one of the gambling houses and wouldn't be back until the wee hours of the morning.

It was of little concern to Jenny. Her mind was still back at the church, fixed fast on David Monroe.

Chapter 3

When Sunday arrived, Jenny managed to sneak out of the house long enough to slip into the back pew of the Methodist Church. She kept her head covered and tried to stay hidden behind a stout man.

David took his place in the pulpit and immediately noticed the dark-haired girl who tried so hard to hide from him. He couldn't suppress a grin as he welcomed those who were regulars as well as those who were visiting for the first time.

Jenny tried not to be pleased, knowing he was referring to her perhaps more than anyone else. But in truth, it made her feel warm and happy to know he cared enough to notice her presence.

The time passed quickly, and Jenny listened intently as David spoke of God's love for the world—love that Jesus had demonstrated when He died on the cross to pay the penalty for the world's sins. Jenny felt a bit uncomfortable when David began to speak about forgiveness. How could God forgive anyone for taking the life of His Son? It would be no different than people expecting Jenny to forgive the Indians for killing her family.

David took his Bible and stepped down from the pulpit. He moved toward the first row of pews and stopped.

" 'I am the good shepherd: the good shepherd giveth his life for the sheep,' " he read from John 10:11. "The world didn't take anything from Jesus. He gave it all. He gave His life and love so you and I might live forever in forgiveness and reconciliation with our heavenly Father."

A few people in the crowd murmured "Amen," and Jenny wondered at their enthusiasm. The congregation seemed to be in perfect agreement with David's words.

To emphasize his meaning, David read more from John 10 and concluded with verses 17–18: " 'Therefore doth my Father love me, because I lay down my life, that I might take it again. No man taketh it from me, but I lay it down of myself. I have power to lay it down, and I have power to take it again. This commandment have I received of my Father.' "

Jenny couldn't take in the meaning of the words, but she thrilled to David's rich, confident voice. When David concluded the service and asked everyone to bow their heads for the benediction, she quietly slipped out the vestibule door and hurried home. Feeling confused about David and his words, she was too nervous to face him.

Throughout the next week, Jenny worked hard to forget her feelings for David. As she scrubbed clothes at the washboard, she could almost see his sweet smile in the soapsuds. Hanging the laundry on long lines in back of the house, Jenny hummed the melody of the song they'd sung at church Sunday. She couldn't remember the words, except for the line about Jesus paying for her sins. She mingled this with her thoughts of David and a Savior's love for his people.

When Friday arrived, Jenny realized she could no longer put aside her thoughts of David and decided to go for a visit. By the time she had carefully finished ironing the last of the laundry and placed it in a huge basket, Natty was still sleeping off the night before.

Jenny briefly examined her appearance in a small mirror. She wished she looked older. Jenny studied the red gingham dress she wore and noted with satisfaction that it made her look more mature. Her brown hair was tied back at the neck and fell long and straight to her hips. She whirled around and watched as the skirt of the gown fell perfectly into place.

Jenny smoothed the eyelet lace that trimmed the square-necked bodice and pinched her cheeks even through they needed little help to be rosy. She then pulled on her wrap, secured the basket on her head, and went on her way to make the deliveries.

So excited was Jenny about the prospect of seeing David, she could scarcely remember where each bundle of clothes belonged. She hurried through town, barely pausing to say hello to the people she passed. She avoided the Indians who had gathered to trade their wares. It didn't matter they were Pueblos, known for being peaceful and friendly. They were Indians.

When she'd delivered the final bundle of shirts to Father Martinez at one of the missions, Jenny nearly ran to the Methodist Church.

David had questioned Pastor Ed about Jenny Oberling. Ed knew a little about the girl and had utilized her laundering services when he could spare the money for someone else to wash his clothes.

"She lives just down the street. I'm not sure which house it is, but it shouldn't be hard to find. Why don't you try to find her?" Ed asked as he helped David finish putting away the breakfast dishes.

"I'd like to try," David said as he considered the possibility. "I know she needs a friend. It doesn't sound like she has any real companionship."

"No, I suppose not," Pastor Ed agreed. "The woman she lives with has a less-than-sterling reputation. Natty Morgan has a flare for the wilder side of life. I've spoken with the woman on several occasions and always met with a stone wall when it comes to church and Christianity."

"Do you suppose she would forbid Jenny from coming to church on a regular basis?" David questioned as he replaced the dishtowel on a peg.

"Nothing would surprise me," Ed replied. "Perhaps there is a way to get on Mrs. Morgan's good side, but I'm not familiar enough with the situation to know how."

David nodded. Just then a light knock at the back door caught both men's attention. David opened the door and couldn't hide his pleasure.

"Jenny!" he exclaimed. "We were just talking about you."

"About me?" Jenny questioned as she set her basket on the ground beside the door and let her shawl fall away from her face and onto her shoulders. "Why?"

"I was just explaining to Pastor Ed that I wondered if I would see you again. You didn't tell me where you lived, so I couldn't stop by to invite you to join us for Sunday services," David replied, uncertain what else to say.

He didn't feel comfortable enough to tell Jenny it was really his concern for her well-being that made him want to call. Then again, David wasn't sure it was only Jenny's well-being that drew him to her.

"Please come in and sit down," Ed said as he came forward and offered Jenny his arm. "You're out awfully early today. Have you been making your laundry rounds?"

"Why, yes," Jenny said sweetly as she allowed Ed to offer her a chair. "Pastor Monroe "

"Call me David," he interjected.

Jenny raised her liquid brown eyes to his and felt her heart beat faster. "David," she spoke softly, "asked me to show him around the city. I thought if he had time we might walk this morning."

David glanced briefly at Ed before accepting Jenny's invitation. "I'd be happy to."

"Good," Jenny said feeling a bit awkward.

"You know, Jenny," Ed began, "we have a gathering for our local youth. You might enjoy coming and meeting some people your own age. They meet here at the church on Sunday evenings. Sometimes they have outings and sometimes they just get together to study God's Word."

"I'll think about it," Jenny replied and lowered her gaze. "I'm not sure it would be all that easy to get out Sunday evenings. Natty usually has friends over and often needs me to put together refreshments."

"Don't feel pressured, Child. I just wanted you to know you're more than welcome."

"Thank you," Jenny said and raised her eyes only enough to meet David's.

"Well, if you're ready," David said with a smile, "I'll put on my coat and take you up on your offer."

First, Jenny led David to the city's adobe square, pointing out local oddities and points of interest. The day had warmed, and the cloudless sky was an intense blue. David listened to Jenny speak of the rich Spanish history of Santa Fe, noting she avoided discussing the Indian population.

He was sorry when Jenny led the way back to the church with the announcement she was needed at home.

"Will you come for the service on Sunday? I'm not speaking that day, but Pastor Ed does a wonderful job and I know you'd like him."

"I'm not sure," Jenny said nervously. How could she explain to David that the Christian faith confused her? She didn't like confronting her anger and her past, and Christianity demanded she do both.

"I hope you can. Especially on Sunday evening. There are quite a few people your own age," David said. Jenny turned quickly to pick up her basket, hoping to hide her disappointment in David's reference to her youth.

"I'll think about it," she murmured. Securing her basket atop her head, Jenny made her way down the walkway.

"Well, think real hard about it," David good-naturedly called out to Jenny's retreating form.

Jenny didn't make the services on Sunday morning or Sunday evening. Natty Morgan was in a fierce mood about the money she'd lost during one of her gambling parties. Jenny knew better than to cross her, and when Natty announced she was throwing a card party on Sunday night, Jenny didn't argue.

As Jenny prepared the refreshments, anger surged within her. She didn't know which infuriated her more: the thought of not getting to see David at the service or the fact that he looked upon her as a child.

Jenny finished spooning jam into the tarts she'd baked earlier and set the buffet for Natty's friends. Everything was in place, so Jenny made herself scarce as Natty's boisterous guests began arriving.

Slipping out the back door, Jenny took a seat in their small courtyard. The night sky was filled with stars, and a huge harvest moon rose just over the horizon.

Inside the house, Jenny could hear the raucous laughter of Natty's drinking friends. How she hated her life with the vulgar woman. Jenny relaxed against the cold iron of the chair and sighed.

She tried to imagine the gathering at the Methodist Church. What would it be like to mingle among people her own age, as David had called them? Long into the night, Jenny sat and dreamed about the church group and David Monroe.

The next morning, scarcely an hour after Jenny had started her morning tasks, she was surprised by a knock on her door.

"Good morning, David," Jenny replied shyly. "What brings you here?"

"I wondered if you would have time to walk with me this morning? I know you have your chores and all, but I wondered if you could spare a few moments."

"I suppose I could," Jenny said as she went to the peg where her shawl was hanging. "Only I can't stay away too long."

"That's fine," David replied with a grin. He held the door open for Jenny and offered his arm to her as he walked beside her.

Jenny hesitated for a moment. She longed to pretend he could see her for the mature young woman she was and not the child that sixteen conjured in his mind. If only she could make him aware of her maturity. Shyly, she accepted his arm and cherished every moment as he led her down the street.

David and Jenny walked down to the river, and when David suggested they sit and talk, Jenny eagerly agreed. Perhaps now she could prove herself to be older and wiser than David Monroe realized.

"It's really beautiful down here," David said as he took a seat on the ground beside Jenny. "I happened down here the first day I was in town. I've been coming back whenever time allows."

"It is nice," Jenny agreed and spread her calico skirt out in an attractive manner.

"I missed seeing you yesterday," David began, "and I couldn't get you out of my mind."

Jenny's heart gave a leap. "You couldn't?" she whispered.

"Truth is, since the first day you walked into the church looking like a drowned rat, I haven't been able to put you far from my thoughts." David said with a smile.

"Drowned rat, eh?" Jenny questioned, cocking her head to one side.

David's smile broadened. "But a very fetching drowned rat." Jenny blushed and said nothing. "Look, Jenny," David continued, "I've been very worried about you for reasons I can't explain. I guess the Lord has laid a burden of concern on my heart for you."

"I don't understand," Jenny replied. "Why would God want you to worry about me?"

"He cares for you, Jenny," David stated evenly. "He wants the best for you, and perhaps, this is His way of getting you to see that."

"I haven't had much religion in my life since the Indians killed my family. I'm not sure I can trust enough to believe all those things you say about God," Jenny admitted.

"Trust is a big part of Christian faith. People are always wanting answers for the things that happen in their lives. Something bad takes place and people want to receive an immediate answer from the Almighty for the wherefores and whys."

"Trust is hard when you've got nothing to base it on," Jenny said as she picked at the scraggly yellow grass.

"God's love is the best foundation you could ever have. Trust matures and grows with each day that you give yourself over to Him. God loves all His children and wants them to know and believe in His love."

"Even the Indians?" Jenny questioned and eyed David's face.

David's expression softened. "Even the Indians, Jenny. You can't condemn an entire race of people for the actions of a few. A renegade band of Apaches attacked your wagon train and killed your loved ones—not all Indian nations, not even the entire Apache tribe. Jenny, just as there are evil people among the whites, there is evil among other races as well."

"I've never thought of it that way," Jenny had to admit. "I've always thought all Indians were alike."

"Up in the town of Cimarron, some pretty tough characters caused a lot of trouble. Would it be fair if the rest of the nation judged the people of the New Mexico Territory by those few troubled souls in Cimarron?"

"No, I suppose it wouldn't."

"Jenny, I know you're hurting and I know your loss is great. But you've grieved your loss for six years and held a consuming bitterness for just as long. You'll never be happy or at peace until you let go of that bitterness. And Jenny," David paused, "I think the reason you came into the church that first day was because you're seeking some peace of mind. Isn't that true?"

Jenny looked out across the valley. David's words had hit a nerve. How could he so easily identify her heart's deepest secrets? Finally, she spoke.

"I would like to sleep without the nightmares. Just once, I'd like to go to bed and not fear falling asleep."

"Jesus can give you that kind of peace, Jenny, but you must let go of your anger. I know it won't be easy, but I'll help you any way I can, and God will give you the strength you need to conquer your fears."

"He can't give me back my family, though," Jenny said sadly.

"But your family belonged to God," David offered. "You said your mother was a Christian."

"Oh, my pa and brothers were too," Jenny said with a glimmer of hope in her voice.

"Then you'll see them again in heaven. Didn't anyone ever tell you one day we'll all be reunited with our loved ones in heaven? If you belong to God, you're His on earth and in heaven. In John 11:25-26, Jesus said, 'I am the resurrection, and the life: he that believeth in me, though he were dead, yet shall he live: And whosoever liveth and believeth in me shall never die. Believest thou this?' "

"Do you believe it?" Jenny asked, feeling completely at ease with David's tender approach. "Do you believe God can take away the hurt?"

"I know He can, Jenny. I believe in salvation through Jesus Christ with all my heart. It's the reason I became a minister. I wanted very much to share the Gospel with a hurting world."

"I have to admit, nothing else has worked. I want very much to get on with my life and not always be concentrating on the pain and memories of what used to be."

David smiled and reached out to take hold of Jenny's hand. "I knew you felt this way. I felt so strongly that God wanted me to share this with you."

"What do I do now?" Jenny questioned.

"Well," David said with a smile, "further in the book of John, Jesus is preparing to raise a dear friend of his from the dead. Jesus went to the tomb and told the people there, 'Take ye away the stone.' Jenny you need to take away the stone. You need to forgive what happened to your family and allow God to deal with the people involved."

"It won't be easy," Jenny said, tears sliding down her cheeks.

"No, not in your own power but in God's unlimited power, you have all the help you'll need."

"I want God to take away my stone. I want to be free once and for all, but I need time to think about this."

David let go of Jenny's hand and reached out to wipe a tear from her face. "Then we'll tell God all about it and trust Him to minister to your heart."

Chapter 4

David began to appear on Jenny's doorstep on a regular basis, and to Jenny's relief he never again mentioned her need of people her own age.

Most mornings they would venture around the city of Santa Fe. Jenny would point out different buildings and explain all she'd learned during her six-year stay in the city. The city was much bigger than David had anticipated, and with the expanded population came a bigger need for God.

One morning, Jenny took David to the Mission of San Miguel on the east side of the city.

"This mission is nearly three hundred years old," she explained as she paused for David to study the building. The first level held a second, smaller floor and on top of that was yet another smaller level. The pattern was repeated twice and gave the small mission a tower. Behind the first and second stories, the building spread out to form the remainder of the chapel.

"It's hard to imagine anything being here that long," David said as he considered the adobe and stone frame.

"It's thought to be the oldest mission in the United States," Jenny stated, "although much of the original mission was destroyed during the Pueblo Revolt. The Spanish rebuilt it in 1710."

"Ed told me the Pueblo had tired of Spanish domination, especially where their religious practices were concerned," David said and continued to study the structure. He felt awed by being able to touch history in a way few people would ever enjoy.

"Yes," Jenny said as she remembered the things she'd been told by others. "The Spanish, primarily the church leaders, were so concerned about the welfare of the people that some of the Indians were hanged as witches. Eventually, the Pueblos decided enough was enough. They held the entire countryside captive and killed everyone that moved along the way."

"I can't imagine the Indians being able to drive the mighty Spanish from this area," David said absentmindedly.

"The 'mighty Spanish,' as you call them, were forced to take refuge behind protective walls. The Indians were slaughtering everything in sight and were unwilling to settle for anything short of the complete withdrawal of the Spanish." Animosity colored Jenny's voice, and David decided to drop the issue.

They walked in silence as Jenny led David back to the plaza at the center of town. They paused to sit on a bench near the gazebo that stood at the center of the plaza.

"I'm intrigued by that building over there. I've heard it called by many names," David said as he tried to reestablish conversation.

"I suppose it usually goes by the name of Casas Reales. It means 'royal houses' in Spanish," Jenny replied. "I've heard it called the Adobe Place and El Palacio. Some descendants of the nobility still call it the Palacio Real or 'royal palace.' The Spanish king directed his people to build it as housing for his appointed governors. This is where the Spanish took refuge during the Pueblo Revolt."

"I had no idea it was that old."

"It's thought to have been built around 1609, some seventy-one years before the revolt," Jenny offered.

"You've certainly learned a great deal about the city," David complimented. Jenny smiled and pulled her shawl close. A breeze coming down from the mountains was chilling her. David immediately noticed and suggested they make their way back to her house.

"You haven't mentioned Mrs. Morgan lately," David said as he took hold of Jenny's arm and helped her across the street.

"Not much to mention. Natty sleeps late most mornings and doesn't know whether or not I'm in the house. I don't see it as her concern anyway. I'm nearly grown and have to start thinking about what I'm going to do with the rest of my life. I can't stay with her much longer."

"I'm surprised you've stayed this long. The woman obviously depends upon you for her living."

"Not really, Jenny said with a shrug. "She's a pretty fair gambler. Most of her money for gambling and drinking comes from her own sources. My earnings keep food in the house and pay the rent. I figure I can do that on my own just as easily as I can living with Natty. In fact, I think it would be a whole lot easier."

"No doubt," David agreed. "But wouldn't it be a bit, well, a bit risqué? I mean, a young single woman living alone in the city doesn't seem fitting."

Jenny laughed. "Apparently, Pastor Ed hasn't told you much about the uninhibited lifestyle of many in this city. Many of the married men not only keep mistresses, but their wives have, well," Jenny paused, blushing slightly, "shall we say, friends of their own."

"I had no idea," David admitted. "Do Mrs. Morgan's friends ever, uh. . ."

David hesitated. "Do they ever bother you?"

Jenny's flushed face darkened. "She has some friends who make me quite uncomfortable. Mostly it's just the way they look at me. No one has ever touched me or caused me any grief, if that's what you mean. Why do you ask?"

David stopped as they reached Jenny's house. He took Jenny's hands in his and tried to find the words to explain his apprehension. "You're a beautiful young woman and it concerns me you're subjected to such a vile lifestyle. Please be careful."

David's worried expression touched Jenny's heart. Perhaps he did care for her, at least a little. "I will be," Jenny whispered and grew uncomfortable in the silence that fell between them.

"Will you have time to walk tomorrow?" David asked as he dropped his hands.

Jenny crossed her arms protectively against her body and raised her brown eyes to meet David's stare. "I should," she replied shyly. It felt so wonderful to have David's companionship, and Jenny was reluctant to enjoy it for fear it would be snatched from her.

"Good," David said with a smile. "There's somebody I want to introduce you to. I'll come by around eight." Jenny nodded and watched for several minutes as David disappeared down the street.

She carried the warmth of David's smile with her as she went up the stone walkway, unmindful of the woman who watched her from the house.

"So that's the way it is," Natty Morgan muttered. Not wanting Jenny to find her, Natty quickly returned to her bedroom and plotted how she would handle this unwelcome change.

The following morning at exactly eight o'clock, Jenny answered the door to find David decked out in his best suit. "Oh my," Jenny said with a frown as she glanced down at her simple, pale blue, cotton gown. "I didn't expect to dress up."

"No need for you to," David said with a grin. "You always look perfect."

Jenny lowered her face but smiled at the compliment. It was becoming clear to her that David shared her deep feelings for their relationship.

"Are you ready?" David asked.

"Yes," Jenny said as she took her heavy wool shawl to ward off the morning chill.

She closed the door quietly behind her and took David's arm as he led the way down the street.

Natty Morgan slipped quietly from her bedroom and watched the young couple move down the road toward Washington Avenue. Why hadn't she realized Jenny was nearly a grown woman?

The robust woman pulled on a silk wrapper and poured herself a cup of the coffee Jenny had kept warming on the stove. How old was the child anyway? Sixteen? Seventeen? Certainly marriageable age, and if that were to happen, what would become of Natty's lifestyle? She depended on the child to wait on her and to keep their meager home together. Natty contemplated the situation for a long time before taking herself back to bed.

David led the way to the Exchange Hotel. "We're supposed to wait here," he said as he turned to Jenny. Her questioning face betrayed her concern. David's brow furrowed momentarily, then it dawned on him that leading Jenny to the Exchange Hotel was most inappropriate.

"I'm sorry, Jenny. I never thought of how this might look to you or anyone else. Why don't I take you across the street to the park and let you wait there? I'll come back here and," David's words were interrupted by a rousing greeting from another huge, blond man.

"David!" The man rushed through the doors of the Exchange Hotel and crushed David with a bear hug. Jenny watched them silently as did a young, blond woman who was standing behind the stranger.

"Daniel, I'm so glad you're finally here. I brought someone for you to meet," David said as he reached back and pulled Jenny to stand beside him. "This is Jenny Oberling, my best friend in Santa Fe. Jenny, this is my older brother, Dr. Daniel Monroe. He's come to answer an advertisement. Seems folks up north of Santa Fe want a doctor."

"Dr. Monroe," Jenny said as she extended her small hand and found it engulfed in Daniel's large, well-manicured one.

"It's nice to meet you, Jenny. And," Daniel said as he pulled the blond woman from behind him, "this is my wife, Katie."

"Wife?" David said in shocked surprised. "You never said anything about a wife in your letter. When did you get married?"

"David," Jenny found herself admonishing the young pastor, "don't be rude. It's very nice to meet you, Katie," she added as she took Katie's hand. "Even nicer still to have someone who's near my own age. At least David keeps telling me I need to circulate among that crowd."

Daniel laughed out loud at David's stunned expression. "I've never seen anybody able to render him speechless. It's indeed a pleasure to meet you, Miss Oberling."

"Yes," Katie agreed and gave Jenny's hand a squeeze. "It's very nice to meet you."

Jenny suddenly grew embarrassed at her bold words, but before she could say anything further, David drew their attention to Katie's condition. "Why, Daniel, you've not only married a beautiful woman, but if I'm not mistaken, she's going to make me an uncle in a very short time."

"That was my prognosis," Daniel said with a smile. Katie blushed, and Jenny noticed her well-rounded stomach as David continued to pat his brother on the back.

"How wonderful," Jenny said and David agreed.

David glanced at the street clock. "Have you had breakfast yet?"

Daniel and Katie nodded. "The long trip exhausted us both so much we fell into bed without a bite of supper," Daniel explained. "This morning we ate like ranch hands."

Katie laughed. "That's for sure. I don't think half of this is as much baby as it is fried eggs and ham," she said, patting her stomach.

"Well then," David offered, "perhaps a walk. I've the best tour guide in all Santa Fe." They all glanced at Jenny who felt her face grow hot under the startling blue eyes of the Monroe brothers.

"I'd love to see more of the city," Katie said, breaking the silence. "I've only seen what little the street lamps afforded me last night."

"I'd be happy to show it to you." Jenny said as she turned to David. "Where should we start?"

The rest of the morning was spent in nonstop chatter about the city and the old relics and buildings that gracefully lined its streets. When Jenny suddenly realized it was nearly noon, she stopped in her tracks with a stricken look.

"What is it, Jenny?" David asked, concerned she'd taken ill.

"I forgot about Natty," Jenny admitted. "She'll be up by now and wondering where I am. There will be a price to pay for this splendid morning."

"I'll take you home right now," David said as he turned to speak with Daniel.

"No," Jenny insisted. "Natty had better not see you coming down the street with me. It would be best if I go ahead alone. Dr. Monroe, Mrs. Monroe, it was a pleasure to meet you. I hope we can spend more time together."

"Only if you call us Daniel and Katie," David's brother said with genuine affection.

"Yes, please," Katie said as she placed her hand upon Jenny's arm. "I'd like for us to be friends."

Jenny forgot her lonely, empty life and basked in the warmth of her new-found friendships. David shook his head in wonder. Could she really be the same scared and angry young woman who had burst into his life only weeks before?

Jenny hurried through the streets of Santa Fe and found Natty Morgan angrily pacing the floor.

"Where've you been?" Natty growled between clenched teeth. "The stove's cold, the coffee's thick as mud, and I haven't had as much as a biscuit to eat."

"Sorry," Jenny said and offered no other explanation. She quickly got a fire going in the stove and threw out the remains of the morning's coffee. "What would you like to eat?"

"I want eggs, toast, and potatoes," Natty said as she took a chair at the kitchen table. "And throw a steak on. I feel as though I could eat a horse."

Jenny went to the larder for the meat and eggs. Satisfied the stove was heating to a proper temperature, Jenny sliced up potatoes and ham and joined the older woman. Startled to discover she was whispering a silent blessing on the meal, Jenny smiled at David's influence in her life.

"I suppose that lovesick expression is for the young man I saw you with this morning," Natty said between stuffing huge forkfuls of food into her mouth.

Jenny's heart sank. Natty knew about David. Working to ease Natty's mind from concern, Jenny didn't deny her statement. "That 'young man' as you call him, is Pastor David Monroe. He's a new minister here working with Pastor Clements at the Methodist Church. He asked me to accompany him this morning and help his brother and sister-in-law learn their way around the city. His brother is a doctor and his sister-in-law is expecting a baby soon."

"I see," Natty replied, somewhat surprised at the detail Jenny gave. It only made her more curious, knowing Jenny was never one to volunteer information.

Jenny picked at the food on her plate, wondering how she was going to get Natty off the subject of her friendship with David.

"How did you meet this Pastor Monroe?" Natty questioned. She watched Jenny intently for any signs of discomfort.

Jenny, who'd long ago learned how to play Natty's moods and tirades, shrugged her shoulders. "I think I met him when I was delivering clothes one day." She tried to sound disinterested, wondering just how much Natty had surmised.

"Seems to me," Natty said as she pushed away from the table and tried to wipe egg yolk from her blouse, "you have a great deal more interest in this Pastor Monroe than in just being his guide around Santa Fe."

"He's very kind, and I enjoy listening to him talk about the cities back east," Jenny said, grateful she didn't have to lie. "I haven't had a chance to talk about things like that since the raid."

Natty always steered away from any reference to the Apache raid, but today she wasn't giving an inch. "What age were you when those Injuns attacked? Better yet, how old are you now, Jenny?"

Jenny nearly dropped her fork in surprise. "How old am I? I'm sixteen, nearly seventeen. You should know that Natty. My birthday's New Year's Day."

"Seventeen? Hmm," Natty said with a strange look on her face. "Seems to me most girls your age are married."

"Seems to me, most girls don't have the responsibilities I have," Jenny said sarcastically. She'd always managed to stand her ground with Natty.

"You think you've got it real bad, don't you?" Natty questioned as she picked at her teeth with the end of her knife. "Where would you have been if I hadn't taken you in? I gave you a roof over your head and food in your belly. I could have left you on the plains to be picked up by the next passing band of Apaches."

Jenny grimaced and Natty knew her words had hit home. One thing Natty knew full well was Jenny Oberling's hatred of Indians.

"A body would think a little more gratitude would be in order," Natty said in a tone of voice that let Jenny know she'd lost the argument.

"I am grateful, Natty," Jenny said as she got up and started clearing the table. "You know I am. We've never had to play games before, so why now? Why not just say what's on your mind."

Natty leaned back and smiled. "I've a mind to find you a husband. A rich one who's willing to pay a high price for a young, unspoiled white woman."

Jenny shuddered at the thought but said nothing. Perhaps if she appeared unconcerned, Natty would drop the idea. Perhaps Natty would go on gambling and drinking and forget Jenny had somehow threatened her security. Perhaps, but not likely.

Jenny went to the well and brought up a bucket of water for washing the dishes. She understood too well Natty had found a new game to play. This time, Jenny's life would be staked.

Chapter 5

With Daniel and Katie in Santa Fe, David had less time to visit Jenny. He'd tried to locate her on her laundry rounds, but to no avail.

He busied himself with his studies and spent more time with Pastor Ed, learning the basics about life in the Indian villages. But no matter how hard he tried, David couldn't stop thinking about Jenny and how good it felt to be in her company.

David stood shaving one morning, staring at his reflection in the small mirror that hung over the washbasin. He remembered the way Jenny had chided him when he'd met Katie. Many men might have found that moment annoying, but David remembered it with fondness because it spoke of the familiarity between him and Jenny. She would never have been comfortable enough to speak her mind had she not felt a closeness to him—of that he was certain.

He finished shaving, had his devotions, and ate breakfast all before the clock in the town square chimed seven. With the morning stretching before him, David decided to walk by Jenny's in hopes of catching her at home.

Donning his coat and hat, David was just about to step out the door, when Daniel appeared on the walkway. "I'm glad I caught you. Can you spare me some time this morning?"

"I guess so," David said and tried not to sound disappointed. "What'd you have in mind?"

"I'm supposed to meet up with the man who placed the ad for a doctor. I got a note from him last night that he'd come in with the cattle drive from up north. I'm supposed to meet him at eight o'clock."

"Who is he?" David questioned as he joined Daniel on the walk.

"Jason Intissar. He owns a ranch north of Santa Fe. In fact, several days north of Santa Fe. He's up in the mountains, has a huge valley spread as I hear tell."

"I've heard of the Intissar ranch. Isn't it called Piñon Canyon?" David asked.

"That's right," Daniel answered and gave David a hearty pat on the back. "You don't know how good it is to see you again. I thought a lot about you

269

while I was doing my residency in Kansas City. I kept wondering if you were eating right and how school was going. I didn't even know you'd left the seminary in Iowa until Ma wrote and told me."

"Sorry," David apologized. "I kept meaning to write, but I had so much work to do."

"You don't need to tell me," Daniel said with a smile. "I've been negligent enough for both of us. You didn't know about Katie, after all."

"She's really nice, Daniel. I'm glad you found someone to love. I always prayed you would."

"You must have put just the right words into those prayers, 'cause Katie is everything a man could want. Do you know, she even wants to be my nurse when I get my practice set up?"

"It doesn't surprise me. She's pretty young, though, isn't she?" David dared the question.

Daniel frowned a bit, "Well, that's another story. I thought she was older. She lied to me about her age. Once we were married, I found out she was only sixteen, and well, the baby was already on the way. But I have to admit, her age has nothing to do with her maturity."

"I guess I can relate to that," David agreed.

"Yeah, I suppose you can. Just how old is that Jenny of yours?"

"What makes you think she's mine?" David asked with a laugh, but in truth he wondered if Daniel had picked up on something he'd missed.

"Just the way she looks at you says it all," Daniel grinned. "Katie was the same way—still is—and it never fails to make this old heart pound a little faster."

David laughed out loud.

"Well, here we are," Daniel added as they paused outside La Bonita Café. "We made arrangements to meet here."

Daniel and David were seated, and although David had eaten breakfast, he agreed to a cup of strong coffee. Daniel had just received his food when an older man and his companion approached the table.

"Are either of you gentlemen Dr. Daniel Monroe?" the older man questioned.

"I am," Daniel said, extending his hand as both he and David got to their feet.

"I'm Jason Intissar," the gray-haired man said with a smile, "and this is Garrett Lucas. He's like a son to me and assists me in most every matter on my ranch."

"It's nice to meet you both," Daniel said as he shook hands with the men. Garrett Lucas, he noticed, hardly looked much older than his Katie. "This is my brother, Pastor David Monroe," Daniel said as he turned to David.

David took hold of each man's hand and greeted them warmly. "I've heard a great many things about you, Mr. Intissar."

"Good things I hope," he laughed, "and please call me Jason."

"Jason it is," David agreed. "Won't you sit?"

The older man nodded, and he and Garrett pulled up chairs. "So you're a pastor," Jason said rather thoughtfully, "I know we're here to deal with your brother's career, but I have a proposition for you as well, if you're interested."

David was curious. "I never overlook a chance for the hand of God to direct me. I'd be happy to listen to your ideas."

"Good man," Jason said as he waved to the serving girl. "How about some breakfast, Garrett?"

"Sounds mighty good to me," Garrett drawled. His wavy brown hair and boyish face made him seem young, but David was impressed by the way he handled himself.

The young girl took their orders and left the men to their discussion. Jason began the conversation by explaining his precarious health.

"My main interest in having a doctor nearby has been my own failing health. I have a bad heart, according to the doctor in Denver. I don't know what, if anything, can be done for me, but I'd feel a heap better having a regular doctor closer to the ranch than Springer or Cimarron."

"I see," Daniel said, then questioned, "where do you have in mind for my wife and me to live?"

"Well, of course it would be up to you, but I'd be happy to see to it something comfortable was built. Money isn't a problem. I can secure land for the house anywhere, but of course, I'd prefer it be in close proximity to my own land."

"How far from Santa Fe would that be?" Daniel asked, considering Katie's upcoming delivery.

"The ranch is a week away from Santa Fe. Is it important that you live near Santa Fe?" Jason questioned.

"My wife is due to have a baby in a couple of months. I'd feel better if we were somewhere close to another doctor. At least until after the baby is born." Daniel replied honestly.

"I don't see a problem with that," Jason said with a smile. "It seems like a reasonable request."

"You know, Jason," Garrett suddenly spoke up, "you have that place about three hours from here on the rail line. Couldn't they stay there until we got another place built for them and Doc's wife has her baby?"

Jason's face lit up. "That's a wonderful idea, Garrett. We only use that place for shipping out livestock after roundup. What do you think about that, Dr. Monroe?"

"Three hours, eh?" Daniel was considering the situation.

"That ought to put you close enough, Daniel," David said, trying to encourage his brother.

"I suppose it would at that," Daniel said with a smile. "I believe we can work something out."

"Good, good," Jason said enthusiastically. "Now, how about the permanent house? Where do you think you'd like it to be?"

"It really won't matter after the baby is here safely," Daniel replied. "I suppose whatever you have in mind would be great."

Jason paused long enough in the conversation to accept his breakfast. "I thought a great deal about this," Jason said as he smiled broadly. "I'd like nothing better than to get a little more civilization near the ranch. Nothing real big, but something more than what we have. I'm even thinking of setting up a town somewhere close to the ranch. Perhaps your house could be my first step toward reaching that goal."

Garrett added with a laugh, "This has been Jason's dream for as long as I've known him."

"It sounds like a good one," Daniel replied.

"Now for you, young man," Jason said turning to David. "What I have in mind is a mission among the Pueblo Indians. A large Pueblo reservation is located near my property and it has been my desire to get the Word of God to these Indians. They are good folks, Mr. Monroe."

"Please call me David."

"They are good people, David. They have a love of the land and work hard to make life better for their people. I've been very impressed with their industrial spirit, but unfortunately, they have little or no interest in Christianity. That's where you would come in. I'd like to build a mission where you could live close to the reservation and be available to visit them on a regular basis and invite them to come to you."

"That's exactly what I feel God has called me to do," David said with such wonder in his heart he could hardly believe Jason's words.

Jason smiled and nudged Garrett. "God is good, Garrett. Just look at how He's blessed us today."

Garrett smiled, "That He has, Jason."

"So you will consider setting up a mission on my land?" Jason asked David seriously.

"I'd be happy to. I'll give it some prayer and reflection and get back to you."

"I'd have it no other way. Now, if you two don't mind, I'm going to give this plate of food my undivided attention," Jason said as he dug into the food.

~

David spent many hours alone in prayer that night. Excitement about Jason's proposal surged through him, and sleep was impossible. Turning through the Scriptures, David found a peace of mind he'd not realized was missing. He knew where he was being led, and rather than moving in a general direction, he had a specific mission to fulfill. God had given him his life's work.

As David settled down and turned out the lamp, he praised God for introducing him to Jason Intissar. Just before he fell asleep, his mind drifted to thoughts of Jenny Oberling. He could see her dark brown eyes so sweet and trusting. He could almost hear her gentle voice, and he longed to be with her.

Was Jenny also a part of God's plan for his future? She hated the Indians. She'd not yet learned to let go of the past, and she would never want a future that included living among the Pueblos.

To accept Jason Intissar's proposal and God's purposeful direction, David would have to give up Jenny Oberling. Yet, to choose Jenny over the mission work would be to turn his back on God. David sighed and pulled the covers over his head. What was the answer?

Chapter 6

"What's the hold up?" David called to the top side of the wagon.

Daniel peered over the canvas covering and grimaced. "If you think it's so easy to tie this load down, then you come up here and do it."

David laughed and walked away. "No thanks," he called over his shoulder, "I'll just go see if Katie needs anything."

"She'd better not have moved from that chair I put her in," Daniel shouted to David's retreating form.

David made his way to the hotel room and knocked loudly. At Katie's soft welcome, he opened the door and peered inside. True to her promise, Katie was sitting where Daniel had left her.

"Are you ready to go yet?" she questioned as she looked up from her needlework.

"Just as soon as that husband of yours ties one of his fancy surgical knots and gets the wagon tarp secured," David said with a grin. "How about you? Are you sure you're up to the ride? It's over six hours, you know."

"I'll be fine," Katie said as she put her sewing aside and struggled to get out of the chair. David went immediately to her side and offered his arm. "Thank you," Katie said as she steadied her ill-proportioned body. "I don't seem to be anything but awkward these days."

"No thanks necessary," David replied, "I'm just mighty excited about this new little one. How much longer do you figure before he'll be here?" Fearing he'd been too personal, he quickly added, "If you don't mind my asking."

Katie laughed. "Just because you don't discuss a woman's condition, doesn't make it go away. The baby is due next month."

"And, of course, my brother wants a boy," David said with certainty.

"Actually, he says he doesn't care either way as long as the baby is healthy. I guess I feel the same way," Katie said as she patted her rounded form. "Although, I am partial to the idea of a boy, myself."

"Me, too," David admitted.

Katie went to the window and looked out on the street below. "I never expected Santa Fe to be this large," she said as she watched the people hurrying on their way.

"Nor this beautiful?" David asked.

Katie turned and smiled. "Nor this beautiful. It really is a charming town. I'd never seen adobe before coming to New Mexico. I love the different colors."

"It's that way because of the various clays. They mix it with straw to make the adobe bricks. It's orange around here, but up at the Taos Pueblo village, Pastor Ed tells me it's more sandy brown. Other places it's almost pink," David offered by way of making conversation.

In truth he still wasn't as comfortable around Katie as he'd like to be. What he really wanted to talk to her about was whether she and Daniel had any interest in God.

As if reading his mind, Katie's expression turned quite serious. "You know, Daniel never told me you were a pastor. At least not until we were on our way down here. In truth, I don't think he knew you were here until your ma told him."

"I can well imagine. Daniel is five years older than me. When you're anxious to make the most out of life, you don't worry too much about leaving a little brother at home before you up and move off to college. I've never told Daniel this, but I was devastated when he left. He was pretty young, but he knew he wanted to go to college. I guess he never thought about what he left behind."

"Oh yes, I did," Daniel said as he came through the door. "I thought about it a great deal. Sometimes I thought about it so much, I nearly left college and came home."

"You never told me that," David said somberly.

"I know," Daniel replied as he came to embrace Katie. He held her against him for several minutes. "I never wanted to make you feel worse than you already did. Ma told me how hard you'd taken my leaving, and believe me, it wasn't easy to go."

David smiled. "But you're here now, and we won't be all far from each other, especially after my nephew gets here."

Daniel laughed heartily. "So you've convinced him that it's a boy," he said as he squeezed Katie's shoulder.

Katie looked up at her husband with wide-eyed innocence, "Who me?"

David grinned at the loving banter. "If you don't mind, we've got a long, dirty ride ahead of us. Pity we can't wait until they repair that stretch of track. I'd much prefer a three-hour train ride to six or seven hours of jostling cross-country."

"Me, too, but you heard the railroad man. There's just no way of knowing how soon they'll be done. I'd like to be settled for Katie's sake," Daniel said and turned to his wife. "Are you ready, Katie?"

"As ready as I'll ever be," she replied with a smile.

"I think I'd better go check that tarp and make sure the doc here got it tied down properly." David interjected. Truth was, he missed Jenny more than he'd like to admit, and watching Daniel and Katie was a painful reminder of her absence.

The trip was grueling, and because of the rough terrain and deeply rutted trail, David and Daniel were forced to stop many times in order to give Katie much-needed rest from the jostling wagon. More than once, Katie chose to walk rather than suffer the bouncing on the wagon seat.

Nearly eight hours after they'd left Santa Fe, the small adobe house came into view.

The mountains rose to the north, and in the death that came with autumn, they added highlights of green pine and flaming vegetation to the desert brown and orange.

The air itself had an arid chill, although the early October sun did its best to warm the earth. As they drew closer, Katie could make out several flowering cactus plants that had been transplanted to grow along a cobblestone walk to the front door.

"Oh, it's lovely," Katie said as she turned to her husband. "I shall truly love living in this land."

David tied his horse to a small hitching post at the end of the walkway and went to help Katie down from the wagon. "Just wait until you see the inside, little sister. You're going to love it!"

"I already do!"

David opened the door and noticed Katie's wearied expression. "You must be exhausted. Come on over here and sit," he said as Daniel came up from behind.

"I knew this was going to be too much for you. Forget sitting. I want you in bed immediately," he said and easily lifted Katie into his arms. "It's a good thing David and I came out here ahead of time and got this place ready."

David opened the door to the bedroom and stepped back. "I'll fix some supper," he offered as Daniel deposited Katie into bed.

"That'd be great," Daniel called over his shoulder. "If it isn't too much trouble, how about bringing Katie a cup of hot tea while I start unpacking the wagon?"

"You don't need to wait on me," Katie argued. "I'll be fine in a few minutes."

"It'll be more than a few minutes before you'll feel fine," Daniel laughed. "Now stay put and relax."

"That's right, Katie," David agreed, "I'd be happy to make tea for you."

It wasn't long before David made good on his offer and brought a steaming cup of tea to Katie's bedside. He helped prop her up, then handed her the cup.

"What made you become a minister?" Katie asked.

David was so surprised that he absentmindedly sat down on the edge of the bed. "Well," he began, "I couldn't imagine being anything else. God's calling to me was so strong that when I tried to ignore it, He kept finding ways to get through to me."

"So you didn't want to work in the church?"

"It wasn't that," David answered softly. "It was more a concern that folks would think me pretentious. I mean, I was always rather serious. Daniel had the reputation of being the fun-loving brother. Me, I was always off spending time alone, thinking about my life and what I wanted to accomplish with the time I'd have here on earth."

"And what did you decide?" Katie questioned as she took a sip of the tea.

"I felt I had to show people there was more to life than working and existing day to day. I wanted them to know the emptiness in their lives wasn't from a lack of things, but from a lack of God in their hearts. I wanted so much for them to know about Jesus and His sacrifice for us."

"You talk about God like you would about Daniel or me," Katie said, rather surprised. "I can't imagine feeling that way. I believe in God, but not like you do. God is important and powerful, and if you don't do what He wants, He punishes you, then you die."

David felt the need to share his heart, and in spite of his concern that he might alienate his sister-in-law, he plunged ahead.

"God is important and powerful," he began, "and if you die without repenting of your sins and accepting His Son, Jesus, as your Savior, you will be punished. But there is so much He offers us. So many good and enjoyable things, not the least of which is eternal life."

"I've heard people talk about living forever in heaven," Katie admitted.

"It's more than that, Katie," David tried to explain. "Eternity with God starts with your acceptance of Jesus as your Savior. You don't have to wait until you're dead to enjoy the benefits and peace that come from being a child of God."

"I'm not sure I understand," Katie said softly.

"Nor me," Daniel's voice called from the door. "I guess I've wanted to ask you some questions since we first arrived, but the time never seemed right."

David felt ill at ease. It seemed strange to be leading his older brother to an understanding of God. The thought of being his brother's keeper came to mind.

"Life can deal you some painful moments," David explained. "You won't escape those even as a Christian, but you can escape the worry and concern when those moments are upon you. It's a matter of faith. Faith in God to trust Him for the answers even when things are so muddled there seem to be no answers."

"Faith?" Katie questioned. "Faith in something you can't see or put your hand on? That's a lot to ask."

"It wouldn't be faith if it didn't require some sacrifice on your part," David said thoughtfully. "You sacrifice your control and worry. God's part is to do everything else."

"Seems unnaturally simple," Daniel replied.

"Not at all," David said with sudden revelation. "When somebody comes into your office with a broken arm, you know what needs to be done and you do it. You wouldn't allow the patient to dictate how you should fix the arm, would you?"

Daniel grinned and Katie laughed. "There's no way Daniel would allow anyone—especially his patients—to tell him how to care for his patients," Katie added before Daniel could answer.

"Why is that?" David questioned.

"Because I'm the doctor," Daniel stated firmly.

"But what about the fact they know better about their own pain?"

"That's sometimes the problem. Because of the intensity of their pain, they often don't realize what's necessary to get them past it," Daniel said, and it suddenly became clear where David was leading the conversation.

"And because of our pain, we don't always know where God is leading us. We can't know everything, but we don't have to. When we belong to God, He takes care of that just like you take care of doctoring your patients."

"But how can we be sure He'll listen?" Katie questioned.

"Jesus said, 'Ask, and it shall be given you; seek, and ye shall find; knock, and it shall be opened unto you,' " David said, quoting Matthew 7:7.

"God wants to give His children good things, but He wants most of all to give them eternal life. In that same chapter of the Bible, Jesus said, 'Or what man is there of you, whom if his son ask bread, will he give him a stone? Or if he ask a fish, will he give him a serpent? If ye then, being evil, know how to give good gifts unto your children, how much more shall your Father which is in heaven give good things to them that ask Him?' "

"The key is to ask. God is only too happy to accept you into His family."

"I think I'm beginning to understand," Katie said as she nodded her head.

"We can't expect God to help us if we don't let Him."

"Just like being a doctor," Daniel admitted, "If people don't come through my office door, I can't offer them my help."

"Exactly," David said with great relief. He'd thought it would be much more difficult to explain, but as Pastor Ed had often reminded him, he never worked alone. God was with him.

"So how do you get saved?" Katie asked. "Do you have to do something special for God?"

"God's gift of eternal life is free," David replied. "We could never do anything good enough or great enough to equal the gift God offers. There's only one way we can have eternal salvation and that is to ask for it."

"That's all?" Daniel questioned in disbelief.

"Basically," David answered. "You must repent of your sins and seek to change your old lifestyle and ways. You must be willing to give yourself over to God and accept His help to start a new life."

"And if you do this," Katie started, "if you really try to change and you honestly want to lead a new life, what happens if you stray or make a mistake?"

"Then you ask God to forgive you and you try again. God's grace knows no limits. Of course, you don't go out of your way to sin just so God can offer you grace and forgiveness."

"I'm not sure I can buy that," Daniel said thoughtfully. "I mean, how can God keep forgiving me? Won't He ever throw up His hands and give up on me?"

David chuckled despite the seriousness of the question. "You and Katie are going to have your own child soon. Say you tell your son or daughter they must stay away from rattlesnakes because they are deadly poisonous. And say you have an obstinate child who thinks he knows best and doesn't listen. If your child gets snake bit, will you take care of his wounds?"

"Of course," Daniel answered.

"What if he gets bit more than once?"

"I'd care for him as many times as it took. Of course, I'd sure be explaining the need for obeying the rules in the meantime."

David couldn't suppress a laugh. "We're no different, Daniel. God explains the need for obeying the rules by giving us His Holy Bible. But He also cares for us as many times as it takes and forgives us no matter how many times we mess up. His love is unconditional and unlimited."

"I want that," Katie said with a glow warming her face. "I want to have an eternity with a God like that."

Daniel turned to face his wife. "Me, too," he said with a sheepish grin.

David felt tears form in his eyes and felt no shame as they fell upon his cheeks. It was a moment so holy he could nearly hear the angels singing in heaven.

Taking hold of his brother's and sister-in-law's hands, David led them in a prayer of repentance. When they'd finished, all bore tears upon their faces and an afterglow of peace.

~

The next morning, Katie's strength had returned. She puttered around the house putting things in their place, not knowing how long this would be her home.

"You certainly have a way with things," David said as he came upon her in the kitchen.

"I love to have my things around me," Katie admitted. "The long preparation for coming here and for finding a place to stay has left me separated from my memory pieces far too long."

David fell silent as he wondered to himself how Jenny might set up a home.

"You miss her a lot, don't you?" Katie observed as she joined David at the table.

"What?"

"Jenny," Katie said softly. "You really miss her."

"Yes," David confessed. "I guess I didn't know it showed so much."

"Well, it does. Daniel and I have even discussed it."

"It's just her life is so bad, and she's so young. I wish I had an easy answer for the situation, but I don't," David said rather dejectedly.

"How does Jenny feel about you?" Katie asked as she eased her body onto a chair.

"I'm not really sure," David answered. "I think she enjoys my company, but I don't know if she feels more than friendship for me."

"Do you want her to?"

"More than I can say," David answered quickly. "I never realized until now, how much I want her to care. I love her, Katie. I love her, and I don't know what to do about it."

"Why don't you tell her?" Katie questioned.

"Do you really think I should? She's only sixteen, and she's not had a chance to meet many men or to court. I wouldn't want to rush her into something she might later regret."

"If you want my opinion, some folks are plenty ready at sixteen. Look at me. When I met your brother, I hadn't courted any other men, but I knew he was the right one for me."

"You certainly made a good choice," David admitted.

"Why don't you pray about it?" Katie asked with a grin. "That is what you'd tell one of us to do, isn't it?"

David laughed. "You're right, of course. I need to commit this to God. After all, if Jenny does feel the same way and marriage becomes a possibility for our future, I would want God's guiding hand upon us."

"I knew you'd figure it all out. And," Katie added, "if my opinion counts for anything, I think Jenny has already lost her heart to you. In fact, I think when you get back to Santa Fe, she'll probably bring up the subject before you get a chance to."

David had never felt such hopefulness. "I pray you're right, Katie. I pray you're right."

Chapter 7

Jenny was quick to realize things had changed between Natty and herself. Natty had begun to watch her with discomfort and mistrust.

More than once, Natty had questioned her about young Pastor Monroe. Jenny was furious with Natty for her constant haranguing and endless tirades, but there was nothing she could do to stop them. She resented being plagued about her feelings for David, which grew stronger and deeper every day.

Jenny struggled to make it through the days and weeks that passed. From the first morning's light, she put her mind and body to work. She heated outdoor caldrons of water and watched in thoughtful silence as the steam hit the cold morning air. It had been over a month since she'd seen David.

She wondered as she moved clothes absentmindedly against the scrub board whether or not she should seek him out and explain her feelings. Jenny shook her head as if answering herself. No, David would just see it as a childish crush. There was no sense in tormenting herself with thoughts about a life with David.

Jenny was startled back into reality by heavy knocking on the kitchen door. Wiping soapsuds from her hands, she made her way from the courtyard and through the house.

Opening the door, she was surprised to find David. Any thoughts of what to say were wiped from her mind when she noticed the grave expression on his face.

"It's Katie," David said in a breathless voice. "Daniel sent word by train. She's having the baby and not doing well."

Jenny's forehead furrowed in worry. "What can we do?"

"I don't know too may people yet, and Pastor Ed is out making calls in the country. He's not due back until Saturday. I thought maybe you'd be able to go on the train with me to Daniel and Katie's."

"Me?" Jenny questioned.

"Yes," David said frantically, "Katie knows you, and it might comfort her to have your company. I know it would be a comfort to me, and I hoped you might agree to come along."

"Of course," Jenny said as she tried to keep from shouting for joy. In such a grave situation, she didn't want to appear unfeeling. "I'll just get a few things."

"Daniel will have all the birthing things," David said as he wondered what Jenny could possibly think necessary to take.

"I know that," Jenny replied softly. "I thought we might need something to eat on the way. How far is it?"

"It'll be at least three hours by train," David said in a worried tone that caused Jenny to pick up her pace. "We'll take the spur from town and join the main line of the Atchison, Topeka, and Santa Fe about eighteen miles to the south. From there, it's another two hours north."

Jenny nodded as she pulled her heavy woolen shawl over her head and shoulders. "I'm ready," she said, handing David the bag she'd packed.

"Should you leave a note for Mrs. Morgan?"

"I suppose I should," Jenny conceded. She jotted a few words on a piece of paper and followed David out the door.

At the depot, a special train had been arranged for the express purpose of getting the pastor and his party back to the seasonal holding pens, which adjoined the property where Daniel and Katie had taken residence. The mood was set in the somber expression of the brakeman and conductor as David and Jenny climbed the stairs and took their seats on the short, four car train.

The train's crews had come to have a special affection for Mrs. Daniel Monroe. Every time they made water stops, Katie would come out and offer them cookies warm from the oven or pieces of her homemade pie. She'd won them over with her easygoing nature and laughing voice. Each crew member felt he owed a special debt to the tiny woman who would soon bring another life into the world.

The train had been stoked and was ready to make the trip before David had been notified, so it was no surprise when it pulled out before David and Jenny had taken their seats.

Jenny was thrown back against the hard wooden seat and stared open-mouthed as the scenery rushed past them. She'd never ridden on a train before, and the rocking motion was relaxing her against her will.

"Jenny," David's worried voice broke through her wonderment.

"Yes?"

"Will you pray with me?" he questioned as he took hold of her hand.

Jenny's heart nearly broke for the man beside her. His concern was clearly etched in every line on his face. "Of course," she replied, wondering what he might expect of her.

David smiled slightly and squeezed Jenny's hand. When he bowed his head, she did likewise and waited in silence for him to speak.

"Father, I need You so much," David prayed in an earnestness Jenny had never heard voiced in prayer. "We all need You. We need You to go before us and be with Daniel and Katie as they work to bring their child into the world. Lord, only You know in Your sovereign wisdom what will happen, what may have already happened. Father, we want Your will and not our own, but we pray You will give us the ability to deal with that will, whatever it may be. In Jesus' name, amen."

Jenny had never before felt the emotions that flooded through her. There was something so powerful in the words David had prayed. She envied the ease with which he spoke to God and wondered if she could have it for her own.

David refused to raise his face for a moment. He relished the moment of prayer with Jenny. Even though she hadn't made a declaration of faith in Christ, he knew she was open to God's message for her heart. He hoped there was a future for them, and that he could spend the rest of his life in intimate moments before his God, with Jenny as his wife.

For hours they rode on, their hands still entwined. Neither made a move to change the situation, and neither spoke for fear it might cause the moment to pass.

Sagebrush and cactus passed outside the window. In the near distance, the snow-capped peaks of the Sangre de Cristo Mountains rose to break the barrenness of the desert. As the sun rose and its brilliance reflected from the icy mountaintops, the scene looked more beautiful than anything Jenny had ever known.

She braved a glance at David, who was watching her with renewed interest. Jenny met his eyes and felt her breath quicken. She loved him so much. There was no doubt about her feelings and no use denying them.

"David, I—" Her words were interrupted by the conductor bursting through the door.

"We're here!" he announced, grabbing the nearest seat as the train shuddered to a stop. The squeal of metal on metal caused Jenny to clench her teeth.

David quickly escorted Jenny off the train and onto the loading platform. The train would wait to take Jenny and David back to Santa Fe because no other passenger train would be through for several days.

It didn't surprise either David or Jenny that Daniel didn't greet them at the door. David gave a knock and walked in without waiting for any word from his brother. The house was quiet except for the crackle and pop of the wood stove, which obviously had been tended regularly.

David strode to the bedroom door and knocked again. His brother joined him in a heartbeat.

"Did you bring another doctor?" Daniel questioned as he looked around the room.

"No, I couldn't find anyone who could come with me. I thought maybe Katie would find comfort in having a woman at her side, so I brought Jenny." Jenny's head snapped up in surprise. He'd called her a woman! David thought of her as an equal.

"I need a doctor!" Daniel said louder than he'd intended. Jenny could see the perspiration on his face.

"You are a doctor," David insisted. "You can do everything that needs to be done. Have a little faith in yourself."

Daniel ran his hand back through his sweat-soaked hair. "I don't think so, little brother. Katie isn't progressing the way she ought to be."

Jenny felt a sudden braveness and spoke. "May I see her?"

Daniel nodded and Jenny went quickly through the door and to Katie's bedside. She tried not to be surprised at the sight of Katie's near-lifeless form. Jenny reached for a basin of water and the cloth that lay beside it. Dipping the cloth in the water, she spoke softly and wiped Katie's brow tenderly.

Delicate lashes fluttered open as Katie drew a ragged breath to speak. "Jenny, how kind of you to come."

"Hush," Jenny whispered as she continued to bathe Katie's face. "I'm glad to be here. I know what a wonderful occasion this is. I wouldn't have missed it for the world."

Katie smiled weakly. "Where is Daniel?"

Jenny looked beyond the bed frame and through the doorway. Daniel stood speaking with David in hushed tones. "He's talking with David. Do you want me to get him?"

Katie shook her head. "No, please don't. I need to talk with you alone."

Jenny couldn't hide her puzzled expression. "With me? But why, Katie?"

Katie drew another deep breath as if it would strengthen her. When it didn't, she closed her eyes before continuing. "I'm not going to make it, Jenny."

Jenny wiped damp ringlets of blond hair away from Katie's face and forced a smile. "Of course you are, Katie. What nonsense. Every mother-to-be feels that way. You just wait until that baby is born. You'll see."

Katie reached up to still Jenny's lips with her fingers. Her hand fell weakly back to the mattress. "No," she said in a resolute manner. "You must listen to me, Jenny."

"Alright," Jenny said as she dropped the cloth into the basin and took hold of Katie's hand.

"Jenny," Katie's soft voice was barely audible, "the baby is dead."

"No!" Jenny stated sternly. "Daniel would have told us."

"Daniel can't think rationally, Jenny. He's been beside himself. I've been ill for two days now." Katie fell silent, and Jenny wondered if she'd lost consciousness.

"How do you know?" Jenny braved the questioned.

"The baby hasn't moved for hours," Katie began. "Daniel told me that they move less as they are born, but Jenny. . ." She paused. With added sadness in her voice, she spoke again. "I'm his mother, and I know he's gone."

Jenny felt tears in her eyes. "Oh, Katie. I'm so sorry."

"That's not all, Jenny. I need you to be strong, and I need you to help me."

"I'll do whatever I can," Jenny answered. She felt a growing love for the young woman.

"I'll soon be joining my son," Katie said with exacting words. "I can't leave, however, unless I know you and David will help Daniel to keep his faith in God."

Jenny felt stabbing pain in her chest. "How can you be certain, Katie?"

Katie smiled sadly. "I can hear the singing, Jenny." Her face brightened. "I can hear all of heaven singing. Oh, Jenny, it's beautiful."

Hot tears fell against Jenny's cheeks.

"Are you afraid?" Jenny asked. She didn't hear the men as they stepped into the room. She clung tightly to Katie's hand and held it to her heart.

"No," Katie said with more surety than Jenny would have thought possible. "My son is there and my King."

Jenny couldn't suppress a sob, "Don't leave us, Katie. Please don't leave us."

"Don't cry, Jenny." Katie offered the comfort and it sobered Jenny as she remembered she was to be there for Katie's benefit.

"I'm sorry," Jenny said as she tried to compose her emotions.

"Pray with me, Jenny," Katie pleaded with her last bit of strength.

"I'm not sure I know how," Jenny whispered, "but I'll try." She thought back to David's words on the train. She couldn't remember exactly how he had started, so she began in the only way she could. "God, I know we don't know each other real well, but Katie here knows You. Please God, don't take her from us."

"No," Katie whispered. "Pray for Daniel, not for me."

Jenny nodded, "Alright, Katie. God, please help Daniel. You know how much he's suffering."

"Please God, don't let my Daniel go astray. Don't let him grow bitter in my passing," Katie murmured. Jenny thought she heard someone leave the room.

Jenny opened her eyes and looked down at Katie's face. It was so delicate and pale, yet there was a peacefulness to her countenance Jenny couldn't explain.

"Thank you, Jenny. Would you please get Daniel? I want to say good-bye."

"I'll get him," Jenny whispered. She turned and found the room empty. David had gone ahead of her to retrieve Daniel.

Daniel was shaking his head as David was trying to convince him to go to his wife.

"I can't watch her die," Daniel said angrily. "I've killed her. Isn't that enough?"

"You didn't give her life," David stated firmly, "and you can't take her life. She's in God's hands now."

"He can't have her!" Daniel shouted back.

"He already does," David whispered in contrast.

"Stop it!" Jenny said as she came forward and put a hand on both men. "Stop it right now! Argue and mourn your losses later, but right now, Katie needs us."

"I can't," Daniel said and his voice cracked.

"Yes, you can," Jenny said as she took control and pulled Daniel toward the bedroom. "You have to for her sake. She wants to say good-bye, and she needs to know you'll be alright."

Daniel looked deeply into Jenny's eyes. "But I won't be alright ever again," he whispered.

"I know how you feel," Jenny replied as she thought of her family. It was a moment only she and Daniel could share. David couldn't understand the loss they faced.

Daniel nodded and followed Jenny to his wife's bedside. Kneeling beside the bed, Daniel took hold of Katie's hand. Tears poured down his face. Jenny cried silently as she stood at the end of the bed. David's hands fell in support upon her shoulders, and Jenny felt warmth spread through her body.

"Don't cry, Daniel," Katie whispered.

"But I've failed you."

"No," Katie answered weakly.

"But I'm a doctor," Daniel said in sorrowed dejection.

"And I'm a woman. Have I failed you because I couldn't give our child life?"

"No!" Daniel said, suddenly sobering.

Katie smiled at her husband's stern expression. "And neither have you failed me, Beloved." Katie sighed and closed her eyes." Thank you for loving me, Daniel, and thank you for our child."

"Oh, Katie! It's me who thanks you for the happiness I'd never thought possible," Daniel said as he leaned forward to kiss her one last time. "I love you, Katie."

"Do you hear it, Daniel?" Katie said as her expression brightened unnaturally.

"Hear what?" Daniel asked as he pulled Katie close.

"The bells. Those beautiful bells," Katie smiled and fell limp in Daniel's arms.

Daniel looked in shock from Katie's still form to David's and Jenny's tear-streaked faces.

"Get out!" Daniel said firmly.

"You need us now," David said as he took a step forward.

"Your God did this. I asked you to pray for her to get well and you prayed for His will. Well, He's had His way and now I'll have mine. Get out and don't ever come back!"

"You don't mean that," David said in shocked horror.

"I do mean it," Daniel said as he narrowed his eyes. "Take her and leave."

"God will give you comfort if you allow Him to," David offered softly. "It's all a matter of faith. Trust Him, Daniel. He won't leave you alone in this."

Daniel gently placed Katie's body on the bed and got to his feet. He stepped forward in a menacing way that caused David to take a step backwards. "I said get out, and I mean it. I don't want your religion or your formulated answers for why my wife is dead."

David took hold of Jenny's arm and pulled her along through the house. Quickly, David retrieved their things and opened the door for Jenny.

Daniel stood firm in his anger at the opposite side of the room.

"I love you, Daniel," David said as he motioned Jenny through the door. "I'll always love you, and so will God."

Daniel's eyes narrowed. "That's not my problem. It's yours and God's."

Chapter 8

David and Jenny rode the rails to Santa Fe in stunned silence. They sat side by side, holding hands as if hoping to gather strength from their loss at Katie's bedside.

It was Jenny who finally broke the silence and sought an understanding of Katie's passing. "David," she whispered in the fading light, "are Katie and her baby really in heaven?"

David's head snapped up, revealing tearstained cheeks. "I know she is," he replied confidently

"How?" Jenny questioned, needing to know.

"The Bible says so," David answered. "Remember when Jesus was dying on the cross?"

Jenny shook her head no.

"Jesus was condemned by His own people because they didn't understand who He was or why He'd come to them. Oh, there were a few who loved Him and knew Him for who He was, but they were too few to stop the others who wanted to put an end to His ministry. When Jesus was on the cross dying for the very people who'd condemned Him to death, two other men were being put to death. One man was only interested in having his flesh saved from death, but the other man was different. He knew Jesus was blameless."

"What did he do?" Jenny asked softly.

"He asked Jesus to remember him when He came into His kingdom. Jesus replied, 'To day shalt thou be with me in paradise.' That thief passed from life on earth to life in heaven with Christ."

"What about the other man?" Jenny asked.

"There is a passage in the Bible, Revelation 21:7-8, that explains what happens to people after they die: 'He that overcometh shall inherit all things; and I will be his God, and he shall be my son. But the fearful, and unbelieving, and the abominable, and murderers, and whoremongers, and sorcerers, and idolaters, and all liars, shall have their part in the lake which burneth with fire and brimstone: which is the second death.' "

"How awful," Jenny said.

"Yes," David agreed as he gazed out the window beyond Jenny.

"David," Jenny spoke, remembering Katie's peace in death. "I want to be saved from hell, and I want to know the same kind of peace and contentment Katie knew."

"I'm so glad, Jenny," David spoke, loving her more than he'd known possible. "Do you believe Jesus can save you from your sins and from the torments of hell?"

"Yes, I do."

"And you want Him to forgive you for your past sins?"

"Yes," Jenny replied. "I want that most of all."

"Are you willing to repent and turn from sinful behavior?" David questioned as he took hold of Jenny's hands. "Even your hatred of the Indians?"

Jenny grew thoughtful. "I don't know if I can forget what has happened, but I will seek daily to forgive the people who took the lives of my family. I certainly don't want to see any more killings happen. It won't bring back my family and it won't make my loss any less. But knowing I'm going to heaven when I die gives me peace I'll see my family again."

"I know God will help you, Jenny," David said with certainty. He led Jenny in a prayer of repentance and felt renewed hope for the future, even in the shadow of Daniel's rejection.

When David had finished praying, Jenny knew there would never be a better time to share her feelings for him. "David," she began, "there's something else I want to talk to you about."

David dropped Jenny's hands and leaned back against the seat. He was drained of all energy from dealing with Daniel, but Jenny seemed to offer him new vitality. "I'm all ears," he said as he turned to meet Jenny's warm gaze.

"I'm not very good at this," Jenny said slowly. "In fact, I've never done this before."

David raised an eyebrow curiously. "Go on," he encouraged.

Jenny took a deep breath and lowered her eyes. She twisted her hands in her lap as she struggled to choose the right words.

"I've never known anyone like you," Jenny began, "and I've never known the feelings you bring out in me." Jenny paused and wondered if she should continue. What if David didn't share her feelings? She'd have to endure another hour or more alone with him, and if he rejected her love, how would she be able to stand the closeness?

"And?"

Jenny sighed and realized there was no reason to avoid letting David know any longer. "I've fallen in love with you, David. I suppose you think I'm too young to know what love is all about, but I do know, I know I love you. I can't stand it when you're away from me, and I feel so good when you're nearby."

Jenny was afraid if she stopped talking, David would say something negative and ruin the moment. She was also afraid to look at him and panicked when she felt him reach over and lift her face to meet his eyes.

Without warning, David leaned over and pressed his lips tenderly to Jenny's. There weren't adequate words to speak his heart, and his kiss was the only offering he knew would be capable of saying everything he felt.

When he pulled away, Jenny fell back against the seat and sighed. He hadn't rejected her. She waited in silence for David to speak.

"You are very young," David said surprising them both. "However, you are very wise and mature. I know you've had to endure a great deal in your life and it has aged you somewhat, but I worry that you've never had the chance to meet other men. Perhaps you only love me because you've never had the chance to know anyone else."

"No," Jenny said firmly. "I love you because you are the right man for me. I know God sent you to me for a purpose."

David said nothing for a few minutes, causing Jenny to fear he didn't share her feelings. "I know He did too," David finally spoke. "I love you with all my heart, Jenny. I have from the first moment I saw you rain-drenched and sorrowed, standing in the church not knowing what you were looking for."

"Oh, David," Jenny said and threw herself into his arms. "I was so afraid you'd tell me you couldn't love me."

David held her close, breathing a sigh of contentment against her ear as he buried his face in her long dark hair. "I will always love you. I pledge that to you now and forever."

"And I pledge my love to you, David," Jenny whispered. "Now and forever, wherever the journey takes us."

"Would you be willing to marry me?" David questioned. "Not right now, but in a year or two when you are a bit older."

Jenny couldn't hide her disappointment as she pulled away from David. "Why do we have to wait? People my age get married every day. Some are a lot younger than I am. I don't want to wait, David. After all, I'll be seventeen in just a few weeks."

"I know all of that, Jenny," David said as he tried to think of just the right words. "I'm nearly finished with my studies and my apprenticeship with Pastor Ed. Jason Intissar, the man who hired Daniel to come to the territory and practice medicine, has a proposition for me as well. Frankly, I'm not so certain you would find it an appealing one, and I feel led to give it a try."

"What has he asked you to do?" Jenny questioned in a worried tone.

"Mr. Intissar wants me to run a Christian mission for the Pueblo Indians who live in the area up north of Santa Fe."

"Then you would leave Santa Fe and I wouldn't see you at all?" Jenny asked, trying to keep her voice even and under control.

"It would only be for a short time until I was able to get things going. Even though Mr. Intissar has kindly offered to provide everything, there is so much for me to learn. I'd need to learn the language just to be able to speak with the people. Then too, I'd need to learn their way of life and what they already believe about religion and God. There will be a great deal of work, and it wouldn't be an easy task under ideal circumstances."

"But I could help you. Don't you see? It would be easier with someone at your side." Jenny tried her best to sound convincing. "I would be able to keep house, cook, clean, sew, and of course, do laundry," she said with a smile.

David couldn't help but laugh. "Of course." Just as quickly his smile turned to a frown as he thought of Natty Morgan. Her influence was bound to take its toll on Jenny's heart and soul. Could he in good faith leave the woman he loved in such a foul place?

"What's wrong?" Jenny asked, noticing David's frown.

"I was remembering Natty. She could be a bit of a problem. If she's expected you to provide for her all these years, she won't be likely to let you go without a fight."

"No, I don't imagine she would," Jenny replied. "But I don't care. I don't owe her a thing. These years with Natty have been spent in misery and pain. I've worked hard for her, and I deserve a life of my own."

"True," David said as he studied the young woman before him. "Still, if you agree to marry me and we wait for a spell, she shouldn't complain too fiercely."

"I wish you wouldn't insist on waiting," Jenny said and bit her lower lip to keep from saying more.

"But you will wait for me, won't you?"

Jenny rolled her eyes and sighed. "You aren't offering me any other choices, are you?"

David smiled as he gave Jenny's arm a squeeze. "The time will pass before you know it. Let's plan to marry when you're eighteen—that's only a little more than a year away. You'll need that much time to plan the wedding," David teased. "And while you wait, read this," David added and handed Jenny a Bible.

Jenny smiled. "Alright," she finally agreed. "I'll marry you when I turn eighteen, but I'm not waiting a single day beyond January 1, 1886." She glanced down at the book in her hand. "Thank you for the Bible. I'll probably have the whole thing memorized by the time you get around to marrying me."

"I'm so happy, Jenny. Thank you for understanding," David said as he pulled Jenny into his arms. "I promise you won't regret your decision."

Jenny laughed and turned her face to David's. "I've no doubt you're right," she murmured as he lowered his mouth to hers in a passionate kiss.

When the train finally pulled into Santa Fe, it was well past nine o'clock at night. David walked Jenny to her home, enjoying the time they shared together, but in his heart was the sorrow that Katie was dead and his only brother had alienated himself from David's support and love.

As they approached Jenny's home, David noticed Natty peering out the window. "You'd better let me explain," David said, opening the gate for Jenny and leading her up the walk.

"Why bother?" Jenny questioned. "She won't be understanding, and she won't care what the excuse is. Natty will only know her meal wasn't on the table and her friends lacked refreshments while gambling at her home."

"I should at least try," David insisted.

Jenny opened the door. A string of curses filled the air, and Natty yanked Jenny away from David's tender touch.

"Where have you been?" Natty yelled. "How can you call yourself a man of the cloth and allow a child such as this to be compromised?"

"I beg your pardon, Madam," David began, "Jenny hasn't been compromised in any way. My sister-in-law went into labor and my brother sent word that help was needed. We took the train to their home north of Santa Fe. We were under constant supervision."

"What possible need would a woman giving birth have for this child?" Natty screeched.

"They were friends. I thought Jenny might offer comfort and support," David responded evenly. "And I might add, she did."

"Jenny doesn't have time for friends," Natty said in a calmer voice. "I don't believe your story, young man."

"It's true, Natty," Jenny said having grown tired of the confrontation. "I've never lied to you, and I'm not lying now. Katie Monroe died a few hours ago. She was my friend for only a short time, but nonetheless, she was my friend. She and her baby now live in heaven."

For once, Natty had run out of words.

Jenny continued, "David, I think you should leave now. I'll see you tomorrow."

David nodded and moved toward the door.

"No, you won't!" Natty said in an ominous tone. "You are not to come here again, young man, and you are never to see Jenny again, anywhere, at any time."

"You can't control her life forever," David said as he narrowed his eyes. He moved toward Natty, then hesitated and turned toward the door. "I intend to make Jenny my wife, and there isn't anything you can do about it. She doesn't belong to you, and she isn't going to work herself to death in order for you to be waited on. I love this woman—obviously something she hasn't enjoyed since the death of her parents—and you will not separate us."

"You are very wrong about that, Sir. Very wrong," Natty said and crossed the room, putting herself between David and Jenny. "I'll have the law here if you aren't off my property immediately, and if you dare to show your face here again, I'll personally shoot you between the eyes."

Jenny gasped and moved forward. "You leave him be, Natty. I've done nothing wrong, and you can't treat me as if I were a child. David, please leave. I'll be fine. I have to talk with Natty, and it would be best if you weren't here."

David nodded and moved to leave. "I assure you of one thing, Madam," he said as he filled the doorway with his full height. "If you harm Jenny in any way, you will answer to me and answer dearly." With that he was gone, and Natty was left to slam the door behind him.

Natty turned, red-faced, to confront Jenny. "I've offered you a home and food for your belly, and this is my thanks?"

"You've offered me nothing," Jenny said, willing to brave Natty's rage. "I've worked myself into exhaustion to keep this place and to provide the food we eat. You spend your days and nights in gambling and all types of depraved entertainment. I've endured it for years, but enough is enough. I intend to find other living accommodations tomorrow!"

Jenny stormed off to her room before Natty had a chance to reply.

Natty sat down on a chair. In mild shock, she began to formulate a plan. There was no way she'd allow Jenny Oberling to slip through her fingers without receiving some kind of return on her investment. The first order of business would be to confine Jenny.

Before first light, Natty promised herself, there would be a lock firmly in place on Jenny's door. A lock on the door and bars on the window if necessary, Natty determined with a smile. Whatever it took to keep Jenny locked inside and David Monroe out.

Chapter 9

Natty sat shrouded in the darkness that was the inseparable companion of her favorite gambling house. The man sitting opposite her at the poker table was impeccably dressed and obviously wealthy. He was also a man of worse reputation than any other who tormented Santa Fe.

"You say she's nearly seventeen?" the man questioned as he raised a glass of whiskey to his lips.

"Yes and *untouched,*" Natty added.

"Are you certain of that?" the man asked, leaning forward and narrowing his dark eyes in a menacing manner.

"I'd stake my life on it. I checked out the pastor who's been keeping her company, and he's got a better reputation than Archbishop Lamy himself," Natty said referring to the beloved archbishop of Santa Fe.

The man nodded and smiled. "And she's not a mixed breed?"

"No," Natty insisted. "She's white."

"Well, if what you say it true, I have a customer who'll pay quite nicely to take your niece off your hands. We have a marriage auction coming up on the fifteenth of January. Can you have her in back of the San Miguel Mission by nightfall?"

"I don't think she'll come willingly."

"We have many reluctant brides," the man said as he reached into his silk vest pocket and pulled out a vial of liquid. "Just put this in her water or coffee. It won't knock her out completely, but it will make her easier to handle."

Natty took the vial and smiled. "And when will I get my money?"

"At the auction." The man finished his whiskey and got to his feet. Giving a slight bow, he left.

∽

Jenny's captivity had passed from days into weeks, until finally she realized she'd missed both Christmas and her birthday. Natty had locked her in her room and hired a man to install bars outside the windows.

Jenny thought she'd go mad trying to free herself. First she'd tried to break down her door, but Natty had called upon one of her associates to reinforce the frame with metal bars similar to those on Jenny's windows.

Jenny had screamed for help, but Natty had threatened to have her moved out of town to stay with one of Natty's friends. Jenny had no desire to be left to the care of the desperate characters Natty called friends, so she remained silent, even when she heard David in the foyer.

As the weeks passed, Jenny spent most of her time praying God would give David the direction and wisdom needed to defeat Natty. But as the sun set night after night, Jenny grew fearful and frustrated.

"Dear God," Jenny murmured, kneeling beside her bed one night, "I know You're watching over me because David said You'd never leave me alone and if I belonged to You, You'd hear my prayers and answer them. Please God, please help David to save me from Natty and whatever plans she's making for me. You have the power over evil and power over Natty Morgan, so please deliver me from this place. Amen."

Jenny got to her feet, blew out the lamp, and got into bed. Thoughts of David and his gentle love filled her mind. Would she ever be reunited with him? David had told her trust and faith formed the key to peace in God. "I trust You, Lord," Jenny said as she closed her eyes. "I trust You."

David paced the floor, reviewing Jenny's predicament. He wished he knew Natty's plans, but the few times he'd gotten past her front door, David had been showered with a tirade of Natty's obscenities that revealed nothing of her intentions.

A sharp knock at the door interrupted David's thoughts. Outside stood Garrett Lucas.

"Evening," Garrett said as David opened the door to him. "I'm Jason Intissar's foreman, Garrett Lucas."

"I remember you," David said as he stepped back. "Come on in and take a load off."

"I'm not usually given to interfering in other people's business, but there are a couple of things I thought we ought to talk about. The first is your brother and the second is your lady friend."

"Jenny? What do you know of her?" David questioned anxiously.

"Well, it's not pleasant," Garrett said, removing his black Stetson and accepting a chair David offered.

"Coffee?" David asked as he poured himself a cup.

"Please," Garrett replied and fidgeted with his hat until David held out the steaming cup. Putting his hat on the empty chair beside him, Garrett took a long drink. "Hits the spot," he sighed.

"You surely haven't come all the way from the Intissar ranch tonight, have you?" David observed as he took the seat opposite Garrett.

"No, I've been staying at your brother's place. That is, until yesterday. I took the train down and have a room over at the Exchange Hotel."

"How is Daniel? I've been quite worried, but he refuses to see me. I've sent several letters to him, but he won't have anything to do with me. He blames me and God for Katie's death."

"I know."

David studied the man before him. He seemed so young. How strange that Garrett would be the one to bring him news of Daniel.

"Does Daniel talk to you?" David asked painfully.

"At first he didn't, but we've come to be real good friends over the past few weeks. I didn't know about the baby and his wife when I first showed up at the house. Daniel wouldn't open the door to me, but after I slept two nights in the barn, he figured I might freeze to death and invited me to sleep in the house."

"What were you doing there?" David questioned.

"Jason had sent me. I was supposed to be checking up on Daniel and Katie, as well as getting Daniel's decision on several possible places for his permanent home. Only now, I guess there won't be a permanent home."

"What do you mean?" David asked, nearly dropping his cup.

"That's why I came to see you. Daniel plans to pack up and move. He said as much as he loves New Mexico, he can't bear to stay where Katie's grave stares him in the face every day."

"But he doesn't need to stay there. Didn't Mr. Intissar want him to move closer to the ranch anyway?"

"That's what I reminded him of. I think I've talked him into coming up to the ranch until spring. I wanted you to know he'd be moving in case you came looking for him," Garrett replied with his eyes downcast.

"Daniel told me he wasn't on speaking terms with you," Garrett continued. "We've talked a great deal about Katie's death and how he blames God for it. I'm a Christian, myself, and I've tried to explain trusting God in the bad times, but your brother is determined to see this as a personal attack. I shared Romans 8:28, telling him God works all things together for good for those who love Him, but your brother looks at me like it's all some cruel joke. I wish I could reach him. Maybe in time, I will."

"I'm grateful for what you've done," David said, getting to his feet. "I wish I could see him. No, actually I wish he would see the truth. I know how he's suffering. Well, not exactly, but enough I feel I could offer some love and support. I want to be with him, but he won't allow me to."

"Don't be too hard on him," Garrett said. "Daniel will come around in time 'cause he's too smart to do otherwise. Just have faith, Pastor." He grinned.

"You're right, of course," David returned the smile. "It's just I've never been good at waiting. I mean, the situation I'm facing with Jenny Oberling is a good example. That reminds me, what do you know about her?"

"I'm afraid my news about Miss Oberling isn't encouraging. Fact is, it's quite the opposite. Jenny is in grave danger, and I knew you'd want to know. I'll help you any way I can."

David paled considerably. "What do you mean?"

"I happened across some information and learned it involved Jenny. I already knew from talking to Daniel you had hopes of marrying her, so when I heard she was to be involved in an illegal marriage auction, I knew it most likely wasn't of her own accord."

"Marriage auction? What's that?" David asked, knowing it seemed like a ridiculous question.

Garrett pushed his cup back and sighed. "It's mostly a front for white slavery and prostitution. Girls think they're bargaining for a husband, but most often they're signing away their lives into all types of heinous activities. No doubt your Jenny isn't going of her own free will, but that doesn't matter to the men who run the auction. As long as the women are provided, they will run their trade."

"I'm certain Jenny would never agree to this auction," David protested, sitting down in a chair opposite Garrett. "What are we to do?"

"You love her, right?"

"Of course, I do. I asked her to marry me on the trip back from Daniel's. She loves me as much as I love her. I've been praying and biding my time." David buried his face in his hands. "Now it would seem I've waited too long."

"You gonna give up, just like that?" Garrett questioned. "I know I wouldn't let the woman I love get away without a fight."

"What do you suggest? I've been to talk to Natty Morgan—she's the woman who's holding her captive. I've tried to talk sense to her, but she won't listen."

"Does Natty ever leave the house?"

"I suppose," David said as he raised his face in hope. "What do you think we should do?"

"I can watch her house," Garrett suggested. "After all, she doesn't know me. I could keep an eye on her, and when she's going to be out, I could come after you. You could come break in and take Jenny out."

"It might work," David agreed as he got to his feet once again. "I can't thank you enough for coming to help me. I would never have known in time and Jenny might have. . ." His voice trailed into silence. "Well, I don't want to think about what might have happened. We won't let it happen, and that's all there is to it."

"Then we're agreed," Garrett said as he stood and put his hat on. "Give me directions to her house, and I'll start watching immediately."

David walked to the door with Garrett. "Our best chance will probably be at night," he decided. "Natty used to do most of her sleeping during the day and spend her nights partying at one establishment or another."

"Then I'll go straightway from here to their house," Garrett said as he stepped into the night darkness.

"You're a good man, Garrett Lucas, and I hope we can be friends for a long, long time."

Garrett smiled and nodded in agreement.

"Now, as for the directions," David said, "you turn left at the corner and head two blocks north. You'll turn left again at the next corner. Her house will be the second on the right."

"Sounds easy enough," Garrett said and buttoned his coat against the cold. "I'll let you know when it's clear."

David watched Garrett disappear into the darkness. He got the strong impression he and Garrett were just beginning their relationship. Despite his youth, Garrett Lucas would make a good friend.

Chapter 10

David's opportunity came the following evening. Around midnight, long after David had given up hope of seeing Garrett, he appeared at the door breathless.

"It's time, David," Garrett said as David tried to pull on his boots. "Mrs. Morgan has planted herself in one of the south side gambling houses. She doesn't look inclined to return home anytime soon, but I suggest we hurry."

"I'm with you all the way," David said, pulling on his coat. "We'll come back here after we get her, and Pastor Ed will marry us. That way, Natty won't have a chance of getting Jenny back."

"You can come to Jason's ranch with me afterward," Garrett insisted. "Since Jason wants you to set up a mission for the Indians, this would be perfect timing." David nodded and followed Garrett into the street.

∽

By Jenny's calculations, it was January 14. She had passed over two months in captivity. Instead of breaking Jenny's spirit, Natty Morgan had only managed to steel her determination to escape.

Jenny had taken to matching Natty's sleeping habits. While Natty ventured away each night, Jenny worked at putting a hole in the wall that separated her bedroom from the sewing room. Natty would never step into the sewing room, and Jenny knew her only chance of escape would be through that wall.

Jenny sighed as she pounded away at the thin, but stubborn, wall. She had taken the brass candelabra and used the base to chip away at the wood. "Lord, give me the strength I need," Jenny whispered. She repeated Philippians 4:13 again and again for encouragement: "I can do all things through Christ which strengtheneth me."

Natty had been gone little less than an hour when Jenny heard noises coming from downstairs. She stopped her pounding and listened. Natty was returning. Jenny's heart sank as she put the candelabra back on the nightstand. Hearing scuffling sounds on the steps, Jenny returned the unlit candles to the candelabra and sat down on her bed.

She waited in silence, wondering why Natty had returned so early. It surely couldn't mean anything good. Her heart pounded harder as the footsteps on the stairs came closer. She pulled her knees up to her chest and held her breath.

Bang! Bang! Bang! The door was still reverberating from the pounding when Jenny called out in a weak voice. "What do you want?"

"Jenny! It's me, David!"

"David!" Jenny called as she raced to the door. "Oh, David, is it really you?" She leaned her face against the door as if it would bring her closer to him.

"It's really me. I'm here with a friend, and we've come to break you out."

"You'll never get through this door," Jenny said, "but I've been trying to break through the wall that joins my room to the sewing room. If you go in there, you might be able to get me out. It's the room to the right."

"We'll give it a try, Jenny. You be sure and stay clear," David called.

"I will," she agreed and moved across the room to where a single candle was burning on a small table.

Jenny could hear the men move supplies and furniture in the sewing room to reveal the small hole she had put through the wall.

"This ought to be fairly simple," Garrett said as he motioned David to stand back. It took only three powerful blows of Garrett's booted foot until the wood splintered and cracked. Both men reached down and pulled the boards away until a hole large enough for Jenny was created.

"Bring whatever you can't bear to leave behind, because I don't intend for you to ever return," David said in an authoritative voice that gave Jenny strength.

Jenny hurried to put her meager wardrobe and family momentos into a bag. The last thing she reached for was the beloved Bible, which had become her mainstay. Placing it in the bag, she handed it through the opening into David's waiting hands.

"Just put your head and shoulders through the opening and we'll lift you out," David said as his heart raced in fear. Too much time was slipping by, and his concern that Natty would return was haunting his every move.

Jenny popped her head through the opening and a broad grin spread across her face. "I've been working at this for weeks, and you come along, put a little pastorly persuasion into it, and here we are."

David reached out and took hold of Jenny's shoulders. "It wasn't me," he said as he eased Jenny through the hole. Garrett cleared away debris that blocked her path.

As the men got Jenny to her feet, she immediately threw herself into David's arms. "I wouldn't have cared if Indians themselves had come to take me away. Thank you so much," she said with tears pouring freely down her face. "I wasn't sure you'd come for me."

David took hold of her face and kissed her wet cheeks. "You must never doubt my love for you, Jenny. Never, never doubt that my love binds me to you. Because of it, we can never truly be separated."

Jenny nodded and reached up to push back David's blond hair as it fell across his forehead. "I will never doubt it again," she whispered.

Garrett cleared his voice uncomfortably. "I hate to break this up, but we need to get out of here before Mrs. Morgan returns."

David dropped his hands and Jenny turned abruptly to face her other rescuer. "Thank you so much for helping us," Jenny said as she leaned forward and kissed Garrett's boyish cheek. "I thank God for the both of you."

"I, too, thank God, Ma'am, but we needn't put Him to a foolish test. I suggest we leave by way of the courtyard," Garrett drawled as he picked up Jenny's bag and led the way.

Jenny let David pull her along through the darkened house, hardly daring to believe the joy that rushed through her. She was being set free—free from a life of misery with Natty Morgan and free from the fear of losing David.

Once they'd reached the courtyard and alley, Jenny let go of David's hand in order to pull her skirts up and nearly fell into a hole. David took hold of her arm to steady her.

When they were nearly a block away from Natty's house, David and Garrett slowed the pace to a brisk walk. Jenny's pounding heart steadied and her breathing evened. "Where are we going?" she whispered into the dark night.

"The church," David responded.

Standing safely in the vestibule of the Methodist Church, Jenny felt as if the nightmare she'd lived the past weeks was nothing more than a dream. She waited patiently as David exchanged a few words with Garrett before disappearing through the sanctuary of the church and into the back rooms.

Garrett tossed his Stetson onto one of the pews and put Jenny's bag beside it. "You're a lucky woman," he said as he gave Jenny a lazy smile.

"I know," Jenny agreed and returned the smile.

"By the way, I'm Garret Lucas."

"I'm indebted to you, Mr. Lucas," Jenny said as she extended her hand.

"Just plain ol' Garrett is good enough for me," he said as he took her hand. "I kinda figure after you and David move to the ranch, we'll become pretty good friends."

Jenny's eyes grew wide in surprise. "What are you saying?"

Garrett frowned for a moment. "I just figured you. . .well, I thought. . ." Garrett's embarrassment.

"Don't worry about it, Garrett. You haven't caused me any problem. Please don't feel bad."

"Why should Garrett feel bad?" David asked as he came through the back door with a sleepy-eyed Pastor Ed.

"I'm afraid I let the horse out of the barn, so to speak," Garrett said, raising his eyes sheepishly to meet curious stares. "I mentioned something about you all moving to the ranch."

David laughed. "Is that all? Jenny, I know this is short notice, but Pastor Ed here has been good enough to get up in the middle of the night and marry us. If you're willing, that is," David said softly.

Jenny looked contemplative for a moment. "Are you sure it's the best thing for us?"

"Are you afraid it might not be?" David questioned.

"No. I feel confident in your choices. I'd love very much to marry you, David." Jenny's smile was all the reassurance he needed.

"Well," Ed said with a yawn, "if you two are agreed, I'd really like to get on with this."

David laughed and pulled Jenny with him to stand in front of Ed. "Then let's get to it. We wouldn't want Natty Morgan to come busting in and ruin our plans."

Jenny stiffened noticeably, and David offered her a comforting smile. "She's not going to ruin our plans, Jenny. Don't worry. God is with us in this."

Jenny nodded, and Pastor Ed began the ceremony that would join the two young people together for the rest of their lives.

Twenty minutes later, David and Jenny Monroe followed Garrett Lucas on horseback. They rode north to a new life serving God. It was the tenderest journey Jenny had ever embarked on, and her heart held a deepening love and admiration for the man she now called husband.

Chapter 11

J enny Monroe brushed on the final touches of whitewash and stood back to survey her work. Three small graves gleamed from the outlines of whitewashed rock. There were also whitewashed crosses at the head of each grave; faithful reminders that her children dwelt in heaven with their Creator.

Wiping the final smudges of paint from her hands, Jenny picked up her things and moved toward the adobe barn. Children's laughter rang sweet from the open pasture behind the two-story adobe house. Glancing out across the fields, Jenny counted the children.

One, two, three—her eyes continued their search until she counted seven. Jenny laughed as the children played the games David had taught them. He loved these young waifs as much as she did. Many had come to them as sickly babes—some as the results of epidemics that claimed their parents' lives—but all of them had one thing in common: they were Indian.

Jenny loved them as much as the three little ones she'd borne and buried. They were God's blessings.

When the children caught sight of Jenny, the sky filled with little brown hands waving with glee. To some, Jenny was the only mother they'd ever known, and they loved her as if they'd belonged to her forever.

How many children had crossed the steps of the orphanage and mission she and David tended? Jenny thought back over the years she and David had worked to establish their ministry with the Indians.

She had to laugh to herself as she went back to work. She had once hated the Indians, blaming them for the death of her family. Now she was mothering seven of them and working with the tribe of local Pueblo. God had been so good to her, but the transition hadn't come without a price.

Within the first four years of her marriage to David, Jenny had developed a strong, sustaining faith in God. She devoted herself to prayer, and each time she'd found herself with child, her faith and belief had been sorely tested.

She remembered the anticipation and longing both she and David had shared as they'd awaited the birth of their first child. Having witnessed Katie's death not long before, they'd also been anxious about the delivery. When birthing day came, Jenny survived. Her baby did not. Jenny would never forget the devastation and heartbreak of burying that little babe who'd never known the sunlight on his face.

To watch their fears be realized had taken its toll on Jenny's and David's renewed hope. He realized he wouldn't lose Jenny as Daniel had lost Katie. The experience also helped him understand why Daniel's despair had so easily turned to bitterness.

Jenny's emotional recovery was much slower, however. She sat for hours in the room that would have been the nursery. Sometimes she cried, other times she ranted, but finally she accepted the event, remembering Romans 8:28: "All things work together for good to them that love God. . ." She still wasn't sure what possible good could come from the death of a baby.

Jenny looked heavenward. The skies had threatened rain all morning and yet the billowy black clouds hung overhead as stubborn sentinels refusing to yield their posts. *We could use a bit of rain,* Jenny thought as she moved across the yard. Her garden was just starting to show wispy shoots of green.

Jenny reveled in the change across the land as winter became spring in dusky hues of mint green and flowering white. It wouldn't be long until spring burst upon the scene in a riot of color and warmth, but for now she was content with the beginnings of life.

Back in her kitchen, Jenny busied herself with the necessary tasks at hand. She checked her roast, then the clock. David would be returning soon, so Jenny rang the bell to call the children.

Everyone had their jobs to do, and from the oldest to the youngest, each child knew what was expected. Jenny maintained if you had the ability to walk and hold onto things, you were old enough to help. Even three-year-old Storm, or Night-That-Storms as the Pueblo called him, was an able-bodied worker and happily carried the napkins and place mats to the table.

Jenny took pride in the children God had loaned her. Some would stay for years, while others were quickly retrieved by family members who'd learned of their fate. Jenny hated to see any of them go and was always happy to see David or one of the Pueblo people appear with yet another needy bundle.

"Is anybody home?" David called out as he came through the front door. Squeals of laughter filled the air, and all the children found hiding places. This was their nightly game, and no one would dream of doing anything different.

Jenny stood in the hallway, arms outspread. "I can't find the children. It seems they've disappeared again."

Giggles and the sound of hushed whispers could be heard throughout the first floor of the Monroe house.

"Mrs. Monroe, it would seem you are always misplacing them. I suppose," David said as he feigned exhausted reluctance, "I shall have to find them for you."

Jenny smiled and her brown eyes danced with love. For nearly ten years she'd been blessed enough to call this man husband, and every moment of her life she only loved him more.

"Ah-ha!" David shouted, and six-year-old Fawn screamed out in pleasure. David tickled her stomach and put her on one of the long table benches. "So, White-Fawn-Dancing, just where are your brothers and sisters?"

"Don't know," Fawn giggled, displaying the wide gap where her two front teeth were missing. "They're hiding. You won't find them."

"Oh yes, I will," David said as he raised the edge of the tablecloth to reveal three laughing toddlers. "Come here, you three." David reached his arms out wide and pulled the children to his chest. He whirled around once before putting the children on the bench beside Fawn.

"More!" all three yelled in unison.

"Not yet," David laughed. "There're still three more to find."

"I know where day are," Storm said in his baby-like voice.

David tousled his ebony hair and said, "Then you may help me." Storm smiled broadly.

Jenny watched the game continue and basked in the warmth that filled her heart. The only thing she was missing was a baby of her own. Quietly, she turned away from the group and finished putting the food on the table. She didn't want the children to see the tears that were in her eyes.

"Please Lord," she prayed in a whisper, "please let me be satisfied with that with which You have blessed me." She could hear the laughter in the front room and forced herself to concentrate on the happy voices of her husband and the orphans.

It should be enough, she realized, but just as readily she knew her discontentment ran deep.

"Papa David told me to help," Raining Sky said as she took a bowl of green beans from the kitchen counter.

"Thank you," Jenny said, composing herself and bestowing a warm smile on the ten year old. Jenny brought the roast and followed behind Raining Sky.

"Oh good," David called. "Come along, children. It's suppertime."

The little ones gathered around the table and joined hands as David led them in prayer. "Dear Father, we thank You for the wonderful meal which

You have provided. We thank You too, for the children who share this food and the love they give us. Bless us all and help us to serve You all the days of our lives. Amen."

"Amen," Jenny agreed, and the children echoed her reply.

"Let's eat," David said as he started cutting the roast. "Pass your plates, and I'll put some meat on them."

"Don't want befajewels," Storm said and made a face.

"They're called vegetables, and you will eat them because they help you to stay healthy and strong," Jenny said firmly.

"Don't like 'em," Storm pouted but, nonetheless, took the offered plate of food.

Later that night, Jenny sat alone in the darkness listening to the silence of the house. The children were all asleep and even David's even breathing signaled he was deep in dreams.

"Why am I struggling so much with this, Lord?" Jenny whispered. "I love the children You've given me to care for. I don't mean to seem ungrateful, because it's not that I don't love my life. I just can't explain what I feel inside. It's like an incompleteness, a longing for that which I've only glimpsed from afar. I want a baby, Lord. A baby of my own that won't be taken up to heaven before I can share my life with him or be retrieved by the Indians to join his real family. I'm like Hannah before Eli in the temple: if You will but give me a child, I pledge to give him back in trust to You. But please, please Lord, let me love him on earth for a time."

Chapter 12

S everal weeks later, Jenny stood admiring her garden. The beans were up high enough to merit staking off the ground, and the onions had already yielded a nice addition to their meals. Jenny leaned over and pulled a few weeds before going into the house to finish her baking.

Spring had come in wet and cold, and Jenny was grateful for the warmth of her toasty kitchen. She pulled two brown-crusted apple pies from the oven and quickly filled the emptiness with five tins of bread dough. Checking the clock, Jenny gauged herself to have time enough to whip up a batch of David's favorite Mexican custard before he'd return for lunch.

A ruckus of children's voices brought Jenny quickly from the kitchen to see what the problem was.

"Look," Fawn called out as she pulled Jenny toward the front window.

Jenny looked out across the front yard to see David approaching with three Pueblo men. She immediately recognized them as members of the council that guided the tribe in all its decision making.

"You children stay here and continue working on your studies. I'll check your work when I come back," Jenny said as she went to meet David. Jenny had only known the tribal leaders to leave the village when it was a matter of grave concern. She knew this time would be no different. She watched as David talked intently with the men, not even pausing to recognize Jenny's approaching form.

Jenny met them at the gate and noted the apprehension in David's eyes. "What is it?" she asked, uncertain she wanted to know.

David cast her a sorrowful glance. "They've come for the children, Jenny."

Jenny swallowed hard. This kind of thing had happened before, but usually the relatives of the children came—certainly never the elders. "Which ones?" she asked hesitantly.

"All of them," he lamented.

Jenny's mouth dropped open in shock. "All of them?"

"I'm afraid so," David said as he put his arm around Jenny's shoulder.

"But. . .but. . . ," Jenny stammered as her eyes filled with tears. "Why?" She looked at each of the tribal leaders with questioning eyes. "Why are you taking them away?"

"Sickness has taken many of our people," the oldest leader spoke. Jenny recognized him as the *cacique*, religious leader of the Pueblo. "Black-Cloud-Raining, why do you want to take all of the children? If there's been sickness, won't they be exposed as well?"

"Many children dead. My people are fewer each year. They die from white man's fevers and walk the way of our father's to the spiritland. We need the children to make us strong again," Black-Cloud-Raining spoke firmly.

The *t'aikabede* raised his hand to speak before Jenny could comment on Black-Cloud-Raining's words. She respected the man whose word was ultimately the deciding factor. As the head of the tribal council the *t'aikabede* would never have left the village if the situation hadn't demanded his guidance.

"We would not have come without many talks. We spent many hours in the Kiva, praying and speaking of what we should do. We know that it is good for the people of our village if we bring the children home."

Despite the fact Jenny knew the religious significance of gathering in the circular adobe Kiva, she couldn't endure the pain in her heart. "But they have a good home here," she protested as her eyes filled with tears. "They belong with us."

"They are Pueblo and they belong with the people of their fathers," Black-Cloud-Raining said with little concern for Jenny's tears.

Jenny opened her mouth to speak again, but David shook his head sadly. "I've already said all of this, Jen," he offered painfully. "They are determined to take them, and we are powerless to stop them."

Jenny looked with pleading brown eyes to each Indian leaders'. She prayed silently that one would take pity on her and leave one or two of the youngest for her to care for. "Surely the littlest ones could stay," she said hopefully.

"No," the *t'aikabede* said firmly. "We will take all the children to their people. We leave now."

"At least let them eat. They haven't had lunch yet," Jenny said as the men moved toward the house.

"They eat while they journey." Black-Cloud-Raining's stern voice and expression caused Jenny to realize she was powerless. How could she stand by and watch them take away her children? How could God let this happen?

"I'll get them ready," Jenny finally said with a heaviness in her voice David hadn't heard since the death of their last child. "You wait here."

Jenny wished she could find it in her heart to offer refreshments, but she felt the old feelings of anger toward Indians creep into her heart. "Let them die of thirst!" she thought and immediately regretted her animosity. "Forgive me, Father."

Jenny called all the children into the foyer. "I have some news," she said trying to sound calm. There was no need to share her grief with the children. "Your families have asked the elders to bring you home. They have come to take you back to the tribe."

"We be gone long time?" Fawn asked, in her wide-eyed, innocent way.

Jenny's resolve nearly crumbled. "I'm afraid so, Fawn. The *t'aikabede* has come to take you home for. . .for. . ." Jenny's voice cracked as she struggled to force out the word. "Forever," she finally managed.

"Will we see you and Pastor David again?" one of the other children asked.

"Yes, of course you will. Pastor David goes often to the Pueblo village, and I will come with him to visit you," Jenny explained.

"Where will we live?" Fawn asked curiously. It was all starting to sound like a game to her.

"You will live in the adobe pueblo's your people have built. Remember? We talked about the houses they live in. They are much like this house, only there are no doors or windows on the ground floor, or at least very few."

"It is to make our people safe," one of the older boys insisted.

"Yes, that's right," Jenny agreed. "You will live a different life there. You will not study from books as you do here. You will not speak English as much as you will the language of your people. Your jobs will be different, also. You boys will do more hunting and fishing, while your sisters work the hides and gather berries and wood."

"I make dem, too," Storm said as his little grubby fingers reached up to pull at Jenny's hands.

Jenny lifted the small boy in her arms and buried her face against his. "I know you will make your people proud," she whispered. "I know all of you will. Now, come give me a hug."

Jenny was rushed from all sides by the children. Even the oldest boy felt no shame in offering affection for his temporary guardian. "Now, go pack your things. The elders are waiting."

Jenny listened as the children's footsteps echoed up the stairs to their bedrooms. She could hear their pat, pat, pat down the hall as they ran in excitement. Why couldn't they seem less excited? No, Jenny reminded herself silently. She and David had worked diligently to teach the children they were to look forward to returning to their people. It would be wrong to expect any different from them now.

She took slow and deliberate steps to climb the stairs to where the children were excitedly chattering about their journey. She helped Storm to secure the small pack he would wear on his back. He looked too little to carry anything for himself, but Jenny knew the elders would expect no less. That was why she and David had always worked to teach the children the Pueblo way. She continued to remind herself it was for just this day they had worked so long and so hard. The children should be with their people to learn and preserve their heritage.

She monitored their packing and helped them to distribute their loads evenly so their little backs wouldn't grow sore. *Children should be cherished and pampered,* she thought, but even as she did, Jenny realized being too soft could prove deadly for these children.

There was a small, parade-like procession back down the stairs and to the front door. Jenny kissed each child and offered some tidbit of advice or reminder of a memory they'd shared together. When she picked up Night-That-Storms, it was all she could do to keep from running—running until she was so far away that no one, not the *t'aikabede* or Black-Cloud-Raining or anyone else, could take him away from her.

"I wuv you, Mama," Storm said in his babyish voice, forgetting to add Jenny's name. She was the only mother he'd known. Would he be upset to leave her?

"I love you too, Night-That-Storms. You are a Pueblo boy with a big heart. Don't ever forget me," Jenny said as hot tears fell upon her cheeks.

"Don't cry, Mama," Storm said, wiping at Jenny's wet cheek.

"Don't cry," Fawn said as she tugged at Jenny's arm. "You say this is good."

"It is good, Fawn. It's just I will miss all of you so much." Jenny put Storm down and composed herself. "Now, go and tell Pastor David good-bye, and be sure and remember your prayers. Don't forget Jesus loves you and God is your Father in heaven." The children promised and went running out the front door to find David.

Jenny watched as David held each child, even the older boys. He held his face close to theirs, talking in low whispers as if imparting some great secret wisdom upon them. In truth, he was praying a blessing over each one.

"Bless you, White-Fawn-Dancing. May God watch over you all the days of your life. Don't forget you are loved and God sends His angels to watch over you and walk beside you," David said in a strained voice. He tickled her one last time just in order to hear her little-girl giggle.

"You funny, Pastor David. I love you."

"I love you too, Fawn," David said and suddenly felt old. He put Fawn down and finished blessing the others.

The leaders signaled it was time to go, and because of the respect the children had been taught by Jenny and David, they quickly fell into place. They walked out the gate and past the stone wall, some so in awe of their tribal elders they looked afraid. Others seemed oblivious to the older men.

Jenny ran to the gate in order to watch the children as far as she could.

The wind picked up and pulled at the strands of her chestnut hair she had so carefully pinned up that morning. She didn't care. As the children marched away, they took her heart and the security she had enjoyed in the face of her losses.

Jenny cried openly as she pulled open the gate and walked the length of the fence to better view the children as they neared the rocky canyon that would block them from her eyes. From time to time, one or more of the children looked back at Jenny and David, offering a wave or a smile. It was a great adventure to them.

As one after the other disappeared into the canyon, Jenny could no longer bear the silence.

"Don't take them. Don't go," she cried out, knowing they were too far away to hear her words.

David put his hands upon her shoulders, but Jenny wanted no part of it. She jerked away and moved forward as if to go after the children. She had taken only three steps when three-year-old Storm turned from the procession and ran back a few steps towards Jenny. He held wide his baby arms and threw out his chest, sending Jenny an open-armed hug he usually reserved for things he couldn't touch.

Jenny sobbed and collapsed to the ground as she mimicked Storm's actions. Her arms ached for the feel of his soft skin and satiny hair. She longed for his baby smell and his constant, questioning voice.

Storm, satisfied he'd shared his best with Jenny, turned and ran to catch up with the others. He didn't look back again, and for this David was grateful. Jenny had fallen headlong into the sandy dirt, releasing in her sobs all the pain David felt tearing at his own heart. Lovingly, he picked her up and carried her back into the house.

Placing Jenny gently in the bed, David did nothing to stop her from crying. She needed to mourn the loss of these children just as she had mourned the loss of her own babies. Walking quietly from the room, David made his way to his study and collapsed in a chair.

"Oh Lord," he cried, "this sorrow is too much to bear alone. Deal mercifully with us, Father." David reached for his Bible and opened it to Psalm 88: " 'O Lord God of my salvation, I have cried day and night before Thee: Let my prayer come before Thee: incline Thine ear unto my cry; For my soul is full of troubles: and my life draweth nigh unto the grave. I am counted with them that go down into the pit: I am as a man that hath no strength.' " David closed the Bible.

"I am that man, Lord. I am without strength. Jenny needs me to be strong, Father, and I have no strength to offer her. Help me to accept this as

Your will and to ease Jenny's pain. Amen."

Long into the night, David could hear Jenny's sobs. He worried for her sanity. Surely it was too much for one woman to endure all she'd lived through.

When her crying could no longer be heard, David made his way to their bedroom. He undressed silently and slipped into bed beside Jenny's spent form. He pulled her into his arms and held her tightly. Somehow they would endure this as they had the other sorrows in their life. He was reminded of Psalm 30:5: " 'Weeping may endure for a night, but joy cometh in the morning.' " The words comforted David as he drifted into a fitful sleep.

Surely joy would come in the morning.

Chapter 13

J oy didn't come in the morning. David found Jenny a silent, stoic reminder of the previous day's events. She got up before David awakened, stoked the stove, and made breakfast, and put on water in the outside caldron for the laundry.

David dragged himself down the stairs after a restless night. He was amazed at all Jenny had accomplished, yet the sight of his wife was shocking. Her eyes were void of life. When he sat down to the table, she silently served him his food and left the room.

David thanked God for the food and asked Him for guidance and peace in dealing with the loss of his family. He couldn't explain to Jenny the pain he felt; it would only add to her burden.

He choked down his breakfast and started his day. The livestock needed to be fed, and their water trough was almost empty. It took several trips to the pump outside the back door for David to finish filling the trough.

David didn't mind the physical labor. It gave him something to keep his mind occupied. Memories of the children laughing and singing as they worked at their chores kept intruding. The morning work always seemed to pass quickly with the sound of their small voices.

From time to time, David cast a glance across the yard and saw Jenny working at some task. When he discovered her carrying two heavy buckets of milk, David rushed to her side and offered a hand. Jenny glanced up long enough to shake her head and pushed past David.

Unable to bear the silence any longer, David decided to go to the nearby town of Bandelero. He went in search of Jenny to see if she'd like to accompany him on the five-mile trip. He found her at the wash caldron, preparing to wash what was left of the children's clothing. Tears threatened to spill from her eyes, but she held herself aloof even as David embraced her from behind.

"I thought we could use a break from the quiet," he said softly, giving her shoulders a squeeze. "I'm going into Bandelero to get some of the things we need. Why don't you ride along and visit with Lillie?" David knew how much Jenny had come to love his brother's second wife.

David himself planned to speak with Daniel about Jenny. He was grateful the Lord had brought Daniel back into the fold. David remembered the day Daniel and Lillie had shown up at the mission after working with the Pueblos during a measles epidemic. Daniel had found his way back to God and had sought David's forgiveness for the separation that had occurred at Katie's deathbed.

Jenny stood silently looking beyond David as if she hadn't heard the question.

"Go on and get your shawl," David encouraged softly. "This laundry can wait."

"Yes, it can wait," Jenny said with anger. "It can wait because the children will never wear them again."

"Now, Jen," David said as he tried to turn Jenny into his arms.

"Leave me alone," she said in a quiet, deadly voice. "Go to town and visit with whomever you like, but leave me alone!"

David started to speak but realized the effort would be futile. He turned and walked away, more downcast than he'd ever been. How would they get past this situation if Jenny wouldn't share her grief?

Instead of hitching the wagon, David chose to saddle his favorite horse. A long, hard ride would do them both good, he thought as he patted the gelding's neck. Lifting his boot to the stirrup, David swung into the saddle and urged the horse into a gallop.

Bandelero had grown considerably in the five years since Garrett Lucas, now owner of the Intissar dynasty, had put the first building in place. Garrett had lost his beloved mentor, Jason Intissar, to the devastating sickness that had prompted Intissar to request a doctor's presence in the first place.

Through the years since first meeting David and Daniel Monroe, Garrett had come to be good friends with both. David knew Garrett had tried to convince Daniel to stay in the territory after the death of his wife Katie. Both David and Garrett had felt the loss when Daniel rode out of their lives. Through the years that followed, Daniel had sent very little information about himself their way, and when it did come, it was always addressed to Garrett. The separation had grieved David, and only through Jenny's prayerful, loving companionship had he been able to concentrate on his ministry with the Indians.

But eventually, Daniel had returned. His arrival had coincided with the appearance of Lillie Johnston Philips. Lillie had been a stubborn one, David remembered, but not nearly as stubborn as Maggie Intissar, Jason's daughter.

David nearly laughed out loud as he reined the horse to a trot. Maggie Intissar had made them all jump through more hoops than anyone cared to admit. At eighteen, she'd come on the scene after years of separation and alienation from her father, only to learn Jason had chosen Garrett Lucas to be her husband. Garrett had had no complaints, but Maggie had been livid.

David was still laughing when he reached his brother's office and home. Sliding off the horse, David tethered the gelding at the hitching post and offered him a brief stroke on the muzzle before going in search of Daniel.

Daniel met him at the door. "What are you laughing about, little brother?"

David paused for a moment. "I was just remembering when Maggie and Lillie first arrived. Maggie in particular. Of course," David said as Lillie appeared from the back room, "Lillie was just as much a cause to be reckoned with as her friend ever was."

Daniel laughed as Lillie appeared with their two-year-old son James, attached to her skirt. "I'd say that's putting it mildly," he said ruefully.

"What are you two talking about?" Lillie questioned, lifting the boy to greet his Uncle David.

David quickly took the boy and received a wet kiss in greeting. It was the grandest welcoming he'd had all day. "I was just remembering you and Maggie when you were younger, more stubborn, and harder to manage."

"Who says she's any easier to manage?" Daniel asked teasingly. Lillie raised a questioning eyebrow to meet the challenge, but Daniel simply pulled her into his arms and kissed her into silence.

David loved the closeness Lillie and Daniel shared. He'd truly wondered if it would ever again be possible for his brother to love another woman after Katie. Then God had sent the recently widowed Lillie into Daniel's life, and the man hadn't been the same since. Both Daniel and Lillie knew what it was to lose a mate and a baby, and it was easy to see that God had put them together to bring healing into each other's lives.

"Where's John?" David questioned as he looked around for Daniel and Lillie's four year old.

"Where else would he be?" Lillie laughed. "He's at the creek watching the fish."

"Me too!" James squealed as he wiggled in David's arms.

"Well, if you two will excuse me," Lillie said, taking James from David, "I will take my son down to the water so that he might see the fish, also."

As Lillie retreated down the path to the small creek that ran through the town of Bandelero, David's face betrayed his mood.

"You might as well come in and spill your guts," Daniel said, pulling David into the office. "I'm sure Lillie left coffee on the stove. How about a cup?"

David nodded and followed Daniel through the office and into the adjoining quarters the family called home. He accepted both the offered chair at the kitchen table and a steaming cup of coffee.

"Thanks," David said mechanically.

"So, what's the trouble?" Daniel asked cutting through all the formalities.

"I'm not sure where to start," David said honestly.

"Is something wrong with Jenny?"

"No. Yes. But I'm not sure it's anything a doctor can fix. The elders of the Pueblo tribe came and took the children away yesterday. They took all of them, Daniel, and Jenny couldn't bear it. In truth, I can't say I'm handling it any better than she is." David put the cup down and sat back dejectedly.

"I see," Daniel began, "and why did the Indians come for the children?"

"You know they're just recovering from an epidemic of grippe. Because they lost so many children, they felt it necessary for the survival of the tribe. They came back with me from my visit and insisted the children return with them to the village. It destroyed Jenny. She fell apart watching the children leave and hasn't been herself since."

"Would you like me to come and give her a sedative?" Daniel asked.

"I doubt she would talk to you, much less take any treatment. She barely spoke to me this morning."

"Perhaps she'd talk to Lillie," Daniel offered.

"Maybe. Do you think Lillie would mind?"

"Would I mind what?" Lillie asked as she came into the kitchen with her children. The boys jumped onto their father's lap, full of excitement about the fish they'd seen at the creek.

"Look, boys, we adults have some problems to discuss, and I need you to go to your room and play. You can tell me all about the fish when I get done here."

"Go along now, boys," Lillie said as she joined Daniel and David at the table. "Now, tell me what you need me to do."

~

Lillie reined her horse to a stop atop the small hill that overlooked David and Jenny's home. She wanted so much to offer Jenny comfort, yet she wasn't sure what she'd say when she came face to face with her dear friend.

"Please Father," Lillie prayed, "please let me help Jenny through this pain. I don't know how You want to use me in this situation, but I trust You to lead me. Give me the strength and the wisdom to know what to say. Amen."

Lillie led the horse down to the house. She looked around for any sign of Jenny, but saw nothing, not even smoke from the caldron fire where David had left her earlier that morning.

Lillie tethered the horse at the barn and began to call out. When she didn't find Jenny in the barn, Lillie went to the house. She opened the door and called inside.

"Jenny! It's me, Lillie. Jenny, where are you?"

Lillie walked from room to room on the first level, calling and praying Jenny would answer.

The house was as still as a tomb. Lillie felt her skin crawl. "Jenny, answer me!"

Lillie had just started up the steps when Jenny appeared at the top of the staircase.

"What do you want?" she asked Lillie softly.

"I wanted to come and be with you. David told us what happened. I thought maybe you could use a friend," Lillie said as she motioned to Jenny. "Come on and talk to me. Are you hungry? I can make us something to eat."

Jenny stood frozen at the top of the stairs. "I'm not hungry and I don't want to talk. I think you'd best leave now, Lillie."

Lillie started up the stairs. "Jenny, you shouldn't be alone. I know how much you're hurting right now. Please let me help."

"You don't have any idea how I feel. You have your family, your children. I have nothing."

"You have David and Daniel and me. Not to mention Garrett and Maggie. And what about John and little James?"

"You don't understand!" Jenny screamed. "They took my children. Nothing else matters. Nothing at all."

Lillie tried to remain calm. "Jenny, please come down and talk to me. I know we can work through this together. God won't leave you alone in this, Jenny. Remember all the wonderful things you told me after I lost my baby?"

"I don't want to talk," Jenny said dispassionately. "Now, please leave. Please understand, Lillie. This isn't the time. I can't talk now."

Lillie nodded, remembering only too well how it felt to have everyone pushing her to explain her pain. After the death of Lillie's first husband, Jason Philips, and the death of their unborn baby, Lillie hadn't wanted to speak to another human being again. And she certainly hadn't wanted anyone telling her about God's sovereign wisdom and unending love.

"I love you, Jenny. Remember that. When you are ready to talk, I'll be there. Until then, I'll hold you up to God in prayer and wait."

"Thank you, Lillie," Jenny said. She turned and retreated up the stairs.

Lillie's heart grew heavier as she returned to her horse and mounted for the ride home. "Oh God," she pleaded, "please help Jenny. Help her to find her way back from the pain. Please Lord, please."

Chapter 14

When David returned home he said nothing to Jenny about the way she'd dismissed Lillie. He knew how worried Lillie and Daniel were, but there was little he could do to change matters.

Jenny said nothing to him when they went to bed that night, but when he reached out to hold her, she pushed him away and hugged the far side of the bed.

How much longer could he stand Jenny's anger? He'd tried to share evening devotions with her, only to have her get up and walk away. When he'd suggested they pray over the evening meal, Jenny had complied with indifference.

"How can I help her, Lord?" David prayed. He tossed and turned throughout the night and finally gave up trying. He slipped downstairs and was still sitting at the kitchen table reading the Bible when Jenny came down to cook breakfast.

David ached to hold her. He was only beginning to realize how much he needed her to help ease his own pain.

Mechanically, Jenny poured David fresh coffee and placed a platter of hotcakes within his reach. She reluctantly sat down at the table and waited for David to offer grace as he had before.

"Jenny," he began instead, "please don't punish me for the children's absence. I didn't want them to go any more than you did."

Jenny stared at him. Lavender circles shadowed her brown eyes, and her cheeks were bloodless.

David continued, "I know we'd feel better if we worked through this together. Would you like to go with me to the village? We could visit the children and see how they're getting along."

"Why torture yourself, David?"

At least they were civil words, David thought. They gave him the courage to continue. "It wouldn't be torture to assure ourselves they're happy, would it?"

Jenny picked absentmindedly at the crocheted tablecloth.

"Jenny, did you hear me? I think it would be good for us to visit the village. We could leave right after breakfast, maybe even spend a day or two with the Pueblo."

Jenny got to her feet. "Maybe it would offer you comfort, David. To me it would only be a mocking reminder. And what of when we leave the village? It would be good-bye all over again. No," she said as she pulled her apron off and went to the back door, "you do what you have to, but don't ask me to subject myself to that kind of pain. I think it's cruel of you to suggest such a thing."

"Cruel?" David asked incredulously. "I honestly thought if you saw them happy and well cared for, you might get on with your life. You know it wasn't just the children who needed you. I need you, too."

Jenny stared at her husband. She wanted to rush into his arms and forget her pain, and for a moment she nearly did just that. She could hardly bear the anguish in his eyes. He was trying so hard to help her. Why couldn't she let go of her anger and allow his closeness?

"God will get us through this, Jenny," David whispered breaking Jenny's spell. She grimaced at the words. That was exactly why she was shutting David out. Just as Daniel had turned him away when Katie had died, Jenny was turning him away at the loss of the Pueblo children. It wasn't David she was pushing away, Jenny realized sadly; it was God.

Jenny turned, opened the door, and walked out. Wandering aimlessly, she found herself at the graves of her children. It had been more than seven years since she'd felt life grow inside her. Jenny's hands automatically fell to her flat stomach. The ache in her heart threatened to bring tears, but she pushed back the urge to cry.

Lovingly, she knelt by the three little graves. The whitewash was holding up well and the constant care Jenny had given each grave was evident. She had planted flowers, and with the warmth of spring quickly turning to summer, they offered an enchanting display of color. Jenny reached down to pull out stray weeds and was so intent on her job she didn't hear David come up behind her.

"I'm packed," he said softly. "I figure I'll be gone a few days. Will you be alright?"

"I'll be fine," Jenny said without malice.

"Are you certain you won't come along?"

Jenny dusted the dirt from her hands and got to her feet. She wanted to make things right with David, yet she couldn't explain the wall she'd placed between them. "I think the time alone will help me a great deal. I'll try to put all of this behind me by the time you get back."

"Will you kiss me good-bye?" David questioned, his face betraying his fear of her rejection.

"Of course," Jenny said and opened her arms.

David held her close for several minutes.

Jenny felt her resolve melting and feared having to face David's questions again. She pulled back slightly and placed a quick kiss on David's lips. It wasn't enough for David. He pulled her back into his embrace and placed a long, passionate kiss upon her lips.

Jenny stepped away breathless. She was amazed at the power David had over her. She didn't want him to leave, but she feared the outcome if he stayed. She turned back to her work at the graves and murmured a good-bye when David promised to return in a few days.

"Remember, if you need anything, Daniel and Lillie are only as far as Bandelero," David said.

"I'll remember, but I won't need anything. I'll be just fine."

Jenny listened to the sound of David's horse galloping across the yard. She lifted her face and watched David disappear into the canyon. When she'd been a young bride living at the Intissar ranch, she'd watched David leave to work with the Pueblos as he established his ministry. Those days had dragged on endlessly until a puff of dust on the horizon revealed her husband was coming home.

Refusing to remember anything more, Jenny buried herself in work and unnecessary cleaning. At night she went to sleep too tired to feel the emptiness of the big bed she'd always shared with David, and in the morning the routine started all over again.

On the third morning after David's departure, Jenny awoke to the silence of an empty house. Instead of getting up and dressing for the day, she lingered in bed thinking about all that had happened. Although she fought it, Jenny was unable to ignore God any longer.

"God," Jenny announced in complete frustration, "I don't want to pray. I don't know what I want to do, but I know I don't want to pray." She waited for a few minutes, hoping the feeling would pass. When it didn't, Jenny threw back the covers and got to her feet.

She paced the wood floor of her room for several minutes before continuing. "I've trusted You all these years, and while it hasn't been easy at times, I always felt Your presence and comfort. But this time I feel numb and betrayed. Does that sound strange?" Jenny paused a moment as if waiting for an answer.

She caught sight of her disheveled image in the mirror. She hardly recognized the woman who stared back. Her long brown hair hung lifelessly around her shoulders, and her usually fresh complexion was sallow.

"Why?" Jenny raged as she swung away from the mirror and threw back the curtains from the windows. "Why must I continue to believe You can make this right, Lord? Why can't I forget what I know to be true? Why can't I walk away from my commitment to You?"

Jenny fought the urge to get the Bible on the nightstand. Why was God forcing her to reconcile things between them?

Unable to resist any longer, she opened the Bible to Lamentations 3:22: " 'It is of the Lord's mercies that we are not consumed, because His compassions fail not. They are new every morning: great is thy faithfulness. The Lord is my portion, saith my soul; therefore will I hope in Him. The Lord is good unto them that wait for Him, to the soul that seeketh Him. It is good that a man should both hope and quietly wait for the salvation of the Lord.' "

Jenny put the Bible down. These were the same verses God had led her to after the death of her first baby. She contemplated them, remembering the pain of dealing with the death of her child. She'd been so young, and David so hopeful.

" 'It is of the Lord's mercies that we are not consumed,' " she repeated. She had relied heavily upon those words.

Jenny resumed her pacing. Forcing herself to remember her first delivery, she thought of how difficult the labor had been and how all she could concentrate on was the thought of holding her new baby. That baby had never taken her first breath. A tiny, silent girl had been laid to rest in the sandy soil in back of the newly constructed mission house.

Jenny remembered not only the devastation, but also her faith that God was with her. She had mourned for a long time, but within months, she'd learned she was expecting another child. Certain she'd faced the worst, Jenny had begun to anticipate the birth of her child without fear.

The second child, also a girl, had come more easily but much too early. Jenny had held the lifeless baby only a moment before they'd taken her away and buried her. Jenny had been too weak to attend the simple funeral. Her body had slowly healed, but Jenny had not been as accepting of the will of God.

Jenny remembered her feelings at that time well: anger, doubt, betrayal. She had pummeled God with her questions: Didn't her choice to serve Him mean He would protect her from harm and pain? If not, why trust Him?

But in the face of losing her Indian children, Jenny's spiritual maturity wouldn't allow those questions to be raised again. She understood God often led His people through the fire in order to purify them.

Jenny's thoughts turned to the last of her children. A son had been born with a healthy, enthusiastic cry, and Jenny had rejoiced with David, confident God had blessed them with a child at last.

Within hours, however, Jenny had been devastated for a third time. Her newborn son had stopped breathing. Jenny had once told Lillie Monroe there hadn't been a shred of pride or arrogance left inside her after that experience. Lillie had wondered how Jenny could trust God after the death of yet another child, and Jenny had replied simply, "How could I not?"

Jenny's pacing stopped in front of the mirror. She tore her mind from its memories and faced the present. "I must go on trusting," she declared to her reflection. "David and I should have leaned upon each other and upon You, Father," she whispered. "David tried to help me and I sent him away; now You are all I have, God. At least for this moment."

Jenny picked up the Bible and flipped through the pages until she came to Psalm 51:12: " 'Restore unto me the joy of Thy salvation; and uphold me with Thy free spirit. Then will I teach transgressors Thy ways; and sinners shall be converted unto Thee.' " Jenny prayed the words as she read.

Putting the Bible aside, she got dressed with renewed strength. She wished David would come home so she could explain to him she was sorry for the way she'd acted. She still ached for the halls to resound with the voices of children, but at least those children were still alive and she would see them again.

Jenny got busy with her chores and was in the barn finishing the milking, when she heard the unmistakable sound of voices. Thinking perhaps Daniel and Lillie had come to check on her, Jenny picked up the buckets of milk and made her way to the front yard.

She rounded the side of the house and came face to face with three Indians. Jenny immediately recognized them as Apache by the markings and clothing they wore. She screamed, dropped the pails of milk, and turned to run.

When a brave caught up with her and grabbed her arms, Jenny couldn't stop screaming. She was caught in the past—a ten-year-old girl, watching her family be cut down by Apaches. Blind with rage, Jenny scratched and kicked to get free.

The brave hit Jenny hard across the face. She knew only blackness as her body went limp. The brave threw Jenny over his shoulder and made his way back to his companions.

One man led David and Jenny's matched bays from the barn. The brave who held Jenny threw her across the back of one of the bays and tied her securely. He issued several quick commands and waited while his men ransacked the house and barn. Smoke betrayed the fact they'd set fire to the buildings.

Jenny began to stir, causing the leader to call out to his companions. The men came running with sacks full of provisions which they tied onto the other horse. The leader directed one of his braves to ride and the other to run alongside. He then mounted behind Jenny's unconscious form and gave a bloodcurdling yell.

Chapter 15

Jenny was jarred into consciousness by the constant thud of her ribs against the bare back of the horse. Her mind demanded she protest, but Jenny forced herself to remain calm and silent.

They were moving at a good clip across the canyon floor, and with every misstep the horse made in the rocky soil, Jenny became only too aware of the Indian who shared her mount.

At the words of the leader, the horses were slowed to a walk. Finally, they stopped altogether. Jenny hoped her captors would take her down from the horse, so she pretended to be waking.

Her moans caught the attention of the leader. He jumped from the horse and untied Jenny's bonds. As gently as Jenny would have handled a newborn, the Indian brave lifted her from the horse's back and set her feet on the ground.

Jenny forced herself to focus on her captor's face. The hateful dark eyes she'd expected were absent. In their place were eyes full of compassion. He spoke to her in Apache, but Jenny knew only a few words and couldn't reply. He switched to broken English, but the result was worse. Jenny finally asked the brave if he spoke Spanish.

"Sí," he replied.

Jenny breathed a sigh of relief which abruptly ended because of a wave of nausea. The constant jostling of the ride had been too much for her stomach. She dropped to the ground and vomited until she could scarcely breathe. Pale and gasping for air, Jenny was grateful for the water offered to her by the Apache leader.

She knew he was making a great gesture. The Apache prized water above all else. Under normal circumstances, hostages weren't allowed more water than was necessary to keep them alive.

Jenny rinsed her mouth and drank deeply from a canteen she recognized as her own. Feeling marginally better, she struggled to her feet and steadied herself against a rock.

"Muchas gracias," she said as she handed the canteen to the leader. "I'm Jenny Monroe."

The man eyed her for a moment, took the canteen, and secured it around his neck before speaking. "I am called Two Knives by the N'de."

"Who are the N'de?" Jenny braved the questioned.

"The N'de are the people, the Apache," he replied.

"I know of no Apache reservations for a hundred miles or more. Where do you live?"

"Beyond the big river," Two Knives said. Jenny nodded, knowing he meant the Rio Grande. "We used to roam the land of our fathers without the white man's laws. Now N'de must live as animals in a cage on white man's reservations."

"But you're still raiding." The words were out before Jenny realized. She silently prayed she had not provoked Two Knives's anger with her words.

"My grandfather refused to be counted on the reservation. He thinks N'de sell their souls for rancid meat and white man's wickiup. N'de cannot hunt, cannot dance the dance of their fathers, and cannot walk the land the One-From-Whom-All-Things-Come gave to them." Jenny opened her mouth to reply but one of the braves signaled the approach of danger.

Two Knives clamped a hand over Jenny's mouth and dragged her along the rock ledge to a place where they'd be out of sight. The other men covered their tracks and hid with the horses behind a boulder on the opposite canyon wall.

As the rider came into view, Jenny's quick intake of air let Two Knives know she recognized the rider.

"Who is he?" Two Knives whispered, barely lifting his hand from Jenny's mouth.

"My husband," she answered in an obedient hush. One of the braves who waited in the shadows across from Two Knives and Jenny leveled his rifle to kill David and claim a much needed third horse. Jenny tensed, knowing she couldn't save her husband. She turned pleading brown eyes toward Two Knives. His face remained impassive, but he signaled the brave to let David pass.

David rode through the canyon oblivious to the danger surrounding him. *He seems happy or at least at peace,* Jenny thought. As David passed safely through the canyon and disappeared, Jenny's strength gave out and she fell back against Two Knives. At least for now, David was safe.

Two Knives took his hand from Jenny's mouth and signaled his braves to move out. He carried Jenny down the ledge to the canyon floor and set her down. He looked at her thoughtfully.

Jenny, in turn, studied the man before her. He wasn't as young as she'd thought. His long, straight hair betrayed some gray, and while he was lean and well muscled, his face was etched with lines of experience and age.

"Come," Two Knives commanded, and Jenny walked quickly to keep up with him. The braves moved the horses skillfully down the side of the canyon and onto the rocky floor. They spoke in Apache to Two Knives as they joined him.

From what little Apache Jenny understood, she knew they were questioning him about his decision to let David go free. Two Knives quickly put an end to their questions with an angry scowl. He lifted Jenny onto the back of her horse and leaped up behind her. She was thankful Two Knives didn't re-tie her hands and feet. She knew this was a sign of trust, and she had no desire to betray that confidence.

Once through the canyon, they turned south, picking out the easier trails through the mountainous land. The sun beat down, and while the men seemed not to notice the heat, Jenny grew increasingly weak.

Two Knives sensed Jenny's struggle and signaled his braves to change course. He led the party to a small cave whose entrance was hidden by surrounding vegetation. Two Knives slid down the horse's broad backside and reached up to pull Jenny down. Jenny felt ashamed when her knees buckled, and Two Knives lifted her into his arms. He displayed only disinterested reserve as he entered the cave and placed her on the ground.

The air was cool, and Jenny welcomed the rest. She was confident she wasn't in any real danger. Two Knives could have easily killed her at the mission. With this realization, Jenny crumbled to the floor of the cave and slept.

Several hours later, Two Knives was shaking her awake. Jenny sat up with a start, forgetting where she was. She put the back of her hand to her mouth to stifle a scream. Two Knives seemed unconcerned and handed her a piece of the smoked meat they'd taken from her larder.

"We go now," he said and helped Jenny to her feet.

Jenny nodded and accepted the meat. Her stomach was growling hungrily. She followed Two Knives outside where the horses waited impatiently.

Knowing the matched bays were a docile pair, Jenny was alarmed to find them stomping the ground and snorting at the dust. "What's wrong with them?" she asked in English only to repeat herself in Spanish.

"They smell the water. Big river is just beyond the pass."

Jenny suddenly realized how far the horses had traveled without receiving much water. She wondered at their ability to continue and thanked God for providing the needed refreshment to keep them strong.

Two Knives lifted Jenny across the horse's back. Instead of mounting in back of her, he led the horse. Night was coming quickly and a missed step could mean the end to a much-needed means of transportation.

Jenny had a great deal of time to think as she clung to the horse's mane.

How long would they travel before Two Knives was reunited with his renegade band? Why had they taken her? Would she ever see David again? Woven throughout Jenny's thoughts were the vivid memories of a terrified ten-year-old girl who's vowed to hate the Indians, especially Apaches.

Brilliant stars filled the moonless night, and Jenny could hear the rushing water of the Rio Grande in the distance. They walked the banks of the Rio Grande until Two Knives stopped to water the horses. Jenny felt them cruel to allow the bays such a small amount, but said nothing as Two Knives joined her on the horse's back. The bays were spirited and agitated as they were forced to move away from the water.

"Pull up your skirts," Two Knives said to Jenny. He waited for her to obey before edging the bay back to the river.

The remaining braves doubled up on the other bay and followed Two Knives. Jenny gasped at the icy cold as the horse waded in chest high water. Her legs grew numb by the time they reached the opposite bank.

Two Knives helped her down and instructed her to rub her legs with her dry skirt and petticoat. Without hesitation, Jenny sat on a rock and vigorously rubbed her legs until she felt the blood warming them. She was thankful she'd not argued when Two Knives had instructed her to hike up her skirt. Surprised by his thoughtfulness, Jenny contemplated the Indian warrior as he once again allowed the horses to drink from the river.

Three days later, Two Knives was reunited with his people. Jenny was startled to find most of the renegades to be elderly and feeble. She said nothing as Two Knives helped her from the bay and led her to an old man.

"Grandfather," Two Knives said as he embraced the man. "I have brought you a gift."

Jenny realized she was being given to the old man and tried to appear congenial about the matter.

Two Knives turned to her and spoke in Spanish, "You are to care for my grandfather and his two wives. They are old and cannot gather the wood and food as they could when they were young. I will bring fresh meat and you will prepare it for them. Do this and you will be treated well."

Jenny nodded and moved to stand beside the aged warrior. "I will do this with a glad heart," she answered. Two Knives nodded in appreciation and showed a hint of a smile.

～

Summer arrived, and Jenny worked hard to help the old man she simply called Grandfather and his aging wives, Wandering Doe and Mescal Blossom. Grandfather had once been an important chief among Water's Edge People, his clan. His wife Mescal Blossom was a medicine woman who taught Jenny many things about using herbs and roots. Wandering Doe was Mescal Blossom's sister. As was often the case, she was wife number two to her older sister's husband.

Jenny kept a watchful eye toward the horizon, hoping and praying David would come for her, yet she feared if David engaged the cavalry at Santa Fe, the elderly band of renegades would be murdered. Funny, she thought to herself, she didn't hate these people who held her captive.

With each passing day, Jenny also realized she could no longer ignore the changes in her body that pointed to another baby. The Indians were sure to notice her once trim figure was being transformed. It frightened her to think about bearing another child, so she plunged into her duties with new zeal that surprised her as much as it did the aging Apaches.

Jenny had worked hard to learn the Apache language, so when Grandfather stopped her one day as she gathered firewood, she no longer felt the need to struggle with each word.

"You work like one of the people."

Jenny knew he was offering her a compliment.

"Thank you, Grandfather. It pleases me to help you."

"Sit with me," he motioned and eased his body onto the ground.

Jenny quickly joined him but offered no help. It would have disgraced him as a warrior to accept the assistance of a woman, especially a white woman.

"You carry a child," he said matter-of-factly as his white hair, secured by a leather beaded band, blew across his shoulders.

"Yes," Jenny replied softly. She had tried so hard to forget the child she carried, but God wouldn't let it pass so easily from her heart.

"Mescal Blossom told me this when you first arrived," the old man announced. Jenny's mouth dropped open in surprise, but she said nothing. "My wife is very wise about such things. She bore nine children, and Wandering Doe, another five. She is very wise."

Jenny nodded and asked, "Where are your children now, Grandfather?"

"They live on the reservation," he spoke stiffly. "They live as dogs under the white man's table, waiting for the scraps of food the white man throws them."

"Why didn't they stay with you?" Jenny asked curiously.

"Some did for a time. Others were taken away in chains. They did not desire to go, but they had no choice. Many died in great battle. Most of my children walk in the spirit world under the earth."

"Tell me of it, Grandfather," Jenny encouraged, wanting to understand the Apache way. She was beginning to realize she had the opportunity to witness to these elderly people.

"The underworld has two homes for the spirit people. One is beautiful and green. The people who have performed great deeds and have met the approval of N'de go there. The other is a barren desert where witches torment their souls. One must live a good life and die a good death to avoid that place."

"Have you ever heard of Jesus, Grandfather?" Jenny asked gently.

"The white man's God has great power, but we do not accept His way. I will rest now. You will help the women," the old man said, dismissing her.

Jenny walked away silently. She had a renewed spirit as she realized God had led her to these aging people in order to put her past in order as well as to lead them to an understanding of salvation. Her hand fell to her rounding abdomen as she thought of a way to witness to Grandfather. Who could know the mind of God?

Chapter 16

First, David smelled the smoke. Then he saw it billowing to the sky. He urged his gelding to go faster and rounded the canyon wall in time to see brilliant red and orange flames burst through the second-story windows of his home.

"Jenny!" He pushed his nervous horse to the gate and tied him securely before running toward the house. The lance caught his eye immediately. It had been driven into the ground as a calling card of the owner and destroyer of his home. Apache!

"Jenny!" he yelled repeatedly as he frantically searched the grounds. The fear that she was inside the flames drove David to find some sign that would prove otherwise. Nearing the barn, he found it. Two spilt buckets of milk. Completing his search of the yard, David rode hard to Bandelero to call on Daniel's and Lillie's help. His mind couldn't shake the image of his beloved Jenny being taken captive by those she'd always feared most—Apaches.

Barely taking the time to tether his horse, David burst through the door of Daniel's office. The room was empty.

"Daniel! Lillie! Come quick!" David cried as he moved through the house. Lillie and Daniel met him in the hallway.

"What is it?" Daniel asked.

"It's Jenny," David said frantically. "The Apache burned down our house and took her."

"The Apache? There's no Apache reservation around these parts. Are you sure?" Daniel questioned, taking hold of David's shoulders.

"They left a lance. It was Apache alright. They must be renegades; not all the Indians accepted living on reservations," David declared. "I was just getting back from visiting the Pueblos and found the whole place up in flames. Apparently, Jenny had been milking when they came. I found the buckets of spilt milk in the yard between the house and the barn."

Lillie paled at the thought of Jenny being taken captive. "Dear Lord," she breathed a prayer, "please protect Jenny."

David's distraught face pushed Daniel into action. "We've got to get word to Garrett. If there's a renegade band of Apache, he'll want to protect his own family. Lillie," Daniel said turning to his wife, "you let the sheriff know. I'll ride with David to Piñon Canyon." Lillie nodded in understanding.

"We can take my horses and let yours rest," Daniel said as he pushed David to the door. "Bring your horse around back and we'll stable him and saddle the others." David nodded, grateful Daniel had taken charge.

Within minutes, Daniel and David were off in the direction of Garrett and Maggie Lucas's ranch, Piñon Canyon. Lillie watched as they rode away.

"Dear Lord, please surround them with Your protection," she whispered and went in search of the sheriff.

~

Maggie Intissar Lucas plucked another of her hair pins from the hands of her two-year-old son and sighed. Putting it back in place, Maggie pulled the boy into her arms.

"Gavin Lucas, why can't you be more like your sister?" the red-headed Maggie asked.

"Baby Doolie!" Gavin said proudly.

Maggie shook her head, "No, not baby Julie; your older sister, Daughtry."

"Dotty," Gavin said, giving it his best.

"That's close enough," Maggie smiled. "Now, why don't you go be a good boy and stay out of trouble?"

"Because he's good at being a boy," Garrett Lucas said, bounding into the room to take his son. He tossed Gavin high into the air and caught the giggling boy in his arms. "Boys have a harder time staying out of trouble."

"I imagine that is especially true given the fact he's your son," Maggie teased.

A bearded Garrett Lucas let out a laugh as he put Gavin down. Gavin's little legs were already running before his father let his feet touch the floor. In a flash, Gavin was out the door and off to find his sister. Garrett pulled Maggie into his arms and kissed her.

"And what kind of remark is that to make in front of a man's son? If I didn't know better, I'd think you gave birth to another girl on purpose," Garrett laughed.

"Maybe I did," Maggie said, cocking her head to one side. "You always said I was the stubbornest woman you'd ever met."

"Stubborn enough to test the patience of God Himself," Garrett agreed and whirled Maggie in the air.

"Stop it," Maggie chided. "You'll wake up Julie."

Garrett stopped and Maggie melted against him. How good it was to be Mrs. Garrett Lucas! She felt her heart might burst from the love she felt for this man.

The peaceful moment was broken as five-year-old Daughtry came running in with Gavin close behind. "Mama! Papa! It's Uncle David and Uncle Daniel," she called out breathlessly.

"Here?" Maggie questioned as Daughtry pulled on Garrett's hand.

"Yup," Daughtry replied.

"Yes," Maggie corrected.

"Yes," Daughtry repeated the word. "They're riding real fast too."

"Something must be wrong," Maggie said, looking with concern at her husband.

"I'll see what the problem is. You keep the children here," Garrett instructed, and Maggie turned to see if the baby was still sleeping. The soft, downy-headed Julie slept soundly.

Maggie took Gavin in hand, and Daughtry wrapped herself around her mother's skirts. Maggie's heart beat faster at the sound of raised voices in the yard. What could have happened that would bring both Daniel and David to Piñon Canyon in the middle of the day?

The three men came into the house and the look on Garrett's face told Maggie the news wasn't good. "You children go to the playroom and wait for me there," Maggie instructed.

"No!" Gavin protested, but followed his sister at the sight of his father's frown.

When the children were out of earshot, Maggie turned to the grim-faced men. "What is it?"

"Jenny's been taken by Apaches," Garrett said.

Maggie's face paled.

"How? When?" she questioned, plunging her hands deep into her apron pockets.

"This morning. I'd been out at the Pueblo village for several days, and when I came back this morning, the entire place was on fire," David blurted out. Daniel put a hand on his shoulder.

"Are you sure they took her? She wasn't in the. . .in the. . ." Maggie couldn't finish the question.

"No, I'm sure she wasn't in the house. They surprised her outside. They must have come upon her while she was doing the chores," David replied.

"What about the children?" Garrett asked.

"The Pueblo had already come to take them back to the village. An epidemic took the lives of so many children the elders insisted the orphans return to their people."

"That must have devastated Jenny," Maggie commented.

"It did," David said softly. "But that's an entirely different subject. We have to go after her. That's why I'm here."

"The first order of business is to secure the ranch and get Maggie and the kids to town," Garrett stated.

"They can stay with Lillie and the boys," Daniel offered.

Garrett nodded. "Thanks, friend."

"But I don't want to leave the ranch," Maggie protested.

"We don't know what dangers lurk in the area," Garrett said as he tried to soothe Maggie. "I don't think they'll still be in the area, but Bandelero will be safer. Besides, I'll feel a heap better knowing you and the children are safe while I'm gone."

"Gone?" Maggie asked fearfully. "Where are you going?"

"I'm going with David and Daniel to find Jenny." Garrett's words hit hard. Maggie blinked back tears. "It's going to be alright, Maggie. God will watch over you and Lillie. You'll be fine."

"It's not me I'm worried about," Maggie said, her voice cracking. "I know you need to do this, but I wish none of you were going. Now, if you'll excuse me," she stated with renewed resolve, "I'll get the children's things together."

Garrett touched her cheek, and Maggie paused long enough to look into his eyes. "Dear God," she silently prayed, "please bring him back to me. Bring them all back safely."

When Maggie was gone, Garrett turned his attention to David and Daniel. "I'll check with the ranch hands and see if anyone wants to ride with us. Then we'll send someone to Santa Fe to notify the cavalry."

"The cavalry!" David exclaimed. "That'll take days."

Garrett glanced at Daniel and then offered David an apologetic look. "I'm sorry, Buddy. You have to face facts. Finding Jenny may take weeks, even months."

"Months?" David and Daniel questioned at once.

"There haven't been any Apache around here since the roundup of '86. The soldiers moved them west of the Rio Grande to the reservation. These have to be renegades, and they aren't going to stay in the near vicinity. At least, that's what I'm banking on. We're going to pack plenty of provisions and plan to be out for weeks, possibly longer."

"I can't believe it," David said and sank to a chair with his head in his hands. "I can't ask you two to go with me. I can't take you away from your families for that long. I thought maybe a few days, a week at the most. I didn't consider the danger. I can't ask you to do this."

"You didn't ask," Garrett stated firmly. "Now let's get moving. The longer we take, the colder the trail."

Within an hour, Garrett had rounded up five men to accompany them in the search for Jenny Monroe. Their first step was to evacuate Maggie and the children to Bandelero. For greater safety, Garrett had Maggie and the children ride in the bed of the wagon, which he drove. The other men surrounded the wagon on horseback, their Winchester lever action rifles ready for a fight.

The trip from Piñon Canyon, although tense, passed uneventfully. At Bandelero, Garrett traded the wagon in for his horse and rechecked the supplies.

Maggie held fast to Lillie's hand. They'd been best friends nearly all their lives. Lillie alone could understand the apprehension in Maggie's heart. Silently, they stood and shared each other's fears and hopes.

Garrett motioned for his men to join in as David led them in prayer. The men took off their hats and bowed their heads as David spoke.

"Father, we ask for Your help in finding Jenny. Please guide us and protect my friends from danger. Lord, I ask that You go to wherever Jenny is and surround her with Your angels. Keep her safe and let her feel confident we're coming for her. In Jesus' Name. Amen."

"Mount up," Garrett called out. He turned to take Maggie in his arms. "I've told the children to be good and to remember their prayers. I guess the same thing holds true for you," he said with a grin.

"Please be careful," Maggie said, unable to smile at Garrett's humor. "I can't bear to think of you being gone for so long. Please hurry home." She sobbed the words despite her resolve to be strong. Garrett held her closely, breathing in the scent of her cologne.

"Please be careful," Lillie echoed her friend's words. "Oh Daniel, I love you so. Please, please come home safe to the boys and me."

Daniel reached up and held Lillie's face in his hands. "I'll come home soon. You'll see. Just remember to pray for us and take good care of the children." He lowered his lips and kissed her gently.

Reluctantly, the women let go of their husbands. They clung to each other as they watched Garrett and Daniel mount their horses. Long after the dust of the horses had obscured any possible view of their husbands, Maggie and Lillie waved good-bye. Then they fell into each other's arms and cried. They cried for each other and they cried for themselves. Mostly, they cried for Jenny, knowing they might never see her again.

Chapter 17

A s the summer months brought uncomfortable heat, Jenny's body filled out in a way that left no one questioning her condition. She'd begun to feel movement, although she denied to herself that a baby was the reason for such activity. Instead, Jenny worked harder to insure the elderly Apache people had food to eat and warm blankets in store for winter. She also spent more time trying to witness to Grandfather.

Grandfather's stoic silence first led Jenny to believe he had little or no interest in her beliefs. Yet as the summer wore on, Jenny found Grandfather asking more questions. He wasn't averse to adding another god to his collection of worshipped spirits, but he saw no reason to leave his own beliefs behind. Jenny prayed God would guide her to say the right things, but she knew while she planted spiritual seeds, God was the gardener.

Two Knives appeared occasionally to bring a deer or antelope for Mescal Blossom. Jenny learned Mescal Blossom was Two Knives's mother-in-law. While her daughter had died several years earlier, Mescal Blossom was still esteemed.

In Apache families, the mother-in-law was given the honor of accepting the game and deciding who in the family would receive a portion. With Mescal Blossom's hands growing more and more twisted from age, she appointed Jenny to care for the kill.

Late one afternoon, Jenny was sitting on the ground scraping hair from a wet deer hide when Two Knives approached with an armload of brush for firewood.

"Two Knives, gathering firewood is a woman's job. You needn't dishonor yourself as a warrior by gathering brush," Jenny protested as she looked up from her work.

Two Knives placed the wood beside the wickiup and nodded slightly. "The only dishonor comes in allowing the old and weak to suffer when I am strong and capable of helping them. The old ways are good ones if you live in a tribal family with many warriors and women. Here, the old and dying cannot work as they could when they were young. We will work for them." He walked away without waiting for Jenny to reply.

Jenny thought his words quite sensible and resolved never again to question

Two Knives when he performed extra tasks. Turning back to her work, she continued to scrape the hair from the hide and didn't hear Grandfather sit behind her in the doorway of the wickiup.

She began pounding out the rougher spots on the hide and thought of verses in the Bible that spoke of making the rough places smooth. Absorbed in these thoughts, Jenny was startled by Grandfather's voice.

"When my people were many, before the white man forced them to the reservation, I would tell many stories; histories of N'de and the Sun Spirit. The children would gather round me and listen with reverence while I told of the animal spirits and why we ask the hunted to forgive the hunter.

"And why was that, Grandfather?" Jenny questioned.

"It is only right to ask the animal to forgive us. We do not take its life because we are angry or seeking revenge. No, we kill the animal for our food and clothes. This he does not mind, so he forgives us. Apache believe all things have spirit. One-From-Whom-All-Things-Come gave all things to N'de to take and use."

"Is that why your people raid?" Jenny asked.

Grandfather looked out across the desert and up into the sky. "If the Great Spirit has given us all things, N'de have only to use as they need."

"But you took me captive. I'm not a thing. I am a human being and a child of God." Jenny said bravely.

"You are not a human being. You are not N'de," Grandfather answered flatly.

"Grandfather, I have listened to N'de ways," Jenny interjected, "and I've been a good captive."

"You speak the truth," Grandfather admitted.

"I know N'de have their beliefs, but I have mine too. I believe in one God. My heavenly Father is God over all. He sent His Son, Jesus Christ, to save all people, not just N'de, but all people from their sins."

"I do not know this word 'sins'," the old man replied.

Jenny prayed for the right words. "Sins are the things we do that we know are wrong. Things that go against God's law. Jesus came to this world so we might be forgiven for those sins."

"Forgiven?" Grandfather questioned.

"N'de ask the animals to forgive them before the N'de kill them, but the N'de really need to ask God to forgive them before they lose their own lives. Forgiveness is when those sins are canceled. They are not accepted as right, but they are forgotten."

"This is not the way of N'de. When white man does wrong to Apache, we do not forgive. It is not our way."

"I know," Jenny said softly. "But Grandfather, if you do not accept God's gift of forgiveness and forgive those who've wronged you, you cannot see God."

"I am an old man. It is not easy to accept new ways, but I know your spirit is sweet. Do you believe this forgiveness is possible for N'de?"

"Of course, I do. What you don't know about me, Grandfather, is my family was killed by N'de." Jenny waited for a response, but the only sign of Grandfather having heard her was the slight nod of his head. Jenny drew a deep breath and continued. "I was a small child, and an Apache raiding party attacked our wagon train at dawn and killed almost everyone."

"It was our people's way," Grandfather said.

Jenny got the distinct impression it was his way of apologizing.

"I understand that, Grandfather. What I'm trying to explain is I forgive the Apache for killing my family and I will not seek revenge for them." Jenny suddenly realized her words were true. For so many years she'd wondered if forgiving the Apache was possible.

"You have a good heart," the old man said as he considered Jenny's words. "You have been good to the Apache, and I believe your words are true."

"Grandfather, as much as you believe this a good thing that I do, God has done a much greater thing for all mankind. God sent His only Son to die so we might live in heaven with Him. When we ask God to forgive us, He does. He doesn't seek revenge for our mistakes. Instead He offers us life in heaven."

"I will consider your words," Grandfather said as he struggled to his feet.

"Thank you, Grandfather." Jenny watched the old man walk away. She was elated. The old man had never given such a positive response to her words of salvation and God's forgiveness.

"Thank You, Father," Jenny prayed. "Thank You for allowing me to help these people." The baby moved sharply within her and Jenny changed the focus of her prayer. "Lord, please help me to feel good about this baby. I'm so afraid to go through this again. I know I prayed for a baby of my own, but now I'm afraid. Here I am separated from my husband, living with the Apache, and carrying a child. Please help me to feel Your peace and not worry about the outcome." Jenny looked heavenward and noticed the sky was filling with heavy black clouds. Forgetting herself, she quickly went to work to finish staking out the hide before it rained.

The storm hit sometime in the night, causing Jenny to bolt upright at the crack of thunder. Through the dim glow of the dying fire, she could make out Grandfather's sleeping form on the opposite side of the wickiup. Pulling her knees to her chest, she sighed. The thunder boomed again and the rain poured until Jenny feared the wickiup would flood.

Beside her, Mescal Blossom and Wandering Doe snored loudly, not noticing the storm. Jenny wished it were that easy for her. Her mind filled with concern for David. Where was he? Was he out in the storm suffering because of her?

Jenny laid back on the woven blanket and thought of her husband. What would he think when he found her and learned of their baby? Would he be happy or would it be cause for grief? Thoughts of David's distress haunted her as Jenny drifted off to sleep. Eventually, the noise of the storm faded, leaving only the steady patter of falling rain.

The next morning when Jenny awoke, the ground had dried. Jenny dressed quickly in a loose doeskin dress, which Mescal Blossom had helped her make. The soft leather felt good against her skin, and Jenny couldn't deny that the style was far more comfortable than the dresses she was used to.

Emerging from the wickiup, Jenny noticed Mescal Blossom was busy using a bone awl to punch holes in thick pieces of undressed skins. Jenny watched in fascination as the old woman's gnarled hands labored at the task with relative ease.

"Some days," Mescal Blossom said, never stopping to look up at Jenny, "the Great Spirit gives me strength in my hands. I never want him to think me ungrateful, so I work hard to prove I am worthy."

Jenny nodded and squatted down beside her. "What are you making?"

"I make good boots for your feet. See how toes of boot turn up to face the sky?" Mescal Blossom questioned, showing Jenny her own moccasined feet. Jenny nodded. "Comanche call N'de *Ta'-ashi*. It means *Turned up*." The old woman smiled slightly as if it were some great joke among the N'de.

Jenny was touched that Mescal Blossom was spending her rare agility to make her a gift. "Why do you make boots for me, Mescal Blossom? You should make them for Grandfather," Jenny suggested.

"Grandfather told me to make these boots for your journey," Mescal Blossom answered frankly.

"What journey?" Jenny questioned, but the old woman simply shrugged her shoulders and went back to work. Jenny's curiosity was piqued, so she went in search of Grandfather.

She found him sitting on top of a small mound of dirt, isolated and away from the rest of the clan. He looked to be praying or meditating on something, so Jenny decided to walk back to the wickiups and continue her own tasks. Grandfather, however, held out his hand and beckoned her to join him.

"I didn't mean to disturb you, Grandfather," Jenny said as she sat down on the ground near the old man.

"You did not disturb me. I wanted to talk to you about the one God."

Grandfather's words caused Jenny to forget what she'd come to ask him about.

"What did you want to discuss?"

"N'de ways are dying, and white man's ways are all around. My people cannot live another winter in the cold, so I must move them to the reservation."

"I think it would be best," Jenny admitted.

"It will always be a matter of sight," Grandfather replied. "White man sees new land for many more white men. He does not see that N'de already live here. He tells us to go and we go, but he cannot see that the land still does not belong to him. Land and all that exists belongs to One-From-Whom-All-Things-Come. I am a tired old man, and I am nearly ready to die. I have thought on your words of the one God and believe your spirit speaks truth. N'de killed your people, yet you serve me with a glad heart. Your God has allowed you to find stillness inside. I want to accept this forgiveness and return with my people to our families on the reservation where we might live our final days in stillness."

Jenny was uncertain whether Grandfather was willing to forsake his Apache religion, but she decided it was for God to deal with Grandfather's heart. "I am glad, Grandfather, and I know God is happy too."

Grandfather nodded and listened as Jenny continued to share the message of salvation with him. After praying with Grandfather and listening to him accept Jesus Christ as his Savior, Jenny felt an exhilaration and exhaustion she'd never known. For the first time since becoming a servant to the Apache, she believed her captivity provided nothing more than a mission field that she'd been prepared for since childhood.

Chapter 18

The next morning, Grandfather met with his people to discuss the move to the reservation. Jenny wasn't allowed to join the circle of N'de, but she could easily overhear the words exchanged.

Two Knives and the other young men were against moving, while the older ones were weary and ready to consider Grandfather's suggestion. Jenny heard Grandfather explain that his family would join with those Apache at the reservation, and if any others desired, they could travel with him. Either way, a move would be required for the entire clan as fall was nearly upon them and the game in the area was exhausted. It was suddenly clear to Jenny why Mescal Blossom had worked constantly to finish the boots.

By nightfall, all but four of the N'de had agreed to accompany Grandfather to the reservation. Two Knives and three of his friends agreed to move west into unsettled land where they could remain free.

Grandfather approached Jenny after the exhausting ordeal. He sat down beside her and watched silently as she ground corn. After nearly fifteen minutes of silence, he finally spoke.

"I was wrong to say you were not a human being. You have worked as one of the Apache since Two Knives brought you to me. I cannot force a human being to remain against his will. I will let you go."

Jenny's mouth dropped open in surprise. Funny, she thought, she'd never once questioned what might become of her after Grandfather joined up with his people on the reservation.

"I can go home?" she questioned.

"Yes," the old man smiled. He signaled Mescal Blossom to bring the boots. "These are for your journey. You have many miles to go. I will give you one of the horses, but you will still have to walk. Mescal Blossom's boots will make your way easier."

Jenny took the knee-high boots and smiled appreciatively. "Thank you, both. I will wear them and remember my N'de friends," she said as she cast aside her well-worn shoes and slipped on the boots. "They fit perfectly!" Jenny exclaimed as she got to her feet. "Now I really look N'de."

Grandfather laughed, and Mescal Blossom nodded in agreement. "You will leave tomorrow morning. Two of my braves will go with you as far as the big river. From there the trail will be easier, and you will be able to find your way."

"But I know nothing of the trails, Grandfather," Jenny protested. "Can't they take me closer to home—at least as far as the Pueblo village?"

"No, the risk would be too great. Your people will be looking for you even after these many moons. It would not be safe for my braves. You told me God is great and powerful. He will take you on your way when the braves leave you."

Jenny nodded. Grandfather was right. She wasn't giving God credit for her freedom or for the fact He would guard her on her journey home. "God will protect me, Grandfather. My Father in heaven will lead me home."

The following morning before the sun was up, Grandfather gave his braves final instructions. Jenny was carefully put on one of the bays. She had no choice but to ride straddled, fearing that without a saddle she'd fall from the horse and lose her baby.

She hugged Mescal Blossom and Wandering Doe as she carefully leaned down from the horse. In the distance she saw Two Knives and felt disappointed he wouldn't be the one to take her back. She waved good-bye to him and then to Grandfather.

"I won't forget you, Grandfather. You helped my heart heal. I will pray for your safety on the way to the reservation and that your people will be strong and live long enough for you to share the truth of God with them."

"I will tell my people of the God who forgives their sin and of His Son Jesus who gave His blood."

"I'll miss you and your people," Jenny said honestly. She was anxious to be with her husband and friends, but she regretted she would never again see the old man and his people.

The sun was just peeking over the horizon when Mescal Blossom brought Grandfather a handful of pollen. As was their Apache way, Grandfather faced east and blew the pollen toward the sun. "I will ask for a blessing," Grandfather said, "not from the sun which warms our land, but from the Great God's Son who sent you to N'de." Jenny smiled and nodded.

They were on their way before the sun was fully risen. Jenny was uncomfortable riding the huge bay but said nothing. Her Apache escort ran on foot beside her, so it would seem ungrateful to complain. Jenny had learned long ago the Apache walked almost everywhere they went. Apache men could often travel fifty miles on foot in a single day. Their loping run didn't wind them.

As she rode, Jenny allowed herself to think of David, a luxury she'd not often indulged in. The fear of never seeing her husband again had been too painful, so Jenny had concentrated on the matters at hand. Now, however, she was going home—home to David.

Would he have changed much? Jenny worried David would have spent every waking moment in worry and grief over her. She could imagine his heartache at finding his home destroyed and his wife missing. Then a panicked thought struck her. What if David thought she'd burned in the fire?

"Oh God," she whispered, "please don't let David give up. Please let him know I'm alright, Lord. Don't let him believe me dead."

~

David bolted upright. "Jenny!" he cried, bringing his closest companions awake.

"What is it?" Garrett asked as he got up and wiped the sleep from his eyes.

"Yeah," Daniel added with a yawn, "what's all the noise about?"

"I just felt, I mean. . ." David shook his head as if to clear the sleep from his mind. "I can't explain it, but I thought I heard Jenny."

Garrett smiled sadly. "Don't worry, David. We'll find her." Daniel nodded and stretched.

"I know we will," David spoke confidently. "I can't explain why, call it the peace of God or whatever, but I feel more positive about this than ever before. I know she's alright, and I know we'll find her very soon."

Daniel seemed to catch his brother's enthusiasm. "We best get crackin' then. The sun's already up, and we're wasting time."

Garrett nodded in agreement. "From the looks of it," he added, "the boys already have the coffee made and the other horses ready. We must be getting too old for this."

"I'll say," Daniel said as he tied up his bedroll. "I'm still not used to sleeping on the ground." Garrett and David both laughed at this, knowing Daniel had lived a more pampered life. "Besides," Daniel added, "I'm a heap older than you two."

"He's got us there, Garrett," David said as he picked up his saddle and started to walk away. "Maybe we should start calling him Gramps." David ignored Daniel's bedroll as it struck him in the back. His heart was lighter than it had been in months.

~

Three days out on the trail, Jenny's ears caught the roar of the Rio Grande. Apprehension filled her heart as she realized her companions would be returning to the Apache.

The Apache men, who'd hardly spoken a dozen words the entire trip, gave Jenny explicit directions for getting home. Jenny accepted the reins the men had alternately led the horse by. She thanked them for their help and followed their directions to a shallow crossing of the Rio Grande.

343

The bay picked his way through the icy waters while Jenny concentrated on staying seated. The bay's right shoulder dropped, then the left as he made his way across the uneven river bottom. Jenny was grateful not to have her long gown to worry about. The fringed bottom of the Apache dress she wore resisted the water, as did the knee-high moccasin boots.

After only minutes, Jenny landed safely on the opposite bank of the Rio Grande. She turned to wave to her traveling companions, only to discover they had disappeared. Feeling isolated, Jenny whispered a prayer before heading the bay toward home.

"Father," she said softly, "I'm in Your hands completely. You know I can't get on and off this horse without help, so I pray You will deliver me into the hands of those who love me." Jenny looked out across the dry, sandy land. The sage had faded to a dusty green, and the small clumps of grass were dried brown.

By the position of the sun, Jenny could tell it was very early, so she pushed the bay to cover as much land as they could before nightfall. The day passed in a blur of scenery that Jenny compared to landmarks in the directions she'd been given. She had passed Two Fingers Rock and the path where the crooked trees grew. She put the white canyon behind her where volcanic rock had formed chalky white walls with narrow passageways. An icy chill caused her to shiver as the wind came down from the mountains.

Mescal Blossom had given Jenny two warm Indian blankets before she'd departed the company of the N'de. One she used as a cushion between herself and the horse's bristly backside. The other she hugged close in order to keep warm.

The horse, ever faithful, trudged on. He bore up well under Jenny's slight weight, but the strain of the climb into the mountains caused him to breathe heavier. Jenny considered dismounting, but she worried because she had never dismounted a horse without the security of a stirrup. With her rounded abdomen, Jenny feared she might harm the baby if she fell in her efforts to get off the horse.

As if recognizing Jenny's thoughts, the baby moved sharply, causing Jenny to gasp. She'd tried not to think about the child she carried, but she knew God wanted her to take joy and hope in this baby.

Just then the horse whinnied, sensing something up ahead. Jenny braced herself, wondering what she should do. Obviously, the horse sensed something she couldn't see.

The horse began to prance nervously, and Jenny concentrated all her efforts on staying seated. Whatever lay ahead was making the horse anxious, and that only caused Jenny to think she should be concerned, too. She managed to slide off the bay. Holding tightly to the horse's reins, Jenny waited and listened. The rustling of the wind in the lodgepole pines caused the horse to whinny.

Jenny tried to lead the bay forward, but he refused. She decided to wait for a few moments in hopes that whatever was spooking the horse would pass.

Suddenly, voices could be heard, and Jenny's heart pounded harder. She strained to hear what was being said. Was it Indian or English? Horses could also be heard, and Jenny knew then what the bay had been reacting to.

She started to push the horse toward a thicket of trees and brush, but something caught her attention. She remained perfectly still, hoping to hear better. Then it came to her. The voices were louder and clearer, speaking not only the English she'd longed to hear, but in voices that she recognized. David!

Jenny pulled the bay with renewed strength and ran in the direction of the voices. "David!" she called out. "David, it's me Jenny!"

The group of travel-worn men rounded the bend in disbelief. David threw the reins of his horse to Daniel as he flew out of the saddle toward his wife. He didn't notice anything but her face. It was Jenny! At long last he'd found her!

"David," she sobbed and fell into his arms.

"It's you, it's really you!" David exclaimed as he covered Jenny's dirt smudged face with kisses. Suddenly, he stopped and put Jenny at arm's length. "Dear Lord," he whispered as he realized she was pregnant.

Garrett and Daniel interrupted David and took turns hugging Jenny. "Thank God we found you, or was it the other way around?" Garrett asked as he gave Jenny a hearty embrace. "And just look at you. You wear those Apache clothes well. I almost mistook you for an Indian."

Daniel laughed and gave his sister-in-law a quick appraisal before hugging her. "Why didn't you tell us about the baby? We'd have never let you go off gallivanting."

The men didn't notice David moved away several steps, but Jenny did. She tried not to react, but she was hurt that he seemed put off. Did he think her baby was Apache? Surely he'd be wise enough to realize from her size this baby was without a doubt his.

"David?" Garrett questioned as he finally noticed the look on his friend's face.

David looked up but said nothing. How could he explain to them the fear he felt? After the weeks they had spent on the trail looking for his wife, David knew his behavior was not only questionable, it was uncalled for.

"You look like you just swallowed bad water," Garrett said as he stepped over to where David stood. "Are you alright?"

Jenny watched her husband, trying desperately to figure out what he was thinking. "David?" she questioned as she came forward. "What is it?" She reached out to touch him, but found David's face expressionless.

"We'd best make camp," he said and walked away, leaving Jenny, Daniel, and Garrett to stare dumfounded after him.

Chapter 19

Well, you don't look any worse for wear," Maggie said as she finished frosting the chocolate cake they would eat for supper.

"I feel great," Jenny admitted. "I hope you know how grateful I am to you and Garrett for taking in David and me. I couldn't believe the mess left over at our place.

"You have to remember the first few months were spent looking for you. It was so hard waiting, wondering," Maggie said as she put the knife down and came over to where Jenny was sitting. "I have to admit, it wasn't only my fear for you, but for the men as well. I guess that sounds selfish."

"Not at all," Jenny said and shifted her weight uncomfortably in the chair. "The only way I maintained my sanity was to put my thoughts of David and my loved ones far from the reality of what was happening. I feared I might endanger myself if I didn't cooperate, and to do that required concentrating on my duties."

"I can only imagine," Maggie replied with a shudder. "I guess what's important is you're safe and you're going to have a baby. I'm so excited for you."

"I just wish David was as excited as everybody else is," Jenny said sadly. "I know he's worried. I was too, but now I believe God has answered all my prayers. See, Maggie," Jenny began, "I never realized the hostility toward the Apache that I held on to after all these years. I can't imagine how hateful I would've become if I'd continued to hold on to it."

"God has a way of making us face our bitterness and deal with it," Maggie admitted.

"Yes, he does," Jenny agreed. "I'm afraid that's what David is going through right now. I never saw it before, but I'm beginning to think perhaps David has held resentment toward God for the death of our children. It seems like I've been blind to something I could've helped David with a long time ago."

"Don't be too hard on yourself, Jenny. God brings each of us around in due time. It's His plan, not ours." Maggie's words were just what Jenny needed to hear.

"I'll pray on it," Jenny said as she struggled to her feet. "I'll pray on it and trust God to help David heal."

Maggie nodded and went back to her cake, while Jenny went in search of her husband.

David was sitting alone in the library. Jenny watched him for several minutes before going to stand beside him. It wasn't like David to sit and do nothing. Jenny knew he was troubled and prayed she could offer him some relief from his fears.

"May I join you?" Jenny asked, placing her hand lightly upon David's shoulder.

"Suit yourself," David said indifferently.

Jenny took a seat on the brocade chair opposite David. "I've missed you," she whispered.

"I know," David replied. "I'm sorry, Jenny."

"I want you to know I understand," Jenny said as she studied her husband.

"I'm glad you do, because understanding eludes me," David said flatly.

"I'm not going to press you in this matter, but we've been together for a long time. I remember how patient you were with me while I came to terms with my hatred of the Indians." Jenny hoped David would say something. When he didn't, she continued. "What you don't know is I never really dealt with it until my stay with the Apache."

David suddenly showed a bit of interest.

"I thought I had," Jenny said as she reflected on the matter. "I was certain I had laid the ghosts of my dead family to rest, at least until the day I came out of the barn to find the Apache in my front yard. I never recognized the anger and bitterness until then."

"And?" David asked, wondering what her point was.

"Something happened inside of me, David. I realized I still blamed God for so much of my heartache. The children, our babies, Natty, the raid—you name it, I blamed God for all of it. Here I was the wife of a pastor, ministering God's love to all who would listen, and I still didn't truly believe in it."

David looked away uncomfortably. Jenny got to her feet and walked toward the door.

"I love you, David. Never forget that. Never doubt that my love binds me to you and because of it, we can never truly be separated." Jenny recited the words David had shared with her the night he'd rescued her from Natty Morgan. Jenny's words lingered in the air, long after she had left the room.

David knew Jenny was right. He was harboring anger toward God. But it was impossible for him to deal with it, and listening to Jenny talk about it only made him feel worse. Perhaps that was why he had distanced himself from her. Worst of all, for the first time since deciding to become a minister, David couldn't talk to God.

~

"I hate the way he sits there and mopes," Maggie said as Garrett finished harnessing the horses to the wagon.

"I do too," he answered and came to put his arm around Maggie. She was holding six-month-old Julie, who was just learning how to pull at her mother's hair.

Garrett pulled off his glove and reached out a finger to his daughter. Julie grabbed on and pulled her father's finger toward her mouth.

"Oh no, you don't," Garrett said as he took his hand away. Julie started to fuss, and Maggie soothed her gently.

"I think she's hungry again," Maggie said and started for the house. Garrett walked with her to get the door and both were surprised when David met them in the doorway.

"I was just coming to get you, Friend," Garrett said as he approached David. "I'm going over to Bandelero, and there's something there I want to show you."

"I don't know, Garrett. I don't much feel like seeing a lot of people."

"Then we won't," Garrett said, leaning over to kiss Maggie good-bye. "I'll be back around supper," he said and turned to David. "Come on. It'll do you good to get out. Maggie will let Jenny know where you are."

"Sure I will, David. You go on with Garrett and I'll whip up a batch of your favorite flan for supper," Maggie said, remembering David's love of Mexican custard.

David finally relented and followed Garrett to the wagon. "I don't know that this is a good idea," he said as he climbed up onto the wagon seat.

"Of course it is," Garrett replied and flicked the reins to put the horses in motion. "I've got quite a proposition for you," he added, but refused to elaborate.

David passed the trip to Bandelero in silence. Garrett, respecting his friend's suffering, chose to spend the time in prayer. He knew it wouldn't be easy to convince David of the positive aspects of his proposal, and he prayed God would show him the best way to deal with his troubled friend.

They stopped first on the south side of town and waited long enough for Daniel to join them. David raised a questioning glance toward Garrett but said nothing. He paid little attention to the conversation Garrett and Daniel shared, nor to the direction in which they were headed. When Garrett brought the wagon to a stop, David lifted his head to find a nearly completed church building.

"Well," Garret said as he jumped down from the wagon, "what do you think?"

David looked first at Garrett, then to his brother.

"Think of what?" he asked.

"What do you think of your new church?" Daniel said and joined Garrett on the ground. "We thought about it, then we prayed about it, and finally we did something about it. This church is the result."

David shook his head in confusion. "I don't understand what this has to do with me."

"The town needs a parson," Garrett said matter-of-factly. "I had to wonder if maybe God wasn't leading you in a new direction what with the fact that the mission has been burned and there aren't any orphans, at least not at the present."

"So you just listened to God telling you what was best for me? Is that it?" David asked, allowing more anger into his voice than he'd intended.

"Well, little brother, I'd sure guess you weren't doing a heap of listening to Him, yourself. Now I'm not trying to act like I've got a monopoly on God's ear, but I've felt called to help in this project as well. And, I might add, with you in mind."

"I see," David said, trying to control his voice.

"Why don't you come on inside and give it a look over. It seems the least you can do after I drove you out all this way," Garrett said with a grin. "I think you might even like it."

David shrugged and reluctantly joined Garrett and Daniel on the ground. "Alright, show me your church."

Garrett led the way and pushed open the door to the new building. "I figure, we get a couple coats of whitewash on the outside," he said as he entered the building. "Maggie and Lillie want a bell in the tower so people know when it's time to come to church, and I told them we'd think about it."

"You know how they are," Daniel said, picking up the conversation. "They'd have curtains at the windows and pillows on the pews if you gave them a free hand."

David was amazed at the work Garrett and Daniel had gone to on his behalf. "I don't know why you went to all this trouble," he muttered as he inspected a solid oak pulpit at the front of the church.

"You need a congregation, and we need a church. I figured the two went together. I don't expect you to take this on without praying about it," Garrett said. "I just think it might offer you the most ideal solution to your problems."

"And," Daniel interjected as he came to stand beside his brother, "it won't be much longer before your baby will be here. I want you and Jenny to move in with Lillie and me as soon as possible. I'm going to keep a good eye on that wife of yours and bring your baby into the world safe and sound. I'm getting pretty good at it, if I do say so myself."

Garrett laughed. "I'll say."

David tried to smile, but fear gripped his heart. They didn't understand. They hadn't gone through the things he had. They couldn't know what it was like to face the possibility of losing another child.

"Mr. Lucas," a voice called from the front door, "could I have a word with you?" A tall, well-dressed man whom Garrett recognized as the owner of Bandelero's only bank waited at the door for Garrett's answer.

"If you two will excuse me a moment," Garrett said and went to see what the man needed.

Daniel took the opportunity to speak to David. He motioned him to take a seat. "I know what you're thinking. I can see it in your eyes. I had the same look in mine when I found out Lillie was pregnant. All I could think about was Katie. Of course, all Lillie could think about was the baby she'd lost in the carriage accident that took her first husband's life."

David nodded, but tightness in his throat wouldn't allow him to speak.

Daniel took a seat beside his brother and continued, "I never wanted to love another woman after Katie died. I never wanted to deal with God again, either. I was such a new Christian, and I didn't have the strength to get through my anguish. I hated myself for turning you away, and I hated God for taking my wife, or at least I thought I did. I couldn't understand why God would allow such a thing to happen, but now that He's sent me Lillie and the boys, I can't imagine life any other way."

"I don't think I can bear it," David finally spoke.

"I know," Daniel answered. "I never thought I could either. But no matter how far you run, you can never outrun God. I know you're trying to outrun Him right now, but it won't work. We both know it."

"It's hard to trust, and I was wrong to ever make an issue of it with you when Katie died," David said sadly.

"No, you weren't. You were telling me what I needed to hear—what God wanted me to hear. I hope I'm returning the favor. Jenny is feeling pretty alone right now. I know, because she cried in my arms and told me so."

David's head snapped up. The thought of his wife seeking comfort from another man unnerved him. "I guess I haven't been what she's needed."

"No, you haven't," Daniel said firmly. "I can still remember the look on your face the day we found her. But more than that, I'll never forget the look on hers. The pain and alienation was enough to make me want to throttle you."

"I didn't mean to hurt her. I don't want to hurt her. I'm just so afraid, and that seems so unmanly. What if this baby dies too?" David questioned with tears in his eyes. "I don't think either one of us could live through the agony.

What if Jenny dies during the birthing? All these questions keep going through my mind, and I don't understand why God can't see my pain."

"He does see it," Daniel said as he put his arm around David. "He's never left you, David—you stopped trusting Him to take care of the situation. Like you told me once, you've got to trust Him. It won't be easy, but it's the only way you'll have any peace."

David nodded. "I know you're right." He looked up toward the front of the church. A wooden cross had been erected behind the pulpit—a reminder to him the answer had been given long ago. "I'd like a few minutes alone."

Daniel nodded, gripped David's shoulder, and left.

"Father," David began as he got down on his knees and looked up to the cross, "forgive me for doubting Your wisdom in this situation. Forgive me, too, for the anger I've held inside all these years. Like Jenny, I didn't realize the way I'd allowed resentment to root itself in my heart. I think back to the children Jenny bore, and it hurts so much to remember their passing. I know they're safely in heaven with You, but God," David broke down and cried, "I miss them so, and I miss the way Jenny used to be before she lost them." Moments of silence passed as David cried before God.

When David was spent, peace filled his soul. God had filled his emptiness. David got to his feet and wiped his face.

He came out from the church and found Daniel and Garrett waiting for his decision. They stood talking at the wagon but fell silent as he approached.

"I'll pastor your church until you get someone who's better suited. I'm still not convinced my ministry isn't with the Indian people, but I'll pray about it and do as God directs me."

Garrett grinned and Daniel nodded.

"Now," David said as he climbed up on the wagon seat, "I'd like to get home to my wife."

Chapter 20

With little ceremony, Jenny and David were settled into Lillie and Daniel's house in Bandelero. For the first time since coming home from her stay with the Apaches, Jenny felt all was well. David's faith had been restored, and with it, Jenny's strength. She'd never realized how much she looked to David for her courage.

Jenny looked out the window and down the street where a distinct hammering could be heard. She knew David and Garrett were working feverishly before the onset of winter to build a small parsonage. God had truly provided for all their needs, Jenny realized. Patting her oversized abdomen, she thanked God for meeting the desires of her heart, as well.

She sat down uncomfortably and waited for the tightening to pass. Her labor had started an hour earlier, but Jenny didn't want to worry David with a lengthy wait, so she had said nothing to him when he left to work on the house.

The pains were coming closer together, however, and Jenny knew she needed to let Daniel and Lillie know so they could prepare for her delivery. Gingerly making her way down the hall, Jenny found Daniel in his office. She grinned when Daniel looked up from his supply ledger.

"Did I miss the joke?" he asked, returning her smile.

"Hardly," Jenny answered. There's no way you're going to miss this one."

Daniel stared at her for a moment before realizing what Jenny was getting at. "Are you having contractions?"

Jenny nodded. "About every five minutes. They started about breakfast time."

Daniel looked at his watch. "That's been little less than an hour, and already they're coming every five minutes?"

Jenny opened her mouth to reply, but pain ripped through her and she doubled over instead. Daniel was at her side in a flash, calling for Lillie and helping Jenny to a bed.

"Make that every three minutes," Jenny said as the pain eased.

Lillie came into the room chiding Daniel for yelling until she caught sight of Jenny on the bed. She immediately went to prepare the things Daniel would need for the delivery.

"Should I send for Garrett and David?" she asked as she went to put a pot of water on the stove.

"Send John for them. I don't think we have enough time to spare you," Daniel answered. Jenny was already grimacing through another contraction.

Lillie nodded and added, "I'll get her into a nightgown as soon as I send John."

Suddenly, Jenny screamed, and Lillie ran in search of her son.

Daniel came to Jenny's side and removed her shoes. "Oh, Daniel," Jenny said as she gripped his arm. "I feel like I'm being torn apart inside."

"Just try to relax," Daniel advised, knowing how ridiculous it was to suggest such a thing. "I've sent John for David, and—"

"No," Jenny interrupted. "Don't let him be here. I can't bear for him to suffer again."

"Jenny, David has a right to be here. He wouldn't want it any other way, and he'd have my hide if I refused to let him be at your side," Daniel said as Lillie entered the room with Jenny's bedclothes.

"I don't, I. . ." Jenny's words faded into a cry which she muffled as she bit into the back of her hand. "I thought I'd have more time. The pains are so much worse. I think the baby is coming now!"

Daniel checked her condition and nodded to Lillie. "We don't have time to change her, Lillie. She's going to deliver any minute. Did you send John?"

"Yes," Lillie answered and wiped a cool cloth across Jenny's forehead. "They should be here any minute."

"Ask them to wait in the sitting room," Daniel said and saw gratitude flicker in Jenny's eyes. Lillie's face questioned her husband's words, but she went outside to wait for David and Garrett.

In less than a minute, David and Garrett came on the run with little John held securely in Garrett's sturdy arms. Lillie met them on the walk. "Daniel wants you to wait in the sitting room," she said as she pulled David along with her.

"No, I want to see Jenny. I want to be with her," David protested. "Something's wrong, isn't it?"

"No," Lillie said gently. "Daniel seldom allows the father to attend the actual birth. You'll be within earshot, though. You'll hear everything from Daniel chewing me out for handing him the wrong instrument, to your baby's first cry," she added lightheartedly.

"But, I was there for her before, and I want to be there for her this time," David argued.

"Maybe it would make it easier for Jenny if we waited in the other room," Garrett said as he put John down. "In fact, it would probably be very helpful to Lillie and Daniel if we were keeping an eye on the boys for them."

"Yes, it would," Lillie added before David could offer further protest.

"You'd best go help Daniel. I'll keep an eye on David," Garrett said as he opened the door and ushered David into the sitting room. Lillie nodded and went to retrieve the water from the stove.

"John, you mind your Uncle David and Garrett. I'll be helping Aunt Jenny and Papa, so you be a good boy and play nicely with James."

"I will, Mama," John said as he went to his room in search of his brother.

Lillie came back through the room with a kettle of hot water just as Jenny let out a scream. David would have jumped to his feet, but Garrett held him back.

"I'd best get in there," Lillie said with no other explanation.

Daniel was working feverishly with Jenny when Lillie came in with the water. "I was beginning to wonder if you'd deserted me," Daniel said as Lillie poured water into the basin.

"David and Garrett are watching the boys in the sitting room," Lillie explained and stopped dead in her tracks as Daniel delivered Jenny's baby. The baby's hearty cry filled the air.

"It's a boy," Lillie said excitedly as she wiped Jenny's brow. "Oh Jenny, he's beautiful."

"You'd better take him," Daniel said suddenly. "Something's not quite right."

His serious tone caused Lillie to drop her cloth immediately. The baby continued to cry and he looked healthy to Lillie, but Jenny was still in pain.

Daniel was intent on his work, and Lillie found it impossible to read his expression. Was Jenny dying? Lillie tried to ignore her fears and wrapped the baby in a blanket. Daniel's laughter in contrast to Jenny's cry caused Lillie to nearly drop the infant.

"What in the world are you laughing about?" Lillie asked as she hugged the crying baby close.

"This," Daniel said as he delivered a second crying baby. "Mrs. Monroe, you have twins."

Jenny joined Daniel's laughter. Lillie caught the joy of the moment. "Twins! And this one is a girl! Oh, Jenny, congratulations!"

David came bursting through the doorway with a stunned expression on his face. "Did I hear you right? Did Jenny really have twins?"

Garrett was right behind him with an apologetic look on his face.

"She certainly did!" Lillie exclaimed. "You have a son and a daughter."

Jenny wiped tears of joy from her eyes. "God is truly amazing," she whispered as she took her son from Lillie's arms.

David came to Jenny's side, while Garrett ushered John and James back into the sitting room. "Is she. . .I mean. . ." David awkwardly searched for words to ask about Jenny's condition.

Daniel read his brother's thoughts. "Jenny is fine, David. She's in good shape, and from the sound of it, so are the babies."

Jenny handed her son to David and accepted her newly wrapped daughter from Lillie. "Oh, David. They're beautiful."

David nodded and wiped a tear from his eye. "So are you, Jenny."

"Any regrets?" Jenny asked as she pulled back the covers to better see her son.

"No," David said with a grin. "You?"

"Not one. Like Hannah in the Bible I asked for a child, but God gave me two. I'm truly a blessed woman."

"What are you going to name them?" Lillie asked.

Jenny looked at David and smiled.

"I think Hannah would be appropriate for our daughter," David said as he reached over to touch the baby's fine, brown hair.

Jenny nodded. "I'd like that," she said, then reached up to touch her son's cheek. " 'She bare a son, and called his name Samuel,' " she quoted 1 Samuel 1:20, " 'saying, Because I have asked him of the Lord.' "

"Hannah and Samuel," Lillie declared. "I think those names are most fitting."

"And I think it would be most fitting to allow this new family a bit of time alone," Daniel said, pulling Lillie toward the door. "I'll be back to check up on you in a little while."

Jenny and David nodded but said nothing as they continued to study their babies.

"I can't say I'm not afraid," David finally spoke. "I mean, seeing them like this is almost more frightening. Now I have the future to worry about."

"No," Jenny said as she placed her hand upon her husband's arm. "The future belongs to the Lord."

"But everything is different now," David said and looked deep into Jenny's brown eyes. "So many things have come to an end: our home, the work with the Indians. So much has changed."

"But change isn't necessarily bad," Jenny chided. "Change brought us Hannah and Samuel. Change gave us a new ministry here in Bandelero."

"Do you think Garrett was right? Has God led us in a new direction? Are we to abandon our mission with the Indians and minister to this town instead? And what about the children? I can't bear the thought of losing them to death."

"Death is a powerful force," Jenny agreed as she nestled Hannah against her breast, "but then, so is love."

David thought for a moment, taking in the sight of his wife and children. The joy he felt was like none he'd ever known. " 'Set me as a seal upon thine heart,' " he quoted, remembering Song of Solomon 8:6. " 'As a seal upon thine arm: for love is strong as death.' " David smiled. "You're right, Jen."

"I pledge you my love, now and forever," Jenny said as she lifted her face to David's. "It doesn't matter where the journey takes us, it only matters that I make it with you."

David cupped Jenny's face in his free hand and pressed his lips to hers. Wherever God led them, no matter the distance, no matter the cost, they journeyed with God. His love had already proven stronger than death.

The Willing Heart

Chapter 1

Rich ebony darkened the view from peak to peak as if someone had draped black velvet, strewn generously with diamonds, above the mountains of Temperance, Colorado. Alexandra Stewart gazed longingly toward the sky. It reminded her of a luxurious gown she had once seen worn by an opera singer in Kansas City. But that was when her family had lived happily and prosperously in Missouri, not in the mining town of Temperance.

In the distance the church bell was ringing, beckoning the population of the small mountain town to join together on that fateful Sunday night. It was March, 1880 and the town of Temperance was nearly a ghost town. Alexandra, usually called Zandy, was uncertain if she really cared whether the town died or not. Mining towns came and went and, as always, its fate followed the ore of the day. These days, silver was booming. Gold was always popular but in Temperance it seemed neither ore was to be had. With such being the case, the people had exited *en masse* just as they had come a scant six months ago.

Zandy's father, Burley Stewart, had been one of the masses to give in to tales of striking it rich and living the life of the well-to-do. He'd closed his small dry goods business in Missouri and moved his family to the mountains of Colorado.

The trip had been hard on all of them. They were seven in number on the journey out and, as of last night, they became eight. Ruth Stewart, Zandy's stepmother, had given birth to Molly, and so, after being the only daughter in a mob of wild boys, Zandy had a sister.

"Zandy!" It was her father calling.

"I'm out here, Pa," Zandy called as she made her way into the house. The word "house" was really stretching the definition of the three-room shack, but it was the only shelter they could afford, and Zandy had worked hard alongside her stepmother to make it a home.

"Get these boys on down to the church, and I'll be along shortly," Burley Stewart directed his daughter. Faithful man that he was, Zandy thought him the best of all possible fathers. The only exception was her Heavenly Father.

"Come on, boys. George, you hold my hand," Zandy said to the smallest boy.

"I'm almost five," George protested, "I don't need anybody holding my hand," he pouted. "I can hold my own hand," and he demonstrated by doing just that.

Zandy couldn't help but laugh and rumple the brown hair of the small boy. "Alright, George. You do that." She herded the boys through the thin wooden door and cast a brief glance over her shoulder at her father. "I'll see you at the church," she said and was gone.

~

The walk wasn't all that far, but the night air was cold and the mountain pathways were slick with ice and snow. Zandy pulled her woolen coat close and soon found George holding up eager arms to be held and kept warm. Zandy lovingly pulled the boy into her arms and snuggled him inside the folds of her coat.

All five were quite grateful to reach the church and walked into the building in total silence. Since they were very small, the children had been raised to respect the house of God. The three older boys were quick to pull their caps off their heads and, with a reverence that seemed almost strange for children, made their way to the pew. Zandy knew this peacefulness wouldn't last. The boys were, after all, just boys, and their attention span was never great.

Zandy took her place beside them, making sure ten-year-old Joshua was separated from eight-year-old Bart and George was well within reach to keep him from parading around the church at will. That just left six-year-old Samuel, who was generally less trouble than the rest and Zandy motioned him to sit beside Bart.

The few people who still lived in Temperance were taking their places in the church. Some waved to Zandy or spoke a brief hello and soon Burley Stewart joined his children as the minister closed the doors behind him.

Pastor Brokamp made his way to the pulpit and smiled. He was a short, stubby man, with a balding head and a whiskerless face. The lack of a beard or mustache seemed to set him apart as a man of God almost more so than any other feature about him.

"Friends, it's good to see you here tonight," the pastor began. "I must say I nearly took a spill off Mabel into Meiers Gulch before finally putting my feet on solid ground again." At this the tiny congregation laughed knowing only too well the temperament of the donkey Pastor Brokamp affectionately called Mabel.

"Nonetheless, I'm here and so are you. I was searching the Word of God last week, seeking to find an appropriate verse to teach on and the Lord bestowed a beautiful passage upon my heart."

"Did God talk to Pastor Brokamp?" George asked his father in a loud whisper.

"I reckon so, George. Better listen up and hear what the Lord had to say to him."

George's eyes widened as he nodded somberly.

"Psalm 55:22 says, 'Cast thy burden upon the Lord, and He shall sustain thee: He shall never suffer the righteous to be moved.' I thought a great deal about this verse, folks, and felt confident the Lord wanted me to see something important in it. You know when the silver played out here in Temperance, most of our rowdier folks took their leave. Temperance is now just a shadow of the boomtown it once was but the atmosphere is purer and the lifestyle better. I know a lot of you are suffering and most of you don't know from day to day how much longer you'll be able to hold out, but I don't think the Lord will allow you to suffer or to be moved. We need to cast this problem upon Him and know He is faithful to deliver us."

A few "amens" resounded in the log-framed structure and Pastor Brokamp smiled. Before he could continue, however, a blast of winter air hit the congregation from the opened church door.

Zandy turned to see a tall, dark-haired man enter the building, close the doors behind him, and stroll boldly to the front of the church.

For the briefest of moments, her hazel eyes met his brown-black ones. Before she quickly lowered her gaze, Zandy noticed the slightest smile form on his lips.

Everyone expected the stranger to take a seat but, when he kept walking until he reached the pulpit, most couldn't contain their surprise. A rustling murmur of comments moved through the church as the stranger spoke momentarily with Pastor Brokamp.

"If I may have everyone's attention," Pastor Brokamp said excitedly. "I believe the Lord is about to reveal Himself in a mighty way."

Zandy forgot the young boys who fidgeted beside her and felt drawn, almost captivated by the man. She watched him as intently as did the rest of the congregation, but he seemed more than once to focus his attention in her direction. Why did she feel he would forever change her destiny?

"Friends," the stranger began in a rich, baritone voice, "I am Riley Dawson."

So the face has a name, Zandy thought to herself, wondering at the same time what could have brought this well-dressed man of means to the tiny town of Temperance.

"I have recently purchased a great deal of the property in Temperance and have it on the best authority that silver will once again run rich from this town."

You could've heard a pin drop, Zandy thought to herself as the people stared in stunned silence. They feared to hope that the man was right and at the same time couldn't help but wonder what it possibly had to do with them.

"I wanted to come to you straight off and explain my plans and solicit your help," Riley continued before anyone could speak or move. "It is my desire to make Temperance, Colorado a boomtown again."

This created a stir and more than one person poised the unspoken question of "How?" in their eyes. While his attention seemed turned to the opposite side of the room, Zandy allowed herself the privilege of studying Riley Dawson. He, however, quickly returned his gaze to where she sat, causing Zandy to go crimson realizing he knew she'd been considering him quite intently. His slight smile did nothing to ease her embarrassment, and even Burley turned to his daughter to find her most uncomfortable from the attention.

Riley would have laughed aloud had his plan not been so important. He was most captivated by the dark-headed woman who sat amidst four bored children. *Surely they aren't hers,* he thought as he waited for the rumbling excitement to die down. *No,* he reasoned to himself, *most likely they were her brothers or, perhaps, a neighbor's children.* This thought seemed to offer him yet another direction of consideration and wasn't at all helping him to concentrate on the task at hand.

"I would like," Riley began, "to hire as many of you who care to work. There will of course be mining jobs, but also there will be a need to place people in supportive jobs like running stores, cooking, laundering, schooling—all the things that a prosperous boomtown would have."

A man in the front row who Zandy knew ran a small general store, spoke up. "Who's going to grubstake the stores with the supplies they need for this boom? I ain't got the money to bring in freighters full of goods."

"Mister?" Riley questioned for a name.

"Edwards, Tim Edwards," the man said rather grudgingly.

"Mister Edwards, I plan to grubstake the business dealings in this town. Of course, I will do this for an interest in the business," Riley added.

"Of course," Mr. Edwards replied sarcastically. "Nothing ever comes free. I guess you'll want most of the profits for such a thing."

"Not at all," Riley said in what sounded like disinterest. "I will expect to be paid a fair price for the goods, but beyond this, I only expect ten percent of your profits."

The crowd burst into excited chatter. Was this man being honest with them? Could this be the deliverance they'd prayed for? The news even surprised Zandy who, although she was no business authority, had always had a good head for figures and an avid interest in business. Riley Dawson was offering the town a way back onto its feet and for a relatively inexpensive cost.

Riley continued to explain his plans for the "company" town as he called it, assuring everyone there would be work for all and everyone would share the wealth. After announcing he would have another meeting the following evening, Riley stepped down from the pulpit and was immediately rushed by several members of the community.

Pastor Brokamp, seeing the evening's meeting was of little interest in light of Riley Dawson's announcement, offered a word of benediction and joined the gathering crowd to ask Riley questions.

Burley Stewart scratched his chin thoughtfully. "Sounds too good to be true," he muttered under his breath.

"It does sound good," Zandy offered while trying to free her long braided hair from George's playful hands. "Are you going to go talk to him?"

Her father hesitated a moment and, before he could answer, found that Riley Dawson had come to him.

"I'm Riley Dawson," he said as he extended his hand and Burley took it quickly in greeting.

"I'm Burley Stewart." Zandy heard her father answer. "This here is my oldest daughter, Alexandra, and my four boys."

"And your wife?" Riley questioned, all the while watching Zandy's lowered face.

"She's back at our place. Just gave birth to a new young'un last night," Burley said proudly.

"Congratulations, Mister Stewart,"

"Ah, just call me Burley, everybody does."

"Alright," Riley said with a smile.

George jumped from Zandy's lap and fairly flew across the pew to tell Riley all about his new sister. "She's got no hair," George said in his little boy voice, "and I think she's ugly."

Riley laughed heartily and Zandy reached out and pulled George back into her arms. George protested but Zandy knew how to manage him.

"I wouldn't worry too much about her looks right now," Riley said as he stared with brazen intensity into Zandy's face. "Just look at her big sister. She's turned out pleasant enough. Just give her time."

Zandy blushed scarlet and felt her face grow as hot as if she had a fever. She buried her face against George as he arched in protest against her firm grip. *What a bold thing to say about someone in front of their father,* Zandy thought silently.

If the moment caused Riley anything more than the slightest thought, Zandy couldn't tell. The words continued to haunt her, however, long after she'd followed her father and brothers back to the cabin.

As she dressed for bed, Zandy continued to think about Riley Dawson. She pulled out of memory every detail of every word he'd spoken. She remembered how his eyes had stripped away all thought of pretense and left Zandy feeling emotionally bared to his penetrating scrutiny.

There was something very powerful in this man and something very dangerous, Zandy decided. She sat down and brushed her long brown hair, pulling the brush through over and over as she pondered the man behind the name of Riley Dawson.

Chapter 2

T his is going to change everything," Burley Stewart told his wife as she nursed their new daughter. "Riley Dawson has promised jobs to anyone who wants one. I'm telling you, Ruth, our bad days are behind us. We'll soon be eating our white bread again, you'll see."

Ruth seemed unconvinced. At thirty-six, she felt worn out and tired. To even hope that Riley Dawson could deliver them from poverty was too much to expect. "Burley, we have six kids, though Zandy I'm sure will be marrying in a year or two, and they have to have food to eat and clothes to wear. We aren't getting any younger, and we need to be realistic."

Zandy tried not to listen in on the conversation but in a small, three-room house, with nothing but tar paper walls and canvas to buffer the words, it wasn't difficult to overhear every word that was said.

Zandy understood how her stepmother felt. Back in Missouri the entire family had known relative security and comfort. Ruth, in fact, had left a very comfortable home in order to marry her father. Ruth Stewart had once been Zandy's schoolteacher and, after the death of Zandy's mother, she'd quickly become a godsend to both Zandy and her father. Zandy loved Ruth with all her heart and daily thanked God for her. It wasn't often a person was blessed not only with one loving mother, but two.

Burley continued to explain Riley's propositions while Ruth, ever the conservative when it came to risk, was trying to understand her husband's dream. Zandy found herself praying that Riley Dawson was everything he claimed to be and that the town of Temperance, Colorado was indeed about to be delivered from poverty and certain death.

~

After going through her day's chores in a preoccupied manner, Zandy made her way with her father and the boys to the meeting at town hall.

The meeting hall was larger than the church, but not by much. The room was thirty feet across and another forty feet long but, with no more than thirty permanent residents, half of whom were children, the hall was plenty big enough to accommodate everyone.

Riley Dawson stood at the front of the room surrounded by six rough looking men, all of whom wore gun belts complete with revolvers.

Zandy steered the boys to seats at the back of the hall and watched as her father made his way toward the front. Zandy knew he intended to sit close to the front in order to be a part of any discussion or decision, but Zandy was happy enough to stay toward the back of the room.

She'd barely taken her seat when she looked up to find Riley's eyes fixed unyieldingly upon her. So as not to offend him, she offered the briefest smile, then turned her attention to Bart, who was trying to show her his latest scratch. Totally immersed in the young boy's conversation, Zandy didn't realize Riley had come to stand beside her.

"Why not come sit up at the front?" Riley questioned.

The richness of his deep voice caused Zandy to tremble slightly. "I have to take care of my brothers," Zandy said as she nervously pulled George onto her lap. "It's really best for everyone else if we stay back here. You know, in case the boys get noisy."

Riley smiled, and Zandy couldn't help but notice the brilliant white, perfectly lined teeth. He wasn't what people would call a handsome man, he was in fact much too rugged looking for that, but he was attractive. Zandy tried not to make an open study of his appearance, but it was difficult to hide her curiosity.

"I yield to your wisdom, Miss Stewart," Riley said in a rather formal tone. "However, you would be doing me a great honor if you would allow me to call on you in the future."

Zandy was stunned. She knew there were very few women in the town on which a gentleman could come calling, but of those available souls, Zandy also knew she wasn't the most attractive or promising.

"I suppose it would be best to talk to my father," Zandy replied softly. Then concern crept into her mind and washed her soul with doubt. Perhaps he hadn't meant to call on her in a romantic way.

Riley seemed to sense her misgivings and smiled again. "Of course, you are right. I must apologize for having forgotten my manners." Zandy let out a sigh of relief before Riley continued. "I must take my leave for the time, however. It seems to be necessary to get this meeting started."

Zandy nodded but said nothing more. Her throat felt strangely dry and even when Joshua pressed closer and asked her how much longer they'd have to sit there, Zandy found it impossible to answer.

The meeting itself was only slightly longer than the announcement at the church. Riley introduced the six rough looking characters as the new law and order in the town. Zandy knew three of the men as former residents, in fact, one man, Jim Williams, had even taken Zandy to a church social last fall. The other two, Tom and Jake Atkins, were brothers who always seemed to be in a row with someone and often with each other. Rounding out this number were Mike Muldair, K.C. Russell, and Pat Folkes.

Riley explained these men would be his eyes and ears among the townspeople, and if anyone had a problem that needed Riley's attention, they could take it to one of his six hired men, first. Although Temperance had never had much in the way of a law official, no one seemed to mind Riley's plan, nor the fact he simply announced how things would be and didn't ask, even once, for anyone's opinion.

The rest of the meeting passed in mild chaos. Riley directed everyone to put themselves in the hands of his six men, who, in turn, showed the townspeople how to go about signing up for work.

While Zandy continued to contemplate Riley Dawson, George grew bored and fell asleep in her arms. Something about him seemed quite appealing, yet there was something else that seemed sinister and foreboding.

~

Two days later, mule-train freighters brought in several wagonloads of supplies. The general store's shelves were restocked to overflowing and two new hardware stores opened up.

The town's former seamstress teamed up with two other women to open a tailoring and laundering business, while at Riley's suggestion, a bakery and restaurant were assigned to two different families.

Within three weeks, the silver mines were showing color and word was out that Temperance was well on its way to becoming a boomtown equal to Leadville and Central City.

Burley had taken a job in the mines and Riley, sensing his ability to lead, put him in charge of the day shift. As men began to pour into the town looking for work at the mine as well as filing claims of their own, Burley was content to be able to provide his exorbitant earnings of five dollars a day, to feed and clothe his family.

Others in town fared just as well. Those who'd been part of the original plan did better than those who came after the news of the boom reached Denver and other places, but Riley was more than generous with everyone. In fact, the generosity was so well received that when the regular weekly town meeting took place, the citizens of Temperance voted to change the name of their town to Dawson, and they elected Riley their new mayor.

In the meantime, Zandy was enjoying the fact that the spring thaw had begun. Every day, Corner Creek would melt, and the run-off would make muddy rivers of the town's streets. Then, at night, it would freeze over again producing a light frosting of ice on the pathways throughout Dawson. Zandy had heard the old-timers say it could go on like this for a month or more, but she didn't mind. It was the forerunner to the warmth and greenery that would be spring proper. That alone made any inconvenience worthwhile.

Zandy hummed through her work and, in spite of the fact that the tiny three-room house was drafty and dowdy, she did her best to add cheery touches here and there.

When they'd first arrived, despite the fact both Zandy and Ruth seriously doubted the stability of the shoddily placed house frame, they had nailed several small crates, bottom sides to the wall and had made cupboards and shelves in which to put their meager supplies. Then Ruth, having read in one of her ladies' magazines about the fashionable elegance of tasseled draperies, took a small piece of calico and clipped a tassel from a once-stylish dancing slipper, then sewed these together to form her own touch of refinement. This was then placed, just as the magazine suggested, across the top of the old crate, with the tassel hanging ever so conspicuously over the side. Both Ruth and Zandy had thought themselves to be quite stylish with this new addition.

Zandy smiled at the memory as she picked up a seed catalog and sat down at the kitchen table. It was only a matter of minutes before Ruth walked into the kitchen and joined Zandy at the table.

"I see you're looking through the catalog. Just what did you have in mind, Zandy?" Ruth questioned and tried her best to suppress a cough. She was pale and sickly, still not having quite recovered from childbirth. This greatly worried Zandy, but she said nothing that gave away her concern.

"Well," Zandy began, "aside from the vegetables we planned, I thought about planting some herbs and maybe even a rosebush or two. Does that sound terribly frivolous, Ruth?"

Ruth smoothed out the flour-sack tablecloth and smiled. "Not at all. I remember how beautiful the roses were back at our house in Missouri. Could it have been only last summer when we said good-bye to them?"

Zandy reached out her hand to cover her stepmother's. She felt the same twinge of pain at the memory of home as Ruth did. Temperance, or Dawson as it was now called, had never felt like home, and Zandy doubted seriously it ever would.

Ruth began to cough again, and Zandy couldn't help but frown. "You need to see a doctor, Ruth," Zandy said with great concern in her voice. "That cough is getting worse, and Molly needs you to be healthy. I heard Riley say a company doctor would be arriving within the week. I'm going to check into it and see that he comes here first thing."

"We can't afford to be extravagant, Zandy. We've only managed to put aside a few dollars. I can't expect Burley to waste his hard-earned pay on a doctor. I'll be fine."

"Getting a doctor for you is not extravagant. I've already put the boys to work reading and printing their letters in the back room. I'll be just a few minutes and hopefully when I return I'll bring the town's doctor with me."

Zandy got to her feet and untied her apron. Ruth really did look quite ill and a grave thought crossed Zandy's mind. What if Ruth died? This country was hard on everyone and the weaker the individual the more the elements took their toll. Ruth was a city girl and while she'd been able to bear five children with little trouble, this time was different. Fear of the grippe or consumption ran rampant during the winter months, especially in the poorer conditions of towns like Dawson.

Molly began to cry from the bedroom, so Zandy helped Ruth to her feet. "You try to rest as much as possible after you feed her," Zandy said as though she had reversed roles with her stepmother.

"I will, Zandy. I promise."

Zandy pulled on her coat and made the muddy journey into town.

~

Dawson was really no different than any other mountain mining town. It was dirty and had all the characteristics of having been slapped together overnight, which of course it had been.

The life of a mining town was often short-lived; thus most of the buildings in town were nothing more than tents. Once a town proved it's color by showing a solid vein of ore, then building materials would be freighted in to make more substantial buildings.

When the town had been called Temperance, it had known a wealthy time, so in its favor now stood several wood and-brick buildings, clapboard houses, and even a stately mansion that seemed to rise up out of the ground at the north end of the city. Zandy glanced in the direction of the mansion knowing full well it was now the residence of Riley Dawson.

"Miss Zandy!"

Zandy glanced up to see Jim Williams walking toward her.

"Hello, Jim," Zandy said with a smile. "It feels like the temperature has warmed up quite a bit."

"I'll say. Corner Creek is flooding again," the dark-haired Jim said, knowing it wasn't any real news.

"Yes, I've seen the mess. It's a good thing you told me what to expect. If you hadn't, I would have worried we were about to slide on down the mountain with the mud." Zandy allowed Jim to walk alongside her while she continued to make her way toward the boardwalk. "Jim, have you any news of the doctor?" Zandy questioned, suddenly remembering Jim's connection to Riley's administration of Dawson.

"He arrived just this morning. He's up at the Travis mansion," Jim said and paused, "I guess I mean Dawson mansion."

"Yes, I heard Mister Dawson had taken up residence there. I'm sure he was the only one who could afford the price. Do you know if the doctor will be staying there? I mean I heard some of the new lawmen were staying in the cottage behind the big house."

"Riley's been real generous," Jim said as he helped Zandy to step up on the boardwalk. She allowed his touch only for a moment before making the pretense of smoothing out her long linsey-woolsey skirt. Jim took the hint and dropped his hand before expounding on Riley Dawson's many virtues. "Riley Dawson must have had quite a grubstake. You know he won the deeds to the first five mine claims?"

"Won? You mean he gambled for the mines?" Zandy questioned, finding herself far more interested in Riley Dawson than she wanted to be.

"That's right. I hear he's quite a card player. I figure it's how he got enough money together to buy all of that new fancy mining equipment. Not to mention all of the money he's been shelling out for salaries and store goods," Jim replied, looking around to make certain no one would overhear him. "He's paying me four dollars a day. Imagine that! Four dollars a day and I don't even have to go down into the mines and breath the dust. I wasn't even making four dollars a day when I was double jacking with your pa," Jim said, hoping Zandy would think more favorably toward him after remembering the closeness he'd shared with her father.

Zandy cringed at the thought of the dangerous job. Double jacking was usually done by two and sometimes three men. One man would hold the long steel drill bit while the other man would pound the bit with an eight-pound hammer, alternating with a third man if available. All this was done in order to make blasting holes in the face rock of the mine. Once this was done, the holes were packed with "giant," a lethal and unstable explosive known to most as dynamite.

"I remember," Zandy said as she issued a silent prayer that her father would tire of this dangerous life and take them all back to Missouri.

Without sensing Zandy's disillusionment, Jim continued. "There aren't going to be any double jackers in Riley's mines. He's bringing in Burleigh drills."

"What are they?" Zandy asked, wondering if they would bring her father help or harm.

"Steam-operated drills. They're something to behold. I saw one up in Georgetown. They cut down the time it takes to drill the blasting holes and decrease the risk of losing fingers or busting a guy's hand while jacking."

"Sounds good, but are they safe?" Zandy asked as she stopped in front of the general store.

"Safe as anything ever is in a mine," Jim offered with a look that told it all. "I'm just glad to be doing what I'm doing." Zandy nodded and started to go into the store. "Say, weren't you wanting the doctor?"

"Yes," Zandy said as if suddenly remembering why she'd come to town in the first place. "Could you send him to our place? Ruth isn't well."

"I sure will. Hope it's nothing serious," Jim said and smiled. "I was kind of hoping you'd be coming to the dance Saturday night."

"I'd really like to Jim, but if Ruth is still doing poorly she'll need me at home," Zandy said and silently prayed that Ruth would be well enough.

"Can I check with you on Friday?" Jim asked hopefully.

"I'd like that, Jim," Zandy said, matching the smile on his face with one of her own.

Chapter 3

The knock at the door startled Zandy. The rest of the family, including a much-restored Ruth, had already departed for the Saturday night festivities and she wasn't expecting anyone. Opening the door, Zandy took a step back, surprised to find Riley Dawson standing in the doorway.

"I'm sorry if I frightened you," Riley began. "I happened to notice your family had already left for the dance and wondered if you would be joining them."

Zandy noted Riley's refined appearance and the stylish cut of his expensive suit. There wouldn't be another in Dawson dressed as well as this man. "I was just frosting a cake," Zandy finally spoke. "I promised to bring it for the refreshment table."

"I see," Riley said as he appraised Zandy's gown. The bright red basque and the red plaid sateen of the bustled skirt were as lovely as any Riley had seen in Denver.

Zandy noted the look of appreciation in Riley's eyes and laughed to herself. Perhaps Riley wouldn't find her so smartly dressed if he knew she'd had to make her own bustle by tying a string through an old tin can. The silence made an awkward barrier between them, and Zandy found herself wishing Riley would leave. Instead, Riley asked if he could wait for her and accompany her to the dance.

Zandy frowned slightly, remembering Jim intended to meet her at the dance. "I'm not sure that would be appropriate," Zandy said reluctantly.

"And what could possibly be inappropriate about it?" Riley said with a grin. The smile quickly turned into a frown, however, as he stepped into the house. "How can you live like this?" he questioned without waiting for an answer to his first question.

Zandy was taken back by Riley's open criticism. "I beg your pardon?" The cake was totally forgotten as Zandy followed Riley as he boldly made his way through the small house.

"This is deplorable. How many people are living here?"

"Eight and I'd like to ask you by what right do you have to trespass?" Zandy questioned rather indignantly. "I don't recall having invited you to take a tour of our accommodations, so I would like you to leave."

Riley turned from the poverty before him and stared boldly into Zandy's fiery green eyes. His eyes narrowed slightly as he considered the woman before him. He liked the spunk that Zandy displayed in the fearless defense of her home.

"I didn't mean to offend you," Riley began, "it's just I can't believe the conditions here. It's not that you haven't done wonders with it," he said as he waved his hand, "but to be honest, Miss Stewart, I can't imagine this is a healthy place in which adults, much less children, can live."

Zandy dropped her guard. She had to admit Riley was right and the sorrow showed clearly on her face.

"I'm sorry," Riley said softly. "I know it must be hard to live like this."

"I do worry about the children," Zandy said as she walked back to the kitchen. She picked up the bowl of frosting and, after stirring it briefly, poured the contents on the top of her cake and smoothed it out with a knife.

"I could help," Riley said in an ominous way that made Zandy regret having been honest.

"I don't think we should discuss it any further," Zandy stated firmly as she finished with the cake.

"There's no need to feel uncomfortable, Miss Stewart. I own this property." Zandy's eyes opened wide in surprise. "You?"

Riley crossed his arms. "Why should that surprise you? I own most of Dawson."

"I just presumed my father owned this place. We owned our house back in Missouri," Zandy's little girl voice appealed to Riley in a way he couldn't explain.

"I'm sorry to disillusion you. This house is on part of the claim I took control of."

"You mean you won, don't you? I heard you gambled for the claims you now own."

Riley shrugged his shoulders. "So what if I did? These are hard and lawless times, Miss Stewart. Men come here with gold and silver fever so fierce they stake everything they have. They don't care what it costs them to buy the equipment they need and they don't care what they have to do to get a claim."

"Are there truly so many godless people?" Zandy whispered more to herself than for any answer Riley might offer.

"Godless and worse," Riley admitted.

"What could possibly be worse than living without God?" Zandy questioned, suddenly fearful that Riley was one of those among the godless.

"Believe me"—Riley cocked his head ever so slightly and with an intense darkening to his dark eyes continued—"you don't want to know.

There are men out there who would not only sell their own souls, but the soul of anyone else who stood in their way."

Zandy felt a chill go down her spine. She knew she'd led a sheltered life, but never had she really stopped to imagine such sufferings and dealings were really going on in the world.

Only the table stood between Zandy and Riley, and the rich aroma of the butter frosting was quickly overwhelmed by the expensive cologne Riley Dawson wore. Zandy was fast realizing just how out of place she felt with Riley.

"I'm sorry again if I've frightened you," Riley said, thinking Zandy looked much like a person who'd seen a ghost. "A young woman like yourself can't be too careful these days. But again, I could do much to help you."

Zandy nervously dropped the knife and it made a clattering sound on the table before falling silently to the dirt floor below.

Riley reached out and took hold of Zandy's hand. He could feel her tremble beneath his touch and the response excited him. "Come sit with me," Riley said in such a way Zandy could only follow him as he led her to the makeshift sofa at the opposite side of the room.

"Miss Stewart," Riley said as he motioned for Zandy to sit, "may I call you Alexandra?"

Zandy nodded silently, then added, "Most folks call me Zandy."

Riley smiled, once again revealing perfect teeth. "I shall call you by both. Alexandra for more serious moments and Zandy for less formal occasions."

"And which is this?" Zandy found herself whispering.

"This is quite serious," Riley said as he came to sit beside Zandy.

"I see," Zandy said as she tried to put a bit more space between herself and the tycoon. There was something very dangerous about this man, yet Zandy didn't really comprehend what it was that made her so cautious in dealing with Riley Dawson.

"Alexandra, you can change everything for your family and for yourself. I can provide a new home, plenty of food for the children, and coal for the stove."

"And just what is it I have to do?" Alexandra asked suspiciously.

"It's nothing all that difficult. I want a companion, someone I can lavish with gifts and attention. Someone who will act as hostess in my house for the many parties I intend to have. And someone who will be there after the parties are over. Do you understand me, Alexandra?" Riley asked in a low whisper that made Zandy feel very uncomfortable.

"But you barely know me, Mister Dawson," Zandy began. "I can't imagine asking me to take such an important position in your life without having even the slightest knowledge of who I am and what my past is."

"I know enough. I know you're pure and innocent. You've never been married, although that does amaze me. You're loving and giving; always quick to lend a hand to your father and stepmother; and you care well for your brothers and sister. Beyond that I know you're by far the most beautiful woman I've ever met."

"Now I know you've gone mad," Zandy laughed. "There are many more beautiful women in this world, not to mention this town. I'm not at all the refined and fashionable woman who would do justice to your image."

"The material parts I can create. Refinement and fashion are often nothing more than the clothes on your back and the shoes on your feet. Think about it. Don't you feel quite smart in your party dress? Don't you in fact walk differently when you put slippers on your feet in place of brogans?"

Zandy thought of the heavy brogans she usually wore to fight through the muddy streets of Dawson. The unflattering boot shoes were nearly impossible to tell right from left and they weighed at least a pound a piece. She had to admit Riley was right about the shoes. The look on her face told him everything.

"See, I was right, wasn't I?" Riley said and without waiting for an answer, continued, "I can buy you the finest clothes ever created for a woman to wear. Rich sateens and velvets, opulent silks, and fine ermine for trims. I can put jewels around your neck to rival the Queen of England's. But, more than this, I can put balanced meals in the stomachs of your brothers and sister. I can give them proper clothing and a house with real walls and bedrooms."

Zandy shifted uncomfortably. This was her first real proposal and she was quite taken back by the dashing man who promised her everything a woman could ever want.

"But what of love?" Zandy found herself speaking without thought.

"That's a rather bold question for a young girl," Riley replied with a quizzically raised eyebrow. "What makes you think I wouldn't consider such a thing just as important as you do? The chemistry must be right between a man and a woman in order to spend their days and nights together." Zandy blushed crimson at the words. "Just remember," Riley continued, "you are the one who brought up the subject."

"I didn't expect you to get vulgar," Zandy said stiffly. She tried to get to her feet but Riley took hold of her arm and pulled her back.

"I believe, given the importance of this situation, you would do well to stay and hear me out," Riley said in a rather brusque manner.

The tone of his voice left Zandy cold and she turned to find his hand still gripping her arm rather tightly. "You're hurting me, Mister Dawson," Zandy said with exacting control given to each word. In truth she felt like crying or at best running, but Burley Stewart had not raised his daughter to be a coward. "Take your hand off of me if you expect me to continue considering your proposal. I can't agree to marry a man who would treat his wife so rudely."

Riley laughed out loud and not only removed his hand but jumped to his feet. The action so surprised Zandy she could only stare openmouthed.

"I'm not looking for a wife, Alexandra," Riley said, composing himself once again.

"You're not looking for a wife? Then what is this all about?" Zandy questioned.

"Alexandra, you are so very naive and innocent. I find that very attractive. It's one of the biggest reasons I chose you," Riley stated as calmly as if he were discussing production at the mine.

"Chose me for what?"

"I want you to be my mistress, Alexandra."

"You what?" Zandy questioned as she got to her feet. "I can't believe you came here to insult me in such a manner. Of all the nerve! Get out of my house!" Zandy was nearly hysterical as she rushed to the door and opened it to the cold April night air.

"It isn't that simple," Riley said firmly as he refused to move. "I am used to getting what I want and I want you."

"I don't care what you want. You may own most of this town, but you certainly don't own me. You can't force me to live with you."

"And just why can't I?" Riley asked in such a matter-of-fact way that Zandy began to fear perhaps he could.

"Kidnapping is against the law," Zandy whispered.

A smiled played at the corners of Riley's lips. "You forget, I am the law here. Besides, it wouldn't be kidnapping."

"Taking someone against their will is kidnapping and anyway, you aren't the only law. I believe in a higher form of law—God's law. I am a Christian as are my father and stepmother, and they'd never allow such a hideous thing to take place."

"Alexandra, you don't seem to understand just how miserable I can make life for you and your precious family."

Riley's words chilled Zandy through and through. Slowly, she closed the door, detesting the look of satisfaction on Riley's face.

"My family has certainly done nothing to merit your wrath, Mister Dawson."

"Call me Riley."

"Riley," Zandy said, hoping by yielding to this small request Riley would be content to drop the matter. "My family is not the issue here, and I don't believe you're being fair by including them."

"Fairness has little to do with this issue nor with life. I have found very little to be fair. Consider for yourself the difficult job your father has in the mines. He works long shifts in dank and dangerous circumstances for a mere pittance of what the job's worth. On the other hand, I have amassed a fortune by sitting down in refined clothes, eating the best food, and drinking the best the house has to offer, all while turning over a few cards. There is nothing fair about it but, nonetheless, that's life."

"It's not our life," Zandy said with a sudden renewal of strength. "God doesn't intend for us to live our lives at the expense of others. We are to treat others better than ourselves and to be kind to our enemies." She emphasized the word "enemies" hoping Riley would take it as a personal reference.

"I would remind you, Alexandra," Riley's voice was now a deadly sword poised at Zandy's heart. "I can put an end to your family. Children don't survive long without food and shelter. Your father hasn't put aside enough money to get his family out of Dawson and, though your stepmother is feeling better, without medication the consumption will no doubt kill her."

"Consumption? The doctor said nothing about consumption," Zandy said as her hand flew to her throat. The growing ache there was threatening to choke her.

"Your stepmother is a very sick woman. My doctor has medicine that will help her but I can easily deny the help and your stepmother will die."

"What a cruel and vicious man you are. Why, I wouldn't even want to court you much less live in an unholy manner with you. How can you live with yourself?" Zandy backed against the door as Riley stepped toward her.

"It's true I can be rather cruel, but I can also be very generous and loving. You must turn the tables in this situation, however, and realize it isn't me, but you who will deny your family these things." Riley opened the door and stepped into the darkness. "It's a great deal to consider, is it not?"

Zandy looked at him in total confusion. "Me? How can you possibly say this cruelty would be my fault? You are asking me to go against the law of my God and Savior. You want me to deny the principles of God's Word for the desires of a lustful man? And somehow, in my denial of such an immoral path, you tell me my family's fate is in my hands."

Riley sunk his hands deep into his pockets and smiled. "Life is full of compromises and concessions, Alexandra. There are worse fates in life than to be my mistress. In fact, I think you would find the kind of life I could give you would far outweigh the spiritual misgivings you might have."

"How very irreverent you are toward God, Mister Dawson. God is my

rock and my deliverance from evil. I don't fear you or anything you can do."
With that Zandy slammed the door in Riley's face and threw herself into the
nearest chair to pray.

"Dear God, what manner of evil is this man? Please protect us from
Riley Dawson and keep me safe from his advances."

Suddenly, the words of 1 John 2:16 and 17 came to Zandy from somewhere in her memory. " 'For all that is in the world, the lust of the flesh, and
the lust of the eyes, and the pride of life, is not of the Father, but is of the
world. And the world passeth away, and the lust thereof: but he that doeth
the will of God abideth for ever.' "

It is quite clear Riley Dawson was not of the Father, Zandy thought, and
she shuddered to think of the future he intended for her.

Chapter 4

The cold of winter eventually melted into the delicate warmth of spring days. With it came the anticipated gardens and outdoor activities everyone had missed during the seemingly endless winter.

Zandy tried to keep her mind on the rows of newly planted vegetables, but her memories kept taking her back to Riley Dawson and the fact he expected her to become his mistress.

She'd wanted so much to talk to someone about the situation, but, with Ruth's illness, Zandy refused to make more of a burden for her stepmother and her father was always working or sleeping. Besides, Zandy reasoned, he would be quite angry with Riley for such a suggestion and it could very well cost her father his job.

Before picking up her hoe and returning to the house, Zandy gave the last plant a brief pat of dirt around its base. Next, there were shopping chores to complete, and Zandy hated these more than anything for the way they forced her to come under the scrutiny of the townspeople, in particular, Riley's hired men. She'd learned rather quickly Riley was having her watched for there were far too many times she'd looked over her shoulder to find one of the six so-called lawmen, watching and waiting for her next move.

Then, Zandy remembered, there were the inevitable times when she was alone and Riley would just happen to appear from out of nowhere to badger and hound her about his request.

Zandy looked in briefly on Ruth and Molly. Both were sleeping soundly and Zandy had to admit the medicine the doctor prescribed had made quite a difference in her stepmother's health. The boys were at the neighbor's house, so Zandy made a list of the things she needed, found her market basket, and braved the short walk into town.

~

When Zandy reached the end of the narrow lane, she was almost stunned at the way Dawson had grown almost overnight. Tents had been erected everywhere and the main street of downtown was flooded with people. Dawson now sported seven saloons and four eating establishments, as well as a new bank building and a bevy of shops Zandy would have never expected to see in the small town.

As if on cue, Jim Williams exited the jailhouse with K.C. and Pat at his side. Before Jim crossed the street to join Zandy, he said something to the two men that took them off down the street in a hurry.

"Hello, Jim," Zandy said apprehensively as Jim approached.

"Hello," Jim said as he touched his finger to his hat. "I haven't seen you in awhile. Have you been sick?"

Zandy grimaced and said, "No, I just don't like having Riley Dawson keeping tabs on me."

Jim tried hard not to look surprised but Zandy could tell he wasn't at all happy she'd brought up the subject. "Sorry, Zandy. I don't like this game, either."

"Then why do you play it?" Zandy asked rather brusquely.

"Look, Zandy, I have to work and I don't have enough to leave Dawson. Not yet anyway," Jim offered.

"I'm sorry, Jim. It's just I don't like people keeping track of me. I suppose Riley will be here shortly, so I'd best get my shopping done before he ruins my whole day," Zandy said and went into the general store.

Jim followed her inside still trying to explain his position. "You know how much I like you, Zandy. I can't stand the fact Dawson has his eye on you but there's not much I can do about it. I don't have enough money for us to get married and besides, if we got married, Riley would fire me just as quickly."

Zandy whirled on her heel. "Married? We've never even talked of such things. You're being mighty bold today, Jim Williams." Zandy knew he didn't deserve the anger she was pouring out upon him but, after weeks of Riley Dawson's games, Zandy was rather tense.

Jim lowered his head, reminding Zandy of George when he was in trouble. "I just thought maybe if you knew how serious I was you could tell Riley you weren't interested in him."

Zandy moved the basket she'd brought with her from one arm to the other, before taking hold of Jim's arm and pulling him with her to an unoccupied spot in the store. "I told Riley Dawson I wasn't interested, Jim. I told him I detested him and wanted him to leave me alone. I have never met a more deplorable man in my life. But," Zandy sighed, "he doesn't care. I can't tell you everything, but Riley Dawson is a dangerous man and I don't intend to get tangled up with the likes of him."

When the bell on the door rang, Zandy knew without looking up Riley would be the one to enter the store. That's the way it always went whenever Zandy came to town. How she wished Ruth would get well and feel like making the trip. Zandy had even sent Joshua once before only to have the store owner refuse to allow the boy to access the Stewart credit line.

"You'd best check in with your boss," Zandy said as she left Jim and started to pick up the items on her list.

By making sideways glances, Zandy could see that Jim was talking with Riley at the front door. She moved quickly around the store picking up sugar, thread, and a package of needles.

"Can I help you, Miss Stewart?" Zandy glanced up to find Mister Edwards, the store's owner.

"Yes," Zandy said as she studied her list. "I need three yards of white flannel."

"More diapers for Molly?" Mister Edwards questioned good-naturedly while he went to the task of cutting the material.

"No," Zandy smiled. "Flour sacks will work well enough for that. I plan to make this into nightgowns for her. She's growing so fast, I'm having trouble keeping up with her."

"I can well imagine. Say, we've got cotton stockings at three pairs for a quarter," the man replied as he handed Zandy the material.

"Not today," Zandy said as she checked the list. "I do need some canned milk, though."

"Sure thing. How many?" he questioned as he reached behind the counter for the milk.

"Better give me six cans," Zandy said as she tried to make mental calculations on the total. She tried not to look toward the door but she wanted most desperately to know whether Riley and Jim were still talking.

Riley stood alone leaning against the door frame and he smiled broadly when Zandy looked his way. She immediately regretted the contact as her heart started to pound harder.

Placing the basket on the counter, Zandy waited while Mr. Edwards totaled her goods. He pulled out a black account book from the shelf behind the counter.

"Let's see, that's one dollar and thirty-five cents."

"Do we have enough balance on account?" Zandy questioned, hoping she wouldn't have to part with the few precious coins she'd brought with her.

Mister Edwards looked up to check out Riley's response and, when he nodded, the older man wrote down the amount in his ledger. "You have more than enough here, Miss Stewart."

What a farce, Zandy thought to herself. How much longer was Riley Dawson going to insist on this madness?

Edwards placed all of Zandy's purchases in the basket and, with a smile, handed it back to her. "You come back soon."

Zandy nodded, took the basket, and braced herself against having to face Riley.

It had become a routine between them, Zandy would approach the door and Riley would give her a wide sweeping bow before holding the door open for her to pass. Zandy said nothing as the moments played themselves out and it wasn't until they were outside Riley spoke to her.

"I've missed seeing you." His voice was warm and inviting but Zandy knew it to be a dangerous trap.

"Sorry," she murmured and started to cross the street for home.

"Oh no, you don't," Riley said as he took hold of her arm and freed her hand from the weight of the basket. "I don't intend to let you get away that easily. You're having lunch with me."

"I'll do nothing of the kind," Zandy said, jerking her arm away from Riley's hold.

Riley's eyes narrowed slightly before he resecured his hold on Zandy's arm. "Don't make a scene. I just want to talk to you. Now, come along like a good girl and allow me to buy you lunch."

"No respectable woman would share refreshment with you," Zandy said, trying desperately to remain calm. "Besides, they're expecting me back at home."

"Then I'll walk you home and announce you are coming to lunch with me."

"No!" Zandy exclaimed a bit more excitedly than she'd intended. "I'll come with you now."

"That's better," Riley said in the same self-satisfied tone he always took on when he got his way.

Zandy allowed Riley to help her cross the street and even managed to keep from saying anything when Riley continued to hold onto her long after it was necessary. She drew the line, however, when Riley suggested they dine in the lobby restaurant of the Neville Hotel, Dawson's newest sleeping establishment.

"I will not go into that place with you," Zandy said in a hushed whisper. Her voice was so low Riley had to bend over to hear her repeat the words.

"And just why not? They have excellent food," Riley stated firmly.

"I'm not about to be seen going into a hotel with you. The Bible says we should avoid even the appearance of evil. I'll not have people saying I participated in something of this kind. If you insist on taking me to lunch, then take me somewhere that won't shame me."

Riley looked thunderstruck for a moment and just as quickly covered his surprise with determination. "It's either the Neville or my home. You make the choice."

Zandy looked into his eyes hoping to see some glimmer of hope she might persuade him to change his mind. There was nothing there, however, except the danger she'd noted on the first night they'd met.

"What's it going to be, Alexandra?"

"Why do you insist on this pursuit, Riley?" Zandy asked boldly. "You know I'm not interested in your proposal. You know how I feel about the lifestyle you lead, so why continue with this game?"

Riley smiled and even the look in his eyes seemed to change. "It's not a game, my dear. It happens to be most important to me."

"You could have your pick of the saloon girls and most any other respectable woman in town. Why continue to torment me? Look around you, Riley. There are more beautiful women in Dawson than ever before. Why not reconsider your choice? I promise not to be offended."

At this, Riley laughed and released his grip on Zandy's arm. With this bit of freedom, Zandy snatched the basket from Riley's hand and headed quickly down the boardwalk.

Undaunted by the fact she knew Riley would angrily dog her heels, Zandy rushed headlong into the busy intersection, narrowly escaping an oncoming freighter only because Riley lifted her out of the way.

"Let me go!" Zandy exclaimed as Riley swung her around.

"I'm being heroic and saving your life. Have you no appreciation?" Riley said with a smile, but Zandy thought she read concern, almost fear, in his eyes.

"I'd rather you lent your heroic deeds to saving my virtue," Zandy replied.

Riley could see his hands were full and his demands had been met head-on. "You are the most stubborn woman I've ever met."

"Good," Zandy said and tossed her long braided hair over her shoulder. "I get the feeling it's about time someone stood up to you."

"People pay a price when they do," Riley said ominously.

Zandy began to make her way up the narrow mountain lane, not wanting to know what the price for her tenacity might be. Riley, however, had no intention of letting her challenge go unanswered and followed her.

"You see, Alexandra," Riley began, "I am a force to be reckoned with."

"So is a rattlesnake," Zandy said, braving a glance. Riley, however, didn't appear all that angry even in light of her frank protest.

"That's true and, like a rattlesnake, my bite can be most deadly."

"Meaning?" Zandy questioned as she stopped.

"Meaning, you can't ignore me and hope I won't strike. I want you for my mistress, Alexandra. I won't change my mind and I won't choose another," Riley said matter-of-factly.

Zandy indignantly placed her market basket on the ground and, with arms akimbo, made her stand. "Why don't you just force yourself upon me, Mister Dawson? I mean, you find any and all opportunity to plague me with your presence. You have me watched so you know when I'm alone and you hound my every step. I'm obviously not much to fight and I certainly am no match for your strength. So, like the many other godless men you spoke of before, why not just take what you want and leave me alone!"

Zandy wasn't sure what kind of a reaction she expected but whatever it was, it certainly wasn't the laughter which came from Riley at that moment.

"You look positively grand, standing there with that wild look in your eye and the wind blowing across your face. You're flushed and out of breath and everything about you is radiant. I can't imagine even looking at another woman when you are nearby," Riley said in a way that made Zandy wish he would remain silent. "No, Alexandra, I won't force anything. Women come quite willingly to me. I can wait until you have a willing heart."

"It will never happen!" Zandy exclaimed as she reclaimed her basket and turned to leave.

Riley stopped her with a hand on her shoulder. "Remember my warning. I can make life most difficult for you and your family. I'm not asking for that much, Alexandra. Not really."

Zandy turned to face him. "Not asking for that much? I think you're either daft or completely incapable of reason. I will give myself willingly to the man of my choice and he will be my husband in the eyes of God."

"Very well then, as they said when the silver first showed color, the rush is on," Riley said with a slight bow. "I hope you can live with the choice you've made."

Chapter 5

Riley's retaliation came first in the form of shortened work hours for Burley. Instead of the regular eight-hour shift Burley was used to, Zandy's father was stripped of his supervising duties and cut to six-hour days. In turn, Burley's paycheck was reduced as well.

Zandy saw the concern in her stepmother's eyes, but said nothing that might add to their grief. Her father tried to take it all in stride telling his family God would look out for them as He always had but, in her heart, Zandy felt responsible.

The first few weeks weren't a problem. Ruth had managed to put aside a nice nest egg and so they drew on it as they needed and tightened their belts as best they could.

Toward the end of June, however, the nest egg was depleted and Burley's hours had been cut to half days. When Burley approached K.C. Russell about the matter, K.C. just shrugged his shoulders and told Burley he'd take it up with Riley and get back to him. Of course he never did and, while her father was totally confused, Zandy knew only too well the reason why.

The next blow came when they approached the store in order to buy groceries on credit. One by one the stores closed their doors to the Stewart family and no amount of pleading would reopen them.

Zandy was more than just a little troubled by the turn of events and she still couldn't bring herself to explain to her father that Riley Dawson was purposefully trying to force her into a compromising situation. It wasn't that she hadn't wanted to talk to her father. She had even tried once or twice to talk to him when he was alone but she could never seem to find the right words. In the back of her mind Zandy blamed herself for the suffering and continuously wondered how she could right the wrong.

She sat in silence as her father put the last of the coal in the stove. "It'd be wise to take the young'uns to look for wood today, Zandy."

"Sure, Pa," Zandy replied as she looked up from the meager ration of oatmeal.

"I'm still hungry," Joshua whined as he cleaned out the last bits of oatmeal from his bowl.

"Here, have mine," Zandy said as she pushed her bowl over. "I'm not very hungry."

Zandy was cleaning up the breakfast dishes when Ruth's gentle hand fell upon her shoulder. "You can't go on giving your food to the kids. You'll get sick."

"They need it worse than I do," Zandy said, refusing to look her stepmother in the eye.

"What is it, Zandy? You haven't seemed yourself for weeks. Is there something I can help you with?"

"No, not really," Zandy said as she put away the dishes.

Ruth sighed and took a seat at the table. "I know you're probably just as worried as I am. I honestly don't know what we're going to do. The kids never have enough to eat and, unless they beg something off the neighbors, they seem to suffer so."

"The garden should provide more," Zandy said as she joined her stepmother at the table, "especially since the weather has warmed up."

"But what do we do after that? What about this winter? If we only knew why Mister Dawson has cut your father's wages. Burley has tried three times to see Mister Dawson at his home, but those hired thugs of his just keep turning him away."

"I'm sure something will work out soon. I've been praying and I know God won't let us down." Zandy hoped she sounded convincing.

"I know He won't, Zandy," Ruth said with a smile. "God has never turned His back on us. I don't expect He'll start now. Look, I have a little bit of change. I want you to go to Tim Edwards and explain that the kids have to have something to eat. Get whatever you can in the way of cornmeal and canned milk. I know it won't be much, but it'll be filling."

Zandy nodded and took the coins. "If Mister Edwards will even allow me in the store."

"He can't turn cash away," Ruth offered and Zandy prayed she was right.

~

After putting the boys to work collecting firewood, Zandy made her way into town. She remembered the verses her father had read for their morning devotions. Psalm 141, verses eight and nine stuck in her memory. " 'But mine eyes are unto thee, O God the Lord: in thee is my trust; leave not my soul destitute. Keep me from the snares which they have laid for me.' "

"Yes, Lord," Zandy breathed, "keep me from the snares Riley Dawson has laid for me."

The bell jingled as Zandy opened the door to Tim Edwards's general store. Zandy felt a bit of relief to see no one else was inside the store, with the exception of Mister Edwards who was looking quite uncomfortable.

"Good morning, Mister Edwards," Zandy said as sweetly as she could muster. "I need cornmeal and canned milk."

"Miss Alexandra, I. . .uh. . ." The man looked completely at a loss for words.

"Here's the money. Just give me whatever you can," Zandy said, undaunted by his discomfort.

"I'm not supposed to trade with you," Edwards finally blurted out.

"Why not?" Zandy questioned.

Just then Riley Dawson stepped out from the back room. "I think we both know the answer to that question."

Zandy whirled around ready to do battle for her brothers and sister. "I have no idea what you mean, Mister Dawson. Has my family somehow offended you?"

Riley frowned as he studied Zandy for a moment. She was thinner, of this he was certain. Just the way her clothes were beginning to hang on her was evidence of this. No doubt she was giving away her share of food.

"No, Miss Stewart," Riley finally answered. "I'm simply being prudent."

"I have the cash, Mister Dawson. Now, may I have the goods or not?" Zandy refused to back down.

"Give her the food," Riley said, never taking his eyes from Zandy for even a moment.

Tim Edwards nodded and Zandy could clearly read the relief in his eyes. He took her money and handed over the cornmeal and milk. Zandy turned on her heel, determined to ignore Riley's intense scrutiny but, as she moved toward the door, she could feel his eyes burning into her back.

"Allow me," Riley said as he was at her side in a moment. "I'll carry those things for you. Just to show you there's no hard feelings."

Zandy glared at him but allowed him to take the basket of goods from her hands. She wasn't about to give him the satisfaction of a scene.

Outside, Riley took hold of her elbow and helped her down from the boardwalk and across the street. Zandy remained silent, determined to say nothing until Riley did. They were halfway to her house before he finally spoke.

"You know it doesn't have to go on like this."

Zandy nodded. "I know. What's sad to realize is you know full well what you're doing to my family and all because of your lustful inclinations. How do you feel when you sit down to your five-course dinners knowing because of your cruelty, my brothers and sister are going to bed hungry?" Zandy had stopped walking by this time. The truth was she wasn't feeling very capable of continuing without a rest. Thinking back, it'd been over three days since she'd eaten much of anything.

"You should ask yourself that question, Zandy."

Zandy felt herself grow faint. *Please, God,* she prayed silently, *don't let me faint in front of this man.* She immediately reached out for the basket and Riley didn't stop her from taking it.

"You don't look well. When was the last time you ate?" Riley questioned her sternly.

"That's none of your concern. I'm quite well, thank you." Zandy turned to continue toward home, only to find Riley keeping pace with her.

"What about your stepmother? She can't be doing too well by now. My doctor tells me she would have used up the last of her medicine a week ago."

Zandy's shocked expression bothered Riley but, for the life of him, he couldn't make himself give in. "What a deplorable man you are. Will you deny us the pine box to bury our dead as well?"

Riley was the one notably surprised this time. "No one has died, yet." His words weren't in character with his brazen attitude earlier. "No one needs to die, Alexandra."

"No one needs to go hungry, either. I doubt in all seriousness," Zandy said as she reached her yard, "that even if I gave in to you my family would be provided for. You have no heart, Riley Dawson. People like you don't keep their word because they have no values, no principles. May God have mercy on your soul, Riley."

Riley stood in silence watching as Zandy made her way into the house. Somehow he'd thought the whole matter would have ended weeks ago. He'd misjudged the stuff of which Alexandra Stewart was made.

~

As if predestined by Riley's words, Ruth Stewart fell gravely ill. Zandy took over the chores of caring for Molly and even began to wean her on cornbread, brown sugar, and canned milk.

"Poor little one," Zandy said as she held the crying infant who burrowed her face eagerly against Zandy's breast, hoping to find something other than the calico blouse. Ruth had been too sick to even nurse Molly and the child was suffering. It served to remind Zandy that if she would only give in to Riley's deviant proposal, Molly and the rest would have what they needed to sustain life.

As Zandy spooned small bits of mushed cornbread into Molly's mouth, she begin to contemplate accepting Riley's demands. *Lord, I know that kind of life isn't right, but neither is it right for a baby to go hungry or for a woman to die from lack of medicine. God, it really is my fault and the answer is so simple. I know it would only hurt me but right now everyone is hurting.*

Zandy looked down at her baby sister and felt the tears slide down her cheeks to fall upon the baby's face.

Suddenly, Zandy felt she knew what she had to do. Finishing Molly's feeding, Zandy bundled up the baby and took off in the direction of the Dawson mansion.

Zandy wondered silently what Riley would think when he saw her coming up his pathway. Her dark blue skirt had been altered to fit her better but the blouse still looked two sizes too large. Zandy knew he'd be very much aware of her appearance but she felt it her mission to deliver into Riley's hands, or at least bring to his attention, the young baby he was responsible for starving.

As she approached the cultivated gardens that surrounded the mansion, Zandy had second thoughts about her plan. Before she could turn around though, Mike Muldair met her on the path.

"And what'll ye be doing here today, Lassy?" he questioned in his heavy Irish brogue.

"I need to see Mister Dawson," Zandy replied while shifting Molly to her other hip. Molly was looking around at the brilliantly colored flowers, totally oblivious to her older sister's discomfort.

"Why would ye be needin' to do that? Mister Dawson is a mite busy," Mike said as he stroked his red beard.

"I don't care. Tell him Alexandra Stewart is here to see him. I'm certain he'll want to talk to me."

"Alexandra Stewart? Well, why didn't ye say so?" Mike said as he motioned Zandy to follow. "Come along, Lass. Ye'll not be wanting to keep the man waiting."

Zandy said nothing but followed the Irishman through the gardens and up the stairs to the mansion's veranda. "I'll wait here," Zandy said firmly. "You tell Mister Dawson I'll see him out here."

Mike Muldair looked surprised and chuckled to himself. Then, turning to open the large double doors, he spoke to himself, "And did ye hear her? Tell Mister Dawson I'll be seein' him out here. Imagine that."

He was still talking to himself as he disappeared out of sight and Zandy couldn't suppress a shudder as she considered what she was doing.

When Riley appeared in the doorway, Zandy noted his casual attire. She'd never seen Riley out of his finely tailored suits, but standing there in a simple cotton shirt and black pants, Zandy could almost forget he was the high and mighty man who controlled Dawson, Colorado with an iron fist.

"And to what do I owe the pleasure?" Riley said as he leaned back against the door frame.

Zandy was at a loss for words. What had she planned to say? Molly started to fuss and pull at Zandy's hair. "I thought," Zandy said slowly, "you should see my little sister. I wanted you to know your actions were grieving even a helpless infant, not to mention four little boys who don't understand why they can't eat regular meals like their friends do."

"I see," Riley said as he came forward and reached out to smooth back the strand of Zandy's hair that Molly had pulled loose. "And you thought somehow this would make me change my mind?"

"I hoped you would do the decent thing and help them by giving my father his job back and allowing us credit at the stores. My stepmother is dying, Riley, and you've got to allow the doctor to help her."

Riley felt a moment of discomfort as Molly reached out to grab his finger. He quickly pulled his hand back, making Molly think he was playing with her. Her gurgling baby sounds made Riley smile.

"She'll be dead in no time at all," Zandy said matter-of-factly. "A baby can't live long without food or without a mother."

Riley looked thoughtfully for a moment. "I'm sure that is true. I will give you food for your family and milk for your little sister." Zandy felt a wave of hope wash over her weak frame, but it was short-lived as Riley continued, "Just as soon as you take your sister home and move into my house. I will send Mike to personally deliver ten dollars worth of groceries to your family. I will also send the doctor with the medicine your stepmother needs."

"You're a ruthless man, Mister Dawson," Zandy said and turned to leave.

"And you are a selfish, spoiled young woman. Your loved ones are hurting, suffering from hunger and sickness because your pride and selfish morals won't allow you to help them. After they're dead, Alexandra, do you think people will praise your piety? Will they erect a memorial to the one person who could have saved her family, but vainly chose to ignore their need?"

"Vanity has nothing to do with this," Zandy said as tears welled in her eyes. "I believe God has a plan for His children and I believe in His word, the Bible. What you propose to me is against everything I hold dear and true. I will never be willing to throw those beliefs aside."

"Then their blood will be on your head," Riley said and left Zandy to contemplate his words.

Chapter 6

Mountain summer was a glorious time but it's pleasures were lost on Zandy. The quaking aspen trees whispered a Colorado melody and all that passed beneath their pulsating boughs were captivated, if not hypnotized, by the sound.

Zandy remembered when Pastor Brokamp had told her that the aspen were quaking because Christ passed beneath one on His way to Calvary. Still others told Zandy it was because the cross itself was made of aspen wood. Either way, Zandy had come to find a certain comfort in the sound.

The one ray of hope was the garden plot was just starting to provide food for the Stewart family. Zandy was more than happy to labor long hours in the garden in order to provide the bounty God grew there. Somehow, it made her feel vindicated and less responsible for her family's plight.

One evening after a lean supper of vegetable soup, the Stewarts were surprised to find a visitor at their door.

"Pastor Brokamp, please come in," Ruth said as she finished putting the last of the dishes on the shelf.

"I heard times were difficult for you. We took up a collection and brought you some things. If you'll come outside and help me unload Mabel, I'd be much obliged," Pastor Brokamp announced.

Ruth's face clearly showed the gratitude she felt. "Thanks be to God," she said as she moved with Zandy and Burley toward the door.

"No, Ruth. You just sit. Zandy and I can get whatever Pastor Brokamp has brought us. No sense wearing yourself out when you're just starting to feel better."

Ruth, who'd begun to enjoy a bit of health, nodded. It was as if the warmer, dry mountain air had eased some of her congestion. Zandy believed it was God's response to her faithful obedience. She knew God wouldn't let them go on being hungry or sick.

Zandy and her father were surprised to find Pastor Brokamp's donkey packed to overflowing. There wasn't even an inch of room for the irritating horseflies to pester the jenny's back.

After they finished helping Pastor Brokamp carry the goods into the house, the preacher offered a prayer for their health and prosperity and took

Mabel back down the path to Dawson.

"I've never seen so much food in my life," Ruth began as she sorted through the abundance.

"The store has this much food, Ma," Joshua offered as he helped to put away the cans of fruit and milk.

"This place will look like a store for sure when we get all this food put away," Burley Stewart told his oldest son.

Zandy went to bed that night with a full stomach and a grateful heart. God was so very good to have provided for her loved ones. It only served to confirm she'd done the right thing by standing up to Riley Dawson.

"Thank You, God," Zandy whispered as she snuggled down in the covers. Before continuing her prayer, she glanced across the room to see that Joshua and Samuel were already sound asleep. "I just knew that I was doing the right thing. Thank You for giving me a sign of encouragement."

~

Zandy's hopefulness lasted only until the next day when she found out Riley Dawson had closed down the church. Pastor Brokamp took the announcement in stride and refused to leave his small cabin. Instead, he announced that anyone who wanted to be his house guest on Sundays would be very welcomed.

Later that morning, Jim Williams appeared at the Stewarts's doorstep to give Zandy a sealed envelope from Riley.

"What does he want?" Zandy said as she looked at the writing on the envelope.

"I don't know. He just called me in and asked me to deliver this to you. He said you were to read it right away. I can't say I was happy to oblige him, but I didn't get much of a choice," Jim said in a rather discouraged tone.

Poor Jim, Zandy thought to herself. If Riley hadn't come along imposing his will upon everyone, Jim might have found a way to marry her. Now, however, Zandy doubted Jim would ever feel comfortable with her again.

"I'm supposed to get on back to the jail," Jim finally said and turned to leave.

"Jim, I. . ." Zandy wasn't sure what it was she wanted to say, but somehow she wished she could console him.

"There's nothing to say, Zandy. You don't owe me any explanation. I know how demanding Dawson can be. Just be careful."

Zandy was touched by Jim's concern. "I will be." She wanted to say more, but Jim was already headed back to town.

Zandy opened the envelope and read the contents.

I want to see you at the church. Now!

Riley

"Of all the nerve," Zandy said as she opened the lid on the stove and shoved the letter and envelope inside. She poked the letter down into the ashes until it caught fire and burned.

"That's all the attention I'll give you, Mister Riley Dawson," Zandy muttered as she tied her apron on. A wave of ominous guilt washed over her, however, causing her to rethink her words. "Oh, alright," she said as she took off the apron and slammed it down on the table.

Zandy quickly braided her hair into a single plait down the back and tied it with a ribbon. She was glad Ruth had taken the children visiting for she had no desire to explain to Ruth or her father as to why Riley Dawson would be summoning her. Zandy hated to be so obedient to Riley's request, but there was really nothing to be gained in raising his ire.

～

She entered the church with a cautious glance. Riley was no where to be seen so Zandy made her way to the front of the church and took a seat in the family pew.

"You certainly took your time," Riley said as he walked into the church, letting the door close with a resounding bang.

Zandy couldn't suppress a shudder. This was a confrontation she wasn't anxious to face. "I came as soon as I could get away," she said, refusing to offer an apology.

Riley walked to the front of the church and took a seat in the pew directly in front of her. "Your Pastor Brokamp made a mistake in crossing me. I've closed the church."

"Yes, I know," Zandy said matter-of-factly.

Riley raised an eyebrow. "You know? My, my, news travels fast in this little town. Do you also know you're the reason."

"Me?" Zandy couldn't suppress her surprise.

"Yes. Brokamp brought your family food last night. He knew better. He'd already been to see me about increasing your father's hours at the mine and I informed him he should stay out of the matter. He chose not to, so I closed the church."

"So, once again, because I am being obedient to God and not to Riley Dawson, a good and caring man is being punished. Fair or not fair, Mister Dawson. I find your idea of a good life very strange." Zandy paused to see if Riley might offer some objection and when he didn't, she continued. "You came here offering people happiness, wealth, prosperity, and, in a way, salvation from their miseries. So far you've managed to make yourself the most despised as well as the best-loved man in all of Dawson. You had the potential to create a dynasty for yourself. You had people eating out of your hand and being happy to do it. Now, you've made a grave mistake. Oh, I realize the masses won't care. They are as you once told me, the godless who would sell their souls for a claim. But, Mister Dawson," Zandy boldly stared Riley in the eye, "the original towns-folk, the ones you made your promises to, they will despise and reject you for harming their pastor and church. You have made a very bad mistake."

Riley studied her seriously for a moment. There was no doubt about it, Alexandra Stewart was an intelligent woman. There was a great amount of truth in what she had to say and Riley couldn't just ignore it. Perhaps it was time to change tactics. It bore consideration.

"Alexandra, I'm sorry that it was necessary to close the church. I'm even sorry others are suffering. It was never my intention for anyone to get hurt. I only wanted to treat one extraordinary woman to a very special life. Hurting people and causing folks to suffer was never a part of my plan."

"Then why allow it to continue?" Zandy questioned.

"Because," Riley said with a heavy sigh, "I can't back down now."

"Why? Is your pride really worth the pain you're causing?"

"I'm causing? I'm not the one causing this." Riley could tell by the look on Zandy's face he wasn't making any more progress than the times before. "I'm not a monster, Alexandra. Why not allow yourself to enjoy my company and the things I can give you. You can't be happy with the constant worry of what the winter will bring. You can't expect another collection to come by way of the townspeople."

"The people didn't send us that collection. God did, Riley," Zandy softened her voice. In a way, she felt very sorry for Riley Dawson. He had no way of understanding her faith in God. "God will always take care of His children."

"I don't consider eight people living in a three-room shack, being cared for, Zandy," Riley said using her nickname, "you could live in a mansion, like a queen."

" 'I had rather be a doorkeeper in the house of my God, than to dwell in the tents of wickedness.' That's Psalm 84:10," Zandy said, feeling a need to share her faith with Riley. "The Bible is filled with verses that speak to us of finding value in the simple things of righteous people rather than the wealth and glory of the godless." Suddenly, it seemed so clear to Zandy what she should have been doing all along was showing Riley the road to salvation.

"Those are just words that poor people comfort themselves with," Riley said, looking slightly disturbed by Zandy's revelation. "How strong will your faith be now that your church is gone?"

"My faith in God doesn't exist simply because a church building opens its doors. My faith in God runs so much deeper," Zandy explained. "Oh, Riley, I wish you could understand. I believe in God and the salvation He's offered me, not because of this building or Pastor Brokamp, or even my Christian parents. I believe in God because the Bible showed me who He was and why He cared about me. I accepted His love and repented of my old, sinful ways and now I have the best that life can possibly offer, all because I have Him."

"So nothing has changed?" Riley questioned, sounding rather awkward.

Zandy smiled and it disturbed Riley more than he would ever allow himself to realize. "A great deal has changed. I know now why God sent you into my life. Before this moment I was constantly asking God why He would allow such a time of testing, but now I see why. God wants you to know Him, Riley."

Riley tried to chuckle at the words but he had an almost fearful feeling that Zandy was right. "We'll see just how long you maintain this point of view."

"Why, what have you planned for me now?"

"Not so much for you, Zandy, as much as for everyone else," Riley said as he got up. He felt the need to get away from Zandy before her words of God and faith changed his mind and his plans.

"Just what do you mean, Riley," Zandy said and rushed to his side. When Riley continued to walk down the aisle, Zandy reached out and took hold of his arm.

It was more than Riley had expected and he quickly turned to pull Zandy into his arms. Their eyes met for only a moment, but a moment was enough. Zandy knew touching Riley had been the wrong thing and, as Riley's mouth crushed down on her's, Zandy's mind went blank.

When Riley released her, Zandy took a step backward and raised her hand to her mouth. More troubling to her than Riley's kiss was the fact she wasn't repulsed by it the way she'd hoped she'd be. The look of confusion betrayed her feelings.

"Think about this moment when everyone turns against you because of their losses. Think about it and remember how you feel right this minute." With that, Riley was gone and Zandy was left to regather her wits.

Chapter 7

Zandy hadn't long to wait until she understood exactly what Riley Dawson had in mind. Word spread throughout the town about the increased percentage of profits that was to go to Riley's personal bank account. Then, there was the increased cost of goods that arrived weekly through Riley's selected freighters. One by one, every family in Dawson was affected and when Riley forced more than one family to turn over their property in lieu of credit extended at the various stores in town, the people became enraged.

At the people's request, Riley held an open forum at the town hall. The building was crowded to overflowing with every inch of standing room filled by one body or another. Zandy offered to take the boys back home while Ruth and Burley stayed on but, just as she turned to leave, Jim Williams approached them.

"Mister Dawson says I'm to make sure you're given a proper place to stand. I'm to escort you to the roped off section at the front."

"But why the special treatment?" Burley questioned.

Zandy felt her heart sink. So this was Riley's retaliation. He planned to publicly humiliate her family. She didn't even hear Jim's reply but simply followed her father and stepmother through the crowd.

How could he be so cruel? Zandy asked herself over and over. "If he had only been kind," Zandy muttered to herself, "I might have actually fallen in love with him."

"What did you say, Zandy?" Ruth leaned over to ask amidst the din of noise.

Zandy shook her head. "Nothing, Ruth." The fact was her statement startled her in a way she couldn't explain. Was it true? Could she really have thought herself capable of falling in love with Riley Dawson?

She hadn't any time to consider the matter as Riley approached the front of the room.

"If everyone will quiet down, I'll begin this meeting," Riley shouted above the noise.

An immediate hush fell over the room and people began to push forward ever so slightly in order to hear whatever might be said.

"I know many of you are unhappy with the new arrangements we've made for your businesses and working hours. I have only one thing to say about the matter. I offered Miss Alexandra Stewart a very tempting proposal and she rejected me. I suggest if you are unhappy you take it up with her." Riley stared squarely into Zandy's shocked face. The hurt in her eyes nearly caused him to wince. Why should it bother him that she was upset? He intended to have his own way in this matter and by whatever means it took to accomplish his goal.

Zandy could see the hurtful and angry stares of her neighbors and friends. Even her family looked at her with eyes that questioned Riley's announcement.

"What does he mean, Zandy?" her father asked in a guarded tone.

"I, uh. . ." Zandy felt at a loss for words. She wanted to cry but wouldn't give Riley the privilege of seeing her break down.

"Let's discuss this at home, Burley," Ruth offered and moved her children out of the roped area.

"What's he talking about, Miss Alexandra? Are you causing us grief just because you don't want to marry Riley Dawson?" someone questioned from the crowd.

Someone else joined in with their opinion. "I don't reckon to see my kids going without like your brothers and sister. Just marry the man and let us be."

A rousing cry of agreement came out of the crowd and Zandy's eyes narrowed slightly as she squared her shoulders and gave Riley Dawson a look that made him think better of having crossed her.

Riley was still contemplating his action after the crowd had dispersed and the Stewarts had gone home. Why had he done it? He knew he'd hurt her and that was never his real intention. Of course, he thought as he walked to his mansion on the hill, he'd never expected her to endure for so long. He'd never in his life had the slightest trouble getting his way with women, but then he'd never met a woman of virtue who interested him. But, that was before Alexandra Stewart had come into his life.

～

Even the children were quiet as the Stewart family entered their little house. A deluge of painful accusations and suspicious eyes had followed them all the way home and when they had closed the door behind them, Burley told the boys to go to the back room and play.

"It appears we need to talk, Zandy," Burley said as he planted his large frame on a kitchen chair.

Ruth left the room only long enough to put Molly down for a nap and soon joined Burley at the table.

Zandy remained standing, feeling as though she were being tried in court for a crime she had not committed. Silently, she prayed that she might be able to say the right thing.

"Is what Mr. Dawson said true? Did you reject him?" Burley questioned.

"Yes, but—" Zandy started to explain but her father cut her off.

"You rejected him even knowing what he would do to your family and the town?" Burley asked and the anger in his voice surprised Zandy.

"I didn't feel his proposal was in keeping with the Word of God," Zandy declared, hoping the words would speak for themselves.

"So you took it upon yourself to interpret the Bible and bring down grief upon your family. Did it ever occur to you that perhaps this punishment came because you weren't doing the will of God?" Burley questioned and Zandy felt the color drain from her face.

"Pa, you don't understand. Riley Dawson isn't all that he seems."

"So now you're an authority on the Bible and on men."

"Now, Burley, don't get so upset. I'm sure Zandy has a good reason for turning away a fine man like Riley Dawson. Perhaps she just needs time to get to know him."

Burley pounded his fist down on the table causing both Zandy and Ruth to jump. "Those little ones in the back room went hungry because of you. You had it in your means to save them from their pain and yet you allowed it to go on. How could you be so cruel? I didn't raise you to be so selfish."

Zandy stared openmouthed at her father and stepmother. Nobody cared what her reasoning was. Nobody cared that Riley wanted a mistress and not a wife. Perhaps they would have if she'd been allowed to explain herself but, instead, her father clearly wanted no explanation.

"I have to face the people of this town every day. Why, the church even took up a collection for this family. Those people must feel like complete fools now," Burley surmised. "I don't understand you. I would think you'd be grateful for the promising life that Riley Dawson could offer."

"Zandy," Ruth said softly, trying to balance out the boisterous voice of her father, "what is it that troubles you so about marrying Riley?"

Zandy sat down across from her parents in a most dejected manner. What could she say? Should she tell her father about Riley's real request? What could possibly be gained if she told her father he wanted her to live in sin with him. Either her father wouldn't care in order to save the rest of the family and town or he'd be so angry he'd give Riley a piece of his mind and lose his job.

"Your ma asked you a question. Are you going to answer her?" Burley said in a calmer tone. Ruth always had that effect on Burley and now, as Ruth clasped her hand in his, Zandy knew he would relax a bit.

"I don't love Riley Dawson," Zandy stated sadly.

"Love? Is that what this is all about?" Zandy's father questioned in disbelief. "What about love for your brothers and sister? What about love for your ma who can't get the medicine she needs? I think you'd best spend some time in prayer and reconsider what sacrificial love is all about."

"Zandy, people don't always love each other the way storybooks tell it. You learn to love, though. I think you could learn to love Riley and have a happy life as his wife," Ruth said in an almost pleading tone.

The word "wife," cut Zandy like a knife. She wanted to scream that he didn't want a wife but instead she remained silent. Only God knew the truth—God and Riley Dawson.

Later that day, when Zandy was working in the garden, Jim Williams appeared out of nowhere. "Care if I hang around a minute?" Jim asked, cautiously.

"No, I guess not," Zandy replied in just as guarded a tone.

"I thought maybe you could use a friend about now," Jim said as he leaned against the crude fencing that lined the front of the property.

"I guess I could at that," Zandy said as she straightened up from pulling onions. "I figured you'd be just as angry at me as everyone else is."

"I'm not mad, Zandy. I guess I just wonder why you don't want to marry Riley. I mean, I know you aren't seeing anybody and it just seems like an awful good life to offer a woman. If I had that kind of money, I know I wouldn't waste any time at all in finding me a good wife."

Zandy smiled. Riley had the entire community exactly where he wanted them. They all presumed from his statement he was doing an honorable, maybe even romantic thing and that Zandy considered herself above the matter or, at best, disinterested in the comfort.

"Just remember, Jim," Zandy finally said, "things aren't always what they seem. You mustn't judge me too harshly."

"I wasn't trying to judge you at all. Frankly, I'm happy you don't want to marry him. I just wish I could marry you instead. But the truth is, Riley said if I spend any more time with you he'd fire me."

"I'm sorry, Jim," Zandy said and gathered her gardening tools. "You'd probably better leave before someone sees you here and reports it back to Riley. I don't want anybody to suffer any more because of me."

"I'm not really worried," Jim said, but Zandy knew it was a lie because his eyes continued to dart from side to side as if he were watching for Riley.

"You may not be, but I am. I'm very worried. I'm not sure where all this is leading, but I don't want you involved."

"I hope you know I'll always care about you," Jim stated softly.

Zandy smiled again. He was so young and handsome and very naive about the power behind Riley Dawson. *He shouldn't have come at all,* Zandy thought to herself. "I'm glad you do, Jim. Thank you." With those few words, Zandy didn't even wait for his response but went quickly into the house.

As Zandy closed the door behind her, she could hear her stepmother still trying to soothe her father's worried mind. The boys were beginning to raise a ruckus in the back room and Molly was fussing to be fed.

Leaning against the door, Zandy breathed a prayer, "Father, I know I'm not to disobey my father and I know I mustn't dishonor Your Word. Please help me, Lord, to know what to do, Amen." Zandy sighed and put the tools away. It was going to be a long summer.

Chapter 8

Day after day, Ruth and Burley went out of their way to ignore Zandy in hopes that she'd make the right choice and marry Riley Dawson.

More than once, Zandy had lain awake in her bed, hearing her father and stepmother talking in hushed whispers about what they would do when the food ran out. Zandy always felt as though she'd had the wind knocked out of her when her father would say he didn't know what had gotten into Zandy.

Zandy knew they still cared about her, but it was a fine line she had to walk in order to keep the subject of Riley Dawson from entering the brief bits of conversation they had at mealtime.

One morning as Burley was leaving for the mines, Zandy happened to be sitting on the front door stoop contemplating the mess she found herself in.

"What are you doing out here?" her father asked as he stepped past Zandy and paused directly in front of her.

"I was just thinking about when I was a little girl. You know, before Ma died." Her father nodded but said nothing. Zandy sighed. "I was so sure we'd always live in the same house, do the same things, be the same people. I never thought things would change so much."

"Me neither," he admitted sadly and placed a hand on Zandy's shoulder. "I know things are difficult right now, but I want you to know I'll never stop loving you."

Zandy needed so much to hear those words. She felt a tear slide down her cheek as she leaned her face to touch his hand and whispered, "I love you too, Pa."

The moment was far too brief, then, without another word, her father walked out the gate and down the path to work. Zandy hugged herself tightly wishing the feeling of warmth could go on forever, but a chilling reminder of Riley Dawson haunted her mind. Hours later, Zandy was to remember the moment as one of the most precious in her life.

~

Most of her days passed in monotonous routine, but this day was different. Without warning, the silence of the day was broken. The loud explosion, followed by the eerie blast of the mining whistle in midday, could only mean one thing—there had been an accident!

Zandy looked up at the same time Ruth did, wondering silently if it would be their family member who had been hurt. Ruth gave Zandy a guarded look. She'd done her best to keep an air of harmony in the house but her own heart was well tested in light of her childrens going without the things they needed. Now, it was only a matter of time before they would learn whether or not Burley was involved in the mining accident.

Zandy opened the front door and looked down the pathway, hoping and praying her father was safe. Minutes ticked by and, after fifteen minutes had passed, Zandy decided she could wait no longer.

"I'm going to the mine and see what happened," she said as she folded her apron and placed it on the table.

Ruth only nodded.

Zandy was just reaching for the door when she heard the commotion on the path below. Her heart sunk and a lump fixed itself in her throat. She dared a look at her stepmother to find tears forming in her eyes.

"Not Burley," Ruth whispered and her hand flew to her mouth to stifle a cry.

A man came rushing ahead of the others to warn Zandy and Ruth to make a place ready.

"He's hurt pretty bad, Missus Stewart," the man said apologetically. "He drilled into a missed hole."

Zandy cringed knowing only too well what that meant. Missed holes were cavities that had been packed with dynamite but hadn't exploded as expected. Her father would have ignited enough spark while drilling the heavy rock face to set off the unexploded dynamite. In turn, the explosion would have torn the drill operator apart. If they were bringing him home, however, he must still be alive.

"Have they sent for the doctor?" Ruth questioned and began to cough. The consumption was now active again and giving her a great amount of trouble.

"Uh. . .no, Ma'am," the man grew quite uncomfortable. "The doc won't come here unless Mister Dawson gives his approval."

Ruth stopped dead in her tracks. She turned both accusing eyes to face Zandy and, for once in her life, Zandy felt anger directed toward her from her stepmother. The look really said it all and Zandy wanted to look away, but couldn't.

"Do you mean to tell me my husband is going to be denied a doctor?" Ruth asked the man, all the while looking at Zandy.

"Sorry, Ma'am. The men are nearly here, you'd best make the bed ready."

Ruth began to cry, which only aggravated the cough. "I'll pull down the covers," she managed to say.

"I'll help you," Zandy offered.

Ruth turned on her heel and held Zandy at arm's length. "There's only one way you can help. I think you know exactly what that is."

Zandy had no time to reply as the men burst through the door, bearing the stretcher that held her father.

"Oh, Pa," Zandy cried as she caught sight of her father's bloodied body. He was mercifully unconscious and for all intents and purposes, looked dead.

Zandy tore out of the house on a dead run to the Dawson mansion. Riley just had to listen to reason. He couldn't be so heartless as to refuse a dying man care. Reason eluded Zandy as she flew across the garden path and, without so much as a knock, burst through the doors to the mansion.

"Riley!" she screamed. Tears were flowing down her face and her hair fell wildly about her shoulders. "Riley Dawson, I demand to see you now!"

Riley stepped from behind double oak doors with a stunned expression on his face. When he saw how upset Zandy was, he crossed the room in several quick strides. "What is it?"

"My father has been blown up! You must send the doctor to my house," Zandy said as she gripped Riley's arms tightly.

The touch was almost more than Riley could stand, but he did nothing to remove her hands. His real thought was to pull her into his arms and comfort her. Zandy looked so scared and upset Riley nearly lost his resolve. His heart cried out to him to be merciful, but his mind told him this was the very chance for which he had waited.

"Alexandra," he began.

"Don't Alexandra me," Zandy said as she dropped her hands. "Don't tell me anything except you're going to send the doctor to my father."

"I can't," Riley said, then bit his tongue to keep from taking it back.

Zandy shocked them both by pounding her fists against Riley's chest. "You brute! You monster! You don't care about anything but having your own way. My father is dying and you don't care."

"You know what I'll expect in return if I send the doctor to your father," Riley said as he took hold of Zandy's wrists.

Zandy fought against his hold, all the while sobbing until the tears came in a wave of hysteria. "He'll die! He'll die! Don't you understand? You have women in town who can satisfy your lustful desires, but my father is going to die if the doctor doesn't come to him now! Please, Riley," Zandy stopped abruptly. "Please don't let him die," she managed between sobs.

Riley released her arms and pulled her against his chest. He couldn't bear the pain in her eyes. "Hush, you're making this much too difficult. Everything is going to be alright."

Zandy allowed Riley to stroke her hair and hold her. She couldn't explain why she wasn't repulsed by the action, nor why she found comfort in it, but then her mind was beyond rational thought, she reasoned.

For several minutes they stood in the vestibule of the Dawson mansion, while Zandy's tears played themselves out against Riley's broad chest. Zandy felt too exhausted to move, yet she knew every passing minute might be the determining factor as to whether her father lived or died.

"I know you aren't a bad man, Riley," Zandy said as she pulled away slowly. She dried her eyes with the back of her sleeve. "I don't understand why you've chosen the path you have. Maybe you didn't have good folks to bring you up like I did. Maybe you've had a falling out with God and feel like He's deserted you. I just don't know, but I do feel strongly you aren't really enjoying this any more than I am. It's become a matter of pride and your pride will eventually break you."

Riley pushed his hands deep in his pockets to keep from reaching out and pulling Zandy back into his arms. He looked at the young woman before him, the red-rimmed eyes, the wild hair, and in his mind he felt something he'd never before felt for a woman—genuine compassion.

"You're right, Alexandra," Riley spoke softly. "I'm not enjoying this at all."

"Then why not give in and end it?"

Riley gave a stilted laugh, "I suppose because I've always mastered my destiny and I'm not about to have someone else do it for me now."

"But God masters everyone's destiny, Riley," Zandy said, momentarily forgetting her father lay dying. "You don't have control over anything at all, Riley. God does."

"God certainly didn't keep your father from getting hurt in the mines."

"There is a purpose for everything," Zandy said and suddenly realized the truth of her own words. "Even this has a purpose."

"A purpose that might cause you to give in and join me here?" Riley questioned.

Zandy stepped back, shaking her head. "You can have most any other woman, Riley. Please don't force me to give myself over to be your mistress in order to save my father's life. It just isn't that simple. Court me or marry me, but don't ask me to shame myself before my God."

The words shocked Riley. Would she actually be willing to marry him? "If God is the way you say He is, knowing everything and all, then He'd know becoming my mistress wasn't your idea. He'd know and He wouldn't blame you. So why concern yourself with saying that you'd shame yourself. You know full well the responsibility would be mine and I don't care."

Zandy swallowed hard. Riley made it sound so simple. Wasn't it true God would indeed know the difference? Wouldn't it be easy to just give in and deal with the consequences later?

A picture of her father, bleeding and unconscious, came to mind. Was one sacrifice worth the other? Zandy turned to leave and Riley couldn't help but follow after her. Before he could speak, Zandy stopped at the door.

"I'm praying for you, Riley. I have been ever since the first night I met you. Praying you'd be the salvation for our town we needed, praying that God would open your eyes to your willful and sinful spirit, and praying God would allow you to find mercy upon the people in this town and me." Zandy said the words in such a way Riley felt completely engulfed by each and every one. "My father's life is in God's hands. That's something I forgot before coming up here. I guess my fears got the best of me, but I want you to know I'm going to keep on praying for you, Riley. I know there is good inside you and I know God can deal with you and bring out that good."

With those final words, Zandy stepped out into the night and hurried toward the path that would lead home.

Riley could only stare after her. Why had her words so disturbed him?

"Such foolish feminine notions," Riley muttered as he watched Zandy disappear from view. But as he closed the door, his heart and mind were at war for control and Riley silently wished he'd never come to Dawson, Colorado.

Chapter 9

When Zandy walked back into her house, she could hear the commotion of the men as they tried to help Ruth in the back room. Zandy quickly put a kettle of water on to boil and found an old sheet she could tear into bandages.

"God, please help me. I need to do my very best in order to help my father and stepmother. Please guide me and help me," Zandy said the words but, in the back of her mind, she felt the nagging doubt of faltering faith.

She wanted so much to believe, yet never had her faith been tested so severely. Surely the Word of God was true. It just had to be true and Zandy had to be able to trust God would deliver her from the pain and confusion.

Riley's words came back to haunt her, though, and Zandy wondered silently if she shouldn't be the one to give up and accept Riley's proposition. At least everyone in town would be treated better and she felt confident Riley would send the doctor to help.

Hearing her father cry out in pain brought Zandy rudely back to reality. She was so tired and so confused. What seemed simple and orderly in the printed words of the Bible somehow didn't seem to fit the lawless life of Dawson, Colorado.

Ruth's ceaseless crying, mingled with the violent coughing spasms, sent Zandy to the door. If the only way she could get help was to offer herself to Riley Dawson, then she'd call Riley the victor and give in. Opening the door, Zandy was shocked to find the doctor on the other side.

"I was sent to care for your father," the doctor said as he entered the room.

Zandy breathed a prayer of thanksgiving. "Please hurry! He's right back there."

Zandy brought the doctor to her father's bedside and cast Ruth a glance as the doctor ordered everyone from the room.

Ruth's eyes held gratitude as well as pain. Zandy knew she was suffering for both her husband and herself. Zandy tried to look hopeful as she looked from her father's mangled body to her stepmother's face.

"Bring me some hot water," the doctor ordered as he went quickly to the business of caring for Burley.

"I'll get it," Zandy said as she hurried from the room.

She pulled down the wash basin and filled it with water from the stove and rushed back to her father's bedside.

"Could've been much worse," the doctor said as he stripped pieces of clothing away from Burley's chest. Ruth clung tightly to her husband's hand, as the doctor began to wash away the rock and bits of dirt that had embedded themselves in Burley's skin.

Just then one of the neighbor women came to announce she was taking the children to her house. Zandy refused to look into the accusing eyes of the woman who, up until a few days ago, had been a good friend. Ruth offered her thanks and quickly turned her attention back to Burley.

"Hand me that bottle," the doctor said and pointed Zandy in the direction of a corked blue bottle.

Zandy quickly complied and watched as the doctor generously poured the contents on Burley's wounds. "This will fight proud flesh," the doctor said, referring to the dreaded blood poisoning that had caused more than one to lose a limb or die.

Ruth began to cough so violently Zandy noticed blood on the back of her sleeve when Ruth lowered her hand from her face.

"Get her to bed and give her this," the doctor said and handed Zandy a packet of powder. "Mix it in a glass of water and have her drink it."

"I'm not. . ." Ruth sputtered and coughed, trying hard to protest leaving her husband's side.

"You're going to bed or I'll not do another thing to help this man," the doctor said sternly. "I won't save his life only to have him wake up to find his wife dead."

Ruth went begrudgingly with Zandy, but once she was seated on one of the beds in the boys' room, she nearly collapsed. Zandy brought her the medicine and helped hold Ruth steady as she drank the contents.

"Tastes awful," Ruth said as she handed Zandy the empty glass. Zandy couldn't help but notice the gritty residue in the bottom of the glass.

"I can well imagine," Zandy said as she placed the glass on the bedside table.

Easing Ruth back into the bed, Zandy was surprised to find her stepmother clinging tightly to her arm. "Zandy, I'm so sorry," she said between coughs. "Please forgive me for the way I've acted. Please."

Zandy smiled and pulled the covers over Ruth's bone-thin body. "There's nothing to forgive. I love you, Ruth. You've been a dear mother to me. You just rest and I'll see to Pa."

Ruth nodded and Zandy was relieved to find Ruth was well on her way to losing consciousness.

"What did you give my stepmother?" Zandy questioned as she rejoined the doctor.

"Sleeping powder. I knew it would ease the cough and put her out of her misery for a short time. I can better tend her later. Your pa is cut up pretty bad, but I think he'll be alright. I'm going to stay with him through the night, so you might as well get some rest."

Zandy shook her head. "There is something I need to do. Will you be alright if I leave the house? I want to tell the children things are going well, and I want to. . ." Her voice fell silent. She didn't want to tell anyone she intended to go and thank Riley for saving her father's life.

"Things are well under control," the doctor said. "You go and do what you must."

Zandy quickly made her way to the neighbor's house and after assuring the children things were going to be alright, she made her way to the Dawson mansion.

Her entrance into the house was a far cry from her earlier one. She waited patiently at the door until the butler appeared to admit her.

"Please tell Mr. Dawson I need to speak with him," Zandy requested.

"The hour is quite late, Miss. . . ," the butler began, but Riley's appearance in the hallway ended anything further he might have said.

"It's alright," Riley said and waved the butler away. "Come on in, Alexandra. I was expecting you." His dark eyes pierced her soul.

"I wanted to thank you for sending the doctor. My father is doing much better, and the doctor gave my mother something to help her sleep."

"Why don't you come on into the library with me. I was just taking some coffee and cakes. You look like you could use some refreshments," Riley offered and his casual generosity surprised Zandy.

"I can't stay long, but it does sound good," she found herself saying without thought. She allowed Riley to lead her through the double oak doors which opened into the library. The room was glorious and Zandy thought she'd never seen anything quite so beautiful.

"Please, sit," Riley said as he pointed to a blue high-backed chair. Zandy did as he directed and accepted a cup of coffee in a fine bone china cup. Riley placed the delicate saucer on the table beside her chair and brought her another small plate with several miniature cakes. It all seemed so pleasant.

Zandy took a drink and grimaced at the bitter taste. She'd never acquired a fondness for coffee, especially without benefit of cream and sugar.

Riley took the seat across from her without noticing her expression. "So, tell me about your father. What did the doctor say?"

"The doctor said it could have been much worse. He thinks Pa will make it. He also promised to look in on Ruth," Zandy said and took another drink. "I can't thank you enough, Riley. I knew you had a streak of good in you, and I knew God wouldn't let me down."

Riley tried not to frown, but the look crossed his face before he could hide it. "I'm glad he's going to make it."

Zandy felt the tension ease from her body as she allowed herself to relax, knowing her father was receiving the best of care. "I really should get back," Zandy said as she yawned. "I'm totally spent, but I had to thank you." Taking one final drink from the cup, Zandy noticed the gritty residue in the bottom of the cup. A feeling of dread filled her as she struggled to focus on the cup. "I need to go home," she said as she got to her feet and tried to balance herself.

"Sit down, Alexandra," Riley ordered. "Sit down before you fall down."

Zandy tried to put the coffee cup on the table but missed and the clattering sound seemed to reverberate in her ears. It was abundantly clear to her Riley had drugged her coffee.

"Why?" she asked with sad accusation in her eyes. "Why?"

Riley put his cup down and stood up slowly. "Because you wouldn't listen to reason."

"I came here to thank you," Zandy said in a slurring manner. "I thought you were being kind. I. . ." Zandy swayed and gripped the side of her chair.

Riley stepped forward to take hold of her, but Zandy pushed him away and nearly fell backward. "Leave me alone," she struggled to say. Her words sounded foreign to her. "Dear God, help me," Zandy worked hard to retain her balance and remember what she wanted to pray. " 'For He shall give His angels charge over thee, to keep thee in all thy ways.' " Zandy quoted from Psalm 91:11, trying to plead with God for protection. "Keep me, Lord. Save me from Riley Dawson's lustful passions."

The words were barely audible, but Riley recognized them easily. It was as if his ears alone could make out each and every word with total clarity. She was praying as she had said she'd done before.

Zandy felt herself pitch forward and knew she couldn't help herself. Riley's strong arms reached out and took hold of her shoulders.

"I can give you a wonderful life, Alexandra," Riley tried to salve his conscience. He'd thought this would be a simple task but it was proving to be more and more difficult.

Zandy's head fell forward as she struggled to stay awake. She snapped her head back and opened her eyes wide as if it would help her to see clearly.

"I'm still not willing," she said, delivering the words in all their simplicity to Riley's heart. "Not willing, just drugged."

The words hit their mark. She wasn't willing. Once again it was just a matter of Riley's forced will. Hadn't he told her he'd wait forever for her heart to be willing?

Ever so gently he reached up to push back a loose strand of dark hair. "You are so beautiful. Why can't you understand?"

Zandy felt herself falling; she could no longer stand. It would only be a matter of seconds and she'd be unconscious. "Save me, God," she murmured and fell against Riley.

Riley easily lifted her into his arms. What should he do now, he wondered. He knew what he'd planned to do, but now found his selfish desires impossible to satisfy. Never in his life had his conscience so bothered him.

"Mrs. Malloy!" Riley called out for his housekeeper. Even at this late hour, Riley knew the older woman would be within earshot.

True enough the grandmotherly woman seemingly came from out of nowhere to answer her employer's call. "Yes?"

"I'm afraid Miss Stewart has collapsed in exhaustion. Will you help me put her to bed?" Riley asked as he cradled Zandy in his arms.

"Of course, Sir. I'll pull down the covers in the Blue Room," Mrs. Malloy stated in a refined manner. Taking the lead, Mrs. Malloy went up the stairs ahead of Riley.

"Not willing," Zandy whispered in her nightmarish state of mind. She was dreaming and all around her were people condemning her for not helping her family.

Her words were only loud enough for Riley to hear and he grimaced at the impact of what he'd done. "I know, Alexandra. I know."

Mrs. Malloy had pulled back the covers and the sheets on a huge canopy bed and turned to Riley, "Shall I bring her one of my nightgowns?"

Riley shook his head. "No. We'll just leave her dressed," he said as he deposited her on the bed. "Can you watch over her through the night?"

"Certainly," Mrs. Malloy replied. "I'll go get my knitting and sit right here."

"Thank you. You may, of course, take tomorrow off to replenish your rest."

"Thank you, Sir. I'll be right back."

With that the older woman left the room leaving Riley alone with Zandy. Riley looked at the sleeping figure. She looked so young there on the huge bed. Why did the term "sacrificial lamb" come to mind?

Gently he reached over to cover her. "Don't hurt me," Zandy murmured in her sleep. "Please, don't hurt me."

Riley felt a stab of guilt. He'd caused her such fear and pain. How could he live with the person he'd become?

"Shh," Riley whispered as he leaned down. "I won't hurt you."

Just then Mrs. Malloy returned, and Riley took the opportunity to escape the obvious reminder of his deception. Taking himself to his own bedroom, Riley slammed the door and began to pace.

"I don't know why this has to be so hard. Why did she have to say no, and why did she have to say the things she said?" Riley muttered as he paced.

He went to pour himself a drink, then thought better of it and threw the whole bottle, along with the glass, into the fireplace. "I don't care what she said. I am no good and there's no way I can be redeemed. I'm too far gone."

The silent reminder of Zandy's prayers came back to haunt him. She'd actually prayed for him as well as for protection from him. How could she do that? How could she care enough to ask her God to change him? And why did she have to see through his façade of ruthlessness and know there was gentleness and compassion buried deep inside?

Well into the night, Riley contemplated his actions and Zandy's words. His mind had been so fixed on having her and now she lay helpless in his house and, for reasons beyond Riley's understanding, he couldn't touch her.

Chapter 10

Sleep eluded Riley, and when the clock in the hall chimed four, he could no longer stand the solitude. Quietly, he slipped into the Blue Room where Mrs. Malloy sat dozing beside Zandy's sleeping form.

The housekeeper stirred and Riley moved to where she sat. "You go on to bed. I'll sit with her now," Riley ordered.

"Are you certain, Sir?"

"Yes, very much so," Riley said, never taking his eyes from Zandy.

He took the seat Mrs. Malloy vacated and shook his head when she asked him if he'd like her to bring coffee. When the housekeeper was finally gone, Riley leaned forward and put his head in his hands.

His plan had seemed so simple. So why had everything gone so wrong? Why, when a beautiful woman like Alexandra Stewart lay just inches away, was he suddenly unable to carry through with his plan?

She'd prayed for him.

Why had she prayed for him? He didn't deserve her kindness or her prayers. She was so pure, and Riley knew there wasn't another woman like her in all of Dawson.

"What have I done?" he questioned aloud.

In her mind, Zandy heard the voice and wondered where it had come from. She felt rested and wonderful but, when she opened her eyes, her heart sank. Overhead was a canopy of starched white lace. This was definitely not her home.

She sat up with a start and was further shocked to find Riley Dawson watching her from a chair beside the bed.

"Why am I here? What have you done?" she questioned.

"I was just asking myself the same question," Riley mused. "You spent the night here after you collapsed."

Zandy's mouth dropped open. Then suddenly the memory of the drugged coffee returned to her mind. "Oh, no! This can't be true," Zandy said as she threw the cover back. She was still fully dressed and that offered a bit of comfort to her mind.

Riley sat back in the chair and watched her with a perplexed look on his face. What should he do now? He'd had the opportunity to do her a grave

414

injustice. Would she appreciate the fact he'd left her alone, or should he allow her to believe the worst?

Zandy sat fixed to her spot. She tried to remember the night before and frowned. "You drugged me."

"Yes," Riley said, offering no apology.

"Why?"

Riley shrugged. "It seemed like a good way to get you relaxed. You know, less inhibited. I thought maybe you were just afraid of what people might say."

Zandy rolled her eyes and sighed. "Well it would appear, Mister Dawson, you have created quite an incident here."

"Yes, so it would seem."

"Why are you here?" Zandy questioned.

"I couldn't sleep. I kept thinking of you. I guess just knowing you were so close kept me from being able to relax."

"Are you sure it wasn't your conscience that wouldn't let you rest?" Zandy knew she'd hit a nerve by the look in Riley's eyes.

"I don't know," Riley finally admitted. "I guess I've never had to deal head-on with a woman and her God."

Zandy laughed out loud, and the sound of her laughter was like music to Riley's ears. Why couldn't they spend more time laughing and enjoying each other's company instead of fighting.

"When you deal with me, Riley, you will always have to deal with my God as well. He's always with me, guarding me, protecting me, and loving me."

"He let this happen," Riley stated. "Now your reputation is ruined. People will find out you spent the night in my house and it won't matter what room you took residence in. You know the people of this town. They will presume the worst."

Zandy nodded and quietly agreed. "Yes, I suppose that much is true. People are always inclined, or so it would seem, to judge you guilty until they find a reason to do otherwise."

"So why not give in? Why not become my mistress now that everyone will assume you are anyway?" Riley questioned as he crossed his arms.

"I don't care what people think, Riley. I only care about what God knows to be true. He knows the truth. I've done nothing wrong."

"But how can you be sure I haven't?" Riley questioned seriously.

Zandy smiled. In so many ways, Riley reminded her of one of her little brothers. For all his worldly knowledge and goods, he still lost the meaning of the most important things in life.

"God would never allow you to harm me, Riley," Zandy stated firmly as she threw her legs over the side of the bed. "You see, my faith is firmly planted in Him. Oh, I must admit it hasn't been easy. I nearly gave in when you wouldn't send the doctor. I kept thinking about what you said and how all of this would be your responsibility. That was true, but God reminded me that He was faithful and I could trust Him."

"Even if it had cost your father his life?"

"Yes," Zandy nodded and then asked, "Have you had any word on my father?"

"Yes. He's doing fine. Both of your parents are resting comfortably."

"Praise be to God," Zandy said in complete reverence. "Thank you, again for sending the doctor."

"How can you thank me, after what I've done?" Riley questioned as he leaned forward.

Zandy studied him for a moment. From the looks of his rumpled clothes and messy hair, she knew Riley must have slept quite fitfully, if at all. His conscience was bothering him, and it amused her that he finally let his guard down long enough for her to see a bit of the real Riley Dawson.

For reasons beyond Zandy's understanding, she reached out her hand to touch his face. The action surprised Riley, but he didn't move away. "You are so lost, Riley Dawson. My heart cries for you. You are like a little boy who's searching for the safety of home. I know this isn't what you want to hear, but God loves you despite your past and the things you've done. You need to repent and accept His love, because until you do," Zandy said as she looked deep into his brown-black eyes, "you will always be just as unhappy and miserable as you are right this minute."

Riley was stunned into silence by the words of the young woman before him. She didn't talk like a woman who hated him, yet wouldn't he, himself, hate anyone who'd treated him as badly as he'd treated Zandy?

Her touch was so soft, so gentle and loving, yet Riley knew she would have done the same for anyone. Why did he find himself wishing she might care singularly for him? Never before had he even considered what she might feel. It was always his own desires that mattered. When she dropped her hand, Riley found its absence almost painful.

The minutes ticked by and the tension that had existed between them seemed to lessen. It was almost as if the façade of harshness had been destroyed, leaving only the most vulnerable pieces of their lives to show. Riley didn't know why, but he found himself sharing things about his childhood with Zandy.

"My folks were Christians," he said as he eased back into the chair again. "They were killed by Indians when I was back east in college. Nobody really knew why or what had provoked such an action, but nonetheless it happened."

"Then you grew up knowing the truth?"

"That depends on what truth you're speaking of," Riley answered.

"I'm talking about salvation in Christ. Surely, your parents did share the Gospel with you."

"I suppose they tried, but I was always an independent thinker. I didn't want to limit myself with religion, so I never paid much attention. When I went back east to college, I fell in with the kind of crowd that kept the same values I had." Riley paused, contemplating Zandy's long dark hair as it fell around her shoulders framing the thin, pale complexion of her face. How he hated himself for having caused her this pain. "Of course," Riley added, "that meant little or no values at all."

"I can well imagine," Zandy said with a shudder. "Is that when you began to gamble."

"I suppose that's when I got serious about it. I despised living at college as much as I had living at home, but at least it offered a bit more freedom. I still had to go to chapel on Sunday, but that's where I usually caught up on my reading assignments. I tore off the leather backing to the Bible my parents had given me and covered the book I needed to study from and read my way through the service."

"It's a pity you didn't pay more attention to the inside of the Bible," Zandy mused.

Light was starting to filter in through the drawn curtains and Zandy suddenly realized she'd better get home before full light or everyone would know where she'd spent the night. "I need to go."

"I know," Riley said and made no move to stop her.

Zandy paused in the doorway and cast a glance at Riley. "I knew there was good in you, Riley. I felt it in my heart."

With those words she was gone, and Riley was left alone with an unfamiliar aching in his heart.

～

Zandy met the doctor as he was coming from her father's bedside. "You're up mighty early," the doctor said as he quietly closed the door.

"How's my father?" Zandy asked as she pulled on her apron.

"Doing just fine, Miss Stewart. He lost quite a bit of blood, but he's a good strong man. I'm sure he'll do just fine. I'm concerned about your stepmother, however. I've given her enough medicine to last through the week and then I'll be back."

"What about Riley Dawson?" Zandy couldn't help but question. "He might have other thoughts on the matter."

The doctor frowned. "I gave my life to healing the sick and treating the injured. Riley Dawson has lame ideas about using health as leverage to get his own way. I'll be back, Miss Stewart, rest assured."

"I'm glad," Zandy said with a smile. "Can I fix you some breakfast?"

"No, but thanks anyway. I've got to be getting back to my office," the doctor said as he gathered his things. "If you need me, just send someone."

Zandy nodded and waited until the doctor was on his way before going to check on her father and stepmother. "Pa?" she whispered as she approached her bandaged father.

"Is that you, Zandy?"

"Yes," she said as she took hold of his hand.

"Where've you been? I was starting to get worried." Burley Stewart's words were barely audible.

"I'm sorry, Pa. It's a long story. How are you doing?" Zandy asked, hoping he'd let her whereabouts drop for the moment.

"I'm doing better. I thought I was a goner for sure."

"I wish you'd just take us home to Missouri and forget about working at such a dangerous job," Zandy said as she squeezed her father's hand. Ruth's cough from the other room caught her attention.

"I want to check on Ruth," Zandy said as she reluctantly left her father's side.

"Where are the other children?" her father asked weakly.

"Neighbors came and got them last night. I'll fetch them home in a little while. Now, you just rest, and I'll be right back. Do you think you could eat a little something?"

"Not just yet."

Zandy nodded and went to the room where Ruth was. "Ruth?"

"Zandy, are you alright? Where have you been?" Ruth said as she struggled to sit up. "I asked the doctor about you, and he didn't know where you were."

"It's a long story, Ruth," Zandy started but she could tell by the look in her stepmother's eyes, she wasn't going to get out of it that easy. "I collapsed at the Dawson mansion."

"Collapsed? Are you alright?" Ruth asked a second time and got up from the bed.

"I'm fine, Ruth. God was looking out for me."

"What happened?"

Zandy was grateful for the concern and tenderness that was clearly displayed in her stepmother's face.

Zandy didn't want to lie, but neither did she want to admit Riley had drugged her. For some reason it seemed important to protect him. "I guess the lack of food and rest caught up with me." It wasn't really a lie, but neither was it the whole truth.

"I'm so sorry, Zandy. I know you've been giving most of your food to the children, and I appreciate the way you've worked yourself in the garden. Please forgive me for my harshness," Ruth said as she held Zandy close. "I just worry about the little ones so much."

"I know, Ruth. So do I." Zandy hoped fervently it would be an end to the fact she'd spent the night under Riley's roof, but it wasn't to be so.

～

A day later, a seething Jim Williams was packing his things when Pat and K.C. came into the room.

"Where ya headed?" K.C. asked as he sat down and put his booted feet up on the chair opposite him.

"I'm leaving this hole," Jim said as he finished stuffing his spare shirt and denims into the bag.

"Why you want to go and do that?" Pat asked as he poured himself some coffee and joined K.C. at the table.

"I just do, that's all," Jim said as he strapped on his gun belt. "I'm going to see the boss man now and get my final pay."

"You ain't leaving because of her, are you?" K.C. questioned with a laugh. "No woman is worth rearranging your life for."

"That's right, Jim," said Pat. "Not even one as pretty as Alexandra Stewart."

"Just shut up," Jim said as he slung his bag over his shoulder.

"You can't still care about her, not after you saw her leave the big house yesterday morning." Pat's words strengthened Jim's resolve to leave.

Jim grimaced and slammed the door behind him. He'd never have believed the gossip in town about Zandy had he not seen her with his own eyes. But, sure enough, what he'd seen and what all of Dawson was saying, was true—Zandy had spent the night with Riley Dawson.

Chapter 11

A week after the accident, Zandy sat with her parents at the kitchen table. Molly was crawling on the dirt floor while the boys had gone to pick wild raspberries in the hot August sun.

Burley was a quick healer and well on his way to recovering from the wounds he'd received in the mines. The problem, however, was the lack of income. Ruth too, was looking considerably better and had even managed to work with Zandy in the kitchen. But now they'd joined at the table to contemplate the severe gossip that was spreading through town regarding Zandy's stay at the Dawson mansion.

"Nothing happened," Zandy stated for the second time that morning. "Please understand, it wasn't my idea to stay. I collapsed and no one gave me a choice."

"I'll have to speak with Dawson," Burley said angrily. "I've had just about as much of this gossip as a body can stand."

"You know, Zandy," her stepmother began, "all of this would fade away if you would just marry the man. The town is simply waiting for Riley to release his hold on their profits and work schedules. So much shouldn't pivot on one woman's choice for a husband, but this time it does. I'm certain the townspeople would be most forgiving if you would just marry him."

Zandy held her head in her hands. "I can't marry Riley Dawson," was all she managed to whisper.

"You can and you will," her father stated in a demanding tone he'd never before taken with Zandy.

Zandy's head snapped up. "What do you mean, Pa?"

"I mean, I'm going to go talk to the man today and tell him you'll be happy to marry him."

"You can't, Pa. You aren't even healed yet. You can't go climbing all over Dawson just to confront Riley," Zandy argued.

"I don't intend to confront the man," Burley stated firmly. "I just want to give him the news he wants to hear."

Zandy sighed and leaned back in her chair. The thin yellow gingham of her well-worn dress reminded her of better days. If only she could take herself back to those times. . .times before Colorado and Riley Dawson.

Ruth placed her hand over Zandy's. "You have to understand everyone is suffering and when you marry Riley, everything will go back to the way it was before."

"How can you be so sure?" Zandy questioned.

"What choice do we have?" Ruth asked with tears in her eyes. She reached down and picked up Molly. "Will you see her die of hunger rather than marry a man you don't love?"

Zandy felt a stab of guilt knowing she'd forced Riley to face the same question. "It's more than that," Zandy protested. "Riley isn't a Christian. You both raised me to marry a man whose faith was the same as mine. A man who'd given his life to God. How can I love someone who doesn't love my God?"

"I don't care if you love him or not," her father said firmly. "I've made up my mind, and you will marry him whether love exists between you or not. And, as far as Riley's salvation is concerned, well, that's a thing between a man and his God." The words certainly didn't sound like her father's, but sickness and hunger had done strange things to his heart.

Zandy remained silent, but her eyes were pleading with Ruth to intervene. Ruth only nestled her face against Molly's soft brown hair. Nothing was right.

Just then George came bursting through the door. "Come quick, Zandy. Joshua's fighting with some big boys down by the creek."

Before Burley or Ruth could say a word, Zandy sprang to her feet and flew out the door. She hiked up the long folds of her gingham skirt and ran for all she was worth to Corner Creek.

She could hear the commotion before she could see it and, as she rounded the corner and passed the bridge, Zandy could see that not only Joshua, but Bart and even gentle-spirited Samuel were engaged in a free-for-all with five or six other boys. Rushing headlong into the ruckus, Zandy pulled Joshua out of the grip of a bigger boy.

"Stop this, do you hear me?" Zandy said as she separated the other boys from her brother.

Several of the townspeople had made their way down to the creek and stood off to one side while Zandy tried to sort through the conflict.

"Who started this?" Zandy questioned as she noted Joshua's bloodied nose.

"They did," Samuel spoke up, surprising Zandy. "They said some bad things and wouldn't take 'em back."

"That's right," Joshua said as he pointed his finger to the large boy whom Zandy had pulled from her brother's back. "He said you were a fast woman."

"And that one said you ought to get a job at the saloon," Bart said as he stepped forward in a threatening way toward the indicated boy.

Zandy cast a glance around her to the people who stood just a matter of ten or so feet away. "I see," she said with a guarded reserve to her voice. "People often find it easier to misjudge others than to learn the truth of a matter, boys. The truth is never quite as entertaining as the gossip. These boys aren't to blame, however," Zandy stated loud enough for all to hear her, "their parents are."

"But Zandy, they was saying real mean things about our family," little George chimed in.

"I know George, but don't worry about it," Zandy said and lifted her face to meet the people's doubtful stares. "God knows the truth, George, and what these people think is really of little concern to me. Don't let it bother you again, and please, please don't feel you have to defend me. God will do that."

At this most of the onlookers dropped their gazes and refused to meet Zandy's eyes. "Come on, boys, let's get you home and clean you up."

Zandy put her arms around Joshua's shoulders and gave them a squeeze. "I love you all," Zandy whispered as they climbed the hill. "Thank you for defending me."

Joshua seemed to grow a foot because of his pride of the moment. Bart and Samuel couldn't help but looked quite pleased with themselves as well.

$\sim$

Long after everyone had taken themselves to bed, Zandy sat out on the front stoop with her Bible, considering the words her father and stepmother had spoken earlier in the day.

"Father," she whispered to the heavens above her, "I need so much to feel Your touch, to hear Your voice, to know Your love." The wind picked up, and the quaking aspen fluttered it's rustling melody down the mountainside and across the valley. It sounded so lonely, yet comforting at the same time.

Zandy stared out into the brilliantly lit night and watched for some time as a huge full moon crossed the sky. Across the way, an outline of blue spruce and tall ponderosa pine reached feathery arms upward to the sky, as if pointing the way to consolation and comfort.

Sitting alone in the chilly night air, Zandy hugged her knees and her Bible to her chest and prayed. "There must be an answer, Lord. There must be an honorable way out of this. I don't want my family to suffer. I don't want the people to hate me and hurt my brothers. Please help me to know what I must do."

Opening the Bible, Zandy found the words of 1 Thessalonians 4:3. " 'For this is the will of God,' " she made out in the bright moonlight, " 'even your sanctification, that ye should abstain from fornication.' " It couldn't possibly be any clearer than that. God would not want Zandy to become a mistress even for the noble cause of easing her family's hunger.

"So, if this is Your will, Father," Zandy breathed the prayer, "that I should remain pure and chaste until my marriage, then please show me what I should do to help my family. My father seems determined to discuss this with Riley and I don't know what will happen then."

Zandy could well imagine Riley's pleasure at her father's demand that she do as Riley wished. Her father would never even know he was sending his oldest child into a life of sin. Zandy shook her head. The Word was quite clear. The only noble cause was God's cause. She would simply have to work on Riley's heart and win him to God.

But how? Zandy couldn't help but hear her mind ask the question. "How, Lord? How do I get Riley Dawson to act honorably with me and to accept You as his God and Savior?"

Zandy sat on the stoop for hours and, when she finally took herself to bed, it was a fitful sleep she found waiting for her.

All through the night, Zandy dreamed of Riley Dawson and his smiling, brown-black eyes. She was trying to talk to him but it was to no avail. Riley would always laugh and go to speak with her father. When Zandy finally woke from the nightmare, it was still dark outside.

She looked down at George and Bart who were snuggled close to each other for warmth. How sweet they were in their innocence. Their faces were so soft and peaceful, lost in their dreams of school and play and better days. How could she not do all in her power to make their lives better?

Zandy finally gave up on sleep and got dressed for the day. She pulled out a dark blue skirt and calico print blouse. Zandy gently fingered the worn lace collar. Once, this blouse had been one of her Sunday best. Now it was used for every day with no hope of a replacement in sight. Riley had said he could give her the finest clothes ever made for a woman to wear. *Why should I remember that?* Zandy wondered silently. Clothes had never been all that important to her, yet just now it had been the one thing that brought her focus back to Riley.

She dressed quickly and went into the kitchen to stoke the fire. The last of cherry embers were barely warming the cast-iron stove when Zandy put in several pieces of wood and went to the task of preparing breakfast.

Ruth was the next to appear, bringing Molly into the front room in order to feed her. "You're up awfully early, Zandy. I suppose it was difficult to sleep," Ruth said as she put Molly on the floor and went to prepare her a bottle of canned milk.

"Yes," Zandy admitted as she handed Ruth an already warmed bottled.

"Thank you, Zandy," Ruth said as she took the bottle and picked Molly back up. Taking a seat at the kitchen table, Ruth quieted the hungry baby before continuing. "I've never told you this, Zandy, but I feel it's important."

"What is it, Ruth?" Zandy questioned as she came to sit across from her stepmother.

Ruth looked behind her and then leaned forward, pressing closer to Zandy. "I don't want Burley to overhear me. It might hurt him if he were to hear what I have to say."

Zandy's look of confusion didn't surprise Ruth. She was certain Zandy would never have expected the words Ruth was about to share.

"Zandy, when your mother died and left you and your pa, I felt sorry for Burley and, of course, I adored you. I felt it was important to mother you and keep you from losing heart. You were such a fragile, little thing, so sweet and gentle. Yet, there was a streak of stubbornness and independence. I was afraid if someone didn't step in and help, you might go astray and never grow up to be the kind of woman your ma would have wanted you to be."

Zandy still held the look of confusion. "But what—"

Ruth interrupted her, "Please, let me continue." Ruth repositioned the now sleeping Molly and placed the bottle on the table. "I wasn't in love with your pa," Ruth admitted and Zandy's confusion changed to surprise. "I think he knew that. But, out of love for him now, I wouldn't want this kind of thing thrown in his face."

"Of course not," Zandy assured. "If you didn't love him, then why did you marry him?"

"I married him because of you. You needed a ma, and I already loved you as if you were my own. I'd fallen in love with you the first day you'd come to school with your long dark pigtails and dark green eyes. You were just so precious to me, Zandy, I couldn't risk losing you. Besides, I wasn't getting any younger, and people already called me an old maid. Burley was needy and so was I. The rest just fell into place."

"I see," Zandy said as she leaned her head on her hand.

"I'm not sure you do," Ruth whispered in the dim light. "Zandy, I love Burley with all my heart, but it didn't come overnight. It took years of steady building and working. I just wanted to offer this to you because I know your pa's mind is set on having you accept Riley Dawson's proposal. I thought it might offer you a small bit of comfort to know many people have been faced with similar problems. Love will come, Zandy. I know you, and Mister Dawson seems kind enough."

Zandy sighed and pushed away from the table. "Riley is a troubled man without a real direction for his life. He is kind enough when he wants to be, yet there is a side of Riley Dawson that frightens me," Zandy admitted and wondered if Ruth would be shocked by her open discussion of Riley.

"Men can be that way," Ruth agreed, "but it usually isn't all that bad. Marriage is work, Zandy. You can't base what you think you should be feeling on storybook fables."

"I'm not, Ruth," Zandy said as she poured them both a cup of coffee. "I'm basing it on the Bible. You and Pa have always brought me up to put God first and to stand by the Bible and it's truth. But this time, you and Pa both seem to be ignoring some important things in the Word. Please understand, I don't mean any disrespect," Zandy said as she reached the coffee out to her stepmother.

"I know that, Zandy. I don't know why things are the way they arc, but I do know the Bible says to honor your father and your father wants you to marry Riley Dawson."

"Very well," Zandy said with a heaviness in her heart she couldn't explain to her stepmother, "If Riley Dawson asks mc to marry him, I will say yes."

Chapter 12

Z andy prepared cornmeal mush for breakfast and busied herself by helping the boys to take their places at the table. She couldn't help but consider each bruised face, the only exception was little George who would have gladly bloodied a nose or two himself, had he been bigger.

How she loved her little brothers. She'd always hated being an only child, and when Joshua had been born, Zandy remembered dancing up and down the street telling any neighbor who would listen that she had a new baby brother.

The boys were all abuzz with the details of the fight and it wasn't until their father joined them at the table, they finally quieted down to eat.

Zandy stood silently in the corner watching the rest of the family as though she weren't even in the room. She listened to her father reprimand the boys for fighting, listened to her stepmother expand on the virtues of being peacemakers, and all the while, Zandy knew it was yet another example of how she was responsible for her family's problems.

After everyone was fed, Zandy took herself up the mountainside to pray and consider her stepmother's words. The day was glorious and the mountainside a riot of color as columbine, daisies, and primroses danced in the wind. Making her way up the path, Zandy barely noticed the world around her. Her mind was still deep in thought from her talk with Ruth.

Zandy would have never imagined in a million years her stepmother and father hadn't been perfectly in love when they married. Zandy tried to think back to when Ruth became a part of their family, but nothing in her memories indicated Ruth hadn't dearly loved her new husband. Zandy sat down on a large rock to think about her fate.

Since they had come to Colorado, nothing had been right. It wasn't that the land wasn't beautiful, but the winters were harsh and so was life in a mining town. Zandy couldn't bear the thought of her father risking his life in the dark, dank hole called a silver mine. Surely, nothing was worth the risk of life that mining created, but as long as people cherished the jingle of gold in their pockets and silver on their table, someone would be willing to risk the lives of others to harvest the precious metal.

Zandy knew it wasn't her imagination that the mining life had aged her family. Both her father and stepmother had seemed to grow older by the minute, and now Zandy knew she was only adding to their burden through her conflict with Riley Dawson.

Her mind went back to the first moment she'd laid eyes on Riley. He was such a strong figure, so self-confident and sure of himself. People always seemed to be drawn to men who had plans of action and weren't afraid to push through for their goals to be accomplished. Riley Dawson was this type of man.

Yet, Zandy couldn't help but think of Riley's honesty the morning after he'd drugged her. He seemed so vulnerable in those moments, and something about his weakness and pain drew Zandy to him almost against her will.

She thought of the young man he must have been and couldn't help but wonder what his life might have been like if he'd remained with his parents instead of going to college in the east. She reminded herself that most likely he would have been killed with his parents and, for some reason that bothered her a great deal.

Absentmindedly, Zandy was reaching down and picking a flower when the peacefulness of her day was disturbed.

"I saw you walking up here." It was Jim Williams. "I just wanted to have a word with you before I left Dawson."

"You're leaving?" Zandy questioned in surprise.

"That's right, not that I expect you or anyone else to care," Jim said as he pushed back his hat.

"Why do you say that? Of course we'll care," Zandy said as she eyed Jim carefully. Something about his manner seemed strained.

"Don't play games with me, Zandy. I know all about you and Dawson," Jim said bitterly.

"Don't tell me you've been given over to believing gossip."

"It isn't gossip that you spent the night at the Dawson mansion. I saw you leave the house."

"I see," Zandy said as she discarded the flower and got to her feet. She smoothed her dark blue skirt and straightened up.

"That's all you have to say for yourself? If I'd known you were a fast woman, I'd have never wasted a moment of time on you. I think you've deceived a great many people, including Riley Dawson."

"Why do you say that?" Zandy questioned. She was growing steadily more angry as Jim hurled his accusations.

"Well," Jim began, "the way I see it, he wanted to marry you because he thought you were honorable. But now he knows better. Doesn't he?"

Zandy wanted to slap him, but she refrained from even stepping a single inch closer. "You're no different than the others," Zandy said angrily. "I did nothing wrong! I collapsed at the Dawson mansion, nothing more, nothing less. My father had just been blown up, my stepmother was gravely ill, and I hadn't had a decent meal in weeks. I fainted, Jim. Does that disappoint you?" Zandy hated lying but she wasn't about to incriminate Riley in any wrong-doings. That would only make it sound like she was making up stories to defend her position.

For several minutes, Jim said nothing. Then, with a shrug of his shoulders, he turned to leave. "It doesn't matter. Everybody already believes they know what happened."

"Yes, Jim, and just how is it everyone learned I'd spent the night at the Dawson mansion. You didn't by any chance have anything to do with the spreading of that story, did you?"

Jim again shrugged his shoulders. "I don't see it much matters how everyone found out."

"Look, Jim," Zandy said as she sat back down on the rock. "I tried to be a friend to you and also to Riley. I tried to be kind and honest with everyone. I simply don't care what you or anybody else thinks. So please, just leave me alone." Zandy delivered the words firmly with emphasis on the word "alone." That word seemed to sum up her life more than any other. She was alone, with the exception of her Heavenly Father.

Jim opened his mouth to say something, then apparently thought better of it.

Zandy watched him retreat down the mountainside and put her head in her hands to cry. She'd never been given to tears, but this was too much.

"Why, Lord," she sobbed into her hands. "Why has everyone turned against me?"

Riley Dawson watched Jim Williams as he disappeared down the mountain. Having seen Zandy go up the mountain, with Jim close behind, Riley hadn't known what to expect when he followed them, but the confrontation between Zandy and his former employee wasn't at all what he'd anticipated.

So, Jim was responsible for letting people believe Alexandra had spent the night with me, Riley thought to himself. If Williams hadn't already quit his job, Riley would have fired him. Why did it suddenly seem so important to defend Alexandra's honor?

Riley moved from where he'd been hiding. Zandy's sobs tore at his heart, and yet, they caused Riley to feel very cautious. Not knowing what to do, Riley depended upon his arrogance to shield him from feeling too much.

"I see you're finally alone," Riley said as he approached Zandy.

Zandy dried her eyes on the back of her sleeve and got to her feet. "What are you doing here?" she questioned, trying to compose her voice.

"I saw Mister Williams make his way up the path after you and thought you might need my help."

Zandy started to laugh until big tears streamed down her face. She was very near to hysteria from the tension and pressure when Riley took hold of her arms and shook her firmly.

"Stop it, Alexandra. Stop it now," Riley said, the concern clearly evident in his voice.

Zandy tried to compose herself. She looked Riley square in the face and tried to shake off his hold. "Let go of me!"

"As you wish," Riley said and dropped his hands. "Why didn't you tell Jim the truth?"

"I don't know what you mean."

"You told him you fainted at my house. Why didn't you tell him I drugged you?"

Zandy shrugged. "What would it have gained me? If I'd told people about the coffee, who would've believed me? Who would have cared about the truth when the lies were so much easier to believe?"

"And you've never told your folks I wanted you as a mistress and not as a wife. Why?"

"I was afraid to," Zandy admitted. "I was afraid my father would defend my honor and lose his job or worse. The one thing I didn't count on was my parents giving up on me."

"But now that Mister Williams has given up on you as well as your folks, I guess you have nowhere else to turn."

"That's not true," Zandy said, trying to defend herself. "I'll always have God."

The wind blew across the mountainside and with it the rich scent of honeysuckle and pine filled the air. Riley reached out to touch Zandy's cheek. Zandy was too tired to care and allowed him to stroke her face. "You're at the end of the road, Zandy. You have to make a choice."

"I thought I had," Zandy said softly as she lifted her green eyes to meet Riley's intense stare. Her heart beat faster, and she could feel her hands trembling.

Neither one said anything for several minutes. The world seemed suspended in time, and even the rippling mountain streams and quaking aspen were muted in the silence of Zandy's mind.

"What do your folks think about all of this?" Riley finally questioned as he took a step backward.

"They want me to marry you," Zandy answered honestly. "I promised my stepmother if you asked me to marry you, I would say yes."

Riley looked stunned. "You what?"

Zandy leaned back against the rock. "I told Ruth I would marry you."

"Is that true?" Riley questioned. "I mean, knowing everything I've done to you and what I've tried to make you do."

"Yes," Zandy whispered. "In order to save my family and help the town out, I would marry you, Riley."

Riley seemed so taken aback by Zandy's declaration he had to sit down. Zandy continued to watch him, but said nothing.

"Why?" Riley questioned hoarsely.

"Why?" Zandy asked in surprise. "Why do you suppose?"

"I'm not really sure," Riley replied.

Zandy was surprised at the turn the conversation had taken. Always before, Riley Dawson had seemingly had the upper hand in their relationship. Sensing a softening in his attitude, Zandy forced an issue that had long been on her mind.

"Why do I have to be your mistress, Riley? I will never have a willing heart to do such a thing," she said. "I will, however, offer a compromise and marry you."

"You're being completely honest with me? You would marry me?"

"Yes."

Riley ran his hand back through his hair. "Alright, Alexandra Stewart. I accept your compromise."

"When?" Zandy asked, trying not to show her surprise. She hadn't expected Riley to agree to marriage.

"What do you suggest?"

"I guess the sooner the better. I don't think the children can hold out much longer," Zandy answered as she got to her feet.

"Tomorrow, then?"

"Alright, Riley. Will you make the arrangements?"

"Yes," he answered softly. "Is there anything I can get you to help you ready yourself?"

"No, nothing for myself," Zandy answered as she looked at her husband-to-be, "but if you would send some food to my family, I would be most appreciative."

"Of course," Riley said and watched Zandy resolve herself to the arrangement. Why didn't he feel victorious in the matter? He'd gotten his way—at least in a matter of speaking. As he watched Zandy walk slowly down the pathway, Riley felt a wave of guilt wash over him. Would he really be able to go through with the wedding?

Chapter 13

Zandy stared at her reflection in the mirror. The woman who stared back didn't seem to be the same one who looked into the glass. Ruth had helped Zandy pile her long brown hair on top of her head and arranged it into an attractive bun. Next, they took the wisps that fell down around Zandy's face and used hot irons to curl them into framing tendrils.

Zandy's dress was the same one Ruth had worn when she married Burley. It was a lovely gown created out of a pale blue sateen. The sleeves were long and trimmed in handmade lace, and the bodice was high to the neck with pleated folds and dark blue trim. The dress had been designed for a fashionable cage bustle but, having no such luxury at hand, Zandy and Ruth had compensated by using layers of rolled dish towels pinned to Zandy's petticoat. The final touch was Ruth's only remaining pair of kid leather boots which although a tiny bit large for Zandy, were more than adequate for the purpose of getting married in.

The boys had gone out to collect flowers for Zandy's bouquet and Burley, determined to attend his daughter's marriage to Riley Dawson, had freshly blackened his boots. The entire Stewart household was busy with the details of the upcoming ceremony. No one seemed to pay any attention to the fact that the bride was less than festive in her preparations.

Riley sent word that the wedding would take place at two o'clock in the newly reopened church. Zandy acknowledged the news with nothing more than a nod of her head, and Ruth returned the message bearer with the Stewart family's approval.

Now with less than twenty minutes until the two o'clock deadline, Zandy couldn't help but feel uneasy about having given her approval to marry Riley. Love will come, Ruth had told her, but Zandy couldn't help but wonder if it were possible to hope for such a thing under the circumstances.

The boys burst through the doorway with handfuls of mountain flowers, each proudly bearing his contribution to Zandy's wedding bouquet. They adored their big sister and, while they didn't relish the idea of Zandy's going to live in the house on the hill, each one had enjoyed the food Riley had sent the night before. Riley had even seen to it that a small bakery cake had been included and the boys thought this extraordinary.

"Are you ready?" Ruth questioned Zandy as she came into the room.

"I guess so," Zandy answered, looking about her as if there were something she was forgetting.

"Did you get your things packed?" Ruth asked softly.

"Yes," Zandy replied in a hollow voice. "I'll have somebody come get them later," she added.

"Zandy, please don't hate us for insisting on this marriage. You know we just love you and we want good things for you. Riley Dawson can give you good things and he cares deeply for you."

"Do you really think so?" Zandy surprised them both by voicing the question.

"How can you ask that? He wants to marry you and just look at the lengths he's gone to in order to get you to say yes."

Zandy's puzzled look mirrored the questions in her heart. *How could everyone be so forgiving of Riley's deeds just because they think he is a man in love? If only they knew the truth,* Zandy thought to herself. *How admirable would Riley Dawson be then?*

Ruth pretended not to notice her stepdaughter's less than jubilant spirit. She comforted herself with the assurance it was a case of bridal nerves and nothing more, but the look on Zandy's face made Ruth wonder for a fleeting moment if they were doing the right thing.

"You should see all the people!" Bart exclaimed at the top of his voice. "The whole town is coming to see you get married, Zandy."

Zandy turned, horror stricken, to Ruth. "He didn't invite the whole town, did he?"

"Now, Zandy," Ruth said with a gentle pat to her stepdaughter's arm, "he's just proud to be marrying you. Let him show off if he wants."

Zandy felt her knees give way and Ruth quickly pulled her to a chair. "I'm not sure I can go through with this," Zandy whispered, but Ruth didn't hear her.

"What was that?" Ruth asked as she brought a cold cloth to Zandy.

"Nothing," Zandy murmured. There was no sense in backing out now. Everyone was too happy, too pleased, in fact, that the honorable Mister Dawson was to be happily married to the bride of his choosing.

How can I face him and not faint, Zandy wondered to herself. The cold cloth did little to settle her dizziness. She knew how he'd be, all smug and self-assured. No one, including Riley Dawson, would care how she felt. And how did she feel? More than once Zandy had asked herself this very question.

A part of her was relieved to know her family would be provided for and she herself could go into an honorable arrangement. Yet, in the back of her mind was the knowledge that Riley wasn't saved and he didn't appear inclined to be saved in the near future.

How could she walk down the aisle of the church, participating in a ceremony she'd dreamed of since being a little child, and know what a mockery she was making of the values and principles she'd been taught to follow all of her life.

"It's time to go," Ruth interrupted Zandy's fearful thoughts.

Zandy felt a wave of panic and it was all she could do to follow her stepmother out the door and down the pathway to the church.

Beautiful music was coming from the church. So many people had gathered that they were now standing outside the building, just to catch a glimpse of Riley Dawson's bride. The "oohs" and "ahhs" went unnoticed by Zandy whose troubled heart was consuming her every thought. It was much like a lamb being led to the slaughter.

Zandy tried her best to control her emotions. She squeezed back tears more than once and took deep breaths just to get through the ceremony without fainting. She heard her name being read as if it belonged to someone else and thought the same of the voice that agreed to honor and obey the man who now gripped her arm.

She swayed only once, when Riley promised himself to her until death and felt a small amount of relief when Riley most capably steadied her so no one else would know of her weakening. But Riley knew and that troubled Zandy most deeply. She had no desire to appear delicate and frail in his eyes. She bolstered her courage and, when Pastor Brokamp announced they were man and wife, Zandy boldly lifted her face to receive her husband's kiss. Her eyes, however, remained closed.

Riley placed a brief, gentle kiss upon his bride's lips then turned her to face the applause and shouts of approval from the congregation.

"Please, get me out of here, Riley," she managed to whisper against his ear. The display looked as if she were murmuring some endearment to her new husband, causing the crowds to respond even louder.

Riley looked down at the paleness of Zandy's face and knew she wouldn't last much longer. For once in his life he was feeling quite responsible for his actions and didn't care for the way it made him feel.

"If I can have everyone's attention," Riley shouted above the crowd. "There are to be refreshments in the town hall and a dance in the park this evening." More cheers rose up and Zandy felt herself grip Riley's arm tightly to steady her weakening knees. "We will, of course, join you later. There are picture sittings to take care of and such, so do feel free to go ahead and enjoy yourselves."

Riley pulled Zandy along through the crowd of well-wishers. She could hardly make her legs move and yet, because of Riley's persistance, found herself out on the church lawn being positioned for her wedding picture.

"Now, Mrs. Dawson, if you'll just put your hand on your husband's shoulder, like this," the photographer was saying and Zandy found herself faced with the stunning revelation that she was no longer Zandy Stewart but Alexandra Dawson.

She posed mechanically, waiting in rigid position as the camera was readied. Burley and Ruth stood looking on, while the boys ran circles around the entire group. When the photographer announced he was finished, Zandy breathed a sigh of relief. Now, perhaps she could retreat to the sanctuary of home, but where was home?

Without realizing what was happening, Zandy found herself being embraced by a teary-eyed Ruth. She was saying something to Zandy about the wedding but, for the life of her, Zandy couldn't concentrate on the words. Then her father was telling her how proud he was of her sacrifice and how he wouldn't forget her generosity to her family.

Zandy gazed beyond her parents to her brothers who were now being beckoned to come say good-bye to their big sister.

"But I don't want Zandy to go away," George began to cry. He was only coming to understand Zandy's wedding meant she'd now be taking up residence elsewhere. Up until that moment, the wedding had been nothing more than a big party to him.

As George began to wail and grip Zandy tightly, Zandy couldn't help but cry too. She picked up George and held him close to her, both crying over the inevitable separation. Riley grew uncomfortable and made the excuse of needing to see the photographer before he got away. Ruth and Burley tried to soothe their children, but to no avail.

Soon, Samuel began to whimper too, then it was only a matter of time before Bart joined in. Joshua stood staunchly grown up, trying to appear a responsible example for his brothers, but tears formed in his eyes as well.

Finally, Burley put an end to the misery, forcing George away from Zandy. Zandy could see the action caused her father a great deal of pain and tried to calm George as her father pulled him away.

"Now, George, you know you can come see me whenever you want," Zandy said as she took a handkerchief from Ruth and dried her tears. "All of you can come see me."

"Of course, they can," Riley reaffirmed as he joined Zandy and her family. "You're all welcome in our home any time."

"Thank you, Mister Dawson," Burley said as he placed George on the ground. The pain of his actions showed clearly in his face.

"I think we should be on a first name basis. After all," Riley stated, "we're family."

"That's true," Burley agreed. "I hadn't thought much about it, but you're right."

Ruth was already herding her little family up the path toward home so, after giving Zandy a quick peck on the cheek, Burley excused himself and hurried after his family.

Zandy watched them until they were nearly home. A part of her heart went with them. . .a part of her Riley could never have, no matter what.

After having made their rounds to the various festivities, Riley led an exhausted and thoroughly spent Zandy, home. Neither one spoke as they walked the path to the mansion. The evening was warm and the night sky was a rich ebony with stars so brilliant and close they looked as if you could reach up and touch them.

Scents of honeysuckle and rose assaulted Zandy's nose as they passed through the Dawson gardens and on into the house. Riley ushered Zandy into the library and called for Mrs. Malloy to bring her something cold to drink.

Mrs. Malloy arrived with a cold pitcher of lemonade, praising the freighters for the shipment of lemons that made the drink possible. Seeing neither Riley nor Zandy were in a mood to talk, Mrs. Malloy made her way out of the room as quickly as she'd arrived.

Riley considered his silent wife as he offered her a glass of lemonade. He'd been unable to shake the feeling of guilt that had assaulted him from the first moment he'd agreed to marry her. It was clear to him she'd not come willingly into this marriage, and his pride sorely pricked his conscience, reminding him of his desire for her willingness.

Unable to bear the silence any longer, Riley got to his feet. "I'm sorry to do this, but I must leave for a time. It seems one of my investments is having severe financial difficulties and the matter requires my immediate attention."

Zandy looked up in surprise and nearly dropped her glass. "You're leaving?"

"Yes," Riley said in a rather disinterested way. He felt the desperate need to distance himself from his new wife.

"When will you be back?" Zandy questioned.

"I'm not entirely sure, but don't worry. If you need anything at all, clothes, food, whatever, just ask Mrs. Malloy to send for it. Or, if you prefer, feel free to go shopping. You'll have an unlimited line of credit at any of the establishments."

Zandy's mouth dropped open. "Unlimited?"

Riley's hard look softened. "I tried to tell you I'd take good care of you. I'm a very generous man, Alexandra."

"What about my family?" Zandy couldn't help but dare the question.

"They've already been taken care of. I made you a promise and I always keep my promises," Riley stated firmly as he moved toward the door. "Now, I need to pack a few things. Do as you like with the house. Choose any bedroom you want, decorate, order new furniture, whatever your heart desires."

Before Zandy could reply, Riley was gone. She sank back wearily against the brocade sofa and studied the room. Books lined the walls to the ceiling, oak shelves and a massive fireplace of limestone and native rock demanded the entire west wall.

Looking farther, Zandy was more than aware of the fine, delicate figurines that had been carefully placed to complement the furnishings of the room. Rich tapestries and ornately framed paintings hung above her head and expensive furniture from another time and place adorned nearly every corner of the room.

Never in her life had Zandy felt so out of place. Hearing Riley's heavy steps on the staircase, Zandy was surprised when his muted "Good-bye" filtered through the huge double doors. Only one question came to her mind as she heard her husband leave the house. "What have I done?"

~

Riley made his way to the small cottage behind the mansion. With bag in hand, he came bounding through the door, surprising K.C. Russell. K.C. eyed him curiously, but never voiced the question on his mind.

"I don't want anyone to know I'm staying here," Riley said as he tossed his bag into one of the rooms. "Do you understand?"

"Sure, boss," K.C. said, the surprise still reflected in his stare.

"I'll take Jim's old room," Riley said as he followed his bag into the empty bedroom. Slamming the door behind him, Riley felt ready to pull out his hair. Instead, he flung himself down in the only available chair and wondered aloud, "What have I done?"

Chapter 14

A fter a week of seeing no one, save the house staff, Zandy decided to go see her family. She contemplated her new lifestyle as she walked the narrow dirt pathway to her former home. How strange it was to suddenly be married and living in a place that seemed foreign to her. Stranger still was to be a bride without a husband.

"Lord," Zandy found herself praying as she walked, "I still believe in Your promises, and I still desire to seek Your will above my own. Protect me from the evil in this world and keep my heart ever thirsty for You."

The crispness of the morning air betrayed the fact autumn would soon be upon them. There were other signs as well. The aspen trees were already beginning to show signs of changing color, creeping vines that had once been dark green were now decorating the hillsides in ribbons of scarlet and amber, and the sunlight was filtered and diffused as the daylight hours became shorter and shorter.

Zandy sighed and wondered silently what the winter hours of confinement would bring. Could she really bear to wander around the big house all alone? Even a baby of her own would be something to look forward to, but there wasn't even a possibility of that. She found her cheeks growing hot at the thought of having Riley's baby. She couldn't help but wonder what the town of Dawson might think if they knew she and Riley had never lived together as man and wife.

The Stewart shanty was strangely quiet as Zandy approached the door. She knocked but, when no one answered, she opened the door and walked in. To her shock and surprise, the house was empty.

A search of each room revealed the same thing as the one before it. All personal effects had been stripped away and while some of the cruder furniture remained, there was no other sign that human life had even dwelled within the walls.

Zandy rushed out the door and made her way into town. She hurried to the jailhouse, thinking that perhaps one of Riley's men would know where her family had gone.

Pat Folkes met her at the door. "Mornin', Missus Dawson. What can I do for you?"

"My family has moved," she stated matter-of-factly. "I was hoping you might tell me where they've gone."

"Sure," Pat said as he took a seat behind a worn desk. "I figured Riley would've told you. He had us move them to the old Mulvane house. You know where that is, don't you?"

Zandy nodded. The Mulvane house was one of the best houses in town. Only Riley's mansion could outshine it as far as size and grace. "How long have they been there?" Zandy questioned.

"We moved them in the day after your wedding."

Zandy was so surprised that she said nothing more as she left the jail and made her way to the Mulvane house.

Long before she reached the stone-step entryway of the Mulvane house, Zandy was hailed by her brothers.

"Zandy! Look it's Zandy!" Bart called out.

The other boys dropped what they were playing with and hurried down the walkway to greet their sister. George fairly wrapped himself around his older sister's frame.

"Zandy, are you coming back to live with us?" George asked innocently.

Silently, Zandy wished she were but instead, she shook her head. "No, Silly, I've just come to make sure you're still washing behind your ears."

At this George unwound himself from Zandy and backed off. "I forgot."

"Just as I suspected," Zandy said in a teasing voice. "Where's Mama and Molly?"

"They're in the house," Joshua began. "You should see the house, Zandy! It's bigger than our house back in Missouri and loads nicer."

"There's even a lamp hanging down from the ceiling in the front room," George said, notably impressed by their new chandelier.

"I see," Zandy said as she lovingly patted each of her brothers on the head.

"Zandy!" Ruth exclaimed from the doorway. "Come on in. I've missed you so much."

Zandy made her way into the house and allowed Ruth to lead the way from room to room. All the while she explained how Riley had provided them with every convenience and had even given Burley a desk job in the mining office.

⁓

When Zandy left some hours later, she felt happy to see her family doing so well and, yet, was troubled because she knew they could've had comfort much sooner had she not been so disagreeable.

Resolving to show Riley her gratitude, Zandy decided to do whatever it took to become a good wife. She thought of her behavior the day of her wedding and knew Riley must have been put off by her self-suffering mood.

"Father," Zandy prayed, "I realize I've not treated Riley very kindly. I realize people change and they need to be forgiven and, just like all Your other children, I'm in need of forgiving too. I'm asking You to forgive me for the way I've acted and to help me to be a good wife to Riley. I know You can work miracles, so please help me to love him as one of Your creations and to be a good example of Christ's love so he might accept Jesus as his Savior. Amen."

Zandy felt as if a weight had been lifted from her shoulders. She hurried to the mansion that had become her home and set about making a list of things she needed or thought would be appreciated by her husband.

When yet another week had passed and Saturday morning dawned bright and cold, Zandy was beginning to worry about Riley and where he might be. When she heard voices in the hallway below, she hurried down the grand staircase to see if it was her husband.

Disappointment lined her expression as she realized it was just Mrs. Malloy directing one of the staff to take upstairs some of the things Zandy had ordered from town.

Zandy led the way back to her bedroom's sitting room and instructed the man to leave everything on the large oval table that occupied the center of the room. After he'd departed, Zandy began to open the boxes to inspect the contents.

Most of the boxes contained clothes as Zandy had felt she had nothing to wear worthy of her status as Riley's wife. She had the town's seamstress working overtime to create several new gowns for immediate delivery while leaving a more extensive order for those that could come later.

Zandy opened a large dress box to reveal a dark green velvet gown that had been lavishly trimmed in black velvet ribbon and lace. She couldn't suppress a gasp of pleasure as she pulled it up to her body and whirled around the room.

"You look charming. Like a little girl in a candy store," Riley spoke from the open door of Zandy's sitting room.

"Riley!" Zandy couldn't help but exclaim. "I was beginning to think you were never coming home."

"I'm not here for long," Riley said as he crossed the room to where Zandy stood holding the dress. It was all he could do to keep from pulling her into his arms.

Zandy felt her knees begin to tremble at the closeness of her husband. She swallowed hard and tried to sound calm. "Oh, I see," she replied softly and Riley couldn't help but wonder if it was disappointment in her voice or his imagination.

"I see you've gone shopping," Riley went on.

"Yes. I thought it might be necessary to make myself more presentable to the public. I mean," she paused and blushed crimson, "now that I'm your wife."

"I think that's wise. Have you ordered anything else?" he asked and Zandy felt certain he was genuinely interested.

"More clothes." Zandy laughed. "I'm afraid I came to you with nothing much more than the clothes on my back. Now, how about you? Where have you been all this time. I thought you might have at least come back to the house once or twice during the last two weeks."

"My, my," Riley teased, "don't you sound the part of the nagging housewife."

Zandy shrugged her shoulders. "It's just common courtesy. I couldn't tell anyone where you'd gone. I mean if someone would have needed you."

"I told my men," Riley said as he reached out and fingered one of the black velvet ribbons.

"Oh," Zandy said, rather disappointed that Riley would confide in his men and not in her.

"This dress is lovely. The color matches your eyes," Riley said softly. "Would you like to wear it to the dance tonight?"

"What dance? Where is it?" Zandy questioned a bit more excitedly than she'd intended.

Riley laughed. "It's a celebration dance. We've just opened another silver mine. I've called it the Alexandra Mine."

"After me?"

"Who else?" Riley said with a smile. "It only seemed fitting I should. Now, do you want to go with me or not?"

"Are you sure you can give me the time?" Zandy asked in mock sarcasm.

Riley pulled Zandy into his arms, crushing the velvet gown between them. "I have more than time to give you, Alexandra." He lowered his lips to hers in a hungry kiss that betrayed his desire. Just as quickly he let Zandy go and stepped back abruptly. "Sorry, I got carried away."

Zandy frowned in confusion. "You are my husband." The words were out before Zandy had even realized she was speaking.

Riley said nothing, but the lightheartedness of the moment was clearly broken.

Zandy thought quickly of some way to take Riley's mind off of her words. "I wanted to thank you for all you've done for my family. I went to see them last week and they're all so happy, Riley. I know it was my fault I let things go on for so long. . . ." Zandy's words trailed into silence as she moved away from Riley's quizzical stare.

She was moving in painstaking slowness to place the velvet gown on a hanger, hoping the extra time would allow her to regain her composure. It was difficult to explain to Riley that she was still uncertain she'd done the right thing in marrying him, but now that it was done she did want to honor him and be a good wife in the eyes of God.

"I'm glad you're pleased with my arrangements for your family," Riley said as he came up behind her.

Zandy could feel his breath upon her neck and silently wished she hadn't pinned her hair up. At least if it were down, she reasoned, she wouldn't feel his presence so keenly.

Zandy said nothing and having placed the dress in the wardrobe, she had no other alternative but to turn and face Riley. When she did, she felt her breath catch in her throat. She was attracted to him, she knew that was beyond denying. There was something in his dark hair and eyes that seemed to draw in her heart and mind. She briefly contemplated thoughts of his forcing her into marriage and suddenly wasn't sure she cared anymore.

Riley reached out his hand to touch her face. His fingers were light upon her cheek, causing Zandy to tremble. "Now, what about the dance? Will you accompany me?"

"Of course," Zandy whispered.

"Remember, you have to dance with the one who brings you," Riley's eyes twinkled in amusement, but Zandy knew he was also quite serious.

"I would love to dance with you, Mr. Dawson," she answered boldly.

Riley's ear-to-ear grin betrayed his pleasure with her answer. "That's good, Mrs. Dawson," he said with emphasis on her married name, "because I intend to dance your slippers off."

"I accept your challenge with pleasure," Zandy said with a smile. It had been a long time since she'd danced and an even longer time since she'd felt this happy.

~

Zandy had never danced so much in her life. Now that she was Mrs. Riley Dawson, she was most eagerly sought out and graciously respected. Zandy, in turn, was guardedly kind and received each compliment with cautious hospitality.

As she found herself dancing with one of the store owners who had formerly turned her away from his door, Zandy was amused at the way the man seemed to gush in conversation of the well-stocked shelves and complete inventory of his mercantile. He ended the dance by telling Zandy he'd be most honored if she would remember him when she needed store goods.

At that comment, Zandy rolled her eyes back. She was surprised, however, to find Riley's laughing eyes fixed firmly on her expression and she quickly lowered her face, flushed in embarrassment.

"I believe this dance is mine," Riley said as he came forward to claim his wife.

"You know what they say about dancing too many dances with one person," Zandy teased. "People will believe you're quite gone on me."

Riley leaned his face closer to Zandy's. "And they would be right," he whispered against her ear.

Riley's warm breath on her neck made Zandy quiver. She wondered if Riley was telling the truth or merely making small talk.

When the dance ended, Riley suggested some refreshments. "After all," he said in an amused tone, "I paid for them."

He had just handed Zandy a glass of punch when a loud explosion rocked the ground.

Riley looked down at his watch. "Um," he said as he noted the time. "It's already ten-thirty. Sounds like the boys must have blown quite a bit of face rock tonight."

Zandy nodded. She knew very well that each shift ended their work hours by blasting out new ore. It would then be the responsibility of the incoming shift to pick up the rock and send the ore on for processing.

The musicians were now taking a break and Riley suggested he and Zandy take a walk. Zandy was grateful to escape the stares and whispers of the others. She laughed to herself when one woman had told her married life obviously agreed with her.

Riley and Zandy had barely taken a step out the door when they were greeted by the loud ominous sound of the mine's whistle. The five short blasts followed by a long one was the signal that everyone dreaded to hear—FIRE!

Riley pulled Zandy aside as the crowd of dancers came rushing out to take up the cause of fighting the fire in their evening finery.

Zandy started out after them, but Riley pulled her back. "Where do you think you're going?"

"We have to help," Zandy insisted.

"I'll go help, but I don't want you in danger," Riley stated firmly.

"I can't just sit by and wonder what has happened. There are injured people down there. I might be no good at fighting the fire, but I can help with the nursing duties."

Riley's expression betrayed his concern. He studied Zandy's determined face and agreed. "Let's go. But you stay away from the mine itself."

Zandy nodded and hiked up her skirt to race after her long-legged husband.

∽

The chaos at the mine was quickly organized. Miners who hadn't been injured in the explosion were busy carrying buckets of water from Corner Creek and a line of people had been formed to pass the buckets down.

Zandy quickly learned six men had been killed and another dozen injured when one of the Burleigh drills had exploded causing a chain reaction that ignited a nearby case of dynamite. She went to work, mindless of the new green velvet gown, washing off wounds, applying tourniquets, and helping the company doctor to organize his patients. At one point when the doctor was anxiously awaiting delivery of bandaging materials, Zandy pulled off her petticoat and began to tear it into strips.

The doctor nodded approvingly and smiled. He admired the young woman's ingenuity and disregard for her own material possessions.

Zandy recognized many of the men who'd been hurt and tried to comfort them and later their families, as the night progressed into the wee hours of morning.

Finally, at four-thirty, the fire had been extinguished and the wounded had been cared for as best they could. Litters were brought to carry the injured to a makeshift hospital in one of the empty buildings on the Dawson estate.

Zandy had directed Riley's men, K.C. and Pat, to lead the way and make every necessary effort to aid the doctor.

Riley had stood to one side contemplating his young wife's ability to organize the tragedy. He offered no interference when Zandy sent Mike Muldair down to Edwards's General Store with orders to bring back the supplies they needed.

When everything had calmed to a reasonable level of order, Riley took hold of Zandy's arm and motioned to her it was time to leave.

"Come on, we've done all we can. Better get some rest. There'll be plenty to do tomorrow or I guess I should say, later today," Riley declared.

"I suppose you're right. I hate to leave them, though. I know what it is to worry and fret over your injured loved ones," Zandy said as she allowed Riley to lead her home. "I'll never forget the feeling when they brought my father home."

"You were quite hysterical, as I recall," Riley interjected.

"I was beyond rational thought," Zandy admitted, "or I'd have never come crawling to you." The words were out before she'd thought of how they might be received. Her hand flew quickly to her mouth and her eyes flew open. The regret was clearly stated in her eyes.

"It's alright, Zandy," Riley said as he tucked her arm close against his body and patted her hand. "I deserved that."

"But I didn't mean. . .I mean we're married now and. . ." Zandy fell silent, trying desperately to figure her way out of the situation.

Riley stopped and gently pulled her into his arms. Zandy said nothing, mesmerized by the tenderness she found in Riley's eyes. "Forcing you to marry me didn't really change anything, Alexandra. I'm just starting to figure that out."

Zandy could feel her heart pounding. She was more than just a little aware of Riley's strong, well-muscled body and deeply embarrassed in her innocence.

Riley reached up to wipe a bit of soot from Zandy's cheek and the touch was electrifying. Zandy shuddered at the touch and Riley misread it for revulsion. He frowned slightly, wishing he could make things better.

"I'm sorry," he said as he dropped his arms.

Zandy's expression of wonderment changed instantly to one of confusion. "What?" her one-word question kept Riley from walking away from her.

"I know things aren't right," Riley said as he pulled Zandy with him toward the house. In his mind he was still seeing the faces of the dead men. Men whose lives had been snuffed out in a flash of explosives and fire. One minute they'd been living, breathing beings with families and homes. The next, they were just objects of grief and pain.

Zandy waited for Riley to open the door, but he didn't. She looked at the strange expression on his face, wondering desperately what he could be thinking.

"I'd better say good night. I need to think and I can't do it here," Riley suddenly said. "I won't be back for awhile, so don't wait up for me."

Zandy watched him walk away. He seemed to have aged twenty years in a few short moments. What had she done to cause his pain, and where was he going at this hour? The only place open would be the saloon.

The thought of Riley drinking his troubles away grieved Zandy. She'd never thought about it before, but perhaps that's where Riley had been spending all his time.

Angrily, Zandy stormed into the house, slamming the door behind her. "Good riddance," she said aloud. For a few brief minutes she'd almost allowed herself to believe Riley cared.

Chapter 15

R iley sat in the darkness of the mining office. It was Sunday morning so there wouldn't be anyone coming to disturb him. Yet, it wasn't outside influences that were disturbing his peace of mind—the conflict was coming from within.

He couldn't forget the faces of the dead miners. He couldn't close out the picture of the wives as they held their dead husbands and cried. Life was not the enduring, lasting thing he'd thought it to be. It was in fact, quite fragile and short.

Riley couldn't help but think of the times Zandy had tried to share God's way with him. He'd ignored her just as he had his parents. But that was when he'd felt immortal.

Putting his head in his hands, Riley knew his life was a mess. He lived on the whim of the silver market, not even needing to put his hand to any real work. He'd forced a beautiful, vital woman into marriage knowing full well she hated him. No, Riley thought to himself, Zandy could never hate anyone.

He thought of Zandy's gentle spirit and enduring nature. She'd put up the best fight he'd ever known, and all to maintain her values and faith. He'd never known anyone who'd held their conviction so solidly when adversity threatened to destroy all they loved.

Thinking of Zandy caused Riley more grief than he wanted to deal with. He couldn't shame her by divorcing her, but neither could he bring himself to shame her by expecting her to be a real wife to him. She didn't have a willing heart and, from the way she seemed repulsed by his touch, Riley didn't expect her to have one any time soon.

As sunlight filtered in through the drawn shades, peace continued to elude Riley Dawson. Determined to ignore his fears and mortality, Riley put his head down on the desk and went to sleep.

Riley slept and, as he did, he dreamed of being at home with his mother and father. His mother was reminding him of Psalm Twenty-three's promise.

He could hear her tell him in her sweet, loving voice, "Remember, Riley, when you belong to God there is nothing the world can do to you that will best what God has planned. 'The Lord is my shepherd; I shall not want.' He will never allow you to want for anything, so long as you lie down beside Him."

"Mama," Riley whispered in his sleep. He felt his mind being forced into consciousness, but he wanted so much to stay in the dream with his mother.

"Don't forget, 'Yea, though I walk through the valley of the shadow of death, I will fear no evil: for thou art with me.' " His mother's voice faded with those words.

Riley sat up with a start. Thinking of the Psalm, he rubbed the sleep from his eyes and got up. "Fear no evil?" he said aloud with a laugh. "But everyone thinks I am evil and how can I not fear myself knowing exactly who I am and what I've done?"

Riley opened the door of the mining office and was surprised to find the sun already starting to set. He'd had no idea he'd slept so long. Pushing back the thoughts that troubled him most, Riley made his way up the hillside.

～

When Riley appeared at breakfast the following morning, Zandy couldn't suppress her surprise.

"What are you doing here?" she asked as she swished across the dining room dressed smartly in a pink-and-white-striped day dress.

Riley lifted his eyes from his coffee cup and smiled. "I thought you might enjoy an outing. I know I've not been good company, and I want to make it up to you."

"I see," Zandy answered in a guarded tone. She sat down at the table and accepted a platter of food from Mrs. Malloy.

"You look very nice," Riley offered in a way of conversation.

"Thank you," Zandy said with a blush. She still found it difficult to accept compliments from Riley. "What kind of outing do you have in mind?"

"I wanted to show you where the Alexandra Mine is. It's not yet working full time and today it's closed in honor of the dead. Still, I'd like to show you your namesake."

Zandy frowned. "I don't think I would like to see a mine. I mean, my father has always told me what awful places they are."

"We wouldn't have to go inside. I just thought it might be nice to drive out to it. The day is starting to warm up and it looks like a perfect fall morning."

"We would drive?" Zandy questioned as she buttered a slice of toast.

"That's another part of the surprise. I've bought a buggy and matched geldings for your use whenever you want to get around. It's quite a walk to the Mulvane house and it would be much easier for you to go and visit if you had proper transportation," Riley replied.

"You bought a buggy for me?" Zandy questioned in surprise. "How very thoughtful. I would love to go for a ride with you. Can we go after breakfast?"

"I'd like that very much, Zandy."

Zandy hurried through breakfast and rushed to see her new gift. She thrilled to the feel of the fine leather upholstery in her new blue-and-gray buggy. The matched geldings were smokey gray with white boots, and Zandy nearly squealed with delight as Riley gave them a flick of the reins.

"Oh, this is so much fun," she said in an animated voice. She'd secured a pink bonnet on her head before climbing into the buggy, but now she wanted nothing more than to feel the wind through her hair.

Riley laughed as she pulled the hat off and took down her hair. Zandy ran her fingers through the long brown mass, freeing it to blow in the wind.

~

The drive to the Alexandra wasn't nearly as long as Zandy had hoped. She frowned slightly as Riley brought the horses to a stop.

"It doesn't look like much," Riley said with a shrug of his shoulders. "Mines usually don't look all that appealing."

"I've never cared for the way any of it looks. It's all so dark and depressing," Zandy said as she took Riley's offered hand. He helped her down from the buggy and showed her around the mine's entrance.

"Looks can be deceiving," Riley said as he lead Zandy to the entrance.

"I suppose," Zandy said apprehensively as she held back.

Riley grew acutely aware of his wife's fear. He dared to put his arm around her waist. "I didn't realize you were so afraid," he said as he pulled Zandy close.

"It's just all of the things my father has told me. The darkness and the feeling of being buried alive," Zandy said with a shudder.

Riley stopped and pulled Zandy around to face him. "I would never let anything happen to you. Do you trust me, even a little bit?"

Zandy lost herself in the darkness of Riley's eyes. "I, uh. . . ," Zandy stammered as she grew increasingly aware of Riley's touch. "I trust you," she finally offered. Her mind reasoned that Riley had always been a man of his word.

"Then why not come inside with me? We can take a lantern and it won't seem so dark. I promise to take care of you," Riley said in a husky whisper.

The wind blew Riley's hair into his eyes and, without thinking, Zandy reached up and pushed the hair away from his face. She found herself unable to take her hand away from his face and instead, allowed it to trail down his cheek to his dimpled chin.

For a moment, time stood still and Zandy forgot the past and all that had marred their relationship.

Riley reached up to hold her hand against his face. "I think I could grow to like this," he whispered.

"Yes," Zandy murmured.

Riley continued to hold her hand as he bent down to kiss her. Zandy was soft and yielding in his arms and this time when she quivered, Riley realized with a start that Zandy trembled from pleasure and not revulsion. He wanted to give a yell, knowing that if Zandy could at least find herself attracted to him, then perhaps he could work through the other obstacles that kept them from having a real marriage.

Zandy's mind was a storm of confusion. She felt herself fall limp against her husband and a part of her wanted the moment to never end. Was she falling in love with Riley Dawson?

When Riley pulled away, Zandy blushed and lowered her face. It was hard enough to wonder what Riley expected of her as a wife, but these new feelings were completely unforeseen.

"Come on," Riley said as he stepped away to light the lantern. "We'll just go in a short ways. You might as well see what buys your bread and butter."

Zandy crushed little handfuls of her pink-and-white-striped skirt. She really didn't want to follow Riley into the black hole that presented itself before them but, if she said no, Riley would think she didn't trust him.

Riley waited for her with the lantern in hand. He couldn't explain the feelings of protection that he felt for her. He watched her standing there. The turmoil on Zandy's face was evident, yet Riley silently hoped she'd have the courage to trust him. For some reason it suddenly seemed very important.

Zandy stepped forward slowly. "I'll go with you, but I can't lie and say I'm not afraid."

"You aren't afraid of me, are you?" Riley asked, almost fearfully.

Zandy smiled up at her husband. "No, Silly. The mine is what I'm afraid of," she said as she pointed to the entrance.

"Well at least that's something," Riley said with a grin. "Come on."

Riley took hold of Zandy's arm and lead her into the mine. The air was stale even just a short way into the mine. Zandy wrinkled her nose and shivered at the dampness. She looked over her shoulder as Riley moved them farther down the tunnel. She cringed at the sight of the entryway growing smaller and smaller. There was little comfort in the fact that the lantern was their only light.

Zandy pushed close to Riley's body, grateful for his strong arm to lean on. "Riley, I don't like it in here. Do we have to go any farther?"

"I just want to show you where the main shaft is. This is where we lower the men and supplies deep into the ground. The best show of color is down below," Riley said as he held the lamp higher. "See, it's just over there."

Zandy strained to see in the dim light. They stood right at the edge of the shaft while Riley explained the headframe to Zandy. "This framework is set up to house the hoisting system that takes the men up and down. See, up there, is the sheave wheel. It's the pulley that holds the hoist cable." Riley held up the lantern so Zandy could make out the contraption.

"It doesn't look very safe," Zandy said gravely. She remembered stories her father had told her of accidents where the cage that held the miners would suddenly plummet and kill everyone on board. Knowing that some shafts ran as deep as a hundred feet or more, Zandy backed away uncomfortably.

"There's always a risk," Riley agreed.

Zandy suddenly became aware of the sound of water. "I hear water. Is there an underground spring here?" Zandy questioned, eager to forget the shaft.

"There's always water in the mine. Pumping them out takes quite a bit of money. Come on, I'll show you what you're hearing," Riley said and pulled Zandy with him down a long narrow tunnel.

"I don't like it here, Riley. Let's just go," Zandy said, tightening her grip on Riley's hand. "Please, Riley. I'm scared."

"Don't worry, Zandy," Riley said confidently. "I haven't gotten you hurt yet and what I want to show is just over here.

They rounded the corner and Zandy was amazed to find a small pool of water with a steady stream of liquid dripping in from overhead. Further inspection showed that the water flowed away from the pool and trickled down rocks and black sand to disappear into the darkness.

Riley handed Zandy the lantern and went to the water and cupped some in his hand. "Here, taste. It's sweet and pure."

Zandy felt strange lowering her lips to Riley's hand but, nonetheless, she sampled the water. "It's very good."

Just then an ominous rumbling caught Zandy's ear. "Riley!"

"I hear it. We'd better get out of here," Riley said as he directed Zandy back to the tunnel.

The words were no sooner out of Riley's mouth than rock began to pour down around them and dirt pelted Zandy's face.

"Alexandra, get back!" Riley pushed Zandy behind him just as the timber overhead gave way and rock and debris came crashing down on top of him. Zandy had fallen backward and landed hard on the floor of the tunnel.

"Riley!" she screamed as the debris buried her husband.

Zandy sat fearfully trying to protect the lantern. Without light the mine would truly become a stifling tomb. She thanked God the rumbling stopped quickly and everything quit shaking.

Shock seemed to stun her mind, but in a flash she knew Riley had saved her life and was now buried in her place. Zandy turned up the lantern knowing it would burn the precious kerosene even faster.

Taking account of the situation, Zandy realized Riley's death would present the perfect opportunity to free herself from his control. She knew it would be simple to do nothing, but in her heart she couldn't. She set the lantern to one side and began to pull at the rocks and dirt with her hands.

The longer it took to dig out Riley's body, the more desperate Zandy became. "Please God, please help me save him. Don't let Riley die, I need him." The words startled Zandy but she paid no attention to them.

Finally, Zandy was able to take hold of Riley's legs and pull him backwards and away from the rubble. She hurried to pull the lantern closer and noticed immediately that Riley was still breathing. "Oh, thank You, Father," she whispered.

Zandy brushed the hair away from Riley's face and was stunned to find her hand wet with blood when she pulled it back. Quickly, she tore strips from her petticoat and dipped them in the water to wash the wound.

Concern filled her heart as Zandy realized the ugly gash on Riley's head was quite deep. Blood continued to pour from it even as Zandy tried her best to stop the flow. "Help me, Father. He's dying. Please don't let him die," Zandy began to cry. She held pressure to the wound with one hand, as she worked feverishly to revive Riley with the other.

She bathed his face with the icy water and felt a bit of relief as Riley stirred. Even though he remained unconscious, Zandy was comforted to find the bleeding had stopped.

The damp cold of the mine seemed to penetrate Zandy's bones and, after binding Riley's head, she worked to pull his body across her lap to keep him warm.

"Dear God," Zandy prayed as she looked around, "I need You so much. Please send someone to help us get out and please save Riley." She hugged him close to her breast as a mother would a child. He didn't stir or make any further sound and Zandy felt her heart grow heavy. Would God listen to her desperate plea?

Chapter 16

The dirt sifted and slithered around the rotten timbers as Zandy continued to cradle Riley's unconscious form. From time to time she heard rock break lose and fall, but at least it was a change in the monotonous sound of the water dripping and Riley's ragged breathing.

Zandy had turned the lantern down as low as it would go and leaned back again on the damp, cold rock. As she held Riley, she gently stroked his face, hoping and praying the stimulation would cause him to awaken.

She dozed off and on, more than a little aware of the poor air. She had thought to explore the direction of the stream but she hated to leave Riley in his precarious state of life.

When she finally drifted off to sleep, Zandy was amazed that her dreams were peaceful and calming. She thought of Missouri in springtime and the sweet smell of apple blossoms as they filtered through her bedroom window from the orchard across the river.

Waking with a serenity she'd not known in months, Zandy was startled to find Riley staring up at her.

"You're awake! Oh, praise God," Zandy said as she checked Riley's head.

"I figured I'd died and you were an angel," he teased in a whisper.

"You didn't die, but very nearly. The mine buried you and I thought you weren't breathing when I pulled you out."

"You saved me? Why?" Riley questioned weakly.

Zandy smiled. "I couldn't let you die."

"Why?" Riley persisted.

Zandy frowned slightly. What did he want her to say? "I'm not sure you'd understand," she finally said and added, "I'm not totally sure why except that you're one of God's creatures and He would expect no less of me."

"Oh," Riley said, sounding disappointed. "I suppose," he paused as if trying to gain a bit of strength, "I shouldn't question why, but just be grateful. Thank you."

"No thanks are necessary," Zandy said softly as she rested her hand against Riley's cheek. "I'm sure you would have done the same for me."

"Of course I would," Riley murmured as his eyes fell closed. "But, then I love you."

Zandy was notably stunned, but her expression was of no concern for Riley because he'd already lost consciousness again. She dismissed the words in disbelief then tried to rationalize that his words were just those of a man afraid he was dying. Riley had wanted her for many reasons, but love was not one of them—at least she didn't have any reason to believe it was. Her moments of contemplation were few as Riley stirred to consciousness again.

"Alexandra," Riley moaned her name as he struggled to move.

"Lie still," Zandy commanded. "You've got a nasty cut on your head and you're going to start bleeding if you move."

Riley fell back against her. "I'm too heavy for you."

Zandy smiled. "Stop worrying about it and just relax."

"Tell me about your God, Alexandra."

The words shocked Zandy's senses. Riley was asking her to share God's love with him. He must feel confident that his life is coming to an end. It was often the common response of people who feared that death was shadowing their doorstep.

"Of course," Zandy said and breathed a silent prayer that she'd say the right thing. "I've never known a day in my life when God wasn't an important part of it. When my mother was still alive, I remember sitting on her lap and listening to her telling me stories about Jesus."

"Did you believe them?" Riley croaked the question. "The stories, that is. Did you think they were more than just stories."

"Maybe not at first," Zandy said, trying to remember. "I was very little and listening to stories was a great way to pass an evening. My mother reminded me that I had heard people telling stories of things that had happened while I'd actually been present. She said the stories of Jesus were true and had been handed down to us through the Bible, just like family stories are passed down."

"I've never read much of the Bible," Riley replied.

"I have," Zandy said as she reached over to turn up the lamp a bit. "It's a constant source of comfort to me. It led the way for me to find Jesus as my personal Savior."

"And how did you do that?"

"Jesus told his disciples, as well as the people who came to hear Him speak, they had to be born again. Of course one man, Nicodemus, couldn't help but think in literal terms, and he questioned Jesus as to how a person could become a baby and be born again. Jesus told him that people had to be born of flesh and spirit. When our mother gives life to us we are born of the flesh, but when Christ gives life to us we are born of the spirit for all eternity."

"And you really believe Christ came to save us?" Riley asked, sounding almost hopeful.

"I certainly do. Jesus went on to tell Nicodemus that 'God so loved the world, that he gave his only begotten Son, that whosoever believeth in him should not perish, but have everlasting life.' That's from John 3:16."

"I can't imagine God could overlook the kind of man I've been and save me just because I choose to believe that Jesus is the Son of God," Riley said in a groggy voice.

"Well, you need to repent of your sin as well," Zandy said and then added, "Romans 6:23 says, 'For the wages of sin is death; but the gift of God is eternal life through Jesus Christ our Lord.' We can't be close to God and live our lives away from His truth. It just can't be both ways."

"And God will really forgive us our sins?" Riley asked.

"Of course. The Bible says He will and I believe it."

"Why would God care so much and how could He keep from blaming us later on for something we did, even if we ask Him to forgive us?" Riley blinked several times trying hard to stay awake.

"I can only tell you what the Bible says, Riley," Zandy said as she reached over and dipped a strip of cloth in the cool water. She moistened Riley's lips with the cloth and bathed his face in a loving manner. "Psalms is one of my favorite books of the Bible. Psalm 103 has several verses I truly love. It says God is merciful and slow to anger. It also says, 'For as the heaven is high above the earth, so great is His mercy toward them that fear Him. As far as the east is from the west, so far hath He removed our transgressions from us.' God lets the past be forgiven and He doesn't hold it against us."

Riley fell silent as if contemplating Zandy's words. Zandy was growing cramped and uncomfortable against the hard rock wall. She tried to shift her weight and, when Riley didn't say anything, she realized he was unconscious again

Taking the opportunity to stretch, Zandy eased her body out from under Riley's and picked up the lantern. For the first time since she'd uncovered Riley, Zandy tried to survey the damage.

There was only the smallest opening at the top of the tunnel and the rest of the passage was buried in debris. Zandy sighed in relief knowing that at least a small amount of oxygen was getting through to them.

She went back to where Riley lay sleeping and wished she could do more to make him comfortable. She knelt beside him and prayed. "Dear Father, You alone know Riley and I are stuck in this mine. I'm asking You to send us help, Lord. We need to be rescued and soon or Riley might die. Please God, don't let Riley die, I really need him to live. Amen."

Zandy got to her feet, unaware that Riley had opened his eyes. " 'He shall give his angels charge over thee, to keep thee in all thy ways.' " Riley's remembrance of Psalm 91:11 startled Zandy.

"I didn't know you were awake," Zandy whispered.

"I know. Sorry if I frightened you," Riley said as he worked his way up the wall to a sitting position. "I need to stay conscious, Zandy. I want you to help me stay awake."

Zandy nodded and reached down to tear away more of her petticoat. "I'll get these wet. They ought to help." Zandy said, trying to ignore the fact that Riley had overheard her praying.

She wet the cloth and came to where Riley sat propped against the wall. When she reached out to wipe his forehead, Riley caught her hand in his. "Thank you," he said as he focused his eyes on Zandy's worried face. "I don't deserve your kindness. . .nor God's, but I am grateful."

"You're welcome," Zandy said and her heart felt all aflutter. Riley's touch was the only warmth in the bone-chilling cold of the mine.

"Zandy," Riley said as he offered her a place beside him, "please sit here with me." Zandy nodded, grateful for the added warmth of Riley's body. "You're freezing," Riley said as he pulled her close.

"I know, but there doesn't seem to be anything to do about it," Zandy said, truly feeling the cold more than she had before.

"Well, you sit right here in my arms, and we will keep each other warm." Riley's free hand went to his head.

"Does it hurt a lot?" Zandy questioned.

"Not that much. I've certainly had worse," Riley said with a weak smile.

Zandy doubted he was telling her the truth, but she didn't contradict him. Instead, she leaned against his chest enjoying the feeling that she was in God's care and Riley's arms.

"How long do you think it will take until someone realizes we're missing?" Zandy finally voiced the question that had been haunting her mind.

"Not long," Riley said confidently. "Mrs. Malloy will have a fit if we're not back by suppertime, which is," he paused to look at his pocket watch, "already an hour past."

"How will they find us?"

"Mrs. Malloy knows we were headed here. She'll send someone to check up on us and then—" Riley's words were cut short by the blast of the mine whistle. "There, see. We're well on our way to being rescued."

Zandy sat up and looked around. "But, Riley we're pretty far into the mine. They'll be working forever to dig us out. It might take days and I'm not sure we have days." The panic was clear in her voice.

"Don't you trust God to save you?" Riley asked as he fought to stay awake.

Zandy smiled. How like God to use Riley to reaffirm her faith. "Of course. I'm sorry. I must have sounded like a doubting Thomas."

Riley laughed. "Now that's one person I do remember from the Bible. I always saw myself in his place."

Zandy laughed but said nothing. She leaned back against Riley's open arm. It was hard to believe so many hours had passed since they'd first entered the mine and suddenly Zandy was starting to feel quite hungry.

"What would you have done," Riley finally asked, "if I hadn't forced you to marry me?"

The question surprised Zandy. She thought for a moment, staring out into the shadowy confines of her tomb. "I would have gone home to Missouri."

"You don't like it here?"

"No, it isn't really a matter of like or dislike of the place. I love the beauty here, but Missouri has its beauty too. I just hate the mining life," she said and laughed. "Now I really hate it."

Riley laughed too. "I guess I can understand that. What would you have done in Missouri?"

"I don't really know," Zandy answered honestly. "I've always had someone else taking care of me. If I went back to Missouri I'd be on my own."

"You don't have any family back there?"

"No and I don't figure I'll ever talk Pa into going back. He loves the mountains," Zandy replied. "I do respect his dream, however. I know what it is to have dreams."

"And what are your dreams, Zandy?" Riley asked, suddenly very interested in what his wife had to say.

Zandy swallowed hard. She'd wanted to tell Riley how much she wanted their marriage to work. She wanted to explain that she had feelings for him she'd not anticipated. But, where should she begin and how could she explain her change of heart?

"This is rather difficult for me. I wanted to be courted and fall in love, marry, and have a family. I wanted to be a good mother like Ruth and I wanted to grow old with my husband. I guess that sounds rather unambitious, but it was really all I ever wanted. Now, I'd just like to get out of here," Zandy said sadly.

She waited for Riley to say something and when he didn't she sat up. "Riley?" He didn't answer her and Zandy quickly felt his chest for proof of his deep even breathing. "Oh, Riley, please wake up."

Time passed and still Riley remained unconscious. Zandy was beginning to panic. She tried to wash his face with the cold water and when that didn't help, she gently slapped at his cheek with the palm of her hand. Nothing.

"Oh, God," she cried, "please help him, Lord. He doesn't know You yet. Please don't let him die without salvation."

Chapter 17

L
ong into the night the town of Dawson worked at a feverish pitch to free Riley and Zandy from the mine. The cave-in was massive and no one knew for sure which direction the couple had gone.

Mrs. Malloy was beside herself with grief, feeling that it was her fault something hadn't been done sooner. Ruth Stewart went to the woman and assured her that she had done everything possible and now it was in God's hands. Mrs. Malloy nodded and agreed to pray with Ruth.

Hour after hour ticked by while the men dug and loaded dirt onto ore cars and dumped it over the side of a ravine. The efforts were slowed by the necessity to reinstall timber framing to support the newly cleared tunnels.

Work at the other mines halted and shifts were organized to share the laborious task of digging out the Alexandra Mine. At dawn, several of the church ladies appeared and set up breakfast tables, while still more women appeared on an hourly basis and brought food and drink.

Zandy heard the sounds of workers and felt only a slight bit of encouragement. She called out over and over, but to no avail. Her voice simply couldn't carry through the length of the tunnel filled with debris.

She had tried to dig at her end of the tunnel but, without even the crudest instrument to work with, Zandy was forced to give up her efforts and conserve her rapidly fading strength. Finally, in exhaustion, Zandy fell asleep beside Riley's unconscious form.

Mindless of the hours that passed, Zandy felt weaker than ever when she awoke. The damp cold of the mine seemed slightly relieved by laying close to Riley, but it was then with much concern that Zandy realized Riley's body was burning up.

Fever! Zandy checked the wound and found the telltale redness of proud flesh. Blood poisoning was setting in and Zandy knew brain fever would only be a short ways behind that. Zandy looked around frantically for a way to stifle the poison that was spreading into Riley's system but nothing revealed itself.

Zandy took the lantern and searched the area but found nothing. There weren't any herbs to work with and even a search of Riley's pockets failed to provide even a small amount of chewing tobacco which Zandy knew made a wonderful drawing poultice.

In dejected silence Zandy slipped to the floor and began to cry. She was cold and hungry and, while she tried to encourage herself with the fact that there was plenty of water, the stale air seemed only to further her depression and listlessness.

"How much longer, Lord?" she whispered into the dim light. She'd turned the lamp down hoping to conserve the precious kerosene as well as eliminate some of the smoke it put off.

She felt the tears begin to slide down her cheeks. "I've tried so hard to have faith, Father," she prayed as she cried. "I kept the faith through my ordeal when Riley insisted on my being his mistress, and I even stood fast to Your promises when there wasn't any food and the children were starving. Oh, Father, I know You can make the way clear for the men to rescue us. I know You can save us. I put it all in Your hands, Lord. If I perish now I know I will wake up in Your house and I don't fear death for myself." She paused and felt Riley's burning head. "I pray he's made peace with You, Lord. I pray that You'll forgive Riley. I forgive him, Lord," she whispered. "I forgive him and I love him." The words came naturally and had no startling revelation as Zandy presumed they would. *I really do love him,* she thought.

After two days of working to free Riley and Zandy, the men finally broke through the last few feet of debris to find the couple sleeping side by side, Zandy's arm placed protectively across her dying husband.

Riley's men were quick to carry the two outside and while Zandy struggled to wake up, Riley remained gravely still.

"Take him up to the house," the doctor instructed and K.C. and Pat loaded Riley into a nearby wagon and drove the team hard and fast to the Dawson mansion.

Burley Stewart knelt beside his barely conscious daughter. "Take her to our house," he instructed Tom and Jake Atkins.

Ruth had waited at the house for news of the rescue. The boys remained subdued, yet quietly argumentative with one another, as they waited for news of their sister. Molly was an exceptionally good baby and Ruth felt certain that she could sense the gravity of the household.

When the men came noisily up the walkway, Ruth clasped her hand to her throat. "Is she dead?" Ruth questioned as she ran to her husband's side.

"No, just exhausted and starved," Burley said in a concerned tone that told Ruth everything.

"Bring her in, she can have Joshua's bed," Ruth said as she led the way. Zandy's dirt-caked body was placed upon the iron-framed bed. Tom and

Jake offered their assistance if the Stewarts should need anything more, then took their leave.

Ruth began washing the dirt from her stepdaughter's body. "Burley, please put some more water on to boil and Josh, you heat up some of that soup we had with lunch." Both nodded in agreement and went quickly from the room.

"How can I help?" George asked simultaneously with Bart and Samuel.

"You boys run and get one of my good nightdresses and the smelling salts."

The boys raced from the room, and Ruth peered down at the hopeless dress that Zandy wore. There was no way to repair the numerous tears. There would be ample money and time to get another, Ruth surmised and made the decision to cut the dress from Zandy's body.

She'd just finished cutting the gown from neck to hem and was covering Zandy with a blanket when the boys returned with the things she'd asked for. Ruth shooed them from the room, then went to work trying to revive Zandy.

Ruth waved the smelling salts under Zandy's nose until the weak fluttering of her stepdaughter's eyes gave her hope of Zandy's regaining consciousness.

"Alexandra, you wake up this minute," Ruth sounded gruff, hoping it would bring Zandy around faster.

"Where am I?" Zandy whispered from a raspy throat.

"You're safe with us at the Mulvane house," Ruth said softly.

"Where. . .?" her words faded as she fought to stay awake. "Where is Riley?"

"He's with the doctor. You have to rest here and get some food in you before you can see him," Ruth said firmly.

"Have. . .to. . .have to see. . .him," Zandy insisted.

"No, Darling," Burley said as he brought fresh water in for Ruth to use. "You can't see him just yet. You've got to get your strength back."

"Oh, Pa," Zandy began to cry although she had no strength for it. "Don't let him die."

Ruth and Burley exchanged brief worried looks before trying to minister to their daughter's needs. Zandy could only stay awake long enough to take in a small amount of soup, and after Ruth finished bathing her, she got Zandy dressed and settled into bed for a much-needed rest.

Ruth remained by Zandy's side constantly, and whenever her stepdaughter opened her eyes even for a brief moment, Ruth managed to get some warm soup or beef broth down her throat. There wasn't a moment when Ruth wasn't in a state of prayer, nor when she didn't ponder the anxiety and concern in Zandy's plea to keep Riley from dying. Was it possible that love had come to Zandy in such a short time?

~

After three days of tumultuous sleep, Zandy managed to feel rested. An exhausted Ruth eased pillows behind her stepdaughter's back and helped her to sit up.

"I feel like I could eat a horse," Zandy said weakly.

"That's a good sign," Ruth said in a joyous voice. "I'll fix you whatever you like. We have a full larder. What will you have?"

"Anything and everything," Zandy replied, then changed her mind. "No, I want to see Riley. How is he?" she threw back the covers and struggled to sit up.

"You can't just jump up out of bed after all you've been through. I'm sure Riley is fine. I haven't heard anything all day, but your pa has tried to keep apprised of the situation. I'm sure he'll tell us whatever he knows when he comes home from work."

"But I have to know," Zandy stated firmly. "Couldn't we send one of the boys?"

"They're all in school, Zandy. You'll just have to wait until three o'clock. That's only two hours away and your pa will be back shortly after that."

Zandy nodded and eased back into the pillows. "How long did I sleep?" she questioned as she pulled the covers back.

"This is the third day."

"No!" Zandy exclaimed. "I don't believe it. How could I have slept all that time. Now I really have to find out about Riley."

Ruth put her hand out to stop her stepdaughter. "You haven't the strength to even dress. Now, do as you are told. I promise I'll send someone up to the Dawson mansion, if you'll promise to stay put until I get back."

Zandy nodded. "I will. I promise. Just please hurry." Zandy said in a pleading tone that spurred Ruth on.

Ruth had pulled on her coat and was just about to leave the house when Burley appeared on the walkway. The prematurity of his arrival told Ruth instantly that he would not be the bearer of good news.

"Is it Riley?" she asked fearfully as her husband approached the porch.

"Yes," Burley whispered. "He's dead."

Ruth swayed back against the porch rail. "Dead? Are you sure?"

"The doctor came and told me just a few minutes ago."

"Oh, my poor Alexandra. This will not be easy," Ruth said with tears in her eyes.

"I want to tell her," Burley said firmly and walked past his wife and into the house.

After several minutes, Ruth could hear Zandy's ragged sobs and went to join Burley in trying to offer consolation to their daughter.

～

The days that followed passed in a blur for Zandy Dawson. People told her that was God's way of easing her burden. She performed her duties mechanically, issuing instructions for the funeral, with her father's help. There was nothing comforting about burying a husband. Especially one whose salvation remained a burning question in Zandy's mind. Had Riley found the Lord before he died?

Too stunned to cry, Zandy went through the motions of attending the largest funeral she'd ever known. Hundreds of people turned out to bid their respects to the closed casket of Riley Dawson. When it was all over, Zandy returned to the mansion alone, despite her father's insistence she come home with her family.

She moved through the house in her widow's weeds, touching the things that reminded her of Riley, and when nothing offered any real consolation, she went to his old bedroom and sat for hours in his desk chair.

Looking down at the desk, Zandy started turning the pages of the ledgers that showed the percentages of profits and losses Riley had recorded for each and every business transaction in town. When she finally came upon his bank ledgers, she gasped. Riley Dawson was a millionaire.

"No," she thought aloud, "I am."

A plan immediately formed in her mind to release the townspeople from their debt to Riley. She made out notices for immediate posting and called a town meeting of the business owners.

Within a week, the town of Dawson was singing the praises of their dead mayor's widow. At first everyone had been stunned to learn of Zandy's plan, but they eagerly accepted her generosity.

Zandy knew she was doing the right thing, but it offered her very little relief from the emptiness. Zandy was greatly relieved when Burley and Ruth showed up to offer a hand with anything she might need.

"I'm so happy to see you," Zandy said as she rang for Mrs. Malloy. The older woman appeared almost instantly.

"Yes, Mrs. Dawson?"

"Please bring us some refreshments," Zandy said as she took a seat across from her parents.

"Certainly," Mrs. Malloy replied and was gone.

"You really don't have to give us refreshments, Zandy. We just stopped by to see if we could help you," Ruth said as she reached out to pat Zandy's hand.

"I've been thinking a great deal since Riley. . ." Zandy fell silent. "Since he died," she finally said. "I asked the doctor if Riley accepted Christ, but he didn't know." Zandy felt her eyes fill with tears. "It's really all I wanted for him. I wanted him to understand life without God was already a way of being dead."

"Did you share the Gospel with him, Zandy?" Burley asked his daughter gently.

"Yes, when he was dying. But," Zandy paused as she wiped her cheeks, "I don't know if he was conscious enough to understand what I was telling him or not. I pray that he accepted God, but I just don't know." Zandy put her face in her hands and began to sob.

"Alexandra," Burley began as he knelt down beside his daughter, "you must trust God and place your worries in His hands. Whether you sit here and worry, spending hours in tears and grief or not, ultimately God is still sovereign and still in control. Leave it with Him, Zandy, and let your life go on. You lived your Christianity in front of him, despite what he wanted you to do."

Zandy's head snapped up. "What do you mean?" she questioned, suddenly sober.

Burley leaned back on his heel. "I know he had expected you to be his mistress and not his wife."

"How?"

"You were delirious. You told it all," Burley explained. "When I realized what I had pushed you to do, I couldn't forgive myself."

"Your father's pain was so great," Ruth added, "that he cried for hours. He just kept saying—"

"It isn't important," Burley interrupted. "What is important is God was watching over you, even when I wasn't. You've got to trust Him now."

Zandy nodded. "I know you're right."

"What will you do now?" Ruth questioned softly.

"I want to go home, to Missouri," Zandy said firmly. "I have more than enough money to take all of us home in style. Please say you'll come back to Missouri with me. I'll pay for everything and we'll still have plenty to buy the biggest store you'd ever want. Please say yes."

Burley looked into the pleading eyes of his daughter. "I can't, Alexandra. We've made this our home," Burley said, looking across the small space to his wife.

Ruth nodded in agreement. "We belong here, Zandy."

"Well, at least move into the mansion," Zandy begged. "I'm going back to Missouri, but this big house needn't stand empty. There's a house full of staff that need to maintain their jobs. I have more than enough money to maintain the estate and all the staff for as long as you want them. Please, let me do this for you."

"No," Burley said, shaking his head. "I can't take charity from my daughter."

"Then don't let it be charity. Take over the estate and holdings for me and be my manager. You can have any salary you wish, this house, staff, and full control. I'll need someone honest to look out for my interests."

"She's got a point, Burley. The lawlessness of this town would take advantage of a vulnerable young widow."

"Alright," Burley agreed. "I'll do it."

~

A week later, Zandy took one final walk through the house. She had a large bank draft, more than enough to take care of her needs for a long time. There was really nothing left to hold her here, yet she felt reluctant to let go of Riley's memory.

She went to his bedroom in search of their wedding picture, but when she couldn't find it, she settled instead for a tintype of Riley that had been taken a year or two before Zandy had met him. He was smiling that self-assured smile that had always appeared smug and demanding. Zandy clutched the photo to her breast. "Oh, Riley."

Mrs. Malloy announced from the hall that her parents had arrived to take her to the stage.

"I'm coming," Zandy called and tucked the picture into her coat pocket. Turning to face the room for one last time, Zandy smiled. " 'What time I am afraid, I will trust in thee,' " she murmured the words of Psalm 56:3.

Chapter 18

The fall of 1881 found southern Missouri in a riot of autumn color. Zandy Dawson stood on the front porch of her boardinghouse and breathed deeply of the glorious scents. The last roses of summer persevered to hang onto the white painted trellis at the end of the porch. Their sweet, muted aroma lingered in the morning air and mingled with the smell of fresh coffee and bacon.

Zandy pulled a watch from her pocket and realized it would be only a matter of minutes before the breakfast crowd would be storming down her stairs and across her parlor to the dining room.

She thought for a moment to go inside and assist Ann, her hired help, with the breakfast but knew the woman would resent any offer. Ann prided herself in keeping the house in perfect order and even managed the new guests for Zandy. Zandy only had to keep the books and tend to the shopping, which Ann hated with a passion.

Life in Missouri had been rewarding and refreshing, and inwardly, Zandy knew she'd made the right decision to come back. Although she'd settled far from her hometown, Zandy was content with her choice. In fact, it was hard to believe a whole year had passed since she'd left Colorado.

The boardinghouse was huge and brought in a reasonable profit, although from the newest ledger report from her father, Zandy knew she didn't need the money. She found ways to use it, however, contributing heavily to the church and orphanage.

Zandy smoothed down the red-sprigged calico bodice and resecured the ties of her apron. While she'd kept the name Dawson, she'd discarded her widow's weeds after reaching Denver. She had deliberated long and hard about the decision and finally concluded she would not present herself as a widow.

Rational reasoning told her she'd have enough to explain to people by simply being a new face in town. Then, should she ever decide to remarry, though she'd firmly decided she wouldn't, Zandy knew it would be difficult to explain having been a bride without having consummated her marriage.

And the proposals had come, just as Zandy presumed they would. Not because she was a raving beauty, but more so because she was financially affluent and news like that simply couldn't be contained. One could not just ignore a bank account with several thousand dollars in it and seemingly no end in sight of those funds.

Zandy leaned against the porch post and sighed. Remarrying was not for her. She hadn't realized how much she loved Riley until he was dead. She felt the tears slide down her cheeks as they often had during the last year.

There was no forgetting the husband about whom she had known so little. Logic concluded she would simply be Alexandra Dawson, the new boarding-house owner, and while people might talk about a single woman running such an establishment, Zandy didn't care. She was as happy as she could be and only during peaceful, quiet moments like this did she acknowledge the emptiness in her heart.

At the sound of voices in the house, Zandy knew it was time for break-fast. She went in and took her place at the table, offering grace and helping Ann see to everyone's needs.

~

Later in the day, Zandy took Ann's list of groceries and headed into town to pick up the laundry and do the household shopping.

The town was bustling and was one of the largest Zandy had ever lived in. She gingerly stepped into the street and narrowly missed a freighter as it went streaking around the corner from a side street. Zandy clung tightly to her basket, steadied her nerves, and went on about her business. It was just another day.

On her way home, Zandy stopped by the house of her seamstress and picked up the new gown she had ordered some weeks earlier.

"Mighty good to see you, Zandy. Can you sit a spell and have some cake and coffee?"

"Sorry, no," Zandy told the older woman. "Although, I must say it is hard to pass up a chance to eat your cake."

"I'll just pack some for you to take home," the white-haired woman smiled.

Zandy smiled and waited while the woman wrapped two pieces of lemon cake in a tea towel. Zandy placed them in her already crowded basket and bid the woman good day.

As Zandy moved down the street of white picket fences and huge cot-tonwood trees, she felt as though she was being watched. Turning abruptly to glance behind her, Zandy found nothing to indicate her concern. Nonetheless, she picked up her pace and hurried to the safety of home.

Ann chided her when she relayed her concerns. "You should take a buggy or ride one of the horses. It isn't safe for you to walk all that way alone."

"But I like to walk. Today is probably one of the last warm ones we'll have," Zandy argued. "I didn't have any problem. I just said I felt like someone was watching me."

Ann, who acted like Zandy's senior but, in fact, was a year younger, sniffed in disgust and, after taking her slice of lemon cake, retired to the kitchen to finish baking.

Zandy shook her head and went to her own quarters. Two rooms at the back of the house with a large enclosed porch, were Zandy's domain. The privacy afforded her here was both a refuge and a bittersweet reminder of all that she'd lost.

She put the cake on a table, then carefully unwrapped the new dress. Lovingly, she spread the blue gown on her bed. This would be a dress reserved for Sundays and special occasions she'd decided. The princess style gown sported many gores with tight-fitting steels placed in the waist to show off Zandy's slender form. The dress was cut low and made without sleeves in order to be worn with a white shirtwaist. This would allow her to make it either a very elegant affair with a silk and lace blouse, or a more simple one out of plain cotton.

The noise of a wagon in the front yard caused Zandy to stop daydreaming. She went in search of Ann and found her already preparing to check in new boarders. Zandy knew this was the routine as her boardinghouse was the best in town, and though outside of the main city proper, it was always crowded with both short- and long-term customers.

Proud that her reputation for cleanliness and good food had spread all the way to Kansas City, Zandy scarcely ever found the house less than half full.

She stayed behind the scenes lest she offend Ann by trying to crowd her. The new boarders, three women and two men, were capably handled by Ann and soon they were cleared from the entryway and directed to their rooms upstairs. Zandy was about to go to the kitchen for a bite of lunch when a third man caught her eye as he entered into the foyer.

The bearded man was covered in dust and had his hat pulled low. He walked with a slow, deliberate stride to the desk where Ann offered him a pen to register. Something about him seemed vaguely familiar, and Zandy tried to place him, wondering suddenly if it was someone she'd known in Colorado.

As soon as the man had registered and gone upstairs, Zandy hurried to the desk and turned the register book around to read the name.

The only mark given was an X where a name would have normally been signed. Zandy sighed. Perhaps she'd be able to find out something more later.

Still in turmoil at suppertime, Zandy asked Ann to bring a tray to her room and to lead the boarders in grace. Ann nodded and was so quick with her work that Zandy had scarcely taken a seat when Ann appeared with her dinner.

"Thanks, Ann. I truly appreciate this," Zandy said, knowing Ann hated it when a boarder would take a meal in his room.

Ann nodded then quickly pulled the door shut and retreated down the hall. Zandy took the tray with her to the enclosed porch and sat down to enjoy the sunset.

The sky looked as if it were ablaze. The flaming orange sun seemed to catch the horizon on fire with ruby streaks bursting out across the blue-and-gold sky.

With a sigh, Zandy reached out to take hold of Riley's picture. She traced the edge of the frame and wondered silently if Riley were in heaven. Tears fell again as Zandy realized it had been nearly a year to the day since Riley had died. Hearing the door open behind her, Zandy knew it would be Ann checking to see if she needed anything.

Not wanting Ann to see her crying, Zandy struggled to control her voice. "I don't need anything, Ann. I'll bring the tray to the kitchen when I'm done."

At the sound of the door's closing, Zandy leaned back against the wicker chair. She felt the loneliness like a twisting knife in her soul. It wasn't good for her to continue pondering Riley's death, but it seemed impossible to get past it. Maybe Ann was right. Maybe what she needed was a good strong man to help her spend her money. She laughed out loud—her money indeed!

"Hello, Alexandra."

The rich, baritone of a man's voice rang out and Zandy thought she must be going mad. She did nothing for a moment until the man came to stand beside her. Fearing the end result, Zandy slowly raised her gaze to find that the face did indeed match the voice.

"Riley!" Zandy jumped to her feet and threw herself into her husband's arms. She covered his clean-shaven face with kisses, while tears fell down her face leaving their salty wetness on Riley's face.

"Whoa," Riley said as he set Zandy away from him. "I certainly didn't expect a response like this or I'd have come a lot sooner."

Zandy clutched her hand to her throat suddenly fearing she'd faint. "You. . .you were the man in the lobby. I knew you looked familiar." She gasped for air, feeling the darkness of unconsciousness trying to claim her.

"Here," Riley instructed, "sit down and I'll get you some water."

"No!" Zandy said and grabbed Riley's arm tightly. "Don't leave me. If this is a dream I'm not ready to give it up yet."

Riley knelt beside her, touching her wet cheeks gently. "It's no dream, Alexandra. I'm really here."

"You can't be. I must be mad," Zandy said sadly and leaned back hard against the chair.

"You aren't mad," Riley grinned, "just the most beautiful woman I've ever known. You look even prettier than the day we were married."

Zandy dropped her hold, but said nothing. She simply couldn't believe her husband had come back from the dead. Before she could say a word, Riley pulled up a chair and sat directly in front of her.

"I'm sorry this is such a shock. I had to come and tell you that I've accepted Christ as my Savior. I did in fact accept Him that day in the mine when you told me about Him."

Zandy stared, dumbfounded. Was this some form of kindness from the Lord to let her know that Riley was safely in heaven? She'd wondered for so long, fearful that he'd never received salvation, that perhaps her mind was failing her.

"Did you hear me, Alexandra?" Riley asked as he took hold of her hands.

His touch felt real enough, Zandy thought as she looked first to her hands and then to his face. "What?" she finally questioned.

"I've come to ask your forgiveness. I know how much I wronged you. I've dealt with everything else in my life," Riley said and then added, "everything but you."

"Forgive you?" Zandy heard her voice ask, but the words sounded as if they belonged to someone else. "I forgave you a long time ago. I prayed you'd come to know Christ and my only hope was that you'd find salvation before you died."

Riley smiled. "I did. Thanks to you and your perseverance. God knew what He was doing when He sent you into my life."

Zandy suddenly realized it was all real. Riley was alive and sitting on her back porch, holding her hands. She didn't know whether to cry anew or laugh.

"Why?" was the only word Zandy could manage for a moment. She took her hands from Riley's and reached out to touch his face. "Why did you let me believe you were dead?"

Chapter 19

Riley sat silently, staring into Zandy's eyes. How could he explain everything he'd gone through? The weeks of recuperation stood out in his mind, so he began the detailed explanation.

"I regained consciousness when Doc had me taken to the mansion. I told him that I wanted him to get me away from Dawson and tell everyone I'd died. I couldn't deal with my feelings, Zandy. I'm sorry," Riley offered the words as a humble apology.

"I still don't understand. It hurt so much when they told me you were dead. A part of me died too. It was like having my heart ripped out."

"I had no idea you'd feel that way," Riley admitted. "I figured you'd be relieved. I thought I'd forced you into a loveless marriage because of my lustful intentions. The night of our wedding I knew I'd fallen in love with you and I hated myself."

"For falling in love with me?" Zandy questioned trying hard to hide her surprise at Riley's declaration of love.

"No," Riley said taking her hands from his face. "For taking you as my wife. . .without a willing heart. I couldn't stay with you and make matters worse." Riley's words were whispers. "Although, walking away from you was the hardest thing I've ever done."

Zandy stared at him with a puzzled frown. "You deliberately chose not to consummate our marriage?"

"Can you imagine it any other way?" Riley said with a laugh. "I was used to taking whatever I wanted. Wild horses couldn't have stopped me, but God wouldn't let me defile you."

"But we were married and I had agreed to whatever that meant," Zandy said boldly.

"I know, but you were still forced. You had no other way out. I'd created an awful situation for you and made myself your only savior."

"That's where you're wrong, Riley. I had the only Savior I needed. I had Jesus and there was nothing else that could change that. I agreed to marry you because it seemed the logical thing to do."

"Exactly my point," Riley sighed. "You didn't marry me for love, except maybe the love of your folks and siblings. I just couldn't live with myself, knowing I'd forced you to marry a man you didn't love and probably never would."

"I've thought about you every day since the accident," Zandy said. "I was so stunned when they told me you were dead, nothing seemed right from that moment on. People kept telling me I'd feel better, but I didn't. I went through your papers, made all the changes I thought necessary, and begged my family to return to Missouri with me. When they refused, I made the decision to go it alone," Zandy relayed the information knowing full well Riley would have already learned all of this on his own.

Riley nodded. "I know. I kept up on your whereabouts through Doc. Zandy, please understand I needed to straighten out my life. I'd made a lot of mistakes and when I accepted Christ, I knew I could no longer ignore those mistakes. I saved dealing with you until last, because you are the most important. I didn't want you to think I was just telling you what you wanted to hear by declaring my salvation in Christ, or for that matter, my love for you."

The second reference to love was too much for Zandy. "You love me?" Somehow that was harder to believe than the fact that Riley had come to know the Lord, though both thoughts thrilled Zandy's heart.

"I think I have loved you from the moment I first saw you wrestling those wild brothers of yours. I walked in expecting to take the town of Temperance for all it was worth. I planned to wring it dry, force everyone to become so dependent upon me that without me they'd be forced to leave. The power seemed so important to me, until I suddenly found something I couldn't overpower—you," Riley said honestly.

"And you're certain what you feel is love and not just guilt?" Zandy asked bluntly.

Riley studied her soft face for a moment. She'd pinned up her hair loosely so that wisps of hair fell in a frame around her face and her green eyes were so intense and dark that Riley could forget his very purpose if he stared too long.

"I know it's love. You are my wife, Zandy," Riley said as he got to his feet and pulled Zandy up with him. "Is there any way you could find it in your heart to accept me as your husband? I don't mean right away. I wouldn't ask that much of you. But maybe in time, after we courted for awhile, then maybe we could remarry."

"No," Zandy said firmly as she put her arms around Riley's neck. "I don't want to court my husband. I have a willing heart to be your wife, Riley Dawson, and I have no intention of waiting weeks, maybe even months, until you go through the motions of making me your wife. You accept your responsibilities now, or leave for good," Zandy stated firmly, but with a twinkle in her eye. She knew full well what Riley's response would be.

Riley crushed Zandy to him and lowered his lips to passionately cover hers. He kissed her with a longing that crossed the miles and months since he'd last seen her. "Wife," he breathed the word. "My beautiful, beautiful Christian wife."

Zandy put her head on Riley's chest and sighed. "I knew God would give me the desires of my heart."

Riley wrapped his arms tightly around Zandy. "I praise God for giving you a strong faith. If you hadn't stood by your convictions and God's principles I would have ruined us both. God is truly good to have provided me with a woman of strong biblical courage."

Zandy smiled to herself. God truly was good and His mercies were everlasting. This, He'd proven to Zandy more than once. Now, He'd rewarded her trust by leading Riley to salvation.

"I love you, Alexandra Dawson," Riley said with as much love as Zandy had ever heard in a man's voice.

"And I love you, Riley Dawson," she breathed the words, "with all my willing heart."

A Letter to Our Readers

Dear Readers:

In order that we might better contribute to your reading enjoyment, we would appreciate you taking a few minutes to respond to the following questions. When completed, please return to the following: Fiction Editor, Barbour Publishing, Inc., PO Box 719, Uhrichsville, OH 44683.

1. Did you enjoy reading *New Mexico Sunrise?*
   - ❏ Very much. I would like to see more books like this.
   - ❏ Moderately—I would have enjoyed it more if _____
   _____
   _____

2. What influenced your decision to purchase this book? (Check those that apply.)
   - ❏ Cover   ❏ Back cover copy   ❏ Title   ❏ Price
   - ❏ Friends   ❏ Publicity   ❏ Other

3. Which story was your favorite?
   - ❏ *A Place to Belong*   ❏ *Perfect Love*
   - ❏ *Tender Journeys*   ❏ *The Willing Heart*

4. Please check your age range:
   - ❏ Under 18   ❏ 18–24   ❏ 25–34
   - ❏ 35–45   ❏ 46–55   ❏ Over 55

5. How many hours per week do you read? _____

Name _____

Occupation _____

Address _____

City _____ State _____ ZIP _____

E-mail _____

If you enjoyed

NEW MEXICO

Sunrise

then read:

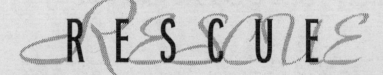

*Four Contemporary Romance Stories
with Life and Love on the Line*

Island Sunrise by Lauralee Bliss
Matchmaker 911 by Wanda E. Brunstetter
Wellspring of Love by Pamela Griffin
Man of Distinction by Tamela Hancock Murray

If you enjoyed

NEW MEXICO

Sunrise

then read:

British

COLUMBIA

*The Romantic History of Dawson Creek
in Four Complete Novels by Janelle Burnham Schneider*

River of Peace
Beckoning Streams
Winding Highway
Hidden Trails

JHEARTSONG ♥ PRESENTS

Love Stories
Are Rated G!

That's for godly, gratifying, and of course, great! If you love a thrilling love story but don't appreciate the sordidness of some popular paperback romances, **Heartsong Presents** is for you. In fact, **Heartsong Presents** is the only inspirational romance book club, the only one featuring love stories where Christian faith is the primary ingredient in a marriage relationship.

Sign up today to receive your first set of four never-before-published Christian romances. Send no money now; you will receive a bill with the first shipment. You may cancel at any time without obligation, and if you aren't completely satisfied with any selection, you may return the books for an immediate refund!

Imagine. . .four new romances every four weeks—two historical, two contemporary—with men and women like you who long to meet the one God has chosen as the love of their lives. . .all for the low price of $9.97 postpaid.

To join, simply complete the coupon below and mail to the address provided. **Heartsong Presents** romances are rated G for another reason: They'll arrive Godspeed!

YES!   Sign me up for Hearts♥ng!

NEW MEMBERSHIPS WILL BE SHIPPED IMMEDIATELY!
Send no money now. We'll bill you only $9.97 postpaid with your first shipment of four books. Or for faster action, call toll free 1-800-847-8270.

NAME _____

ADDRESS _____

CITY _____ STATE _____ ZIP _____

MAIL TO: HEARTSONG PRESENTS, PO Box 721, Uhrichsville, Ohio 44683